THE DEVELOPMENT OF EARLY MODERN EUROPE 1480–1648

Geoffrey Woodward

LONGMAN

Contents

ii

Contents

Contents

Editorial introduction

This aim of this book is to give you as clear a picture as possible of the events and developments in the period you are studying. You may well be using this book to prepare for an examination and the book has several special features, listed below, to help you in this. Most of all, we hope it will help you to develop a critical awareness about, and a continuing interest in, the past.

FOCUS: Each chapter has a main focus, listed in the contents. These are the main issues and 'concepts', like cause and consequence, the evaluation of evidence, the role of the individual, key themes, historical controversies or interpretations and so on. All of these are important in studying and understanding history. Identifying a focus does not mean that the chapter only looks at the past in one way; rather that you are encouraged to find out about topics from a different slant.

TIME CHARTS: Most chapters begin with a time chart. It helps you follow the chronology. Some time charts develop a basic point which is not in the main text. You should also find that the charts provide you with a handy reference point.

KEY TERMS: There are some words or phrases which it is important to know in order to understand a wider topic. These have been highlighted in the text so that you can easily look up what they mean. Sometimes quite simple ideas appear in unfamiliar form or in jargon. Decoding these should help you to make sense of the wider ideas to which the terms relate. Towards the end of the book you will find a separate index of the key terms.

PROFILES: There is not space in a book like this to provide full biographies of the people you will meet. The profiles give you the information you need to understand why an individual is important and what his or her main achievements were. Like the time charts, you might want to use these for reference. As with 'key terms', there is a separate index of people who are the subject of profiles.

TASKS: Nearly all the chapters end with some suggestions for follow-up work and further study. These include:

- guidance on how, and why, to take notes
- suggestions for class discussion and debate

- help on how to use historical evidence of different types
- tips on answering source questions
- hints on planning and writing essays
- specimen examination questions so that you can prepare for assessment.

FURTHER READING: You will find that you need more help on certain topics than can be provided in a book like this. The further reading guides you to some more detailed or specialist texts. The reading is listed with the most immediately obvious supporting texts placed first, followed by others – some of which may be considerably more detailed – and ending with articles and other shorter pieces, where these are appropriate.

MAIN INDEX: Many individuals, issues and themes are mentioned in more than one chapter. The index is designed to help you find what you are looking for quickly and easily by showing you how to collect together information which is spread about. Get practice in using an index; it will save you a lot of time.

The historian's job is to recreate the past. On one level, this is obviously an impossible task. There is far too much of it to put into one book while at the same time much of the information we need has been long since lost. Most of it can never be recovered. It is because there is so much of it that the historian has to impose his or her priorities by selecting. It is because so much more has been lost that he or she has to try to fill in the gaps and supply answers which other people can challenge. The processes of **Selection** and **Interpretation** are the key tasks of the historian and they help to make the subject endlessly fascinating. Every time a historian makes a decision about what to put in and what to leave out that decision implies a judgement which others might challenge. Historians try to get as close to the truth as they can, in the knowledge that others may disagree with what they say. Don't be surprised, then, to find a number of personal views or 'interpretations'. Some of these will make comparisons between the present and the period you are studying. These personal views have not been included in order to persuade you to agree with them. We aim to make you *think* about what you are reading and not always to accept everything at face value. If this book helps you to tell the difference between fact and opinion while keeping up your interest in the past, it will have served its purpose.

Christopher Culpin
Eric Evans
Series Editors

Part One   Renaissance and Reformation, 1480–1559

1 Europe in 1480: politics and religion

If you were able to ask well-informed contemporaries what Europe was like at the end of the fifteenth century, many of them would have replied that a new age was beginning. Although they would still feel that Europe, and particularly western Europe, was the centre of civilisation, many would have concluded that things were changing fast. In the medieval world, which had survived for about a thousand years, authority came from two places:

■ *Christendom* The Pope was the spiritual head of all Christians in western Europe. There was little or no division in the Church. Catholicism was the religion of the western world.

■ *The Holy Roman Empire* In theory, at least, this controlled the 'secular' – that is, the non-religious – world. Notice that this authority was called 'Holy', although the Emperor was not a priest, and 'Roman', although the Emperor did not live or have his court in Rome. The title 'Holy Roman Empire' symbolised the close links which were supposed to exist between religious and political authority.

Most ordinary people lived in villages and would certainly know their parish priest well. They would be aware that this priest was a representative of the mighty Roman Catholic Church. They would, however, have nothing directly to do with the Emperor. Their loyalties were to their locality, village or town.

This world of stability and very limited change seemed increasingly under threat by 1480. Three closely linked agents of change can be identified:

1 The increasing power of monarchs – kings and queens – in particular countries.

2 Some of these countries were developing as separate 'nation states' – rulers were establishing authority over people with similar traditions, perhaps those sharing a common language. These nation states threatened the overall authority of the Holy Roman Emperor, and perhaps the Pope too.

3 As these nation states developed, rulers began to claim 'absolute' power – that is, power limited only by the authority of God. They were bent on reducing, and eventually destroying, any obstacles to their

authority. While they continued to acknowledge the separate power of the Church, they sought ways to gain control over other great landowners (often called 'the nobility') and perhaps over rival princes. These rulers aimed to be 'sovereign' over large areas of territory.

Well-informed observers would have noted all these trends. Some historians have put them together to label the late fifteenth century as the crucial 'turning-point' from the 'medieval' to the 'early modern' world. For British historians, in particular, what was happening in Europe as a whole seemed to mirror what they knew of their own country. In England in 1485 one decisive battle seemed to be the turning-point from a world riven by civil conflict – the Wars of the Roses – into a new era of much greater peace and stability under a dynasty, the Tudors, which would survive for well over a hundred years. As we shall see, those who looked outside their own country could point to rather similar developments in both France and Spain. It is still common to find courses, both at school and university, which are called 'medieval' if they come to an end no later than the early sixteenth century and 'early modern' if they begin no earlier than the second half of the fifteenth century.

Historians, however – as you will discover as you read through this book – love looking at similar events in different ways, producing different 'interpretations' of the past as they do so. For many, historical controversy is the lifeblood of history. Only rarely do historians differ about the *facts* of the past but they frequently disagree about *why* things happened and how *important* certain developments were. In recent years, more historians have begun to stress not the *changes* of the later fifteenth century but *continuities* with the medieval world. As you look at Europe in the 80 or so years covered by the first part of this book, think about which seems to be more important: change or continuity.

Our starting-point is what was happening across Europe in the 1480s.

Europe in the 1480s

In political terms, Europe consisted of four power blocs (see Figure 1.1). Relations within each of these power blocs – and often between them – were very unstable, as we shall see.

- ■ **Western Europe** – the main powers here were France, Burgundy (including Franche-Comté and the Netherlands) and England;
- ■ The **Iberian Peninsula** – Castile, Aragon and Portugal;
- ■ The **Italian States** – especially Venice, Milan, Florence, Naples and those territories controlled by the Pope (the Papal States);

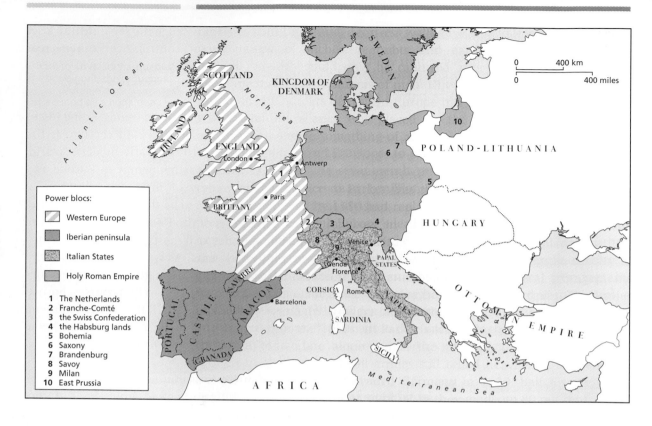

Power blocs:

◫ Western Europe

▨ Iberian peninsula

▨ Italian States

▨ Holy Roman Empire

1 The Netherlands
2 Franche-Comté
3 the Swiss Confederation
4 the Habsburg lands
5 Bohemia
6 Saxony
7 Brandenburg
8 Savoy
9 Milan
10 East Prussia

Figure 1.1 *Europe in 1480*

■ The **Holy Roman Empire** – the power base for the Empire was central and northern Europe and this brought it into conflict with areas frequently thought of as on the fringes of Europe: Scandinavian rulers in the Baltic, Polish rulers in the East and (perhaps most important) the only important non-Christian rulers in Europe – the Ottoman Turks, Muslims from Asia who contested territory in the south-east of Europe.

France

At times during the Middle Ages, the kings of England had ruled over more of the territory of what we now call France (see Figure 1.2) than the kings of France did. However, by the 1480s the challenge from England had been beaten off and Burgundy was also in retreat. The kings of France were secure in their heartlands.

The most important French king in the fifteenth century was Louis XI (1461–83). He had consolidated French power. When the Duke of Burgundy died, Louis took over the duchy and offered to marry the Duke's daughter, Margaret. This marriage would give him Flanders, Franche-Comté and Artois and thus secure France's northern and eastern borders. This was necessary because another daughter of the Duke of

Figure 1.2 *France in 1480*

Burgundy, Mary, had married Maximilian of Habsburg, the ruling family of the Holy Roman Empire. Their son, Philip, would become ruler of the Netherlands. Louis XI's successor, Charles VIII (1483–98) introduced a further cause of conflict. When the Duke of Brittany died in 1487, Charles invaded the duchy, married the Duke's young daughter and provoked war with Maximilian. France had extended its territory but at the cost of generating conflict with the Habsburg Empire.

Spain

The most important development here was the marriage of King Ferdinand of Aragon to Queen Isabella of Castile. These were the two most important states in Spain (see Figure 6.1 on page 57) and had been major players in the civil war which had racked the Iberian peninsula for much of the century. In 1479 Isabella was finally acknowledged by all as the true Queen of Castile, while Ferdinand became King of Aragon. Together the two rulers began the process of uniting Spain and restoring royal authority. The foundations of what would become Europe's greatest power in the second half of the sixteenth century were being laid. Ferdinand and Isabella's task was made easier because the kingdom of Portugal was now investing more of its energies in the exploration of territories overseas, especially in west Africa. This activity deflected Portugal from the damaging interference in Spanish affairs it had exercised earlier.

Italy

Italy (see Figure 1.3) was obviously a geographic unit but it was politically a confusing mixture of small states, many of them built on great trading towns of the thirteenth and fourteenth centuries. Conflict between these had been normal for centuries. The main Italian territories at the time were:

Figure 1.3 *Italy in 1480*

■ **Venice** – the greatest; now sufficiently strong to dominate much of north-east Italy.

■ **Milan** in the North-West was controlled by the Sforza family who were great patrons of the arts but also frequently brutal and aggressive rulers.

■ **Florence** was controlled by another of the great Italian families – the Medici. Its power in parts of northern Italy had become substantial. Duke Lorenzo de' Medici (1469–92) was known as 'The Magnificent'. He was a powerful, but tyrannical, ruler. After his death, his son Piero struggled to hold on to the state's influence and was to prove an important element in the growing instability of Italy at the end of the century.

■ **The Papacy**   We must remember that, in their own territories, the Popes were not only the rulers of the Church but significant secular rulers. New Popes did not 'emerge' because of some divine revelation which everyone had to accept. Once a pope died, his successor was elected by a 'college' of Cardinals. Although in theory the cardinals were expected to choose the best qualified pastor and church leader, in practice papal elections for many years had been the source of some of the most shameless power-broking in Europe. This was because leading families, not only in Italy but outside it, schemed to have one of their members elected. It was normal for younger sons of princes and aristocrats to go into the Church and for their families to engineer rapid advancement for them. So there was no shortage of powerful candidates to be Pope. Families which were disappointed during a papal election often nursed a sense of grievance which broke out into conflict. The image of the Papacy easily became tarnished. The conduct of worldly popes – such as Sixtus IV (1471–84) who raised his own army and who distributed lavish gifts and powerful church jobs on his own family – only lowered it further. By the end of the fifteenth century, the Papacy was a source of at least as much conflict as spiritual leadership and comfort.

■ The **Kingdom of the Two Sicilies** – Naples and Sicily (see Figure 1.3). These southern kingdoms were remote from the main centres of power within Italy but they were a source of rivalry and dispute nevertheless. The throne there had become disputed once the succession passed down an illegitimate line. The kings of Aragon and the Popes were only two of many rulers who hoped to profit from the fact that kings who were illegitimate usually faced powerful challenges to their authority.

The Holy Roman Empire

Like the Popes, the rulers of the Holy Roman Empire (see Figure 1.4) were elected. However, since 1437, the immensely powerful Habsburg family had provided the Emperors and would continue to do so throughout the sixteenth century. In practice, the Habsburgs became dynastic, rather than elected, rulers of the Empire (*i.e.* the succession remained in the one family). This should have been a source both for continuity and stability, and in one sense it was. The Habsburgs were the most important family in Europe for more than a century. In another sense, however, the opposite was true. The 'Habsburg Empire', as it came to be known, was not a unified territory. It included about 300 states, some of them large and threatening, some small and obscure. Most of them clung fiercely to their local privileges. One or two of the biggest rulers, such as the Duke of Brandenburg, could raise bigger armies than the Emperor himself. Eighty cities – such as the important north German trading centres of Hamburg, Bremen and Lübeck – were virtually independent of any imperial control. The 13 **cantons** into which Switzerland was divided were likewise not controlled by the Emperor and the cities had declared themselves independent. In these circumstances, it is hardly surprising that the long-lived Emperor Frederick III (1440–93) decided to concentrate his energies on what we would today call his 'core territories' – the family lands of Austria, Styria and the Netherlands (see Figure 1.4). These alone made him one of Europe's most powerful rulers.

KEY TERM:

Canton

A **canton** is an heraldic term denoting the upper part of a shield. The term has come to mean an area, or subdivision, of a country. The Swiss Confederation was divided into 13 areas known as **cantons**.

Figure 1.4 *The Holy Roman Empire in 1480*

The edges of Europe

Many opportunities for instability presented themselves in the far north, east and south of the continent. Among the most important at this time were:

■ King John of Denmark: he had become ruler of Norway as well in 1483 and planned something of a Scandinavian clean-sweep with designs on Sweden.

■ King Casimir of Poland – an area which frequently had to fight for its independence.

■ Ivan III, Grand Duke of Muscovy (1462–1505). He successfully challenged the long-established authority of the Tatar rulers and in 1480 proclaimed himself 'sovereign of all Russia'. Russia was, for most Europeans, a remote, primitive and barbarous country. However, its potential for effective involvement on its western and southern borders was enormous, as subsequent rulers would prove.

■ South-East Europe – here in 1453 the most significant change of the century had taken place. The Ottoman Turks captured Constantinople, on the border of Europe and Asia and the historic centre of eastern Christianity. The Ottoman rulers – the Sultans – were casting ever more greedy eyes over southern Europe. Some, like Bayezid II (1481–1512), harboured hopes of overrunning the whole Christian world and converting it to Islam. This was no idle boast. By 1480, Turkish armies had taken Serbia and Albania, reached the banks of the river Danube overlooking Hungary and had even landed in southern Italy. No one responded to the call from the Emperor and the Pope for a Christian Crusade against the Muslims. As the historian Maurice Keen wrote: 'That consciousness of Christian union, in matters political as well as religious, which marks off medieval from modern Europe, did not exist any more.' Only Hungary and Venice had any success against the advancing Turks. Hungary put on a show of military strength; Venice offered the Sultan an annual bribe. Would the Turks threaten the heartland of western Europe? No one knew, but many Christians feared the answer.

The aims and means of the rulers

Everywhere in western Europe rulers were moving to assert the un-limited extent of the powers they exercised, acknowledging the superior authority only of God. Kings and Princes in Spain, Italy, France, England and the German states stressed the sovereignty of Roman law, which recognised the power of princes over their subjects. The influential writer Philip de Commynes (1447–1511) stated that rulers who observed the law and demonstrated the traditional leadership qualities of courage and morality served the best interests of their people. The rulers themselves preferred survival to lessons in political theory but often concluded that appearing just and generous to their subjects was the best way to achieve this objective.

Rulers also had a strong determination to see their own sons succeed them. These dynastic ambitions were pursued in three ways: by war, marriage and diplomacy. If *war* was primarily the sport of kings, it was only because few others could afford to raise and pay for the troops. Certainly wars were not fought for the benefit of the people; though, from a prince's point of view, war carried positive gains: the nobility acquired military commands, and a successful campaign brought glory, titles and land. War was, however, expensive and unpredictable. A quarter of Pope Sixtus IV's annual expenditure went on military costs and Louis XI's army of 40,000 troops was only made possible because he could guarantee their payment. 'No money, no Swiss,' ran a contemporary saying, reminding us that the Swiss mercenaries were the best and the most expensive army for hire.

Marriage offered the prince a more stable prospect. A skilfully arranged contract between rival families might reduce the possibility of war – as the marriages of Ferdinand to Isabella of Castile, Charles VIII to Anne of Brittany, and Maximilian to Mary of Burgundy showed. The unscrupulousness of Louis XI, celebrated in Machiavelli's *Prince*, was amply demonstrated when he married his crippled daughter to the Duke of Orleans in the knowledge that the ducal lands would pass to the French crown upon the Duke's death.

Such devices were traditional princely pursuits but the late fifteenth century also witnessed a new development in several Italian city states. From around 1450, Milan, Florence, Naples, Venice and Rome began to appoint ambassadors to each other's courts. Governments had always used spies and informers to acquire accurate details about family alliances, arguments and trade agreements, but as intelligence gathering became more sophisticated, the role of ambassadors was viewed in Italy as an essential feature of diplomacy.

Administration

Medieval government reflected the will of the ruler: the ability to command respect and organise an effective administration largely decided whether the ruler would succeed or fail. All monarchs were served by a body of 'councillors' drawn from the royal household, clergy and nobility. They attended the king as he required them. In many states it was the role of the nobles to give advice and it was the role of the clergy to provide the administration, largely because the higher clergy had good communication skills, especially in Latin, which remained the administrative language in many states. By the end of the fifteenth century, however, knowledge of the law was increasingly prized by monarchs as they attempted to confirm and defend their rights to ancient, feudal inheritance. Increasingly, trained lawyers played an influential role at court.

The nobility, however, could pose a problem for rulers. They were all great landowners and had grown used to recruiting armies of their own, both to defend their territories and – when opportunity offered – to increase them. So they kept what amounted to professional soldiers (armed retainers) to defend their interests. Rulers had to treat the more powerful nobility cautiously. Successful rulers might be able to isolate individual 'over-mighty' subjects and reduce their power. Harsh or unjust rule, however, might provoke the nobles to challenge royal authority. How effectively rulers handled their nobility frequently shaped the destinies of their country. Generalisations are dangerous but the following relationships can be observed at the time this book begins:

- In **France**, kings were advised by royal princes, aristocrats and clergy in the *Conseil du roi* (King's Council). However, local rights and a confusion of local government practices made it difficult for the King consistently to enforce his will over his subjects.

- In **Spain**, the nobility had acquired extensive lands from the monarchs of Castile and Aragon without yet giving up much of their independent powers of action.

- **Venice** and the **Papacy** both had relatively advanced administrations, though of different types. In Venice the tradition had been firmly established of government in the hands of wealthy merchant families. The Papacy had developed an extensive and efficient *curia* (council) and relied on intricate diplomacy and information-gathering services to provide church leaders with the service they needed.

- The **Holy Roman Emperor** ran his estates from his court in Vienna. A chancery (which kept records and provided legal administration), a treasury (running finance) and an extensive secretariat (offering a kind of early civil service) all combined to give the Empire an outward show of effective government. In reality, it proved very difficult to impose any kind of imperial power on many of the states.

- Most of the states of **Eastern Europe** had only elementary governmental structures. The size of the countries and the limited number of

KEY TERM:

Serfs

These were the landless labourers who were virtually slaves. **Serfs** made up most of the population in Russia and only gained their freedom in 1861.

towns and commercial outlets all combined to ensure that rulers depended heavily for support upon the nobility. The monarchs of Bohemia, Hungary and Poland were further restricted by constitutions which required elections from among the landed elite. In Russia, the tsar was able to gain the cooperation of his nobility only by rewarding them with grants of land and giving them almost total control over their **serfs**.

Throughout Europe as a whole late in the fifteenth century, local interests still exercised a powerful influence against the ability of rulers to centralise power in their own hands. In Spain, the Basques resented Aragon; in France, the Bretons were similarly suspicious of Louis XI and Charles VIII. Those from Pisa resented rule from Florence as the Genoese did that from Milan. As yet, no real feelings of 'national identity' were detectable in those countries which were to become nation states during the sixteenth century, even if their rulers claimed to be ruling in their interests.

The condition of the Church

Although the Papacy was in theory the supreme ruler over all the Catholic church, in practice its power had been declining since the eleventh century, when clashes with the Holy Roman Emperor had first begun. Its credibility was seriously damaged during the years 1378 to 1417 when there was a 'schism' with two rival popes vying for authority, each claiming that he was the source of true authority in the Church.

In the fifteenth century, a desire by successive popes to establish their position as princes within Italy and to promote individual family interests worked against the growth of church authority. Pope Sixtus IV, for example, unashamedly favoured his nephew, Giuliano, whom he created Archbishop of Avignon and ruler of two wealthy abbeys. In some parts of Europe – notably Burgundy, France and Spain – the Pope's right to appoint archbishops and other senior posts in the Church was often challenged successfully.

Throughout the Middle Ages the clergy had been criticised both by laymen and by some preachers, but these criticisms seemed to have greater validity during the fifteenth century when church life almost certainly deteriorated in quality. Tales of corruption abounded. Anticlerical writers described:

■ the selling of important offices to the highest bidder – 'simony'

■ holding several church jobs at once – 'pluralism'

- neglecting church duties by not being there – 'absenteeism'
- clergy who lacked money, education and proper knowledge of church doctrine
- lecherous monks and nuns leading scandalous lives in monasteries.

Medieval German dramas – such as The *Rise and Fall of Antichrist* in which the Church showed itself incapable of resisting temptation by the Devil, and Sebastian Brant's *Ship of Fools* which satirised the monastic orders – proved highly popular, suggesting that attenders agreed with the critical messages being put across. Many felt that the Church had entirely lost its way in teaching, in pastoral care and in standards of clerical morality. We should be careful, however, of painting too crude a picture. Shafts of light could be perceived amid the clerical gloom. Some bishops were pious, devout, organised and excellent church leaders. Some German preachers called upon the Emperor to lead a pro-reform movement within the Church. Some monasteries proved themselves capable both of internal reforms and of increasing the spiritual zeal of their members.

The main drive for reform, however, came from the laity, some of whom were becoming increasingly dissatisfied with many orthodox Catholic beliefs, at least as interpreted by the Church. A small minority – like the Waldensians in the French Alps, the Hussites in Bohemia, the Lollards in England and the Fraticelli in Italy – even set up their own organisations. For the most part, however, the fifteenth century saw an intensification of certain aspects of Catholicism, particularly those associated with the rituals of the Church. Few lay people understood the details of the theology which underpinned the Catholic Church, but they retained vivid pictures of Heaven and Hell from the teachings they received about death. Death, indeed, absorbed most people's thinking about religion, perhaps not surprisingly in an age where large numbers of children failed to survive infancy and where infections regularly carried off substantial numbers of adults. The growing number of chantries, established to hear daily prayers for the dead, confirms the preoccupation with death. Every town and church boasted its collection of 'holy relics' – most of them entirely spurious, of course. Wittenberg Castle Church in Saxony possessed 17,443 such relics and celebrated over 100 'holy days' a year. Pilgrimages to holy places such as Jerusalem, Rome, Compostella and Mont-St-Michel were very popular by the end of the fifteenth century. Venetian shipping companies, ever alert to the prospect of profit, offered cut-price trips to them.

A few of the better educated began to search for an alternative route to salvation. This stressed not unthinking obedience to the rituals of Catholicism, but a more 'personalised' religion in which people sought

God through their own study of the messages of the Gospels. These people were often called 'pietists'. They founded 'schools' such as the Brethren of Life, which emphasised the scriptures, Christian values and inner spirituality, rather than a slavish acceptance of Church doctrine. Following some of the earlier leads of the Hussites and Lollards, they laid down an important challenge to orthodox Catholicism. Would either the Papacy or the Holy Roman Empire be able to summon up the strong leadership to meet it? Failure by the authorities risked provoking an avalanche of religious and political changes which neither institution could possibly contain.

Further reading

J. Lotherington (ed.) *Years of Renewal: European History, 1470–1600* (Hodder and Stoughton, 1988) – a useful A-Level text.

R. Bonney, *The European Dynastic States, 1494–1660* (Oxford University Press, 1991) – a very impressive general introduction.

J. Bossy, *Christianity in the West, 1400–1700* (Oxford University Press, 1985) – studies changing religious perspectives in the longer term.

D. Hay, *Europe in the Fourteenth and Fifteenth Centuries* (Addison Wesley Longman, 2nd edn, 1989) – originally published in 1966 and provides an older and thoughtful analysis of the period which immediately precedes this.

J. R. Hale, *Renaissance Europe, 1480–1520* (Fontana, 1971) – a short but impressive and perceptive study.

R. Mackenney, *Sixteenth-Century Europe: Expansion and Conflict* (Macmillan, 1993) – a more advanced study, which is skilfully written.

2 Europe in 1480: economic and social conditions

The evidence for fifteenth-century economic and social history is patchy and for the most part incomplete, so we should recognise that all conclusions must be even more tentative than usual. Statistics were rarely kept, records were imperfectly drawn up and, where details have survived, their value is often very limited. Having taken such considerations into account, historians generally believe that the late fifteenth century was a time of economic change. Social conditions can, of course, either restrict or encourage economic change. In this period they usually did the former rather than the latter, so that even where fundamental changes were occurring, society remained essentially stable.

Population

The most important change was the increase in population. After a century of relative stagnation following the Black Death of 1347–9, the population of most European countries began to grow again in the second half of the fifteenth century. Increases were greatest in northern Europe, especially Scandinavia, and less so in Mediterranean states like Spain and Italy. A combination of factors – peace, a steady expansion of towns and trade, and fewer crop failures – may explain this upward trend although outbreaks of plague, war, bad harvests, and unchanging farming techniques ensured increases were inconsistent and regionally variable.

In 1480 Europe was an underpopulated continent with some 50 million people. About 19 and 20 million, respectively, lived in France and Germany. Figures, however, can be misleading. Most people lived in the countryside and few countries had more than one city in excess of 100,000 people. In the 1480s the most populous cities were Naples (c. 200,000), Paris (150,000), Milan, Venice, Valencia and Istanbul (c. 100,000). Interestingly, none of these was in the Holy Roman Empire. As population levels began to rise, so the demand for food increased. Although money wages continued to rise, this demand pushed prices of food and other necessities up by more, so the real value of wages declined. Coincidentally, the discovery of silver deposits in Hungary and Bohemia in the 1470s added to the rise in prices which, in Germany and parts of France, stood at between 2 and 3 per cent a year.

KEY TERM:

Subsistence economy

This is where the main economic activities are the production of food and goods solely for those that produce them and not for the market.

Trade

Medieval towns had developed as religious, university and political centres as well as a result of economic activity. As they grew in size and prosperity, so the demand for work and goods stimulated an expansion of trade, both locally and nationally. The medieval manorial economy was at **subsistence** level, producing enough food in a good year to feed its own inhabitants and using its surplus to buy or exchange crops and goods from nearby towns at the weekly market. Items on sale varied from region to region, but most were farm produce, textiles and goods from local trades, though spices from the Orient and French wine were always in demand. Some countries, like Poland and Estonia, regularly exported crops, and Sicily had emerged as the main grain supplier in the Mediterranean exporting nearly 10,000 tons a year. Already there was long-distance trade though enormous risks and very high costs restricted it to two main areas which had the necessary maritime and financial resources:

- North-west Europe stretching from the Baltic Sea to the Netherlands and northern France, and dominated by the towns of the Hanseatic League in the north-east and Bruges in the north-west;
- Northern Italy and southern Germany.

North-west Europe

In northern Europe, the cities of the Hansa (Hanseatic League) – led by Lübeck, Danzig, Brunswick and Cologne – had controlled the Baltic–North Sea trade since the thirteenth century. Their merchants transported grain, herring, timber, iron ore, flax and furs from Poland and Lithuania, Scandinavia and northern Germany to all parts of Europe and enjoyed extensive privileges in most foreign ports. However, there were already signs that the Hansa's monopoly was coming to an end. Danish and Dutch merchants challenged German traders in the Baltic. Bruges, the Hansa's principal *entrepôt*, was in decline as Castilian, French and English cloth merchants increasingly favoured Antwerp because of its accessibility by land, sea and river, and its biennial (held every other year) fairs. When Emperor Maximilian forced all foreign traders to move there from Bruges in 1488, Antwerp's golden age began to dawn.

Northern Italy and southern Germany

The Mediterranean had been at the heart of European trade for some 2,000 years. By 1480 the centre of commerce was firmly established in Genoa and Venice, the crossroads of east–west traffic. Genoa's trade largely consisted of the import of silk from southern Spain, wool and

KEY TERM:

Entrepôt

Commercial centre for the collection and distribution of goods and raw materials.

alum for the north Italian textile industry, and spices via its bases on the Aegean and Black Sea. Venice brought in spices, perfumes, silk and dyes from the East. Its merchants then exported them to the rest of Europe's cities.

In the second half of the fifteenth century both centres of trade experienced external threats. Genoa had largely seen off rival competition from Catalonian merchants in the western Mediterranean but found its eastern trade severely affected by the advancing Turks. It had to abandon both its Black Sea routes and a recently established pepper trade with India. Genoese merchants tried to develop banking and insurance but this initiative was too little too late to sustain its commercial dominance. Venice was similarly affected but showed greater resilience by developing local glass and textile industries, and by negotiating a truce with the Turks in 1479. Condemned for this by the rest of Europe, Venice alone was able to expand its commerce with Egypt and Cyprus and so kept its monopoly on the valuable pepper and spice trade. Above all, trade with southern Germany increased rapidly. The towns of the Swabian League, established in 1488, produced linen, fustian and minerals; new techniques enabled miners to dig deeper shafts to extract copper and silver in the Austrian Tyrol, Saxony and Bohemia; towns like Ulm, Augsburg and Nuremberg flourished as centres of arms manufacturing.

Government intervention in trade

In the last quarter of the fifteenth century some rulers realised the advantages which trade could bring and tried to introduce an elementary form of **protectionism**. Louis XI of France, for instance, regulated the quality of cloth production in Paris, Rouen and Bordeaux, protected the Rheims linen trade and exempted Lyon silk merchants from taxation. In Spain, the Catholic Monarchs (Ferdinand and Isabella – see chapter 1) increased the Mesta's (sheep farmers) privileges, granted a monopoly of Castilian wool to the Burgos merchants and gave control of American trade to the *Casa de Contratación* in Seville.

Transport

Sea transport

Most countries introduced navigation laws designed to encourage the export of goods in native ships and so increase shipbuilding. However, it was Portugal and Spain who pioneered new ships and financed overseas expeditions. In the early fifteenth century Portuguese sailors developed the **carrack** and then the **galley**. These innovations enabled them to travel faster than before and increased the size of cargoes from 100 to 800

KEY TERMS:

Protectionism

In order to safeguard native trades and industries from foreign competition, governments took a variety of measures known as **protectionism**. Such protection included imposing import duties on manufactured goods, encouraging native shipbuilding, and granting favoured companies trade benefits. These actions were not generally part of a coherent strategy and were a far cry from the more extensive protection known in the eighteenth century as 'mercantilism', but the principle was the same.

Casa de Contratación

The *Casa de Contratación*, or House of Trade, regulated all vessels, commerce and passengers travelling between Spain and America.

Carrack

A large merchant-ship with four sails which was equipped for warfare.

Galley

A low, single-decked vessel powered by wind and by oars.

tons. Equipped with the necessary navigation instruments – the quadrant, compass and a table of the stars – they were able to undertake long journeys. Perhaps it was the quest to satisfy their curiosity of the unknown – a desire to locate the legendary Prester John, or the search for gold in north Africa – which encouraged them to sail out of sight of land. Perhaps it was the financial support – 'patronage' – of Henry 'the Navigator' (1394–1460), governor of the Algarve. By 1480 Portuguese sailors had explored the coast of west Africa as far south as Guinea, settled the islands of Madeira and the Azores, and established a trade route from Sierra Leone to the Cameroons.

Seven years later, John II (1481–95) gave financial support to Bartholomew Dias, enabling him to sail further south, to the Cape of Good Hope. Portugal stood on the threshold of acquiring the first overseas European empire, and all the benefits and problems which accompanied it. Coincidentally, the Genoese adventurer, Christopher Columbus, was rejected by John in 1484 and failed to convince the English and French monarchs that his plan to sail across the Atlantic in search of the 'Spice Islands' was commercially viable. It was then Castile's judgement and good fortune to back his expedition in 1492. The result helped to transform Spain into the leading European power for the next 150 years.

Land transport

If the overseas trade picture was changing, methods of land transport were not. Roads were poor, often impassable in winter, and littered with bandits. Merchants travelled in convoys and, as all journeys were conducted by packhorses and carts, travel was slow, arduous and costly. An average convoy travelled only 15 miles a day, and transport costs determined the price of goods. For instance, 95 per cent of the cost of timber went on transport charges. Navigable rivers provided cheaper transport so, in areas like the Po valley in Italy, canals were dug. The average travelling time on the Rhine – Europe's busiest river – was 21 miles a day, but its popularity only encouraged provincial and state authorities to impose tolls, which increased the costs and journey times. By 1480 there were over 60 tolls on the Rhine and 15 on the Seine between Rouen and Paris.

Banking

A major development in most European cities in the fifteenth century was the growth in commerce and financial activities. In Italy sophisticated commercial practices had been established by 1300. The characteristic feature in Florence was for members of a family and friends to form a company, invest their money and share the profit. The largest companies like the Medicis had agents and factors in foreign towns and diversified their wealth into providing loans. Interest rates were high; 7 to 15 per cent was usually asked while money deposited with them earned rates of 6 to 10 per cent. Until the fifteenth century, the Papacy had condemned money-lending but by the 1480s, recognising that it was out of step with changing practices, it acknowledged that an interest rate could be imposed to cover the risks and charges. No fixed rate was stated but 5 per cent was considered to be a 'just' price. In fact, interest payments were often concealed in a contract by recording the higher figure for repayment as the actual loan.

In the 1480s the Monti di Pietà (banks which loaned money to the poor) were set up in Italy and endorsed by the Church; in Lyon, merchants charged 15 per cent on communal loans and Muscovite monks levied 150 per cent. Some merchant families made fortunes by providing financial services. In Augsburg, the Welsers, Hochstetters and Fuggers became major bankers, though it was Jakob Fugger who turned his family business into an international concern. He imported spices and cotton, exported silver and copper from 1480 and dominated trade between Swabia and Antwerp (see Figure 1.4, page 8). When Jakob Fugger was asked whether he planned to rest on his laurels having cornered the European financial market, he replied with characteristic candour that he would 'make a profit as long as he could'.

Insurance brokers also flourished to provide another service for traders at risk of loss at sea. They offered much higher rates on less stable round-ships which travelled the Mediterranean. Bills of exchange and promissory notes (IOUs) were used to avoid the need to carry large amounts of cash about. Such paper transactions could also be used to raise money. Although there was reasonable comparability between local rates of exchange, variations did exist and it was possible for merchants to borrow money in Florence, for example, and sell at a profit in Lyon. In Genoa and Venice, shares in trading companies could be bought on the open market. Much of this commercial activity can be explained by a slackening of domestic trade in the second half of the fifteenth century which encouraged merchants to put their wealth into shipping and insurance services. When the level of international trade picked up at the turn of the century, western Europe was well placed to reap the reward.

Agriculture and industry

The agrarian economy saw few changes in this period. The land was tilled by the village community, so many wasteful practices continued. One-

Fulling and tentering

Fulling is the process of cleaning and thickening cloth by beating and washing it. This process is also referred to as 'milling the cloth'.

Tentering is the next process in the manufacture of cloth. After fulling, the cloth is stretched over a wooden framework, so that it sets or dries evenly and without shrinking. A tenter-hook is a bent nail by which the ends of the cloth are held firmly on to the tenter frame. The expression 'on tenter-hooks' means on the edge, nerves taut, waiting to see what will happen.

third of the land was left fallow each year, growing no crop. Animals were grazed on the fallow fields, their droppings providing the only form of fertiliser. Productivity was low, so there was not enough food to keep many animals alive in the winter. The quality of livestock was very low as a result. Rather than change their traditional methods to produce more sheep and cattle, farmers moved on to upland regions, and arable farmers reclaimed land and encroached on waste lands and forests. More than 90 per cent of the population lived on the land and there was only a slow movement of labour from the countryside to the towns.

Very little industry existed in the fifteenth century. Waterwheels, windmills and treadmills were the main sources of energy, and in the principal manufacturing industry – the cloth trade – only the **fulling and tentering** processes involved large workforces. Most employees did part-time work in addition to farming, as sorters, spinners, weavers, warpers, finishers and dyers in their own homes. The mining industry, however, was steadily expanding due to the requirements of war, the demand for metals, and the need for silver. From the mid fifteenth century, the 'saiger' process enabled silver to be extracted from silver-bearing copper ores, and more money was invested in silver, copper and mercury mining. The only large-scale industry in Europe, however, was the Arsenal in Venice where up to 4,000 craftsmen worked in 50 acres [20 hectares] of shipyards.

Society

Everyone in the fifteenth century belonged, in theory, to one of three 'orders':

- the nobles defended the people,
- the clergy prayed for them,
- the labourers, according to William Caxton, provided 'for the clerks and knights such things as were needful for them to live by in the world honestly'.

This clearly-defined and static medieval world picture was idealised by writers who wanted to preserve the old order at a time of economic and political change. Woodcuts commonly illustrated disruptive social behaviour to remind everyone that they should keep their place in society (see Figure 2.1). Similarly, any sect or group that fell outside the traditional power structure, dominated by the nobility and the clergy, were viewed as social upstarts, a threat to the moral order. Doctors, lawyers and officials were therefore widely despised for much the same reasons as Jews, gypsies and beggars: each appeared to be living off the

Figure 2.1 *A German woodcut* Die Veränderung der Stände *(1508) revealing a mythical world in which the normal order is turned upside down. The clergy are ploughing the fields while the peasants conduct church services.*

backs of the people without producing anything tangible in return. The fifteenth century was an age when skilled craftsmen were rewarded according to the quality of their work and though education could unlock the door of social mobility – the painter Sandro Botticelli's father was a tanner – the declining feudal system still possessed tremendous force.

Peasants

Since at least the eleventh century, peasants had served landlords in return for the right to farm an agreed plot of land. The nobility held huge estates and enjoyed wide privileges, while also agreeing to provide their princes with an armed force or other services when they were requested. This social system was known as feudalism. Gradually, the wealth gained from trade and landownership enabled nobles to transfer their personal and military obligations to their princes into money payments. The scarcity of labour after the Black Death also loosened the bonds between the peasantry and their landlords. The degrees of emancipation, by which serfs achieved increasing freedom from restrictions on their lives, varied from country to country.

In general, peasants living west of the river Elbe enjoyed greater freedom than those in Brandenburg, Poland, Prussia and Russia. In France, the

Netherlands, much of Italy and west Germany, the peasantry was treated quite liberally. The *métayage* system, whereby land was held in return for a rent in kind, enabled French peasants to acquire and develop their own land. Conditions in Spain were more variable: in Castile they were fair, but in Catalonia and Aragon service tenure was the norm, and throughout Spain all peasants were subject to unrelenting taxation. Opportunities for social and economic improvement existed for those peasants who lived near a town where their local produce and goods could be sold. In the Netherlands town burghers and country peasants lived side by side free of feudal obligations.

Only in times of famine or rising food prices was there social tension, and then the civic and ecclesiastical authorities tried to keep control. In north-west Germany and central Europe, however, peasants received increasing demands for labour, and serfdom persisted. Low population densities, poor communications and the dominance of the Hanseatic League and Teutonic Knights slowed down the development of towns situated east of the river Elbe. A trade recession in the second half of the fifteenth century affected their main exports – grain, timber and hemp. By 1480 the peasantry was being exploited. Hopes of emancipation would not be realised until the nineteenth century and landlord–serf hostility was never far from the surface.

Slavery still existed in several states bordering the Mediterranean: in southern Iberia, 'Saracens' were captured by Christians and in Granada and north Africa, Christians were seized by Muslims and enslaved. In parts of Messina, Venice, Genoa, Lisbon, Toulon and Marseilles slaves of all colours and creeds – the product of war and piracy – were bought and sold, and domestic slavery was commonplace in Italy and Portugal. In 1488 Ferdinand of Aragon saw nothing wrong in sending Pope Innocent VIII 100 Muslims as a gift. The Pope passed them on to his cardinals.

Bad harvests, famine and disease were endemic features of urban and rural life. Most upper clergy and nobles preferred to live on their country estates away from urban squalor. As principal landowners, they placed great store by the size of their estates, the number of tenants and servants who wore their uniforms ('liveries'), and how well they kept their house. In an age when few nobles participated in trade or business and a gentleman's coat reflected his social standing, poorer nobles like the Polish *szlachta* and Spanish *hidalgos* struggled to maintain appearances. For most peasants and day-labourers, survival hung by a thin thread, often determined by seasonal and local weather conditions.

The family household was the unit of all social groups. Within it, its members lived, worked, played and died. Marriage was for life but, as girls married much earlier than men and many married more than once, extended families were normal. Society was patriarchal: the male worked and the female tended his home and family, though enough woodcuts have survived to remind us that many females worked and some were independent, thus challenging the stereotype image of male control. The eternal battle of the sexes was a paradoxical feature in an essentially stable society.

Task: making notes

An important skill you need to acquire early in your A-Level course is note-making.

Why make notes?

1 Notes will be shorter than the books you have read, and probably shorter than some of your class handouts as well.

2 Good notes help you to make coherent sense of a topic. Working on longer pieces of writing to produce shorter notes should help you to get your ideas in order.

3 Notes give you a chance to practise making your own selection of what is important from what is often a lot of detail. This is a valuable historical skill in its own right and specially important at exam time.

4 Notes will be much easier to revise from when the time comes.

What makes good notes?

■ Notes are for you. So devise a system which is for your benefit. People learn in different ways but notes should always be shorter than the source from which you are taking them.

■ You don't practise how to write essays in notes, so don't worry about complete sentences or even looking up spellings. Don't be afraid to use abbreviations, so long as you are sure that you will remember what they mean later. Try to simplify what you read, but remember that you may need to use them again in a year or more's time. Simplify in ways which will help you remember.

■ The way this book is organised should help you with your notes. It contains some big headings for you to follow. It also gives you specific factual information in the time charts, although a few chapters do not have one because a time chart would give undue prominence to particular events when the main theme concerns continuity and change over many years in several countries. An example of this is the present chapter.

■ It will probably be a good idea to stick with the main headings from the book, and then jot down notes which help you to understand why the heading is an important one.

■ Don't forget that some themes are found in more than one chapter. The good note-maker will know that the index of a book is a useful way of finding out whether there are more references. In this book you will find reference to:
– the main content headings
– the key terms whose meaning you need to know
– the key people who are given brief profiles in the book.
You will find reference to the specific pages on which more information may be found. Become familiar with an index. The index can provide numerous short-cuts to valuable ideas and information.

Example of note-making

Getting started

Let us say that you want to make notes on European trade in the 1480s. You will see that there is a heading specifically on this, so that should be your starting-point. Look at that section carefully. Your notes will probably follow the order of the section. You will also see that in the section there are subheadings and references in bold type to key terms. You will want to make use of them. As you work your way through the section, look for developments which resulted in economic change as well as in continuity.

Now look at the example opposite of notes on this section. The aim was to shorten, simplify and yet give sufficient information to help you when you come back to the topic – perhaps when you write an essay or just before an examination.

Eur. trade in the 1480s

1 Intro: Medieval econ. was subsistence (self-suff.) but local tr. expanded due to demand for farm prod., textiles, goods + foreign spices & wine. A few countries e.g. Pol, Est, Sic, exported cereals.

2 N. Europe: Hansa (centred on Bruges) controlled shipment of grain, herring, timber, iron, flax, furs between Baltic and North Sea, BUT incr. challenged by Den, Neth, Fr and Eng merchants: — rise of Antwerp; decline of Bruges.

3 Mediterranean: Italian merchants imp/exp silk, wool, alum, spices, perfume to Europe but incr. challenged by Turks in the East. Genoa suffered in spite of devel. commerce & banking; Venice survived due to glass & text ind. and its truce with Turkey (1479). S. Germ trade (linen, fustian, copper, silver) growing via Swabian League (est. 1488).

4 G.ment intervention (protectionism): aim? — protect native trade/ind; how? impose high duties on for. goods; low duties on dom. goods & raw materials; develop shipbuilding BUT inconsistently applied e.g. Fr — cloth trade; Castile — Mesta (wool); Casa (House of Tr).

5 Transport: by sea — imp. changes in ship design e.g. Port. carrack, galley & navig. instr. (quadr, comp, star charts), patronage (Henry the Nav.) & exploration (Diaz).
by land — little change due to slow (15 m.p.day), dang., rough, expen. roads; quicker (21 m.p.day) by river, BUT exp. tolls (e.g. 60 on Rhine).

Further reading

M. Keen, *The Pelican History of Medieval Europe* (Pelican, 1969) – a sound general introduction to economic and social topics.

D. O'Sullivan, *The Age of Discovery, 1400–1500*, Seminar Studies in History (Addison Wesley Longman, 1984) – covers the early explorers and contains documentary texts.

H. Kamen, *European Society, 1500–1700* (Hutchinson, 1984) – a very detailed and readable study.

H. Kellenbenz, *The Rise of the European Economy: An Economic History of Continental Europe from the Fifteenth to the Eighteenth Century* (revised and edited by G. Benecke, Weidenfeld and Nicolson, 1976) – a wide-ranging and detailed survey.

G. V. Scammell, *The First Imperial Age: European Overseas Expansion 1400–1715* (Routledge, 1989) – a detailed examination of early exploration.

M. Bush (ed.), *Social Orders and Social Classes in Europe Since 1500* (Addison Wesley Longman, 1991) – a collection of lively essays.

3 A European intellectual and cultural revolution?

Time chart

1304: Birth of Petrarch (d.1374), writer

1377: Birth of Filippo Brunelleschi (d.1446), architect

1378: Birth of Vittorino da Feltre (d.1446), founder of Platonic schools

1386: Birth of Donatello (d.1466), sculptor

1392: Birth of Flavio Biondo (d.1463), humanist

1404: Birth of Leon Battista Alberti (d.1472), architect, writer and humanist

1410: Vitruvius's *Treatise on Architecture* is discovered

1414: *Imitation of Christ* written by Thomas à Kempis (1380–1471)

1428: Birth of Giovanni Bellini (d.1516), painter

1430: Birth of Jean de Okeghem (d.1494), composer

1431: Birth of Andrea Mantegna (d.1506), painter

1433: Birth of Marsilio Ficino (d.1499), humanist

1435: Birth of Andrea del Verrochio (d.1488), painter

1440: Birth of Josquin Desprez (d.1521), composer

1444: Birth of Donato Bramante (d.1514), sculptor

1445: Birth of Sandro Botticelli (d.1510), painter

c.1450: Birth of Lefèvre d'Étaples (d.1536), humanist

1452: Birth of Leonardo da Vinci (d.1519), painter, sculptor and inventor

1453: Johan Gutenberg invents a printing press with movable type

1467: Birth of Guillaume Budé (d. 1540), humanist

1471: Birth of Albrecht Dürer (d.1528), engraver

1475: Birth of Buonarroti Michelangelo (d.1564), painter, sculptor and architect

1483: Birth of Raphael (d.1520), painter

1486: Krämer and Sprenger publish the *Malleus Maleficarum*

Europe in the late fifteenth century experienced intellectual and cultural changes far greater than any previous or subsequent movement in modern history. First described by the Italian Vasari in 1550 as a 'renascita', or 'Renaissance', this development was more than a rebirth of classical ideas: it was a fresh consideration of existing beliefs and a challenge to traditional values. This chapter considers the main ideas that shaped people's minds and the changes which took place in the 1480s. Important questions need to be asked. Were these changes extensive and permanent or confined to particular social and intellectual groups? Was the pace of change rapid, even revolutionary, or was it slower and more variable – as between places and social groups?

Historians have long argued about the origin and nature of the Renaissance but it is now generally agreed that the movement had its roots in the ninth century when Charlemagne encouraged the collection of Roman literature, art and artefacts. In the twelfth century particular interest was taken in Arabic culture and ideas, which resulted in a rediscovery of Greek mathematics, science and philosophy. Two centuries later, the Italian poet Petrarch revived academics' awareness of Roman and Greek civilisation.

By the early fifteenth century the idea of a rebirth was widely acknowledged among Italian scholars. Flavio Biondo termed the thousand years following the fall of Rome (AD 410), the *medium aevum* or middle period, to distinguish it from his own enlightened age.

Humanism

Humanism lay at the heart of the fifteenth-century Renaissance. To Pico della Mirandola, writing in 1486, God had given Adam a central position in the universe so that he could 'more easily observe the world from there' and freely decide whether 'to degenerate into the lower forms of life, which are brutish' or 'to be reborn into the higher forms, which are divine'. The belief that humans could influence their own behaviour directly challenged traditional ideas based on the works of the Greek scholar Aristotle which had governed people's thinking for over 1,500 years. Humanists like Marsilio Ficino questioned Aristotle's view that the universe was fixed and that all substances were permanent. In his Latin translation of Plato, Ficino encouraged the study of Greek philosophy, art and literature to achieve the ideal concepts and values beyond human experiences. He identified the idea of 'Platonic love', the condition of spiritually perfect love. The Greeks had emphasised the importance of the individual and it was this which led Alberti to boast: 'Man can make whatever he will of himself.' Petrarch had earlier claimed that the works of the greatest Roman authors like Seneca, Livy and Cicero stressed moral, social and aesthetic values. These were the keys, he believed, to

KEY TERM:

Humanism

The 'humanista' was a student who educated himself for an active role in the political life of the state. By studying architecture, art, language, rhetoric and literature, he became a more civilised individual than students who were trained only in the civil or canon (church) law. The humanities were viewed as the essence of civilisation and enabled the student to discover the significant differences between classical and later cultures. A study of Plato and Homer, for instance, suggested that humans were not governed by destiny or absolute values and could determine their own fate.

27

Scholasticism and *imperium*

Scholasticism was a logical argument based upon fixed beliefs which rejected everything that fell outside such 'truths'. The thirteenth-century revival of Aristotelianism, and support given to it by St Thomas Aquinas (1226–74) and other theologians, ensured it became the basis of moral philosophy.
Imperium was the power of secular rulers balanced by, and equal to, the rule of priests. In practice, boundaries distinguishing temporal and spiritual authority were far from clear and open to challenge, as Marsilio of Padua showed in his book, the *Defensor Pacis* in 1324.

unlocking society's problems, rather than humility and penance as taught by Christian theologians. As a result, successive generations of Italian historians, led by Bruni and Valla, studied original texts in search of those civic virtues and noble values which had underpinned imperial Rome (see chapter 4).

As a further consequence of studying classical manuscripts, some fifteenth-century scholars began to challenge certain features of late medieval culture, notably **scholasticism**, *imperium* and Christianity. Florence, Naples and Rome established Platonic academies and in Venice and Mantua, Vittorino da Feltre introduced a new curriculum in his schools to teach grammar, history, moral philosophy, poetry and sport. Both rich and poor – girls as well as boys – attended and followed a curriculum which led many to criticise the Christian Church.

Humanism outside Italy

Educational changes were also taking place outside Italy. In the Netherlands the mystic religious order, the Brethren of the Common Life, set up schools in Deventer and Gouda and taught the '*devotio moderna*', a form of personal devotion. Their most celebrated student was Thomas à Kempis whose book, *Imitation of Christ*, was especially influential in shaping fifteenth-century humanism. In Germany scholars like Reuchlin and Erasmus began to study the scriptures more critically. For example, Erasmus's translation of the New Testament into Greek was heavily influenced by Lorenzo Valla's book on philology (study of literature), *Annotations*. Prince-bishops, abbots and city authorities, eager to assert political independence, recognised the advantages of Roman Law. Lawyers like Lupold of Bebenburg and Conrad of Megenburg stressed the nature of *imperium* and Ulrich von Hutten studied Tacitus's *Germania* and the chronicles of medieval rulers.

Humanist studies made limited progress in France and Spain. Guillaume Budé and Lefèvre d'Étaples were humanist oases in a French cultural desert. Though there were cultural links with Italy and much interest in classical literature, the humanist movement cut no ice with the Sorbonne – the guardian of French religious and cultural beliefs. Similarly in Spain, the powerful Salamanca University, shored up by its strict 'Thomist' philosophy [that of St Thomas Aquinas], rejected any study of Greek until the early sixteenth century.

Significantly, there was far less resistance from the scholastics in the cities of Germany, the Netherlands and Italy. In these seedbeds of change the printing press, the greatest invention of the fifteenth century, revolutionised the humanist movement. On the eve of its invention in 1453, literacy levels appear to have been rising and personal libraries were very fashionable. In 1437 Cosimo de' Medici established St Mark's Library in Florence and public libraries had been founded in Venice and Rome. The printing press greatly increased the number of books in circulation and spread ideas much more rapidly and extensively. Elizabeth Eisenstein has argued that although the presses at first reproduced errors and traditional ideas, such features were laid bare under textual analysis and any criticisms served only to stimulate further enquiry. It was these features which made the fifteenth-century Renaissance unique. It is important to remember, therefore, that the fifteenth-century European Renaissance was primarily an intellectual movement and that all subsequent artistic and scientific developments followed from this.

Science and mathematics

Figure 3.1 A 1486 reprint of The Earth According to Ptolemy

Contact with Arab Spain and Islamic culture in the twelfth century had

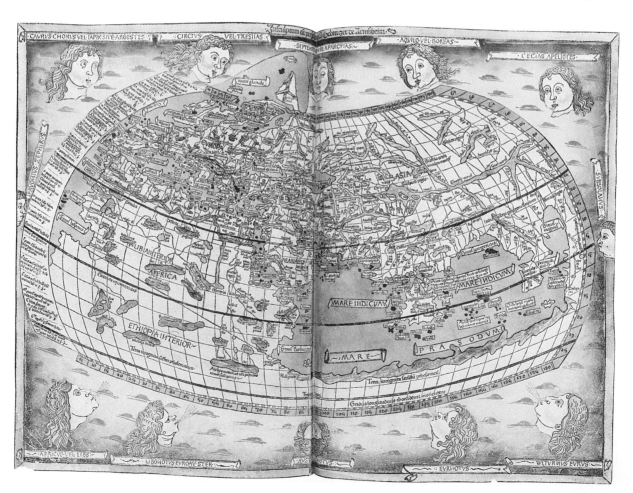

led to a rediscovery of Greek medicine, mathematics, astrology and astronomy. Of particular interest were Euclid's *Elements*, Archimedes's scientific treatises, and the *Almagest*, an Arab version of Ptolemy's astronomical system. By the fifteenth century these and other works were studied in their original texts in order to test long-established truths. Even Bishop Nicholas of Cusa shared Ptolemy's doubts about the earth being stationary but, as this theory conflicted with the Aristotelian and Catholic views, the politically correct bishop decided to keep his ideas to himself.

Another popular work was Ptolemy's *Geography*, which revealed that the world was a sphere and that Africa could be circumnavigated. Read in the late fourteenth century as a Greek text and translated into Latin in 1406, its ideas greatly influenced map-makers and explorers (see Figure 3.1). One visitor to Florence who studied the book was the brother of Henry, King of Portugal, who later patronised voyages to Africa and the Canaries. Caravan routes across the Sahara and China were thus well established, navigational instruments like the astrolabe and compass were widely used, and patrons with a desire to find out about the world around them were ready to back explorers like Bartolomew Dias, Christopher Columbus and John Cabot. A fascination for globes, curiosity in maps and a desire to discover new worlds were all part of the renaissance mind. In geography, as in intellectual life, medieval certainties were being challenged by new forms of experiment and enquiry.

Figure 3.2 *A detail from 'Birth of Venus' by Sandro Botticelli, painted about 1483–4*

The Arts

Italy

Paintings   The main school of visual art in the late fifteenth century was in northern Italy where several artists demonstrated an originality in style and technique that set the Italian Renaissance apart from other periods. Florence was culturally the richest of European cities in the 1480s. Artists working there included Luca della Robbia, Sandro Botticelli (see Figure 3.2), Andrea del Verrocchio and Leonardo da Vinci. Each painter had his own distinctive style. Robbia, for example, worked on terracotta reliefs; Leonardo preferred oils to egg tempera and introduced a novel use of light and shade known as chiaroscuro; Andrea Mantegna, who lived and worked mainly in Mantua, specialised in frescoes (murals) and paintings; his brother-in-law, the Venetian Giovanni Bellini, experimented with primary colours. Rules of perspective, the use of oils, the portrayal of the senses and feelings, and an increasing preference for landscapes and portraits, were all typical of fifteenth-century Italian painting and marked an enormous break with the past.

Figure 3.3 *'Condottiere Gattamelata' by Donatello, 1453*

Sculpture   The dominant influence on Italian sculpture was Donatello. Equally at home with bronze or marble, he applied his new linear perspective to sculptured door panels to create an illusion of depth. In his equestrian statue, the 'Condottiere Gattamelata' (see Figure 3.3), he combined a realistically proportioned human body in a god-like form. Not surprisingly, he became the mentor of the High Renaissance sculptors, Bramante, Raphael and Michelangelo. Italian architecture owed a great deal to Vitruvius and Brunelleschi. The discovery around 1410 of Vitruvius's *Treatise on Architecture* revived interest in the design of ancient Rome and encouraged Antonio Filarete to write his own architectural handbook, laying down rules of perspective based upon the work of his idol, Filippo Brunelleschi. He used precise mathematics to determine these harmonic proportions. For example, in his church designs the height of the nave was twice its breadth.

Music   Music was also undergoing major changes. The 1480s saw the creation of musical notation and a real attempt to break away from traditional Gregorian chants by developing harmonies. The Greek mathematician Pythagoras had claimed that the eight notes of the musical octave represented the sounds created by the eight spheres of the universe. Fifteenth-century musicians believed that the harmony achieved by the geometric ratio between these notes, especially of thirds and fifths, was comparable to the use of perspective in painting and of proportion in architecture. And they were right.

Outside Italy

Outside Italy the royal and ducal courts also experienced a cultural revolution. Burgundy, for instance, developed a style of painting that combined realistic observations and use of oils with classical and spiritual subject matter, best exemplified in the work of Jan van Eyck. The German Albrecht Dürer took his skill as an engraver to Italy in the 1490s, learned the art of proportion and returned to Nüremberg to introduce this technique. Not until after 1494 did France, and to a lesser extent Spain, begin to embrace this culture when their troops and sovereign rulers persistently invaded the Italian states.

Architecture and music, on the other hand, witnessed a greater degree of cultural exchange. The predominant style of architecture since the twelfth century had been Gothic but as each country continued to develop its own variation on this style – Italian villas, French chateaux and Burgundian merchant houses, for example – architects were increasingly attracted to designing secular buildings rather than churches. These revealed the dignity of 'man' rather than his spiritual humility. As with the visual arts, northern Europe possessed its own musical Renaissance and musicians acquired international reputations. It was widely believed that Dutch composers were the finest in Europe: Guillaume Dufray, who built upon the polyphonic mass, and Josquin Desprez, were attracted to Rimini, Bologna and Rome; Johannes Okeghem, who developed compositions based on counterpoint, was lured to Paris. Historians now recognise that in music and the visual arts Europe experienced not one but several renaissances at much the same time.

Popular culture

In 1492 Ficino wrote: 'It is undoubtedly a golden age which has restored to light the liberal arts that had almost been destroyed: grammar, eloquence, poetry, sculpture, music.' While the intellectual elites of the fifteenth century enjoyed a rich and varied culture, those groups further down the social order were more affected by personal experiences. **Broadsides**, **chap-books**, sermons, songs, tales, plays, dances and woodcuts were the principal forms of popular culture. Chivalric romances and ballads were universally enjoyed: Roland in France, Orlando in Italy, Cid in Spain, Ilya in Russia and Holger in Denmark were national folk heroes. Cinderella – a moral tale of child abuse by wicked relatives and the supernatural interference of a good fairy – was popular in France and Germany. Castile's Diego Corrientes (the robber of Andalucía) and Florence's *il piovano arlotto* (a poor country cleric) were variants of England's Robin Hood and Friar Tuck.

Plays were performed in market places, taverns and churches. Churches were common venues for the performance of mystery plays. These had a biblical theme. Wandering minstrels often performed in taverns known as 'cabarets' in France, but the market place and 'piazza' were the preferred location of travelling actors. In most towns, cultural activities were organised by guilds, sometimes in conjunction with the local church but often independently. In Paris the *Confrérie de la Passion* put on mystery plays, in Florence its guilds held pageants for St John the Baptist, and in Spain the feast of Corpus Christi was celebrated by all of its guilds. Carnivals or *charivari* were the most popular festivals, lasting from a few days to several weeks in southern Europe, when they ended on Mardi Gras, the last day before Lent. It was a time of fun and frolic, when individuals and conventions were mocked in an orgy of riotous behaviour until, eventually, the natural order was restored. Street theatre often went in for role-reversal: turning the world upside down. Men dressed as women, animals were ceremoniously sacrificed and gangs of youths, known as 'Abbots of Misrule', roamed the streets. Everyone was fair game, though special targets for ridicule were unmarried people living together, newly-married couples, Jews and gypsies. Even the Church participated with its Feast of Fools, a series of mock church services in which an ass was dressed in clerical vestments. In spite of this disorderly behaviour, carnivals were carefully orchestrated by guilds, like the silk weavers in Lyon, shoemakers in Sweden and butchers in Germany. They enabled local tensions to be released before order was re-established.

Groups who lived outside the network of urban life – like miners, shepherds and mariners – had their own distinctive subcultures. Miners in Kutuá Hora in Bohemia and Annaberg in Silesia, for example, had their own songs, plays and mythology. At Rothenburg in southern Germany, they met each year to dance, eat and elect their king and queen. Similarly, mariners developed a heritage of sea shanties, legendary tales and customs, and shepherds celebrated their own festival of St Bartholomew. The celebration of saints and miracle plays reminds us that most people believed in the supernatural. Saints protected people from evil forces: St Nicholas when travelling, St Sebastian when plague threatened and St George when there was a war. All were popular saints in the fifteenth century, yet certain regions had their own local saints to whom people prayed in times of danger. In Brittany, for instance, they were Nonna and Coventin. Wise women, cunning men and witches were all regarded as necessary aids in the endless fight against evil. They healed the sick, devised spells and predicted fortunes. At a time when intelligent people believed in miracles, demons and astrology, it is hardly surprising that old women who lived alone with their 'familiar' (cat) were frequently believed to be witches. In 1484 Heinrich Krämer and Jakob Sprenger had acquired a papal bull to hunt down witches. Their *Malleus Maleficarum* (see time chart) was a summary of sorcery and witchcraft. This only confirmed the popular belief that witches could fly and consort with the Devil (see chapter 30).

The cultural historian Peter Burke has argued that elitist and popular cultures were not mutually exclusive: Boccaccio translated Greek drama into short stories for popular Italian consumption, Lorenzo de' Medici donned a mask and led the revelry during Florence's *charivari* and Hanz Folz, a Nuremberg barber, had his plays performed at the local festival. While this remains true, it is also evident that the clergy, nobility and bourgeoisie had begun to abandon popular cultural activities. Rates of change varied from region to region but the gulf between elite and popular cultures appears to have been widening, rather than narrowing, at the end of the fifteenth century. Whether this was due to increasing commercial opportunities, a growth in literacy or the challenge to traditional religious beliefs is a matter of debate. What is certain is that the Renaissance was the source of this cultural and intellectual revolution.

Most west European states experienced a cultural revolution in the course of the fifteenth century. Northern Italy saw innovative developments in the visual arts but other countries developed their own cultural styles and techniques, and contributed to, as well as learned from, the Italian movement. While people in towns were aware of artistic changes, their own cultural experiences were rooted in traditional beliefs and practices, and changed very little in the course of this period. In contrast, only a narrow band of writers and scholars appreciated how humanism could affect their understanding of art, religion and philosophy. The intellectual revolution was therefore confined to university circles, Platonic academies and grammar schools. Here traditional ideas were challenged. The majority of people, however, remained unaffected by such developments.

Task: working with visual sources

Examine the visual sources in this chapter.

1 Look at Figure 3.1 carefully.
   a Ptolemy was a second-century Egyptian who drew a series of maps of the Earth. What continents, seas and oceans can you identify? What continents were not known at this time?
   b Why were his river configurations largely incorrect but the landmasses and coastlines drawn more accurately?

2 Look at Figure 3.2 on page 30. What characteristics of the Italian Renaissance are evident in this painting?

3 Both the reprint and the painting were produced in the 1480s. What did fifteenth-century mapmakers and artists gain from a study of earlier civilisations?

Further reading

A. Brown, *The Renaissance*, Seminar Studies in History (Addison Wesley Longman, 1988) – a short and highly readable survey with a good set of documents.

P. Burke, *Popular Culture in Early Modern Europe* (Temple Smith, 1978) – provides an excellent introduction to the subject.

R. W. Southern, *Medieval Humanism and Other Studies* (Oxford University Press, 1970, reprinted 1984) – remains the standard work on medieval humanism.

A. Goodman and A. Mackay (eds), *The Impact of Humanism on Western Europe* (Addison Wesley Longman, 1990) – a collection of detailed essays.

J. H. Plumb, *The Pelican Book of the Renaissance* (2nd edn, Penguin, 1982) – a useful introduction suitable for the general reader.

4 Why did the Renaissance begin in Italy?

Time chart

1304: Birth of Petrarch (d.1374), writer and humanist

1307: Alighieri Dante writes his *Divine Comedy*

1331: Birth of Salutati (d.1405), scholar and chancellor of Florence

1348: Boccaccio writes the *Decameron*

1378: Birth of Lorenzo Ghiberti (d.1455), sculptor and artist

1386: Birth of Donatello (d.1466), sculptor who worked for the guilds and cathedral of Florence

1400: Birth of Luca della Robbia (d.1482), sculptor and artist

1402: Florence gains its independence from Milan

1404: Birth of Leon Alberti (d.1472), architect, writer and humanist

1412: Filippo Brunelleschi (1377–1446) writes his *Rules of Perspective*

1430s: Bruni (1374–1444) composes 'The Praises of the City of Florence'

1431: Birth of Andrea Mantegna (d.1506), painter

1435: Birth of Andrea del Verrocchio (d.1488), painter and inventor

1440: Platonic Academy is established in Florence

1445: Birth of Sandro Botticelli (d.1510), painter

1452: Birth of Leonardo da Vinci (d.1519), painter, sculptor, inventor

1453: Constantinople falls to the Ottoman Turks

1469: Birth of Niccolò Machiavelli (d.1527), writer and politician

1475: Birth of Buonarotti Michelangelo (d.1564), painter, sculptor and architect

1483: Birth of Guicciardini (d.1540), writer, and Raphael (d.1520), painter

1486: Pico della Mirandola composes his 'Oration on the Dignity of Man'

1511: Birth of Giorgio Vasari (d.1574), painter, sculptor, architect and writer

Why was Italy at the heart of the Renaissance in the fifteenth and sixteenth centuries? Before considering the evidence of contemporary sources and the views of historians, three points must be noted.

1 Any historical analysis is subjective by the very process of selecting material, and you should be aware that sources can give a slanted view. Arguments also need to be rooted in evidence.

2 This chapter is concerned with the reasons for the flowering of the Renaissance in Italy. There is not space to examine in detail the views expressed in various studies that the Renaissance did not begin in Italy, that other European cultures were more advanced, and that there was not one Renaissance but a series of rebirths throughout the Middle Ages.

3 You should decide what are the most important features of the Italian Renaissance and then put them in order. Inevitably, this will be a subjective decision but it is a dilemma which all historians have to face. Five main causes will be examined in this chapter.

1 Italy's direct association with classical civilisation

Fifteenth-century Italy was an antiquarian's dream. Wherever one went there were ancient Roman tombs, sculptures and temples, not all in fine condition but sufficient to uphold a respect for classical civilisation. It was, for instance, the remains of imperial Rome – notably the Colosseum, the Pantheon and the Arch of Constantine – which caught Brunelleschi's eye and inspired his architecture. No villas or country houses had survived but classical writers like Pliny the younger and Vitruvius had described them, and ground plans had been discovered.

Ancient texts survived in their thousands and, though every scholar studied Latin, humanists attached particular importance to reading original works before they were amended by later scribes. Fifteenth-century Florentines were especially interested in what classical authors had to say about politics, morality, war and public speaking. Poggio Bracciolini, for example, hunted high and low for manuscripts. 'Please send Lucretius . . . the little books of Nonius Marcellus . . . the *Orator* and the *Brutus* – beside I need Cicero's *Letters to Atticus*', he wrote to Nicolao Niccoli, the leading book-collector in Florence. This passion for collecting books first began with Petrarch in the fourteenth century but, like most Italians, his knowledge of Greek was weak. It was the fall of Constantinople in 1453 and the consequent emigration of thousands of Greek refugees to Italy that proved so decisive in the development of Italian humanism. Not only did large numbers of Italians now come into contact with the Greek language, but they were also presented with a unique opportunity to study Greek manuscripts.

2 Italian genius

In 1860 the Swiss historian, Jakob Burckhardt, identified in his book *The Civilisation of the Renaissance in Italy* a particular explanation for its origin. 'It was not the revival of [Roman] antiquity alone,' he wrote, 'but its union with the genius of the Italian people, which achieved the conquest of the Western World.'

> *'In the Middle Ages both sides of human consciousness – that which was turned within as that which was turned without – lay dreaming or half-awake beneath a common veil. Man was conscious of himself only as a member of a race, people, party, family or corporation – only through some general category. In Italy this veil first melted into air. When this impulse to the highest individual development was combined with a powerful and varied nature, which had mastered all elements of the culture of the age, then arose the "all-sided man" –* l'uomo universale.*'*
>
> Jakob Burckhardt, *The Civilisation of the Renaissance in Italy* (1860).

Modern historians have rejected Burckhardt's suggestion that the Italian was 'the first-born among the sons of modern Europe', responsible for 'the discovery of the world and of man'. No nation has a monopoly on 'genius'. In many respects, Burckhardt was a victim of uncritically accepting the praises which Italian writers had showered upon each other. In the fourteenth century, for example, Boccaccio recognised Giotto's artistic genius whereby 'he restored to light this art which for many centuries had been buried', and praised Dante who 'first opened the way for the return of the muses, banished from Italy'. In the 1430s Bruni described Petrarch as the first 'who possessed such grace and genius that he could recognise and recall to the light the ancient elegance of style, which had been lost and extinguished'. In 1481 Cristoforo Landino claimed that Florentine painters and architects were largely responsible for the city's brilliant reputation – a view repeated in 1568 in Giorgio Vasari's influential book, *Lives of the Most Excellent Painters, Sculptors and Architects*. Vasari believed in the multi-talented artist – *l'uomo universale* – as the sketchbooks and paintings of Leonardo da Vinci or the literary and scientific works of Leon Alberti confirm, but he was mistaken in suggesting that the Italian people as a whole were blessed with a special genius. This was the error which Burckhardt repeated some 300 years later.

Despot

A cruel and ruthless tyrant (unelected ruler) who exercises total power.

3 Political factors

The historian David Maland has argued that much of Italy's strength lay in its unique political condition. Unlike any other area of Europe, northern and central Italy was comparatively free from imperial domination and the influence of the Papacy. There were, of course, variations between states – Urbino and Milan were ruled by **despots**, while Florence and Venice were semi-democratic republics. However, Maland asserts that because:

> 'there was no controlling Italian dynasty, no universal censor, no central court to dictate cultural standards and to discourage nonconformity, the Italian states were free to go their different ways, stimulated by an intense civic pride which prompted them to compete with each other in cultural as well as political rivalry.'
>
> David Maland, *Europe in the Sixteenth Century* (1982).

Certainly many Florentines believed the origin of the Renaissance was to be found in the nature of their political constitution and in their own control of their destiny (political autonomy). 'Of all peoples the Florentines appreciate liberty most and are the greatest enemies of tyrants', wrote Bruni in *The Praises of the City of Florence*. As a Florentine, Bruni may be accused of special pleading but it remains true that once the city escaped from the ruling dukes of Milan, it never tired of singing the praises of freedom. Bruni's reading of the Roman author Tacitus confirmed his belief that civic virtue and culture could only spring from political liberty. It was an opinion shared by Bartholomeo Scala, chancellor of Florence, who later claimed that his city was 'very free ... everyone talks a lot, some in favour, some uncertain, and others pursuing their own different interests'. Pope Pius II could also confidently assert that 'in our change-loving Italy where nothing stands firm and no ancient dynasty exists, a servant can easily become a king'.

Was this true? How liberal was Florence's constitution? In reality, its government was an **oligarchy** dominated by wealthy banking and trading families, which excluded nobles from holding public office and barred women from voting or belonging to trade guilds. While it remained possible for a talented man to shake off his humble origins – Palmieri was the son of an apothecary and Vasari the son of a potter – neither was born in Florence. In contrast, Brunelleschi, Donatello, Robbia, Verrocchio, Botticelli and Leonardo – to name but some of its most eminent citizens – all came from socially respectable families. By the

Oligarchy

In an **oligarchy** government is in the hands of a small, privileged group or elite. Landowners used their position to influence the restricted numbers of electors to support candidates of their own choice in elections. In this way, politicians owed allegiance to aristocratic families. While 'aristocracy' was considered an appropriate form of government, the use of 'oligarchy' usually implies criticism.

end of the fifteenth century, the Italian Renaissance was an elitist movement. If Florence's political autonomy encouraged a degree of social mobility, as some historians have suggested, it does not convincingly account for its wealth of cultural talent.

4 The city state and urban development

We have already seen that Florence was the first city state to celebrate its freedom from despotism with a series of tributes about public service and civic virtue. To Hans Baron, writing in the 1950s, it was this combination of 'civic liberty and the independence of city states' which had enabled Florentine culture to flourish. Civic humanism – the humanist's devotion to the community – figured prominently in the works of Florentines like Petrarch, Salutati and Bruni. Niccoli dedicated his lifetime collection of books to the reformed monastery of San Marco, which became the first public library in Florence, and the celebrated Florentine historians, Machiavelli and Guicciardini (see time chart), both emphasised 'reason of state' as a self-fulfilling quality. Of course, civic pride had long existed in Italy, and was hardly exclusive to Florence. Lodovico Gonzaga, Marquis of Mantua, wished to make his politically uninfluential state a centre of art and architecture. Lodovico Sforza patronised Leonardo da Vinci to adorn Milan. Rulers like the Malatesta of Rimini, d'Este of Ferrara and Federigo of Urbino invested heavily in enriching their palaces and city states. Neither the Papacy nor Venice fell behind in this urban competition: Pope Sixtus IV enticed Florentine artists to move to Rome, and both Raphael and Michelangelo worked on civic as well as papal projects under the patronage of Julius II and Leo X.

In recent years Baron's thesis has been attacked because it failed to give proper attention to other features of north Italian urban life. One of his critics, Gene Brucker, has suggested that the rivalry between Venetian and Florentine guilds was more important. Guilds organised civic life, commissioned paintings, statues and public buildings, and encouraged friendly competitions against each other. In 1425, for example, the Bankers' Guild financed Ghiberti to make a tabernacle which would 'surpass in beauty and ornamentation that of the Wool Guild which always sought to be the master and the superior of the other guilds'. Ghiberti duly triumphed but his success served only to encourage the Wool Guild to rebuild a statue of St Stephen which would 'exceed, or at least equal, in beauty and decoration the more beautiful ones'. Perhaps it is not surprising that Florence's 21 guilds set the pace and standard of artistic taste in Italy.

Competition between guilds was only a short step from rivalry between city states. Most artists were prepared to move from city to city and from state to state in search of employment and fame. Leon Alberti, for instance, designed the Rucellai Palace in Florence, Sant' Andrea Church in Mantua, San Francesco Church in Rimini and many civic buildings in Rome. Like other Italian craftsmen, wherever he went, Alberti transported ideas, practised new techniques and left envious people behind him. Florence competed with Pisa, Milan with Lodi and Venice with Verona. There was also rivalry between Italian universities. Most Italian cities possessed one and some acquired international reputations – Ferrara and Bologna for law and Padua for medicine. Interestingly, Florence's university never attained the status of its rivals in Pisa and Milan, but this did not prevent Florence from leading the Italian Renaissance both intellectually and culturally. Perhaps its other educational institutions had a more vital influence than historians are willing to recognise.

5 Patronage

Artists were craftsworkers looking for paid employment, and northern Italy was teeming with rich merchants and bankers. Patrons were influenced by a variety of motives: civic duty (see chapter 2), self-glorification and religious devotion. Giovanni Rucellai candidly confessed that he built churches and palaces because 'they do honour to God, to Florence and to my own memory'. Cosimo de' Medici was equally forthright: 'I know my fellow citizens,' he said. 'In fifty years' time they will only remember me by the few poor buildings I leave them.' There was nothing miserly about his endowments. He spent over 40,000 florins on rebuilding San Marco Church because 'his conscience pricked him about some money which he had come by not quite cleanly'. His son, Lorenzo, saw literature, art and buildings as a means of self-glorification and spent more than 660,000 gold florins. Looking back over 20 years of patronage, he seemed well pleased with his investment: 'I think it casts a brilliant light on our estate and it seems to me that the monies were well spent and I am very well pleased with this.'

Lauro Martines has recently argued that the fifteenth-century Italian patrons, many of whom were despots, saw artistic patronage as a means of strengthening their political authority, for it gave them an air of respectability and sophistication. Social upstarts like Sigismondo Malatesta, Borso d'Este and Lodovico Gonzaga were apparently just as keen to spend their wealth and display their power as the merchants and bankers of Florence. Malatesta employed Alberti to improve the church in Rimini, d'Este beautified the city of Ferrara, and Gonzaga helped turn

Mantua into an important centre of humanism. Unlike their counterparts north of the Alps, patrons throughout Italy much preferred to invest their money in artistic work rather than land.

6 Commercial prosperity

Wealthy patrons, of course, exist in all societies. In the fifteenth and early sixteenth centuries the princely courts of Burgundy, France and Germany created their own cultural renaissances. What was so distinctive about northern and central Italy was the large number of very wealthy cities in close proximity to one another. From the eleventh century, northern Italy was at the crossroads of European trade: Genoa dominated the west Mediterranean and Venice the east, Milan was in regular contact with German cities, and Florence straddled central Italy. Ironically, a trade recession in the late fourteenth and early fifteenth centuries may also have contributed to Florence's dominance since its wealth was concentrated in only a few families and these were keen to spend their money on the arts. Most other European aristocracies generally preferred to invest their wealth in land. Moreover, the city was blessed with a stroke of great fortune in 1420 when the Florentine Medicis became the Papacy's principal bankers.

Conclusion

It has been suggested that a combination of classical heritage, natural talent, political autonomy, civic pride, wealthy patrons and a commercial environment made Florence in particular and Italy in general the heart of the European Renaissance. Historians disagree over the relative importance of each of these factors, but this is only to be expected. Perhaps we are wrong to look for a single explanation. Do the reasons for Florence's decline throw any light upon the question? Its leadership was challenged when the Papacy became its principal rival in the 1470s. It ended when Lorenzo de' Medici's financial empire collapsed in the 1480s and it was destroyed when foreign armies invaded Italy after 1494. The sack of Rome in 1527 was a telling reminder that war had displaced culture as the principal pursuit of European rulers. By the mid sixteenth century, Spain had imposed its own austere character upon most of the Italian peninsula. In forcing Italian writers and artists to conform to its cultural taste, Spain suppressed the competition between states, stifled artistic liberty and originality, and syphoned off much of their wealth.

Task

1 Look at the factors in this chapter which historians have used to explain why the Renaissance began in Italy.

    a Put the factors in your own order of importance, giving your reasons.

    b Do you think that this list helps you to explain the precise timing of the Italian Renaissance? Explain your answer.

    c These factors have been deliberately separated. Do you think that convincing explanations of the Italian Renaissance need to stress how factors acted together, rather than separately? Explain your answer.

2 What can you work out from this chapter about the kinds of evidence historians rely on when they give reasons for the Italian Renaissance?

3 Why do you think that some historians have questioned the origin and significance of the Italian Renaissance and suggested that there was not one renaissance but a series of rebirths throughout the Middle Ages?

Further reading

A. Brown, *The Renaissance*, Seminar Studies in History (Addison Wesley Longman, 1988) – suitable for A and AS-Level students and contains a good range of documents.

P. Burke, *The Renaissance*, Studies in European History (Macmillan, 1987) – provides the best analysis of the historiographical debate on the origin of the Renaissance.

L. Martines, *Power and Imagination: City States in Renaissance Italy* (Knopf, 1979) – contains many thoughtful comments.

F. W. Kent and P. Simons (eds), *Patronage, Art and Society in Renaissance Italy* (Oxford University Press, 1987) – a collection of specialised essays.

5 Who was Erasmus and why was he so important?

Time chart

1467: Desiderius Erasmus is born in Rotterdam

1487: He becomes a monk in Steyn priory

1493: Enters the service of the Bishop of Cambrai

1499: Visits Oxford

1500: Erasmus publishes the *Adagia*

1503: Publishes the *Handbook of a Christian Soldier*

1509: *In Praise of Folly* is published

1513: The death of Pope Julius II is the theme of *Julius Exclusus*

1516: Erasmus translates the Greek New Testament and Latin Vulgate, and publishes *The Education of a Christian Prince* and *The Complaint of Peace*

1519: Erasmus writes the *Colloquies*

1521: Erasmus leaves Louvain University for Basel

1524: He publishes a *Discourse on Free Will* and clashes with Luther

1527: New editions of the New Testament and works of Ambrose are published

1528: Erasmus publishes *Paraphrases on the New Testament, Ciceronianus* – a defence of Latin rhetoric – and a new edition of Augustine

1529: He produces editions of *Epistles* and *Lactantius*

1535: Publishes *Ecclesiastes* – the art of the preacher

1536: Erasmus dies in Basel

Few men have had such an impact on European history as **Desiderius Erasmus**. This chapter studies his life, his works and beliefs. It seeks to explain how a comparatively reserved and humble scholar came to be the best known and most respected intellectual in Europe.

Erasmus the Humanist

Erasmus was first and foremost a Christian humanist. His education at

PROFILE: *Desiderius Erasmus*

Born in Rotterdam in about 1467, the illegitimate son of a priest, **Erasmus** was educated at Deventer by the Brethren of the Common Life. In 1487 he entered the Augustinian priory at Steyn where he discovered that 'this kind of life was good for neither mind nor body'. Six years later he entered the service of the Bishop of Cambrai, although he was not dispensed from his monastic vows until 1517. Dissatisfied and restless, in 1499 he visited Oxford where he befriended English scholars such as More, Colet, Grocyn and Linacre. They encouraged him to study the Church Fathers and the scriptures, and to master the Greek language. This he did, travelling Europe in search of patrons and seats of learning. As a lecturer in Greek at Oxford, Cambridge and then Louvain, Erasmus developed a low opinion of academic life, describing students as 'dung-eaters'. Ill-health and hostility from the university authorities caused him to leave Louvain in 1521 for Switzerland, where he tried to escape from the controversy surrounding Luther and Zwingli. He died in Basel in 1536.

KEY TERMS:

Devotio moderna* and *philosophia Christi

The ***devotio moderna*** was a form of spiritual devotion. It was believed that Christian piety and spiritual perfection could be attained by prayer, meditation, chastity and poverty. Derived from the works of St Thomas à Kempis, the movement contrasted sharply with the theological sterility of scholasticism. Erasmus believed that 'man' could recover his spiritual condition if he had faith in Christ and studied the Church Fathers. This he called the ***philosophia Christi***, the philosophy of Christ.

the Brethren of the Common Life had introduced him to the ***devotio moderna***, which convinced him that Christianity was essentially a simple belief that had become materialistic and unproductive in the hands of theologians. He believed that it was possible to achieve spiritual salvation, for faith to triumph over ignorance, but only through studying and following the teaching of Christ. His ***philosophia Christi*** was first developed in his *Enchiridion Militis Christiani* in 1503. This 'Handbook of a Christian Soldier' was a manual or dagger ('enchiridion' is Greek for something carried in the hand) with which 'man' could fight against ignorance and evil. As Erasmus explained in his original dedication: it was 'a kind of summary guide to living, so that, equipped with it, you might attain to a state of mind worthy of Christ'. Three themes particularly concerned him:

1 The study of Latin and Greek was only a means to the end of acquiring a deeper understanding of the scriptures.

2 Knowledge of the gospel in conjunction with a spiritually pure heart was the most practical form of Christianity.

3 Though it was not wrong to revere saints and relics, religion had become too much a matter of conventions and ceremonies. It was more important to achieve inner spirituality than to observe forms of devotion outwardly.

> *'Monasticism is not holiness but a kind of life that can be useful or useless depending on a person's temperament or disposition. I neither recommend it nor do I condemn it. You accuse and utter your sins to a priest, which is a man: take heed how you accuse and utter them before God, for to accuse them before him is to hate them inwardly. You believe by chance all your sins and offences will be washed away at once with a little paper or parchment sealed with wax, with a little money or images of wax offered, with going on a little pilgrimage. You are utterly deceived and clean out of the way!'*
>
> Desiderius Erasmus, *Enchiridion Militis Christiani* (1503).

Note that this attack on indulgences preceded Luther by some 16 years (see chapter 8).

Erasmus's popular writings

By the time the *Enchiridion* was in circulation, Erasmus had become a celebrity. Earlier in 1500 he had published the *Adagia* – more than 800 Latin and Greek proverbs, complete with a commentary on their origin and meaning. Written, he said, for readers who were 'in search of more spritely and brilliant modes of expression', his book combined classical and biblical scholarship with illustrations drawn from everyday life. It was a success: by 1525 it had sold more than 72,000 copies. Its popularity encouraged him to revise and expand the text regularly: by 1536 he had increased the number of proverbs to over 4,000. The range of topics covered is breathtaking and it is hard to believe that the first edition was written in just two days. Erasmus's main aim was to whet his readers' appetite for more knowledge and so lead them towards his chosen goal: a better understanding of the scriptures and, ultimately, the truth. He had little time for scholastics who rejected classical authors or who studied them for their own sake in preference to Christian theology.

Examples of proverbs in the *Adagia*:

- to look a gift horse in the mouth
- there's many a slip 'twixt cup and lip
- to leave no stone unturned
- God helps those who help themselves
- to have one foot in the grave
- one swallow does not make a summer

Erasmus's attitude to the Church

The themes of his early works – the immoral condition of the Church, the sterility of scholasticism, the worldliness of secular rulers and the spiritual salvation of personal piety – were more fully developed in his next publication *In Praise of Folly*. Dedicated to his friend Thomas More, it combined satire and realism to expose man's ignorance. 'Folly' represents freedom, sensuality and subversion; she (Erasmus deliberately classified folly as a female) praises flattery, ignorance and madness. In identifying her followers – theologians, monks, princes, courtiers, as well as Christian idealists like himself – Erasmus skilfully changed his tone from light-hearted fun to a fierce swipe at contemporary religious practices, before finally arriving at the virtues of the philosophy of Christ. In laughing at fools, Erasmus was following a popular tradition except, in his case, the line between serious and humorous was not clear cut. Folly, like Thomas More's narrator Hythlodaeus in *Utopia* (1516), was really speaking on behalf of Erasmus and enabled him to make fun of serious issues.

Extract from chapter 54 of *In Praise of Folly* in which Erasmus exposes monastic corruption:

'The happiness of these people is most nearly approached by those who are popularly called "Religious" or "Monks". Both names are false, since most of them are a long way removed from religion, and wherever you go these so-called solitaries are the people you're likely to meet. I don't believe any life would be more wretched than theirs if I didn't come to their aid in many ways. The whole tribe is so universally loathed that even a chance meeting is thought to be ill-omened – and yet they are gloriously self-satisfied. In the first place, they believe it's the highest form of piety to be so uneducated that they can't even read. Then when they bray like donkeys in church repeating by rote the psalms they haven't even understood, they imagine they are charming the ears of the heavenly audience with infinite delight. Many of them too make a good living out of their squalor and beggary, bellowing for bread from door to door, and indeed making a nuisance of themselves in every inn, carriage or boat, to the great loss of all the other beggars. This is the way in which these smooth individuals, in all their filth and ignorance, their boorish and shameless behaviour, claim to bring back the apostles into our midst!'

Many of the passages in *In Praise of Folly* touched raw nerves and the book earned Erasmus a European reputation for scholarly satire. By 1536 it had run to 42 editions. The worldliness of the Church, clerical abuses and papal corruption were central subjects of his next work, *Julius Exclusus*. In

1513 Pope Julius II had died (both in fact and in Erasmus's fictional account). In Erasmus's book, however, the Pope was refused entry to the gates of Heaven by St Peter, on account of his pleasure-seeking life on earth. Erasmus never acknowledged authorship for *Julius Exclusus*, perhaps because it was understandably criticised by the Church but more likely because its publicity diverted attention from his major work in 1516: a new translation of the Greek New Testament.

Extract from *Julius Exclusus* (published in 1513) in which the Pope explains why he should be allowed into Heaven:

'The invincible Julius ought not to answer a beggarly fisherman. However, you shall know who and what I am. I have done more for the Church and Christ than any Pope before me. I have set all the princes of Europe by the ears. I have torn up treaties, kept great armies in the field, I have covered Rome with palaces. And I have done it all myself, too. I owe nothing to my birth, for I don't know who my father was; nothing to learning, for I have none; nothing to youth, for I was old when I began; nothing to popularity, for I was hated all round. Spite of fortune, spite of gods and men I achieved all that I have told you in a few years, and I left work enough cut out for my successors to last ten years longer. This is the modest truth, and my friends at Rome call me more a god than a man.'

This book comprised a Greek text, a new Latin translation of the Vulgate and an extensive commentary on the classical sources and word derivations. By examining vital words and phrases, Erasmus was clearly challenging orthodox beliefs. In *Matthew 4:17*, for example, he translated 'do penance' as 'be penitent' and, in later editions, it became 'change your mind'. This suggested Christ was concerned with inner attitudes rather than the Catholic sacrament of penance. Equally heretical to theologians was his apparent belief that theology should be directly available to everyone. In the preface, he declared:

'I wish that all women might read the gospel, and the Epistles of Paul. I wish that they might be translated into all tongues of all people, so that not only the Scots and the Irish, but also the Turk and the Saracen might read and understand. I wish the countryman might sing them at his plough, the weaver chant them at his loom, the traveller beguile with them the weariness of his journey. Only a very few can be learned, but all can be Christian, all can be devout, and – I shall boldly add – all can be theologians.'

Though far from accurate – the book was based on eleventh-century manuscripts and hastily edited – it was the first of its kind and Europe was ready for it. Protestant reformers like Zwingli, Luther, Bucer and Calvin all found inspiration from it. However, church theologians, especially Dominicans, severely criticised it, and Erasmus was genuinely hurt. It had never been his intention to challenge the unity and universality of the Christian Church but to restore it from within. From now on he deliberately avoided questions of church reform.

A matter of some importance to Erasmus was the constant warfare in Europe after 1494. He believed that peace and love were fundamental Christian principles and that all too often the Church had actively encouraged war. He had discussed this topic on at least three occasions before deciding to write *The Complaint of Peace*. In it he implored all Christian princes, nobles, bishops and theologians 'to work together with united hearts'. His pleas fell on deaf ears.

Erasmus and Luther

Many of Erasmus's beliefs were printed in the *Colloquia* in 1519. This consisted of 60 imaginary dialogues on contemporary issues and proved to be even more popular than the *Adagia*. By 1536 it had run to over 300 editions. Part of its appeal lay in the clarity and humour of his style, but readers also detected a more subversive tone. Even Luther alleged (perhaps tongue in cheek) that he would not let his children read it and Cardinal Contarini rejected it as a grammar book because 'there is much to teach impiety to untrained minds'. Erasmus did not seek controversy, but it never seemed to be far away. It was already clear to him that the 'golden age', which he had referred to in a letter of 1517, was slipping away and that Martin Luther, that 'genius of discord', had much to do with it.

Hard as Erasmus tried to distance himself from Luther's religious views (see chapter 8), he was constantly asked for his opinion. Ever courteous and cautious, Erasmus had no desire to be drawn into this debate but explained that Luther's criticism of indulgences, church doctrine and the Papacy should never have been made in public. They were unfortunate distractions from the true purpose of Christian humanism. In 1518 he wrote: 'Luther has said many things excellently well. I could wish, however, that he would be less rude in his manner.' Two years later, Luther's appeal to the German nation prompted Cardinal Aleander to claim, 'Erasmus laid the egg which Luther hatched'. Erasmus suitably retorted: 'I laid a hen's egg, but Luther hatched a bird of a quite different breed.' In a letter to Aloysius Marlianus, dated 25 March 1521, he bristled:

KEY TERM:

Epicurean

An **Epicurean** is a person devoted to sensuous pleasure. Epicurus was a Greek philosopher who taught that pleasure is the greatest good. An epicure is a person who enjoys sensuous pleasure and, especially, good food and wine.

> *'Christ I know: Luther I know not. The Roman Church I know, and death will not part me from it till the Church departs from Christ. I abhor sedition. Would that Luther and the Germans abhorred it equally. Many great persons have entreated me to support Luther.'*

Among those 'great persons' were friends and reformers like Hutten, Dürer, Bucer and Melanchthon.

Orthodox Catholics sought to enlist Erasmus in the campaign against Luther. Among them were Charles V, Hadrian VI, Clement VII, Cardinal Wolsey and Henry VIII. It was Henry who actually suggested that Erasmus should engage Luther in a literary debate on the subject of free will. The resulting tract, *De Libero Arbitrio* (Discourse on Free Will), was published in September 1524. In what was his first official denunciation of Luther, Erasmus attacked, but in a conciliatory tone, Luther's concept of grace and justification. However, neither Lutheran nor Catholic theologians were satisfied with Erasmus's statement. Luther dismissed his views as those of 'a babbler, a sceptic, some other hog from the **Epicurean** sty'; orthodox Catholics, on the other hand, claimed that his reasoning was ambiguous. 'I am a heretic to both sides,' he lamented. 'Instead of leading, I have stood naked and unarmed between the javelins of two angry foes.'

In truth, Erasmus had gone far enough. He had replied to Luther's arguments, defended his own and, by retaining his composure, hoped his moderation would help to heal the rift in the Church. That it did not was due in his opinion to Luther's 'arrogant, impudent, seditious temperament', rather than his own unwillingness to speak out decisively. He never met Luther and last wrote to him in 1526 although he kept in touch with his friend Philip Melanchthon. For the last decade of his life, Erasmus tried to achieve a compromise between Luther's view of justification by faith alone and the Catholic theology of the fall and the Grace. His efforts were in vain. French, Spanish and Italian theologians condemned his work as heretical. In a letter to Martin Bucer, Erasmus prophetically expressed his anxiety declaring: 'I seem to see a cruel and bloody century ahead, if the provoked section gets its breath again, which it is certainly now doing.' Frustrated and disheartened, Erasmus buried himself in his work. Between 1527 and 1535, he published a new edition of the *New Testament*, *Paraphrases on the New Testament* and *Epistles*, more editions of 'the Fathers', a defence of Latin rhetoric and advice on the art of preaching. This most accomplished of classical scholars and prodigious correspondent – he wrote an estimated 30,000 letters – wanted nothing more than to be left alone with his books, unravelling the mysteries of the Early Fathers. It is entirely fitting that he should have been editing Origen's works and letters when he died in 1536, aged 69.

Part of Erasmus's *Discourse on Free Will* (1524).

'By freedom of the will I understand the power whereby a man can apply himself to or turn away from that which leads unto eternal salvation. It is within our power to turn towards or away from grace just as it is our pleasure to open or close our eyes against light; for it is incompatible with the infinite love of God that a man's striving with all his might for grace should be frustrated. I like the sentiments of those who attribute a little to the freedom of the will, the most, however, to grace.'

Conclusion

This case study raises several important questions. Why, for example, do you think Erasmus was so popular in the first two decades of the sixteenth century but less so at the end of his career? (You should read a biography on Erasmus.) Do you agree that Erasmus's greatness rested on his scholarship and wit rather than on his work as a reformer? (Phillips' and McConica's books, listed on page 53, are useful starting-points.) In what respects, and why, does Erasmus's Christian humanism differ from Italian humanism in the fifteenth century? (Refer to chapter 4 and Huizinga's book on Erasmus.) Finally, Erasmus and Luther had much in common but also disagreed on several fundamental matters. Do you agree that they had 'similar aims but different methods'? (R. D. Jones is particularly good on this theme.)

Task: answering source or document questions

On pages 52–53 are a number of source-based questions. Before you tackle them, read the following hints on how to approach source or document questions.

General hints on answering source or document questions:

1 Always read your documents slowly and carefully at first to make sure that you understand them. When you start doing this, you may find the language unfamiliar. People in the past did not speak or write as we do. You will get better at understanding them as you gain experience and practice. Remember that part of your training as a student of history involves 'getting inside' the period you are studying. This includes becoming familiar with the material which has been left behind from that period for us all to study. Don't give up because some words or phrases are unfamiliar. A decent dictionary is a wonderful research tool, so get to know how to use one effectively. If you still don't understand, discuss what the source is about with your teacher and other students.

2 In answering document questions, you will almost certainly be asked not only to show understanding but also to draw conclusions. You should learn how to relate one source to another – not least because many examination source questions ask you to explain what you can work out using two or more presented sources. That might seem an artificial exercise in itself. It is, however, a valid way of testing a wider skill – the ability to gather information from different sources and then to select what you need for a particular purpose.

3 You will be given information about the origins of a source – its 'provenance' to give it its technical name. This can be as valuable to you as the material in the documents themselves. The extracts in this chapter were all written by Erasmus, but for different purposes.

4 You are often asked to explain the usefulness of an extract. All sources are useful to some extent; most are useful for a range of purposes. Always try to look for positive advantages to using a source, remembering that the source will need to be placed in context. Never run the risk of concluding that, because of some obvious deficiency (gaps in evidence, clear bias of the author, dating of the source at a time different to that being described, and so on), it is 'useless'. Be critical of your sources by all means, but come to them with a positive attitude. Don't emphasise negative features or you may fail to do justice to your own powers of critical appreciation.

5 Examination questions often require candidates to compare two extracts. Comparative questions are best answered by assessing both passages point by point in terms of their similarity and difference. Consider whether one is more complete, more useful and more reliable than the other. You should apply contextual knowledge in support of your answer.

Hints for answering the source questions below:

6 Most source questions are designed to test your understanding of the material you are given. Often this understanding will link to your own knowledge. You must get practice in tackling questions with a particular focus or emphasis.

7 When you have read through the sources, look at question **a**. It includes the phrase 'According to (document) . . .'. This indicates that all you need to answer the question will be found in that document. The question is testing the skill of comprehension and your ability to use the evidence.

8 Look at question **b**. This asks you to draw conclusions from the extract on *Julius Exclusus*. It should be answered from the material within this document. However, the skill tested is different. This is concerned with inference: can you work out a conclusion from the material you are given? It requires you to understand what is being said but, in addition, you have to work out (or 'infer') an attitude or position. You are being asked here to 'read between the lines' to assess Erasmus's rather colourful language. Because a question on the 'value' of a source needs you to set that source in its context, you also need to know about Julius's life, and perhaps about other sources for it.

9 Look at question **c**. This requires you to compare two extracts and to explain the differences in their tone and language. Most of what you need is in the extracts, but this question is more than comprehension: an explanation is required. This is concerned first with the reasons why Erasmus wrote these works, and second with the political and religious climate when they were written. Fifteen years separated the two works and Erasmus was an older and wiser man in 1524. The time chart and profile in this chapter will help you here.

10 Look at question **d**, which is a contextual question. Start with the documents and assess what each tells you about:
   i Erasmus's conservatism (his reluctance to reform the Catholic faith and the Church)
   ii his reforming tendencies (readiness to make satirical jibes at the clergy and Papacy).
   Consider how complete are these extracts, what do they not tell you about Erasmus's beliefs and what further information is needed to provide a full answer.

Exercise on Erasmus

Read the three extracts from *In Praise of Folly*, *Julius Exclusus* and *Discourse on Free Will* (pages 46–50). Then answer the following questions:

a According to *In Praise of Folly*, what monastic practices were corrupt?   *5 marks*

b Look at the extract from *Julius Exclusus*. How valuable is it for a historian studying the life of Julius II? *5 marks*

c Account for the contrasting tone and language of the extracts *In Praise of Folly* and *Discourse on Free Will*. *7 marks*

d How far do these three extracts suggest that Erasmus wanted to conserve, rather than reform, the Catholic Church? *8 marks*

Further reading

J. McConica, *Erasmus* (Oxford University Press, 1991) – this is the best recent biography.

J. Huizinga, *Erasmus* (New York, 1924; Princeton paperback, 1984) – a classic study though now rather dated.

R. D. Jones, *Erasmus and Luther* (Oxford University Press, 1968).

M. M. Phillips, *Erasmus and the Northern Renaissance* (English Universities Press, 1967) – provides a general introduction.

J. P. Dolen (ed.), *The Essential Erasmus* (Mentor, 1964) – contains a wide range of Erasmus's works.

R. L. DeMolen, *Erasmus* (Arnold, 1973) – is particularly useful in providing examples of Erasmus's correspondence.

6 What was the importance of Isabella and Ferdinand for the development of Spain?

Time chart

1469: Isabella of Castile marries Ferdinand of Aragon

1474: Henry IV, King of Castile, dies and is succeeded by Isabella

1476: The *Santa Hermandad* is established

1478: Castilian Inquisition is introduced

1479: John II, King of Aragon, dies and is succeeded by his son, Ferdinand
The Treaty of Alcaçovas between Castile and Portugal

1481: Aragonese Inquisition is revived

1482: Crusade against the Muslims in Granada begins

1492: Conquest of Granada. Expulsion of Jews begins. Columbus 'discovers' the New World

1493: Roussillon and Cerdagne are recovered by Aragon

1496: Joanna, youngest daughter of Isabella and Ferdinand, marries Philip the Fair of Burgundy, son of the Emperor Maximilian

1499: Revolt of the *Mudéjars* begins in Granada

1500: Birth of Charles, son of Joanna and Philip

1502: Castilian *Mudéjars* forced to emigrate or convert; Gibraltar is restored to royal control, followed by Cartagena in 1503

1504: Isabella dies; Joanna, her daughter, is declared queen

1505: Naples is ceded to Aragon by France

1506: Ferdinand marries Germaine de Foix, Princess of Navarre. Philip the Fair dies, and Ferdinand becomes regent in lieu of Joanna

1510: North African ports of Bougie, Tripoli and Algiers are captured

1512: Southern Navarre is ceded by France to Ferdinand

1516: Ferdinand dies and is succeeded by his grandson, Charles I

Historians have been unusually consistent in their praise for Isabella and Ferdinand, the 'Catholic Kings', as Pope Alexander VI rather oddly called them in 1496. 'The most glorious epoch in the annals of Spain,' wrote W. H. Prescott in 1837; 'a happy golden age', claimed Ramón Menéndez Pidal in 1962; John Lynch, writing in 1991, attributed to them 'the makings of a nation state, united, peaceful and powerful beyond any in Europe'. Ferdinand left no one in doubt as to his achievements. In 1514 he stated: 'For over 700 years the Crown of Spain has not been as great or as resplendent as it is now, both in the west and in the east, and all, after God, by my work and labour.' He certainly convinced his great-grandson, Philip II, who allegedly declared, 'We owe everything to him'. Are these praises justified or have historians been deceived by contemporary propaganda? Exactly what was the legacy of Isabella and Ferdinand? To answer these and other questions, five features of their rule will be examined: royal authority, unification, religion, the economy and foreign affairs.

Restoration of royal authority

When Isabella claimed the throne of Castile in 1474 and five years later Ferdinand became King of Aragon, each inherited unstable kingdoms (see Figure 6.1). Ferdinand had to deal with restless Catalonians and his wife faced civil war in Castile. Though by 1479 they had secured their thrones, their authority was far from guaranteed, especially after the death of their only son, John, in 1497. Two of the greatest obstacles to the restoration of royal authority were the aristocracy and the poor condition of the crown's finances. It was once believed that Isabella and Ferdinand weakened the aristocracy by a mixture of threats and persuasion. In truth, their approach had to be more pragmatic since the clergy and nobility owned 90 per cent of the land and could not be so readily dismissed. However, they could be persuaded that it was in everyone's interest to have a strong monarchy.

Isabella and Ferdinand strengthened their authority in various ways:

- Royal lands were recovered, unlicensed castles destroyed and heavy punishments imposed upon law-breakers. Cadiz, Gibraltar and Cartagena were all brought under royal control.

- The Crown assumed control of the military crusading orders who commanded more than a million men. Ferdinand became their Grand Master and took possession of their lands and wealth.

- The monarchs took control of the police force known as *Santa Hermandad* (Holy Brotherhood), established by several cities in Henry IV's reign, first in Castile from 1476 and then for a short period of time

Right of entail

An entail is a settlement of
succession of a landed estate
upon one person. According to
Spanish medieval law, younger
children were entitled to a
'fair' inheritance; but from
1505 the **right of entail** passed
to the eldest son only. Thus
nobles' estates, and the titles
which accompanied them,
were likely to remain in one
family which made its
economic condition reasonably
stable.

in the 1480s in Aragon. This force, recruited from each town and paid
for by all members of society, patrolled the countryside and inflicted
speedy justice. Despised by those who had most to fear, the local
hermandades reminded the nobility that justice was preferable to
anarchy.

In order to retain the loyalty of the aristocracy, however, the Crown had
to make concessions. Ferdinand and Isabella guaranteed their exemption
from taxation and imprisonment from debt, and attracted support by
issuing patents of nobility and land grants in a series of *pactos* (contracts).
The Count of Treviño, for example, received estates in the Rioja, control
over 1,200 vassals (servants) and a handsome reward in return for
surrendering his governorship of Vizcaya. Nobles' seigneurial power
was further strengthened by a law of 1505 which confirmed the **right
of entail**. As a result, by 1516 the Duke of Infantado ruled 93,000
vassals and the Velasco family 258 towns and villages. In addition, the
aristocracy continued to receive the highest political offices and privileges: for instance, the Duke of Najera became viceroy of Navarre and
the Marquis of Mondéjar viceroy of Andalucía.

Royal finances were a second source of weakness. In 1474 ordinary
revenue should have totalled 73 million *maravedís* – principally derived
from the *alcabala* (a 10 per cent sales tax), customs duties and taxes on
silk, sheep and cattle – but in practice, due to the corrupt administration,
the Crown only received one-sixth of the total. The *alcabala*, which was
collected by the nobles and towns, rose throughout the reign but as the
clergy and nobility were often exempt, the burden fell on the towns. Of
greater importance to the Crown was its development of extraordinary
sources of revenue: the military orders, *Hermandad*, Indies, Church and
the Cortes all contributed, but Ferdinand's active foreign policy and expensive lifestyle quickly exhausted his supply. New sources were required.
Juros (government bonds) were issued for the first time in 1489 but the
capital gained was offset by heavy interest payments which totalled one-
third of the ordinary revenue by 1516. After a promising start when tax
collectors were closely supervised and the number of Crown employees
reduced, the financial administration fared no better. Corruption and bribery
ran through all aspects of tax assessment and collection, and by 1516 the
Crown probably received little more than 10 per cent of its revenue.

The monarchs used the Cortes and the *Hermandad* to extend royal
authority to the towns. Where factions existed, they sided with one of the
major oligarchs, replaced annual council elections with appointments by
lot and made certain that only the names of persons acceptable to them
went into the box. They regularly consulted the *Junta da Hermandad* and
personally visited every city in Castile. From 1480 officials known as *cor-*

Figure 6.1 *Spain in the reign of Ferdinand and Isabella*

regidores were appointed to every town: by 1487–8 there were 62, nearly doubling the number in Henry IV's reign. These royal servants were expected to maintain public order, administer justice, supervise the city council and act as the Crown's ears and eyes. The Catholic Monarchs travelled their kingdoms personally dispensing justice. They set up a central court at Valladolid in 1489 and provincial appeal courts at Santiago (1480), Seville (1495) and Granada (1504).

In the years following Isabella's death in 1504, many grandees (high-ranking nobles) exploited the succession dispute, first between Ferdinand and Philip and then, after Philip's death in 1506, between Ferdinand and Joanna. Leading nobles rose up in the north and seized Burgos; in the south, Gibraltar was besieged. By 1507 Ferdinand had resumed control of central government but his authority was severely checked. In Toledo, for instance, local aristocrats sat on the council and openly threatened the peace of the city. Complaints that nobles were encroaching on town property went unheeded and there were reports that *corregidores* were pocketing fines. At his accession in 1516, Charles I inherited an administration steeped in corruption.

Unity or unification?

Considerable advances towards a unitary state occurred after 1474, but by 1516 Spain was still a disunited country. Politically, Castile and Aragon

KEY TERM:

Justiciar

The **Justiciar** was a law officer, appointed by the Crown, in charge of law courts and justice in the kingdom of Aragon. The justiciar resolved disputes between the Crown and its subjects. Once in office, he could not be removed.

were brought together by the personal rule of Isabella and Ferdinand, Granada and Navarre were added in 1492 and 1512 respectively, and the Inquisition operated throughout the peninsula. Coins, seals and banners bore their joint names and arms, they dispensed justice together and pursued a common foreign policy. But behind this display of apparent unity lay deep divisions. Each kingdom had its own language, laws, Cortes and *hermandades*, its own customs and currency, and its own administration.

Isabella and Ferdinand's main aim was to secure and to strengthen their control over their kingdoms. Survival not unity was their short-term objective. Little could be done about Aragon where the monarch was unable to legislate without a Cortes, impose new taxes, raise troops or remove the **Justiciar** from office. Ferdinand called the Aragonese, Catalonian and Valencian Cortes on several occasions in the early years of his reign but left them largely as he found them: uncooperative and resistant to change. The alleged Aragonese coronation oath was a constant reminder of their determination to defend their privileges: 'We who are as good as you, swear to you, who are no better than we, to accept you as our sovereign king and lord, provided that you observe our liberties and laws, but if not, not.'

Not surprisingly, the monarchs viewed Castile as a much more useful kingdom. By far the largest territory, it possessed 80 per cent of the population, most of the wealth, a favourable economic outlook and the potential for effective administration. The Council of Castile, mainly composed from 1480 of *letrados* (law graduates), gave advice on financial and foreign policy, acted as a court of appeal and became the central organ of government. Further councils were formed to administer Aragon (1494), the Inquisition (1483) and the Military Orders (1489–98), and committees of professional bureaucrats gave continuity to the administration. The Catholic Monarchs called the Castilian Cortes 16 times between 1474 and 1516 – it did not meet between 1483 and 1497 when they consulted the *Santa Hermandad* instead. On the 12 occasions it met after 1497, it was principally called to obtain subsidies, confirm the succession and approve Ferdinand's legislation. He spent 30 out of 37 years in Castile and by 1516 regarded it as his most desirable kingdom. The Aragonese, ruled for much of the time by viceroys, resented being treated as inferior people and rejected any attempt to Castilianise them.

Nothing better illustrates the separateness of the kingdoms and their desire to resist unification than the hostility meted out to Ferdinand on the death of his wife. Isabella willed that Castile would be ruled by her daughter, Joanna; Ferdinand was only allowed to be 'governor and administrator' in the event of her being incapacitated. By 1505 he had given up hope of ruling the two kingdoms and Philip of Burgundy,

Conversos, Moriscos and **Mudéjars**

Conversos were Jews who had been converted to Christianity; *Moriscos* were Muslims, mostly of North African origin, who had been converted to Christianity; and *Mudéjars* were Muslims living under Christian rule who were allowed to practise their customary beliefs.

Joanna's husband, made it clear that he was no longer welcome in Castile. Ferdinand married Germaine de Foix and retired to Aragon. There is little reason to doubt that Castile and Aragon would have gone their separate ways had not chance intervened. Philip unexpectedly died in 1506 and Joanna, refusing to part with his corpse, retired to Tordesillas and went mad. Their eldest son, Charles, was only six and until he came of age, Ferdinand assumed control. Even then it seemed unlikely that Charles would inherit a unified kingdom. If Germaine had produced a son, he would have been king of Aragon upon Ferdinand's death and Charles king of Castile. In fact, a boy was born in 1509 but only survived a few hours. Charles Habsburg was to become king of Spain by accident, not by design. It had not been Ferdinand's intention to see Aragon ruled by a foreigner; it had never been Isabella's wish to see Castile united with Aragon. Their legacy was unplanned.

Religious uniformity or toleration?

In 1474 Castile and Aragon were multiracial kingdoms with a long history of *convivencia* (co-existence) behind them. About 200,000 Jews and 20,000 **Conversos** lived in Spain. Many held prominent positions and, though retaining their distinctive dress, customs and beliefs, were largely integrated into Spanish society. Moors and **Moriscos** were less numerous in Castile but some 400,000 Muslims in Granada served as a reminder that most of the peninsula had once been under Islamic rule, and **Mudéjars** still comprised some 30 per cent of Valencia.

Isabella was the dominant voice in religious affairs. Determined to rid her kingdom of Jews and Moors and impose Christianity upon them, she revived the Inquisition first in Castile in 1478 and, three years later, in Aragon. Initially it concerned itself with *Conversos* and *Moriscos*. From 1492 Jews throughout Spain were ordered to convert or emigrate within three months. Although upwards of 50,000 Jews departed, many appear to have returned within a few years, and some 50,000 became *Conversos*. These were the groups subsequently investigated by the Inquisition.

Evidence of treasonous activity between the Moors of Granada and Arabs in north Africa and clashes on the Andalucían border in 1481 convinced the monarchs that a 'holy expedition' was necessary. Isabella helped with the organisation, Ferdinand personally directed the artillery and 'crusaders' volunteered from all over the peninsula. After a decade of bitter fighting, Granada surrendered in 1492 (see Figure 6.2). For the next seven years a generous policy of re-education, conversion and toleration occurred but a revolt in 1499 against rising taxation persuaded Isabella to adopt the hard-line advice of her confessor, Ximenes de

Figure 6.2 *Ferdinand, Isabella and Ximenes enter Granada*

Cisneros. In 1500–1501, 200,000 *Mudéjars* (Moors living in Castile and Granada) were given three months either to emigrate or to stay and be baptised. Those who remained – and they were the vast majority – perpetuated social and racial divisions. Significantly, the expulsion order did not apply to Muslims living in the Aragonese kingdoms. Constituting 12 per cent of the population and living in large settlements, Ferdinand wisely left them alone.

Isabella and Ferdinand wanted to bring the Catholic Church under closer state control and to reform the clergy. Many of the 47 bishops lived comfortable lives and posed a serious challenge to the Crown. The Archbishop of Toledo, for example, commanded 19,000 vassals, an army of

2,000 and 20 castles and fortified towns. The key to the problem lay in the Crown wresting the appointment of bishops from the Papacy. Pope Sixtus IV first gave Isabella the right to nominate the Bishop of Cuenca in 1482, Seville in 1484 and, two years later, all ecclesiastical offices in Granada. Then Pope Alexander VI confirmed the monarchs' right to appoint lesser offices. In 1508 all ecclesiastical posts in America were recognised as part of the royal patronage. By 1516 most appeals were heard within Spain and the Church was, in all but name, controlled by the Crown.

The Spanish clergy, however, remained largely unreformed. The appointment of Mendoza as Primate of Castile in 1482 made political sense as his loyalty to the state was without question but not until his death 13 years later were reforms really begun by his successor, Cardinal Cisneros. A papal bull of 1493 enabled him to investigate each of the monasteries though little was achieved outside the Jeronimite and Mendicant orders. He demonstrated his humanist qualities by funding the *Polyglot*, a translation of the Vulgate Bible into Greek, Hebrew and Latin, and he called upon bishops to act against clerical abuses. Some bishops – like Talavera of Granada – were successful but Cisneros's influence was mainly confined to his own Franciscan order, his own cathedral chapter of Toledo and his newly – founded university of Alcalá. By 1516, the Spanish Church was officially orthodox, virtually under state control and armed with inquisitorial tribunals; but it was also responsible for many *Converso* and *Morisco* communities and a clergy which was largely unreformed.

Was the Spanish economy fundamentally flawed by 1516?

The economic policies of the Catholic Kings have been criticised by some historians on three counts.

1 The economy of the eastern kingdoms was only partially rescued from decline. Barcelona was Catalonia's principal city but plague, piracy, Genoese competition and civil war in the 1460s severely affected its trade and commerce. Like Aragon and Valencia, it was excluded from trading with America and given no privileges at the Castilian fairs. Its declining trade with the Mediterranean was further hit by the expulsion of prosperous Jews and *Conversos*. In the 1480s Ferdinand introduced a series of protectionist measures to improve trade, industry and shipping, but they had only a limited impact and the newly-liberated Catalonian peasants found it hard to earn a living in an increasingly depressed economy.

2 Castile's monopoly of American gold and silver was not put to good use. Admittedly, Isabella and Ferdinand had no precedent for guidance and these were early days in Spanish–American relations, but already bullion was being earmarked for military purposes and insufficient attention was given to developing the transatlantic trade.

3 Most seriously, the Catholic Monarchs adopted a defective economic strategy within Castile, favouring the production of wool rather than cloth and supporting sheep farmers to the detriment of arable. Commerce was centred round the wool trade. Since the fourteenth century, the *Mesta*, a corporation of sheep farmers, had been granted the right to move its sheep from the uplands in the spring to the lowlands in winter along the *cañada real* (royal sheepwalk). In 1489 the *cañadas* were enlarged and a royal councillor made president of the *Mesta*, which paved the way for it to grant permanent access at low, fixed rents to any land previously under pasture. The imbalance between pasture and arable worsened when towns and villages were prohibited from cultivating common land. John Elliott has written that such privileges resulted in a 'wilful sacrifice of Castile's long-term requirements to considerations of immediate convenience'.

While this remains true, serious short-term problems were also apparent by the turn of the century. Rising population, a policy of deforestation and a failure to provide for bad harvests caused major grain shortages after 1504. A dual economy had also emerged within Castile. High-quality Andalucían wool serviced industries in the south and the export markets of Burgos, Bilbao and Seville, but Spain's northern and central regions received only low-grade wool for the poorer domestic market. Thus, the opportunity of enhancing local employment and investment was lost. In addition, heavy regulations designed to protect the cloth industry actually stifled future developments. Trade guilds were established at Burgos and Bilbao to safeguard the woollen industry but excessive rules – like the Ordinance of Seville in 1511 which laid down 120 regulations governing cloth weaving – acted as a brake on manufacturing.

Spain was not lacking in raw materials or industrial investment – silverware from Valladolid, silk in Toledo, leather in Córdoba, ironwork in Vizcaya, soap and ceramics in Seville, and wine from Burgos testify to that – but there was little incentive to develop these trades. Reports from Segovia in 1507 and Burgos in 1516 calling for an increase in the volume of cloth manufactures, a reduction in imports and greater royal support for industry, reveal the concern merchants felt at prevailing trends. Such pleas, however, largely went unheeded.

Foreign affairs: a recipe for greatness or disaster?

Ferdinand assumed responsibility for directing foreign affairs between 1474 and 1516. He viewed France as the major threat to his Aragonese empire in the Mediterranean and to his control of the Pyrenees. By 1493 Roussillon and Cerdagne, occupied by French troops for over 30 years, had been regained by skilful diplomacy. A combination of political intrigue and military victories saw the recovery of Naples in 1505, and the acquisition of Navarre from France in 1512.

Ferdinand's statecraft was legendary. Trusted by few and admired by Machiavelli, the Aragonese king brought new dimensions to the art of diplomacy. Recognising the advantages of having an official representative in a foreign country, he was the first monarch to appoint resident ambassadors. Through them he spun his web of intrigue to secure marital alliances with Portugal, England and the Empire. Trade and marital agreements with Portugal ensured a long period of friendship after years of hostility. The marriage of his daughter, Catherine – first to Arthur and then to Henry VIII – brought England into his fold, and he concluded two marriages with the children of Maximilian I. Finally, following the death of Isabella, he married Germaine de Foix, thereby enabling him to assert his claim to the kingdom of Navarre upon the death of her brother.

KEY TERM:

El Cid

He was an eleventh-century knight, Rodrigo Diaz, who became a Castilian hero as a result of his military successes against the Moors.

Since the ninth century the recovery of land from the Turks, known as the *Reconquista*, had inspired a crusading spirit in Spain. After two centuries of comparative peace, Ferdinand revived memories of **El Cid** by declaring: 'From my youth I was always very inclined to war against the infidels and it is the thing in which I receive most delight and pleasure.' In addition to his victory over the Moors in Granada, he sent help to Rhodes, Naples and Venice, and won control of six ports in north Africa, including Tripoli and Algiers.

The patronage of Christopher Columbus in 1492 and the discovery and settlement of several West Indian islands brought mixed blessings. Granted a monopoly by the Spanish Pope Alexander VI in 1493 of all lands 170 leagues west of the Cape Verde Islands, the way was open for Spanish *conquistadores* to explore the New World. By 1510, however, stories were reaching the homeland that Castilian emigrants had seized property, murdered natives and transported Indians as slaves from neighbouring islands. Ferdinand was powerless to stop this exploitation. Adventurers like Balboa, who discovered the isthmus of Darien in 1513, only served to encourage future generations of *conquistadores*. It seems that imperial needs outweighed moral scruples.

Conclusion

According to court writers Ferdinand del Pulgar and Diego de Valera, Isabella and Ferdinand brought stability and prosperity to a divided and war-torn country. They were the first rulers to control major clerical appointments, to incorporate the Military Orders and to establish the *Hermandad*, *letrados* and *corregidores* in the royal administration. In fact, none of these claims was entirely true. Virtually all of Isabella and Ferdinand's methods and policies had been employed by their predecessors, especially Henry IV, and Spain after the death of Isabella in 1504 was far from settled. Within a few years of his accession in 1516, Charles I faced serious revolts. That he was an absentee foreigner who preferred Burgundian to Castilian advisers did not help the new king but long-term grievances of corrupt administrators, law-breaking nobles and declining trade figure prominently among the rebels' complaints. The legacy of Isabella and Ferdinand was not the golden asset traditionally presented by historians.

Task: essay-writing

'How far was Spain a united country by 1516?'

All A- and AS-Level history students have to write essays. Sometimes they will be examination questions, when you will have about 45 minutes to write an essay; more frequently, you will have several days in which to complete the assignment. Your initial task is to decide what the question is about. Begin by identifying the key words or phrases in the title – in this case, they are 'united country' and 'how far'; and then think carefully about their meaning. The concept of 'unity' needs to be considered first. To do this effectively, it may help if you ask a number of sub-questions. For instance, were the kingdoms unified administratively as well as politically? Did the monarchs' religious policies in any sense unite Spain? Did Castile and Aragon develop separate or similar economies? Was a common foreign policy pursued? Questions of this kind will help you to construct sections or paragraphs which will enable you to develop your ideas and explanations.

Evidence of 'unity' or disunity can best be obtained by reading your class notes, and by making notes from textbooks and historical articles. This is a slow but necessary process and there are no short-cuts. All essays should be a combination of facts and arguments. Getting the right balance is not easy: there must be enough facts to 'prove' an argument but not so many that the reader is left confused. As you read, you will not only gather information; you will also gain ideas, some of which may cause you to rethink your original interpretations. You should not be put off by this. Reading and re-assessment are vital parts of a historian's training. In this essay, your reading will help you to shape your ideas about 'how far' Spain was a united country. This requires you to make a value judgement: 'to what extent' was there partial or complete unity, and, by inference, how far was there an absence of unity?

Once you have decided upon how to interpret this question and you are satisfied that you have acquired enough evidence to support your argument, put your ideas on paper in an essay plan. This can be done point by point or diagrammatically. Experiment to see which method you prefer. Number your points to gain an order of hierarchy; this will enable you to begin with the most important idea and to work logically through your list when you write your essay. Ensure that your opening paragraph answers the question but, to avoid later repetition, keep it short. Finally, once you have worked your way through the points in your plan, conclude your essay with two or three sentences. They should draw together your main interpretations and refer to the key phrases of 'how far' and 'a united country'. This will leave your teacher or examiner in no doubt about your views, which is very important. After all, these are the last words that he or she will read before deciding upon your mark!

Further reading

G. Woodward, *Spain in the Reigns of Isabella and Ferdinand, 1474–1516* (Hodder and Stoughton, 1997) – offers an up-to-date survey of the monarchs and early modern Spain.

G. Redworth, *Government and Society in Late Medieval Spain*, New Appreciations of History (Historical Association, 1993) – a short and informative survey of the problems facing the monarchs.

J. Edwards, *The Monarchies of Ferdinand and Isabella*, New Appreciations of History (Historical Association, 1996) – is particularly good on the disunity of the Spanish kingdoms.

F. Fernández-Armesto, *Ferdinand and Isabella* (New York, 1975) – the only satisfactory biography in English of the Catholic Monarchs.

P. K. Liss, *Isabella. The Queen* (Oxford University Press, 1992) – the most recent biography and rather personal view by an American historian.

J. Hillgarth, *The Spanish Kingdoms, 1410–1516: Castilian Hegemony*, vol. ii (Clarendon Press, 1978) – a very sound survey which sets the reigns of the Catholic Kings in their medieval context.

7 In what respects did the Holy Roman Empire change, 1493–1558?

Time chart

1493: Emperor Frederick III dies; accession of Maximilian I

1496: Marriage of Maximilian's son, Philip to Joanna of Castile (from the Trastámara family)

1500: Birth of Charles to Philip and Joanna

1503: Birth of Ferdinand to Philip and Joanna

1516: Charles becomes King of Spain on the death of Ferdinand

1517: Luther publishes his *Ninety-Five Theses*

1519: Charles is elected Holy Roman Emperor

1521: Charles bans Luther from the Empire

1522: Compact of Brussels: Charles gives his brother Ferdinand control over Austro-Hungarian lands. Tournai riots against tax increases

1523: The imperial knights lose at Landstuhl

1525: Rebel peasants are defeated at Frankenhausen

1526: Louis II, King of Hungary, dies. The first Diet of Speyer meets

1527: Ferdinand is crowned King of Hungary

1529: The second Diet of Speyer is called. Siege of Vienna by Turkish troops

1530: Charles rejects compromise with Luther at the Diet of Augsburg; Lutheran princes form the Schmalkaldic League in protest

1531: Ferdinand is crowned King of the Romans

1547: Charles defeats Lutheran princes at Mühlberg

1548: The *Interim* of Augsburg is issued

1552: France and the German princes sign the Treaty of Chambord

1555: Peace of Augsburg is reached
    October Charles abdicates as ruler of the Netherlands

1556: **January** Charles abdicates as King of Spain
    September Charles abdicates as Emperor

1558: Charles V dies in Spain

KEY TERM:

Interim

Following his victory at Mühlberg in 1547, Charles V offered the German Catholic and Protestant princes a political and religious truce, pending the meeting of the General Council of the Church. An **interim** is an intervening period of time but it was also the name given to the Emperor's offer.

Between the accession of Maximilian I and the death of Charles V, the Holy Roman Empire underwent a major transformation in its political, social, economic and religious conditions. This chapter seeks to explain these changes and to identify particular turning-points which punctuated what may be seen more as long-term continuity. The union of the Trastámara and Habsburg families in 1496, the imperial election of Charles in 1519, the 'protest' by German princes at Speyer in 1529 and Charles's failure to press home his advantage after Mühlberg in 1547, were some of the more significant moments in this period (see time chart). As you read this chapter, judge for yourself why some events may be considered more important than others.

The Holy Roman Empire

The death of Emperor Frederick III in 1493 neither surprised his subjects nor changed their lives. He had been on the throne for 53 years, was in very poor health and for the past five years had largely entrusted power to his son, Maximilian. The Empire at the end of the fifteenth century was a mosaic of territories – each ruled by a sovereign prince, prince-bishop, imperial knight or city council – theoretically owing allegiance to the Emperor, though in practice acting autonomously. Indeed, the Empire seemed destined to political disintegration as rival dynasties threatened the very existence of the ruling house of Habsburg. In 1485 Frederick had been the prisoner of the Hungarians; three years later his son was exiled from Burgundy, and in 1490 Upper Austria and the Tyrol were invaded by his cousin, Sigismund. Although Habsburgs had been emperors since 1438 and Maximilian had been elected emperor-designate in 1486, the territorial basis of his dynastic power was fragile.

His family lands comprised three regions: Upper Austria, centred upon the Tyrol, the Upper Rhineland, the Vorlande, Alsace and East Swabia in the south-west of Germany; Lower Austria, containing the cities of Linz and Vienna; and Inner Austria comprising Styria, Carinthia and Carniola to the south-east (see Figure 1.4 on page 8). To the far west of the Empire were Franche Comté, Luxembourg, and the 11 provinces of the Netherlands, which had passed to Maximilian in 1477. To the south lay Milan and the Swiss Confederation; both were capable of breaking away and becoming independent. To the north and west of Austria, from the Rhine to the Oder and south to the Danube, lay the 300 German states which were the backbone of the Empire. The Habsburgs were only one of several leading families aspiring for hegemony in the area in the 1490s: the Jagiellons, who were kings of Bohemia and Hungary, the Wettins of Saxony and the Wittelsbachs who controlled Bavaria and the Palatinate, were well capable of challenging their supremacy.

The Empire and Europe: diplomatic marriages

In the course of the next 65 years the Holy Roman Empire's geo-political condition changed dramatically: in part due to planned dynastic policies but also to an unforeseen family quarrel. Frederick had once immodestly claimed that 'the House of Austria is universal ruler', and Maximilian believed it was his destiny to preside over a universal monarchy. To achieve this lofty dream, he spent his life forming diplomatic alliances, fighting wars and devising marriage contracts. In an age of dynastic intrigue, he was an arch-intriguer. The death of his wife enabled him to marry Bianca Sforza and strengthen his claim to Milan which his grand-son, **Charles**, would seize in 1521, and legally transfer to Spain in 1555. The union with the Castilian house of Trastámara was crucial to both families. Maximilian married his son, Philip, to Joanna, and his daughter, Margaret, to Joanna's brother, John. As a result, Philip's sons, Charles and Ferdinand, came to dominate the Holy Roman Empire and Europe in the first half of the sixteenth century (see Figure 7.2).

By January 1519, Charles had inherited Burgundy from his father, Spain from his maternal grandfather and Austria from his paternal grandfather. Six months later, he was elected Holy Roman Emperor. Charles believed that by skilful marriages he could bind his empire together, preserve the Christian peace and perpetuate his family dynasty. Portugal and the house of Bragança was his chosen target: he married his daughter and son, two sisters and himself into its royal family. His plans eventually came to fruition when the Portuguese throne fell vacant in 1580 and the country was united to Spain. Diplomatic unions negotiated with Francis I of France, Christian II of Denmark and Mary of England brought only short-term political gains, but the double marriage in 1521 between Ferdinand and Anne of Hungary, and between Philip's daughter, Mary, and Louis II of Hungary, proved more rewarding. In 1526 Louis died

PROFILE: *Charles V*

The elder son of Joanna of Castile and Philip of Burgundy, **Charles** (1500–1558) was born in Ghent. Brought up at the court in Malines by his aunt, Margaret of Austria, he was tutored by Adrian of Utrecht and Guillaume de Croy. Both men were later rewarded with high offices in his administration. In 1515 he assumed control of the Netherlands, in 1516 Aragon and Castile and, when Maximilian died three years later, Austria as well. See Figure 7.2.

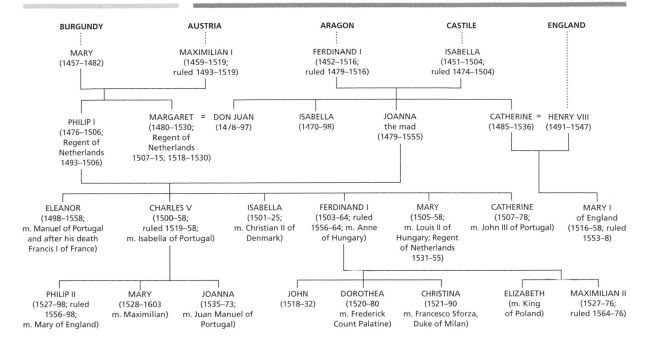

Figure 7.2 *The inheritance of Charles V*

fighting the Turks, which enabled Ferdinand to gain Bohemia. This event well illustrates why political change occurs and how it can take years to run its course. Though the Habsburgs now had a claim to Hungary, they would not wrest it from the Turks until 1699. Dynasticism, then, was a key factor in the continuous growth of the Habsburg Empire.

Family quarrels can alter the course of history; and this is what occurred in 1550–51. Since 1522 Ferdinand had competently administered the family lands, stoically repelled Ottoman attacks and more than adequately deputised for the absent Emperor. His reward was to be crowned King of the Romans in 1531 and to be declared the imperial-designate. Twenty years later Charles changed his mind and announced to the **imperial diet** that he wanted his son, Philip, to be the next Emperor. In the summer of 1550 the two brothers argued, their sons refused to speak to each other and an unholy row broke out. After eight months of bitter bargaining, the Augsburg Agreement was reached by which it was decided that the imperial succession should alternate between the two houses, first going to Ferdinand and then to Philip. The German princes and imperial diet were not consulted but Ferdinand was satisfied.

In 1555 Philip duly conceded all his claims to the Holy Roman Empire in return for Milan. It was a momentous decision. Philip and his heirs had the platform in Spain, Italy and the Netherlands to achieve greatness in western Europe, while Ferdinand could consolidate his family interests around Austria and eastern Europe. As it turned out, the mould had been cast for the next 300 years.

KEY TERM:

Imperial diet

Called at the discretion of the Emperor, the **diet** (or parliament) comprised German princes, knights and representatives from the towns and cities. It was their duty to advise the Emperor and to consider his requests for reforms and financial grants.

The Habsburgs and war

Both Maximilian and Charles devoted their energies to war; the first out of pleasure, the second out of necessity. Neither emperor achieved total success. Maximilian once said, 'a warlike regime and reputation count for far more than does money'. Motivated by a desire to secure and extend his control over Burgundy, he joined any coalition against France, spent money that he could ill afford, and neglected urgent imperial problems. The Italian Wars gave Maximilian his opportunity but he failed to capture Leghorn (1496), was beaten by the Venetians (1508) and lost control of Milan and Lombardy (1516). He spoke endlessly about leading a crusade against the Turks but, lacking the money, men and resolve, it remained an idle dream. Worse, as early as 1495, his fund-raising schemes turned the Swiss cantons against him and they repeatedly defeated him in a series of battles. The Swiss did not particularly want independence but by 1499 Maximilian's incompetence saw that it came about.

Charles V pursued a consistent policy to re-unify the Empire, strengthen Habsburg power and defeat the Turks. His difficulties were acute. After his imperial election in 1519, successive French kings never rested until they had broken the Habsburg encirclement of their country. Francis I (1515–47) and Henry II (1547–59) were prepared to ally with German Lutherans and Ottoman Muslims, even bankrupting France in the process. Unlike Maximilian, Charles fought to defend his family lands and though his wars brought territorial gains in Italy and the Netherlands, he also suffered damaging imperial losses of Metz, Toul and Verdun (see chapter 11). He took his military role seriously, personally leading his troops and constantly travelling from one trouble spot to another. Nevertheless, one or other of his dominions always required his attention and inevitably compromises had to be made.

Spain was his first priority. He spent more time there, made it the centre of his *monarquía* and, by the Compact of Brussels (1522), left the defence of Habsburg family lands in central Europe to his brother. In the course of the 1520s the Turks advanced along the Danube valley reaching the gates of Vienna in 1529 (see Figure 7.3). The impending winter caused them to retreat but they remained nearby for the next three years until Charles, at the head of 250,000 troops, routed them at Güns. Not for the first time, Charles failed to follow up his victory, partly because he was suspicious of an agreement between Francis and the Pope and partly because the German troops refused to cross into Hungary. The Emperor responded cautiously which allowed Suleiman, the Sultan, to launch assaults on the Hungarian towns of Buda (1541) and Gran (1543) and to put John Zápolyai's son on the Transylvanian throne whenever the

KEY TERM:

Monarquía

A monarchy is a system in which a king or queen reigns over a country. Historians often use the Spanish term *monarquía* to describe the lands ruled by Spanish kings. Although their overseas lands are often called the 'Spanish Empire', the monarchs never acquired the title of Emperor, whereas the term *monarquía* includes all dominions under their rule.

Figure 7.3 '*The siege of Vienna*' *1529*

mood took him. Charles appeared willing to sacrifice Hungary because he regarded the Ottoman threat to central Europe as one of his less serious problems. Historians have been surprisingly reluctant to condemn his indifference or to credit Ferdinand for defending the Empire during these difficult times.

Administrative reforms

The Netherlands

Between 1493 and 1555, the Netherlands was governed by a succession of Habsburg regents: Philip (1493–1506), Margaret (1507–15), Charles (1515–17), Margaret again (1518–30) and Mary (1531–55) (see Figure 7.2). The Dutch grandees neither liked nor trusted Maximilian, and attempts to unify the territories were abandoned in favour of granting them political influence and social pre-eminence. Rudimentary machinery for a more centralised government existed in the Netherlands – a council of state, privy council, States-General, law courts, provincial assemblies – but nobles and town burghers controlled the provinces and their parliamentary representatives upheld the principle of unanimity. They were therefore able to preserve their independence and reject burdensome Habsburg taxation. Charles viewed the Netherlands as an important resource. He aimed to bring them under closer control, acquire adjoining territories and create a more cohesive administrative unit. Such a strategy took time to effect and, of necessity, resulted as much from unplanned events as from deliberate design. A combination of military successes and political threats brought him Artois, Flanders and the bishopric of Tournai (in 1521), Friesland (1523), Utrecht (1527), Overjssel (1528), Groningen and Drenthe (1536), Cambrai, Zutphen and Gelderland (1543) (see Figure 7.4).

In 1531 a council of finance was established to organise tax collection throughout the provinces and a high court of appeal set up to hear cases from provincial courts. **Stadholders**, who represented the Emperor in each province, were encouraged to reside in Brussels and bailiffs were appointed by the regent to supervise the town councils more closely.

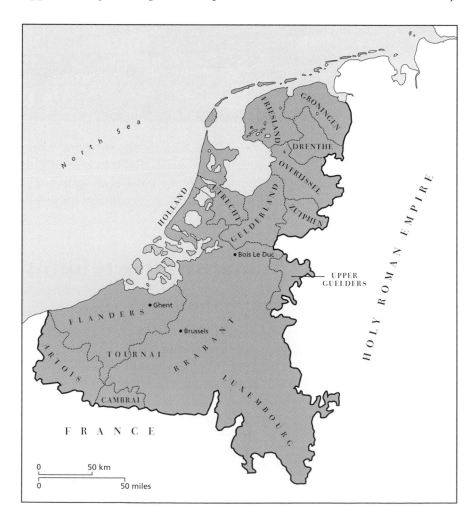

Figure 7.4 The Netherlands in the reign of Charles V

As early as 1522 a state inquisition was introduced to work alongside episcopal inquisitors; its power to arrest and try anyone overrode local magistrates and was naturally seen as an instrument of potential centralisation. Riots against rising taxation in Tournai, Bois-Le-Duc, Brussels and Ghent, and opposition from the States-General against financing a standing army was further evidence that the Dutch would resist imperial plans for unification. The regents sensibly treated them more tolerantly than Charles desired. They understood the need to cooperate both with the nobles and wealthy merchants. Charles could not have a unitary state if he also expected it to finance his wars and, when minor changes were introduced, they had to be with everyone's consent.

Austrian Habsburg lands

Maximilian and Charles had neither the opportunity nor inclination to reform the administration of their family estates in Austria and Hungary, but Ferdinand did. Between 1522 and 1564, he demonstrated what could be achieved by a more realistic approach. He aimed to strengthen his control by enlisting the cooperation of the Hungarian and Austrian nobles to collect taxes, enforce the law and defend their lands. He left untouched the Magyar, Czech and Polish diets and chancelleries in return for noble support. Recognising that Lutheranism ran too deep to be eliminated from his German lands, he concentrated on supporting a revived Catholic Church rather than continued conflict with Protestantism. His flexibility was rewarded. Bohemia, despite its anticlerical tradition, never fell to the Lutherans and Austria began to receive regular ecclesiastical visitations from as early as the 1520s. Heresy certainly existed but the problem was contained.

Germany

Machiavelli observed that the crucial problem facing Maximilian in 1493 was that he had 'no power to enforce his will'. He had no army, no regular taxation and no central administration. But reform was in the air. Increasing lawlessness and the Turkish threat instilled a sense of urgency among leading German princes and bishops which, if handled skilfully, might have been turned to the Emperor's advantage. Unfortunately, Maximilian could not be trusted and too many princes feared they would suffer if he was given both a permanent army and a full treasury. In 1495 at the Diet of Worms, Berthold – Archbishop of Mainz and Imperial Archchancellor (1484–1504) – proposed that an imperial supreme court of justice should be set up and private armies outlawed. The Emperor agreed but rejected a proposed permanent executive council since he thought it would restrict his power. In response, the Diet refused the 'common penny' universal tax and Maximilian went away empty handed.

Five years later at Augsburg, he achieved a better deal. The Diet promised to finance 34,000 troops if he would establish a council of regency of 20 men – three would be nominated by him – who would make and enforce laws in his absence. In addition, the Empire would be divided into six administrative circles (extended to ten in 1512) to supervise justice, finance and the army. Maximilian had the support of a minority of princes who believed they could win control of the administration but the majority feared that he would concede nothing and would instead use these institutions to weaken their authority. By 1504 Berthold, who had been the driving force behind the reforms, had died, Maximilian's money had been spent, the council of regency abolished and thoughts of reform abandoned.

There was little constructive legislation in the 20 diets between 1495 and 1518. The Emperor regarded them as a means of bargaining for money and troops and he was too weak in body and mind to construct a coherent plan of constitutional reform. He rarely finished what he started – even his tomb was incomplete at his death! Maximilian, though, was not without some political authority provided it was backed up by one of the military leagues. In 1504, for instance, he was able to impose an imperial ban on Ruprecht and prevent him from seizing Bavaria because he had the support of 13,000 Swabian troops. A serious peasant revolt in 1514 was suppressed by the same means. Without the assistance of such groups, he was powerless.

Charles V faced similar difficulties. Even before he was elected Emperor in 1519, he had to promise constitutional reforms. At his first diet at Worms (1521), the princes demanded more independence for the supreme court, the restoration of the regency council and the right to appoint 18 of the 22 councillors. Though the court was restored, Charles never allowed it to operate independently and when it was abolished in 1530, no one objected. The political reality, as Charles well knew, was that each secular and ecclesiastical ruler within Germany exercised as much authority as his neighbour permitted. Circles and leagues functioned at the discretion of sovereign princes, imperial knights and free cities. In Germany, the Emperor was a tool in their hands. Thus it was the Swabian League, dominated by the Rhineland princes, which suppressed the Knights' War in 1523 and the Peasants' Revolt in 1524/5.

Only on one occasion was Charles strong enough to effect reforms. At the *Interim* of Augsburg in 1548, he decreed that the supreme court would be strengthened, a regency council set up without princes and a new military league established under his control. Significantly, both Lutheran and Catholic princes closed ranks to oppose him. In practice, none of his edicts was implemented. Was it always inevitable that the princes would restrict his power? It is a debatable point. While it remains likely that their influence would have continued to increase, that sovereign states would have been formed and in time gained their independence from the Empire, what was unforeseen at the beginning of Charles's reign was the speed with which such changes would occur. Undoubtedly, it was Martin Luther who brought this about.

The political impact of Luther

Charles mismanaged Luther from the beginning, though in retrospect it is easy to see why. In 1519 a young, inexperienced Emperor, with the largest *monarquía* since Charlemagne, faced many problems. When he first met Luther at Worms, he severely underestimated his significance stating, 'a single friar who goes counter to all Christianity for a thousand years must be wrong'. He called upon his princes to carry out his imperial ban: 'I have therefore resolved to stake upon this cause all my domains, my friends, my body and my blood, my life and my soul.' No one can deny the Emperor's sincerity or his intent to defend the Catholic faith, but he seriously misjudged the loyalty of the German princes. His rhetoric cut no ice with Frederick, Elector of Saxony, and Ludwig of the Palatinate, who never signed the ban.

Charles was away from Germany between 1521 and 1530 (see chapter 11). Much occurred during these years to suggest that his authority was ebbing away. The heresy laws were blatantly ignored; Luther still lived at large and his beliefs were openly discussed in much of the Empire. After the princes had defeated the imperial knights, Ferdinand astutely observed, 'We have lost the support of an important element on which we could have counted to assist our government.' In the course of the diets of Nuremberg between 1522 and 1524, divisions between estates took place as orthodox and reformed camps were established. On 18 April 1524 Ferdinand achieved a compromise: 'Each prince in his own territory should enforce the Edict of Worms in so far as he might be able.' The Catholic dukes of Saxony, Bavaria and Brandenburg complied, and set up the League of Dessau (1525). Luther's princely supporters – Philip of Hesse, Frederick of Saxony and his nephew John Frederick, and the imperial cities of Augsburg, Strassburg and Nuremberg – responded in kind by setting up their League of Torgau (1526).

Such armed groups were, of course, capable of fighting each other but this was not their intention. On the contrary, their prime aim after 1525 was to maintain civil order in the face of peasant and urban disturbances. Catholics and Lutherans, princes and magistrates joined forces to suppress the Peasants' Wars, which had been caused as much by unfair land taxes, excessive tithes and a total lack of confidence in the usual forms of justice, as by Lutheranism. Traditional secret societies, like the 'Laced Boot' and 'Poor Conrad', sought to replace feudal with customary law and demanded fair and efficient government. Luther condemned this massive popular uprising, calling upon the princes to 'strike, smite, strangle or stab, secretly or publicly' the peasants. They needed no prompting. In 1525 the Swabian League restored control in the Black Forest and Upper Swabia – the main source of trouble – and personal scores were settled with a vengeance. The Bishop of Würzburg alone supervised the execution of 272 peasants.

At the following Diet of Speyer in 1526, Philip of Hesse arrived with 200 horsemen and Lutheran preachers. On the eve of the meeting, he provocatively ate meat on Friday: a practice banned by the Catholic Church. Ferdinand yielded to this display of princely audacity by issuing a 'recess', whereby each prince was asked to enforce the faith 'as he would have to answer to God and the Emperor'. Ferdinand was buying time. He did the same three years later at the second Diet of Speyer when he revoked the 'recess' and called for a halt to evangelical reform. He also insisted that in Catholic lands no freedom should be granted to Lutherans, but in Lutheran lands Catholics should receive toleration. Protests came from six Lutheran princes and 14 cities. When Hesse failed to unite Lutherans, Zwinglians and Strassburgers in achieving a common confession at the Colloquy of Marburg in 1529, the Emperor's position seemed more favourable.

Charles's personal appearance next year at the Diet of Augsburg was his first attempt to resolve the schism. Three reasons explain his failure:

■ his own unwillingness to compromise

■ the influence of his hard-line advisers, like Campeggio, Pimpinelli and the Duke George of Saxony

■ the religious conviction of the Lutheran princes who in December established an armed League of Schmalkalden.

For the next 15 years Charles had to contend with a Papacy which was unresponsive to his call for a general council, a vengeful French king and persistent assaults by the Turks on his Mediterranean lands. As the Habsburgs were thrown onto the defensive, support for Lutheranism spread through the north and west of the Empire. Nothing better illustrates the Emperor's weakness and the princes' growing power than the case of Württemberg in 1534. Philip used the Schmalkaldic troops to seize the duchy and restore Ulrich, an exiled murderer, who promised to join the League. Ferdinand was powerless to intervene and the Swabian League stood by and watched. In 1541 Charles made one final attempt at reconciliation when rival theologians met at Regensburg but their failure convinced him that soon he would have to resort to war.

Between 1543 and 1546 Charles built up military alliances with Cleves, Maurice of Saxony and two Brandenburg princes. He also obtained a guarantee of French neutrality, a papal blessing and arranged for his imperial army to invade from Italy. Though offers of toleration were put on the table at Speyer and Regensburg, he was only playing for time. In June he declared privately, 'If we failed to intervene now, all the states of Germany would be in danger of breaking with the faith'. By April 1547 his army had won a glorious battle at Mühlberg, most Lutheran princes had surrendered, and John Frederick and Philip had been taken prisoner. Within a year, however, this success had evaporated. The dukes of Bavaria and Brandenburg defeated his proposal to set up an armed league of princes, and his *Interim* – a genuine attempt at religious compromise – was rejected by both Catholics and Lutherans. A despondent Maurice of Saxony, who wanted an electorate, was on the point of defection.

If Charles had possessed the political vision to see that the Empire had changed and if he had been willing to concede a degree of independence to the princes – which in practice they were exercising anyway – then he might have been able to retain their support during his wars against France. As it was, he missed his opportunity. Defeat had been snatched from the jaws of victory. In 1550 the northern princes resurrected the League of Torgau to defend Lutheranism. In 1551 Maurice and in 1552 Henry II of France joined them. This was a nightmare scenario. Ferdinand wisely tried to buy time at Passau by negotiating a truce with Maurice but Charles was unprepared for France's swift capture of Metz followed by a sudden drive southwards which forced him to flee to Innsbruck. News that his army had failed to recapture Metz in January 1553 left him a disillusioned and broken man.

Charles could not bring himself to attend the Diet of Augsburg in 1555. Neither his faith nor his health permitted it. Instead it fell to his long-suffering brother to confirm the principle of *cuius regio, eius religio* ('what-ever the religion of a prince should also be the religion of the lands he ruled'), first outlined at Speyer in 1526. Lutheranism was allowed but there was no place for Calvinists, Zwinglians and Anabaptists. Territories ruled by a Catholic in 1552 had to remain and no Catholic state was allowed to convert to Lutheranism, though a Lutheran state could return to Catholicism (a term known as the 'ecclesiastical reservation').

Just how effective this settlement would prove to be depended on the sovereign power of the princes, not the Emperor. In practice, peace in the Empire lasted for more than half a century. Charles never returned to

Germany. In a series of carefully arranged ceremonies he abdicated, first as Duke of Burgundy, then as King of Spain and Duke of Milan, and finally as Holy Roman Emperor, although he retained his imperial title until February 1558, when the electors appointed Ferdinand. By then Charles had removed himself from worldly affairs, entered a Spanish monastery at Yuste and quietly prepared to die. The future, like the recent past, of the German Empire lay with the princes. Throughout the later Middle Ages, they had been consolidating their power but it was Lutheranism which enabled them to assert themselves at the expense of the Emperor. This development could certainly not have been predicted in 1519 (see chapter 8).

Task: roleplaying

Work on Charles V lends itself to roleplaying. Divide into four groups, each one representing well-informed subjects with different views about the Emperor Charles V.

- German peasants in the 1520s
- Italian merchants in the 1530s
- Spanish troops in the 1540s
- German princes in the 1550s

Each group has to use the evidence in this chapter to come up with reactions to the changes brought about by Charles V's election in 1519. You could set up a debate, or each group could make its own report. Remember to make use of the evidence contained in this chapter and any other information you may have. Chapter 8 (on Luther) and chapter 11 (on the Italian Wars) will also be helpful. You should also use the index of this book to look up the topics related to Charles V. You are not allowed to make things up, or say how things 'must have been'! There is plenty of proper evidence about. What makes this topic particularly interesting is that not all the evidence points in the same direction. You might well find that different people in the same group will have different points of view.

Further reading

M. Rady, *Emperor Charles V*, Seminar Studies in History (Addison Wesley Longman, 1989) – provides a short and integrated study of Charles's German problems.

R. Scribner, *The German Reformation* (Macmillan, 1986) – offers a concise and thorough introduction to the religious dimension.

M. F. Alvarez, *Charles V* (Thames and Hudson, 1975) – a sound and detailed biography.

G. Benecke, *Maximilian I* (Routledge and Kegan Paul, 1982).

J. Bérenger, *A History of the Habsburg Empire 1273–1700*, trans. C. A. Simpson (Addison Wesley Longman, 1994) – discusses imperial problems.

H. Wiesflecker, *Maximilian I: Die Fundamente des habsburgischen Weltreiches* (Vienna/Munich, 1991) – is the only satisfactory biography of Maximilian but it still awaits an English translation.

8 Why did Luther appeal to so many German people?

Time chart

1517: Luther pins his 95-point theses on the church door in Wittenberg

1518: A papal commission is set up to investigate Luther; recommends that Cardinal Cajetan debates points of theology with him at Augsburg

1519: Luther rejects papal authority in a public disputation with Karlstadt and Eck at Leipzig. Charles V is elected Holy Roman Emperor

1520: Pope Leo X excommunicates Luther who responds by writing three pamphlets – *To the Christian Nobility of the German Nation, On the Babylonish Captivity of the Church* and *Concerning Christian Liberty*

1521: April Luther refuses to recant at the Diet of Worms
May Luther is 'imprisoned' in Wartburg Castle

1522: Leading Imperial Knights adopt Lutheran views, mostly for political reasons

1524: The Peasants' Wars begin in the Black Forest (southern Germany)

1525: Elector Frederick the Wise dies. Albrecht of Hohenzollern, Grand Master of the Teutonic Knights, and John, Elector of Saxony, are converted to Lutheranism

1526: Philip of Hesse announces his conversion

1528: Margrave of Brandenburg-Ansbach, Count of Mansfeld, Duke of Schleswig and Duke of Brunswick all become Lutheran

1529: Six princes 'protest' at second Diet of Speyer; Luther meets Zwingli at the Colloquy of Marburg but it fails to resolve theological differences between them

1546: Luther dies in Wartburg Castle

In this chapter we investigate the principal ideas of Martin Luther and, through a study of his writings and contemporary documents, attempt to explain why he became so popular in much of Germany.

On 31 October 1517 Luther allegedly (historians are undecided whether this famous event took place or not) pinned his 95 Theses to the door of Wittenberg Castle Church and thereby began a process which developed

Figure 8.2 Johann Tetzel selling
indulgences

Johannes Tezelius Dominicaner Münch/mit sei-
nen Römischen Ablaßkram/welchen er im Jahr Christi 1517. in Deutschen-
landen zu marckt gebracht/wie er in der Kirchen zu Pirn in seinem
Vaterland abgemahlet ist.

O ihr deutschen mercket mich recht/
   Des heiligen Vaters Papstes Knecht/
Bin ich/vnd bring euch jtzt allein/
   Zehn tausent vnd neun hundert car ein/
Gnad vnd Ablaß von einer Sünd/
   Vor euch/ewer Eltern/Weib vnd Kind/
Sol ein jeder gewehret sein
   So viel jhr legt eins Kästelein/
So bald der Gülden im Becken klingt/
   Im huy die Seel im Himel springt/

as the German Protestant Reformation. The target of his attack was
Johann Tetzel, an **indulgence** seller (see Figure 8.2), whose advertising
slogan ran: 'As soon as the coin in the coffer rings, a soul from purgatory
springs'.

Although Luther chose the time and place to criticise the abuses of indulgences, he did not set out to attack the Church as an institution, still less
the Papacy. Nor could he have foreseen what his action would lead to.
Events took over, for the Theses were printed in German, without
Luther's consent. Within two weeks they were circulating throughout
the Holy Roman Empire. Luther, along with Wittenberg University
where he was lecturing, and its patron, Frederick, Elector of Saxony,
found themselves in the glare of public controversy. In October 1518 at
Augsburg, **Luther** publicly defended his rejection of traditional Catholic
teaching about the role of good works and indulgences in a debate with
the papal legate, Cardinal Cajetan. The following year, in another public
disputation, this time at Leipzig, he rejected papal authority at least by
implication.

PROFILE: *Martin Luther*

Born in 1483, son of a wealthy Thuringian silver miner, **Martin Luther** entered the Augustinian priory at Erfurt in 1505 in search of the true path to salvation. The monastic routine failed to satisfy his anxiety about **purgatory** and the fate of his soul, so he left the priory for the newly established university of Wittenberg, where he became professor of biblical studies. In 1516, while studying St Paul's *Epistle to the Romans*, he was struck by the phrase 'The righteous shall live by faith'. This marked the point at which his life was transformed. It led him to the belief that only God, through the gift of faith, could grant salvation. Good works, penance, indulgences and many other current Catholic practices were at best irrelevant, at worst positively harmful. As a result, the only sacrament that counted was the Eucharist (mass). It brought the believer into direct contact with God and was administered in both kinds (*i.e.* the bread and the wine), so that the laity and not simply the priest could fully participate. Luther died in 1546.

KEY TERM:

Purgatory

A place or condition in which, according to Catholic theology, the souls of the departed are purged, by suffering, of the burden of Penance for the sins which they committed during their lifetimes.

Extracts from the Ninety-Five Theses *(1517)*

5 The Pope has neither the will nor the power to remit any penalties beyond those he has imposed either at his own discretion or by canon law.

6 The Pope can remit no guilt, but only declare and confirm that it has been remitted by God; or, at most, he can remit it in cases reserved to his discretion. To ignore such remissions would of course leave the guilt untouched.

27 It is mere human talk to preach that the soul flies out [of purgatory] immediately the money clinks in the collection-box.

32 All those who believe themselves certain of their own salvation because of letters of pardon will be eternally damned, together with their teachers.

67 The Indulgences, which the merchants extol as the greatest gifts of grace, are rightly understood as 'greatest' only as far as money-getting is concerned.

To date Luther had had the worse of the debates and Pope Leo X, content with the situation and anxious to support Frederick's candidature in the forthcoming imperial election, agreed that Luther's fate should be determined by a future German diet. The election of Charles as Emperor Charles V, however, led Leo to condemn Luther officially in June 1520.

KEY TERM:

Excommunication

The Papacy had the right to punish Christians by stopping them from having access to, or the privileges of, the Church. They could be denied the Eucharist (known as 'minor excommunication') or prevented from entering a church and participating in any religious ceremony ('major excommunication'). Luther received the latter punishment.

He was given 60 days to recant or face **excommunication**. Luther decided to appeal to the German people and explained his beliefs more fully in a series of pamphlets written between August and December.

Part of Luther's first pamphlet 'To the Christian Nobility of the German Nation', August 1520

'All Christians are truly of the spiritual estate, and there is no difference among them, save of office alone. As St Paul says, we are all one body, though each member does its own work, to serve the others. This is because we have one baptism, one Gospel, one faith, and are all Christians alike. For baptism, gospel and faith, these alone make spiritual and Christian people. Therefore it is a wickedly devised fable – and they cannot quote a single letter to confirm it – that it is for the Pope alone to interpret the scriptures or to confirm the interpretation of them. They have assumed the authority of their own selves. And though they say that this authority was given to St Peter when the keys were given to him, it is plain enough that the keys were not given to St Peter alone, but to the whole community.'

Luther's appeal

Luther's attack on the Papacy and the Catholic Church found an immediate response among the German people. Luther was a superb communicator. Not only did he preach well over 2,000 sermons, he also used the newly established printing press to disseminate his ideas. During his lifetime, his works went through nearly 4,000 editions in 12 languages, and the use of visual illustrations proved particularly important in carrying his message to the common people, many of whom were illiterate (see Figure 8.3). An opportunist with a pen as sharp as his tongue, Luther was never slow to reply to his critics. His crude use of propaganda and earthy language go some way towards explaining his appeal. Wittenberg became the centre of Lutheranism and many of its university students became evangelical preachers.

Lutheranism would never have spread if it had not had the support of established authorities. Imperial Knights – like von Hutten, Sickingen and Cronberg – adopted Lutheranism in an attempt to revive their authority over the princes. The Elector Frederick, who could have stopped Luther in his tracks, gave him protection and refuge in Wartburg Castle. Frederick remained an orthodox Catholic, but the same was not true of all other princes. To give three examples among many, Albrecht of

Hohenzollern, the Landgrave Philip of Hesse and the Margrave of Brandenburg-Ansbach committed themselves to Lutheranism.

The motives which prompted those in power to follow the path of reform were mixed. Some were prompted by a genuine desire to eliminate the abuses that had disfigured the Catholic Church. Others were attracted by the prospect of gaining control of Church property as well as clerical appointments, and of transferring papal taxation to themselves. Not all rulers were free to act as they pleased. In the south of Germany, in particular, they had to take into account the Catholic orthodoxy and military power of the Wittelsbach and Habsburg families.

The historian Peter Blickle has stressed the importance of rural support for Lutheranism, at least in the early 1520s. Peasants, miners and weavers were attracted by Luther's appeal to 'Godly law' and the apparent egalitarianism of his assertion that 'we are all one body'. In fact, Luther was thinking in terms of spiritual equality, but rising taxation combined with bad harvests in 1523–4 had created widespread distress and resentment in the German countryside. The belief that Luther was a prophet sent by God to redress injustice gave his message a cutting edge. He was hailed as a messiah, and this was one of the factors that brought about the Peasants' War of 1524–6. But, Luther quickly distanced himself from it. He had an innate dislike of disorder, and in any case he was dependent upon the existing rulers for the protection of his infant church and the spreading of his unorthodox beliefs. The defeat of the peasants, however, led to religious indifference in many rural areas by the 1540s.

Extracts from 'The Twelve Articles of Memmingen', a manifesto written by rebel peasants in March 1525.

'First *of all, we humbly ask and beg – and we all agree on this – that henceforth we ought to have the power for the whole community to elect its own pastor, and also to depose a pastor who behaves improperly. He should preach the holy gospel purely and clearly, without any human additions. For constant preaching of the true faith impels us to beg God for his grace.'*

'Third, *it has until now been the custom for the lords to own us as their property. This is deplorable, for Christ redeemed and bought us all with his precious blood, the lowliest shepherd as well as the greatest lord, with no exceptions. Thus the Bible proves that we are free.'*

'Fourth, *until now it has been the custom that no commoner might catch wild game, wild fowl, or fish, which seems altogether improper, selfish and contrary to God's Word.'*

In recent years, historians have attached increasing importance to Luther's appeal to the imperial and territorial cities. By 1546 a majority of the 85 imperial cities and hundreds of smaller towns in the north, centre and south-west had adopted Lutheranism. Each urban group responded to Luther's theology with greater individuality and diversity than used to be believed, though historians are still unsure about the particular importance of local conditions. Of 2,000 German towns, only 80 have so far been studied in detail and any conclusion must be provisional. Steven Ozment has emphasised the importance of evangelical preachers like Bucer, Osiander and Melanchthon in spreading Luther's ideas. Bob Scribner has stressed the importance of preaching friars like Staupitz in Nuremberg and Keyersberg in Strassburg in preparing people's minds. In southern Germany, in the lands bordering the Swiss cantons, Zwinglian preachers were similarly successful.

Some town councils like Nuremberg adopted Lutheran beliefs to control the speed of religious change in the face of disunifying forces, whereas in Hesse the landowners responded to protect their peasants' interests as inflation and a rising population increased economic tension. In the northern Hanseatic cities of Bremen, Stettin, Lübeck and Hamburg, strong anticlerical traditions combined with economic and religious grievances to force the issue. Pressure to introduce reform was certainly evident in Basel, Strassburg and Memmingen where guilds voiced the feelings of their members; Mühlhausen council, for instance, adopted Lutheranism 'so that Christian brotherly love and unity may be planted among us'; and Ulm held a public debate followed by a referendum in 1530.

Not all cities embraced Lutheranism. Places in close proximity to prince-bishops like Mainz, Trier and Cologne in the west, and to orthodox rulers like the Duke of Bavaria in the south, Duke George of Saxony in the north and the Elector of the Palatinate in central Germany, did not dare antagonise them. Uberlingen warned its citizens against the new teaching, while Regensburg, Gottingen and Brunswick magistrates openly opposed it. Even the ruling oligarchs of Augsburg and Speyer took their time and waited until conditions were favourable before declaring for religious reform. They feared not only the wrath of the Emperor but a possible loss of trade if they acted too hastily. Strassburg was exceptional in managing to combine Catholicism with Lutheranism, Zwinglianism, and even for a brief period Anabaptism, until Lutheranism finally prevailed in 1598. In short, in towns as well as states, the fate of Lutheranism depended to a great extent upon the attitude of the established authorities. Where there was a tradition of political independence, town authorities were free to adopt Lutheranism, Zwinglianism or to remain orthodox; where social and political conditions were not favourable, Luther's message fell on deaf ears.

Task: evaluating sources

Study the three sources below and look back to the extracts from Luther's 95 Theses (page 81) and to the Twelve Articles of Memmingen (page 83). Then answer the questions which follow the sources below.

Document A

'I must deny that there are seven Sacraments, and must lay it down, for the time being, that there are only three – baptism, penance and the bread – and that by the court of Rome all these have been brought into miserable bondage, and the Church despoiled of all her liberty. But why should not Christ be able to include His body within the substance of bread, as well as within the accidents? Fire and iron, two different substances, are so mingled in red-hot iron that every part of it is both fire and iron. Why may not the glorious body of Christ much more be in every part of the substance of the bread? Let every man then who has learnt that he is a Christian recognise what he is, and be certain that we are all equally priests, that is that we have the same power in the word, and in any sacrament whatever, although it is not lawful for any one to use this power, except with the consent of the community.'

From Luther's pamphlet, 'On the Babylonish Captivity of the Church', published October 1520.

Document B

'I first lay down these two propositions, concerning spiritual liberty and servitude: a Christian man is the most free lord of all, and subject to none; a Christian man is the most dutiful servant of all, and subject to everyone. And so it will profit nothing that the body should be adorned with sacred vestments, or dwell in holy places, or be occupied in sacred offices, or pray, fast and abstain from certain meats, or do whatever works can be done through the body and in the body. Let us therefore hold it for certain and firmly established that the soul can do without everything except the word of God, without which none at all of its wants are provided for. But, having the word, it is rich and wants for nothing. Hence it is clear that as the soul needs the word alone for life and justification, so it is justified by faith alone, and not by any works. From all this it is easy to understand why faith has such great power, and why no good works, nor even all good works put together, can compare with it, since no work can cleave to the word of God or be in the soul.'

From Luther's pamphlet, 'Concerning Christian Liberty', published December 1520.

Document C

Figure 8.3 *An engraving entitled 'The Spiritual Wolves' by an unknown Dahlem artist in the early 1520s*

1 In what ways, and why, can Luther's pamphlets of 1520 be considered more radical than his 95-point theses of 1517? Refer to both pamphlets (Documents A and B) and to the theses in your answer.

2 What message is the engraving (Document C) trying to put across about the Papacy, Luther and Christ's flock? How effectively does this source convey its message?

3 In what ways do the extracts from the 'Twelve Articles of Memmingen' (see page 83) confirm the view that Luther's teaching helped bring about social rebellion in Germany?

4 On the basis of Documents A, B and C, and using your own knowledge, do you think Luther was a revolutionary leader? Explain your answer.

Further reading

K. Randell, *Luther and the German Reformation, 1517–55* (Arnold, 1988) – provides a good introduction.

J. M. Kittelson, *Luther the Reformer* (Inter-Varsity Press, 1989) – offers a recent assessment of Luther's life and work.

E. Cameron, *The European Reformation* (Oxford University Press, 1991) – a detailed study of Luther's theology and his appeal.

P. Johnson and R. Scribner, *The Reformation in Germany and Switzerland* (Cambridge University Press, 1993) – provides the political context for Luther's appeal in Germany.

P. Blickle, *Communal Reformation* (Humanities Press, 1993) – examines the social/urban conflicts.

R. Po-Chia Hsia (ed.), *German People and the Reformation* (Cornell University Press, 1988) – a set of 12 stimulating essays written by experts.

T. Scott and R. Scribner, *The German Peasants' War: A History in Documents* (Humanities Press, 1991) – useful collection of source material.

9 Zwingli, the Swiss Reformation and the Anabaptists

Time chart

1484: Ulrich Zwingli is born at Wildhaus

1506: Zwingli becomes Glarus parish priest

1518: He becomes stipendiary priest at Zurich

1519: He preaches the gospels from the New to the Old Testament

1522: He openly attacks fasting in *Of Freedom of Choice in the Selection of Food*

1523: The Zurich Council accepts his 67 Theses

1525: Zurich rejects the traditional mass. The Swiss Brethren is established

1526: The town of St Gall adopts Zwinglianism

1527: Zwingli publishes his *Refutation of the tricks of the Anabaptists*

1528: Berne becomes Zwinglian

1529: Zwingli, Luther and Melanchthon meet at Marburg; civil war begins between the Christian Civic Union and the Christian Alliance

1531: Zwingli dies at Battle of Kappel; civil war ends

This chapter is concerned with the first generation of Protestant Swiss reformers of whom the best known is Ulrich Zwingli. It looks at his ideas and explains why they were accepted in Zurich but rejected by other religious groups, notably the Swiss Brethren whose own brand of Anabaptism earmarked them as revolutionaries. Contemporary responses to these and to other sectarians are considered through a variety of sources.

Zurich was one of 13 cantons in the Swiss Confederation which enjoyed a high degree of religious and political freedom in the early sixteenth century. Nominally within the diocese of Constance, it was effectively ruled by wealthy landowners and craftsmen who made up the Council of Two Hundred. This oligarchy was ready to introduce church reforms when **Zwingli** arrived but felt no obligation to follow Lutheran principles

PROFILE: *Ulrich Zwingli*

Born in 1484 the son of a wealthy farmer, **Zwingli** first studied at Vienna and then Basel universities, excelling in Latin and theology. Following his ordination in 1506 at Constance, he was appointed parish priest of Glarus, where he stayed for ten years. During this time, he read as much as he could of Erasmus and agreed with him that the scriptures must be the basis of faith. What was not adequately explained by the Bible could, he believed, be overcome by reason. Erasmus' translation of the New Testament into Greek encouraged Zwingli to improve his own Greek and to learn Hebrew so that he could then study the Old Testament. Like Erasmus, he began to develop pacifist tendencies which brought him into conflict with his town council. Switzerland was renowned for its mercenaries – Zwingli himself twice accompanied troops to Italy – but his bitter experience at the Battle of Marignano in 1515 led him to renounce warfare. Not surprisingly, his views were unwelcome, so he moved first to Einsiedeln and then to Zurich (Figure 9.2) as a stipendiary priest. Perhaps what was more of a surprise was that Zwingli died at the age of 47 in a battle!

Figure 9.2 *A woodcut of Zurich in Zwingli's time showing the Great Minster on the right, and the river flowing through the town with its 5,000 inhabitants*

– a situation ideal for a man of Zwingli's ability. His biblical expertise was unrivalled and he had the self-confidence to defend his beliefs in public.

Zwingli's first innovation in 1519 was to preach the gospels in biblical order, beginning with *Matthew* and continuing to the end of the New Testament, before progressing to the Old Testament. He then attacked the arrival of Sanson, an indulgence seller, and won the support of the Bishop of Constance and the town council. Church reform proceeded quietly until 1522 when Zwingli declared that there was no biblical precedent for Christians to fast at Lent nor for clerical celibacy (he himself was married in 1522). A firm rebuke from the bishop led to his declaring that he would defend these and other beliefs in a theological debate in January 1523. As his 67 Theses were not contested by the bishop, Zwingli had little difficulty defending his beliefs. The mayor and city council duly adopted them as their reformed church.

Extracts from the Sixty-Seven Theses *(27 January 1523)*

1 All who say that the gospel is invalid without the confirmation of the church err and slander God.

2 The sum and substance of the gospel is that our Lord Christ Jesus, the true son of God, has made known to us the will of his heavenly Father, and has with his sinlessness released us from death and reconciled us to God.

18 Christ, having sacrificed himself once and for all, is for all eternity a perpetual and acceptable offering for the sins of all believers, from which it follows that the Mass is not a sacrifice, but is a commemoration of the sacrifice and assurance of the salvation which Christ has given us.

22 Christ is our justification, from which it follows that our works, if they are of Christ, are good; but if ours, they are neither right nor good.

24 No Christian is bound to do those things which God has not decreed; hence one may eat at all times all food, whence one learns that the dispensations about cheese and butter are a Roman imposture.

28 All that God has allowed or not forbidden is right, hence marriage is permitted to all human beings.

36 All the rights and protection that the so-called spiritual authority claims belong to secular governments provided they are Christian.

57 The true holy scriptures know nothing of purgatory after this life.

Although much of Zwingli's theology was outlined in these theses, the city council adopted his ideas very slowly, and then only after a series of public debates. In 1523, for instance, it decided how people should be educated:

> *'Learned, skilful and upright men shall lecture on, and expound the Bible publicly every day devoting one hour daily each to the Hebrew, Greek and Latin texts, very necessary for the proper understanding of the divine word. In addition, schoolmasters, better paid than previously, shall be provided to be an active teacher and leader to the boys.'*

In April 1525 the Zurich city council voted to reject the mass and to adopt Zwingli's view of the Eucharist which he had been developing since 1523. To Zwingli, Christ's words at the last supper *'hoc est corpus meum'* indicated that the mass was a commemorative act, that His body and blood were really present at communion though only in symbolic and representative terms, and that the physical body of Christ was in heaven as the Creed stated and not in the sacraments.

> Part of an open letter from Zwingli to Matthew Alber (16 November 1524).
> *'I think that the heart of this matter [the meaning of the mass] lies in the shortest word, namely "is", which does not always mean "to be" but can also mean "signify". Now let me consider Christ's word [Matthew 26:26]. Jesus took bread etc. with the words, "Take this and eat; this is my body [Luke 22:19] which is given for you." Here I read "signifies" [represents] for "is". "Take and eat. This signifies my body which is given for you." Then surely, the phrase must mean "Take and eat. For this, which I now order you to do, shall signify or recall to you my body which is now given for you."'*

To Luther, Christ was both spiritually and in body everywhere. On this theological point he differed from Zwingli. Four years later, when they met at the Colloquy of Marburg for the first and only time, they agreed on 14 articles of faith but not on the Eucharist. In Luther's opinion, the Swiss reformer 'neither holds nor teaches any part of the Christian faith rightly'; to Zwingli, the German theologian was blinkered and wrong.

The success of Zwinglianism owed much to Zwingli's belief that the congregation and community were inseparable and that religion must be controlled by the state. Each canton and city authority in Switzerland therefore introduced its reformation in an orderly manner. Unlike Luther, who constantly felt drawn to secular authorities to impose his ideas, Zwingli did not have to appeal to the Swiss people or to lay rulers. They applied his theological reforms while the more radical social and political ideas, which were an extension of his doctrine and which gave rise to visionary popular movements, were suppressed.

By 1529 Zwinglianism had been adopted by Zurich, St Gall, Berne and Basel – who joined Schaffhausen, Chur, Constance and Biel and six south German cities including Mühlhausen, Ulm, Augsburg and Frankfurt-am-Main – to form the Christian Civic Union. Opposed to them were the Catholic Swiss cantons of Zug, Lucerne, Schwyz, Uri, Unterwalden and Fribourg, which joined Ferdinand of Austria in the Christian Alliance. Predictably, Zwingli was accused of reverting to type when he defended the use of violence and called his comrades to arms. His ironic death at the Battle of Kappel in 1531 prompted Luther's unkind comment, 'He who lives by the sword, dies by the sword'. Although Zwingli's ideas were continued by Henry Bullinger, the subsequent military defeat of Zurich and Berne saw the Swiss Reformation stagnate, before moving to the free city of Geneva and the evangelism of Calvin in the second half of the century (see chapter 12).

The Anabaptists

In 1523 Simon Stumpf, Felix Mantz and Conrad Grebel announced that they could no longer accept Zwingli's ideas since they were altogether too conservative. By 1524 they had renounced the swearing of oaths, military service, tithe payments, the mass, and most radically of all, child baptism, because none could claim secure biblical foundation. Such expressions of unorthodox behaviour were but a short step from a total rejection of civil authority and the establishment of a separate, self-governing, congregation. Thus in 1525 the movement known as the Swiss Brethren was born. Zwingli condemned it and Zurich magistrates acted quickly. Grebel and his followers were arrested and Mantz was drowned in Lake Zurich in January 1527, the first Anabaptist martyr.

Zwingli condemns the hypocrisy of Anabaptists in a sermon (31 July 1527).

'The Catabaptists speak of God, truth, the word, light, spirit, holiness, the deceits of the flesh, falsehood, impiety, desire, the devil, hell not only attractively but even nobly and magnificently, if only hypocrisy were more surely absent. But if you look carefully into their lives, at first glance they seem innocent, celestial, appealing, even superhuman, but when you penetrate more deeply, you find the evil there so great that it is shame even to mention it. They overturn everything and make things as bad as possible. When a city begins to think more soundly about divine teaching, they come and bring confusion.'

Apocalypse

In the Book of Revelation in the *Bible*, John describes a series of violent events that would befall mankind, as told to him by an angel of God. The Greek 'to uncover' is *apokalupto*, thus the **Apocalypse** refers to the revelation that the ungodly would be destroyed.

Other sects expressed similar ideas. At Wittenberg, Andreas Karlstadt pressed for a more reformed church and assisted by the arrival of the prophets of Zwickau – three followers of Thomas Müntzer who had been expelled from the Saxon town in 1520 – introduced social, economic and religious changes. In 1521–2 Wittenberg saw outbreaks of iconoclasm (the breaking of religious images), an attack on monastic orders, the rejection of the mass in favour of a vernacular service and communion in both kinds, which were all in advance of Lutheran and Zwinglian teaching. Their very popularity with miners, weavers, peasants and students threatened Wittenberg with the unattractive prospect of democracy, and brought the return of Luther from Wartburg. He condemned them in a series of sermons – the *Invocavit*. By March, order had been restored and Karlstadt had moved on.

Müntzer had meanwhile settled in Allstedt in Saxony and begun to advocate adult baptism, the election of ministers, the communal use of property and wealth, and the imminent return of Christ. Unlike Zwingli, who believed all sections of the Old Testament were of equal importance, Müntzer emphasised the *Book of Daniel* and the **Apocalypse**. His belief in redemption through suffering encouraged many of his followers to welcome martyrdom, such that a contemporary could comment, 'they went to the stakes as to a wedding'. Müntzer was a prolific preacher, writer and teacher, whose sermons, hymns and biblical commentaries were printed 'for the whole world'. As a self-confessed 'disturber of the unbelievers', he saw himself as a crusader of truth and Dr Liar (alias Luther) was his enemy. Both Luther and Zwingli condemned him and when the town of Allstedt found his ideas too revolutionary, he again took to the road reaching Mühlhausen, one of the centres of the Peasants' War, in 1524 (see page 83). Although he died in prison in 1525, Müntzer's ideas survived and his disciples moved to more friendly territories in the Netherlands and north Germany, where they joined the **Melchiorites**, **Hutterites**, **Mennonites** and other spiritualist sects.

Conclusion

We could conclude that all dissenters were considered as dangerous and subversive by Catholics and that, among dissenters from what Catholics called 'the only true religion', much internal disagreement prevailed. Very frequently, these disagreements bred intolerance. Luther was too extreme for Erasmus, Zwingli too radical for Luther, and Anabaptism too revolutionary for all three. Each sought to reform the Church, believed theirs was the true faith and that neither heaven nor earth was large enough to accommodate differing views.

KEY TERMS:

Familiarism

Hans Niklas founded the Familist sect in the Netherlands in the early sixteenth century. He believed in **familiarism** (*i.e.* that religion should be a matter of love rather than of faith) and his followers practised free love and polygamy (having more than one wife or husband at once).

Communism

Anabaptists believed in the fellowship of all men, women and children, and that the common possession of goods and land was a more perfect way of life than private ownership. Subsequent generations of social reformers developed this idea and in the nineteenth century, through the works of Karl Marx, a political and economic perspective was added and it became known as **Communism**.

Second Coming

In the last two chapters of the Book of Revelation, John describes how in the wake of the Apocalypse (see key term, page 93) a new Jerusalem – a purified city of God – descended from heaven to earth in preparation for the return of Christ. His anticipated arrival was known as the **Second Coming**, since Christ had informed John: 'Yes, I am coming soon' (*Revelation 22:20*).

Melchiorites, Hutterites and Mennonites

Melchiorites were named after Melchior Hoffmann who first voiced apocalyptic and mystical beliefs in Strassburg in the 1520s. Claiming to be Elijah, Hoffmann called upon the people to opt out of the established church and to join the 'gathered church'. He preached that Christ would return again after a war between the Pope, Emperor, false prophets and the New Jerusalem, and the latter would be victorious. Disappointed that this did not happen, he moved to Emden in 1530. Some of his followers had meanwhile settled in Münster in north Germany. Amid growing social and economic distress, and the sighting of comets in 1531–3, they were elected to the town council.

By 1534 two Melchiorites – Jan Matthys of Harlem and Jan Beukels of Leyden – had taken control and established an Anabaptist regime in which the communal sharing of goods, polygamy, censorship and penal laws in keeping with their interpretation of Old Testament scripture, became the order of the day (see page 96). Nominally pacifist, the sword was never far from their Bible and violence was justified in maintaining order and silencing the godless. Only in 1535 was normality restored through the unlikely combination of the Catholic bishop of Münster and local German Lutherans violently purging the theocracy (state ruled by the clergy). More than 800 Anabaptists were put to death, including 'King Jan' of Leyden, whose tongue was ripped out with red-hot pincers.

Hutterites got their name from Hans Hut, a social revolutionary who believed in Anabaptism, **familiarism**, **communism** and the **Second Coming** but rejected the Bible in favour of the 'inner word'. Arrested in Augsburg where he died in 1528, Hut's ideas remained popular in central and southern Germany, Moravia and Austria, and were continued by Jakob Hutter and his 200 followers known as the Moravian Brethren. Hutter died in 1536 – his body immersed in water, then dowsed with brandy before being set alight – but the Hutterites survived under the protection of Moravian nobles.

Mennonites were followers of Menno Simons (1496–1561), a Dutch Anabaptist who reacted against the excesses of Münster. Although his theology was radical – he agreed with Hoffmann's Christology of the celestial flesh that Christ was born without Mary losing her virginity – he obeyed secular authority and was totally opposed to violence. Tolerant, peace-loving and numbering only a few hundred, the Mennonites were the least harmful of the radical sects, and yet ironically, labelled the 'enemies of truth', were persecuted and ostracised.

Task: evaluating sources

Now that you have read chapters 8 and 9 on the major Protestant reformers in Europe in the early sixteenth century (Calvin will be studied later in the book), answer the following questions.

1 Read the following extract from a speech by Thomas Müntzer on 27 April 1525. He is speaking to the peasant rebels in Allstedt.

'The pure fear of God be with you, brothers. What are you still sleeping for, why have you not recognised the will of God – do you think he has abandoned you, is that it? Ah, how often have I told you that God can only reveal himself in this way, in your apparent abandonment. If not, the offering of your broken and contrite hearts must be in vain. And you must then come into another kind of suffering. I tell you again, if you won't suffer for God, then you will be devil's martyrs. So take care, cheer up, do your duty, and stop pandering to those fantastic perverts, those knaves. Get going, and fight the battle of the Lord!...The whole of Germany, France and the Roman lands are awake – the Master will start his game, and the knaves are for it!...So now On! On! On! – it is time to hunt the knaves down like dogs – On! On! On! have no mercy even though Esau gives you good words – Genesis 33. Do not look at the misery of the godless. They will beg you, will whine and cry like children. But you are to have no mercy, as God commanded through Moses – Deuteronomy 7 – and has also revealed to us. Get going in the villages and towns, and especially with the miners and the other good fellows. We must sleep no more. On! On! On! Let not your sword grow cold, let it not be blunted. Smite, cling, clang, on the anvil of Nimrod, and cast the tower to the ground.'

    a How does the tone and use of language in this speech help to explain the appeal which Müntzer had in parts of Germany in the 1520s?

    b Explain why Müntzer and Luther had different attitudes towards the Peasants' Revolt.

2 Read the following extract. It is part of a chronicle written about 1534 by Heinrich Gresbeck of Münster.

'Thus Jan van Leiden – together with the bishop, the preachers and the 12 elders – proclaimed concerning the married estate that it was God's will that they should inhabit the earth. Everyone should take three or four wives, or as many as were desired. However, they should live with their wives in a divine manner. This pleased some men and not others. Husbands and wives objected that the marital estate was no longer to be kept.

'Jan van Leiden was the first to take a second wife in addition to the one he had married in Münster. It was said that there was still another wife in Holland. Jan van Leiden continued to take more wives until he finally had 15. In similar fashion all the Dutchmen, Frisians and true Anabaptists had additional wives. Indeed, they compelled their first wives to go and obtain second wives for them. The devil laughed hard about this. Those who had old wives and wanted to take young ones had their way. The Anabaptists in Münster, especially the leaders, such as Jan van Leiden and the 12 elders, were planning it well. They had done away with money, gold and silver, and had driven everyone from his property. They sat in the houses, held the property, and also wanted to have 10 or 12 wives. I presume they called this the "right baptism".'

a What characteristics of life in an Anabaptist community are found in this source?

b What are the limitations, as well as the value, of personal chronicles as historical evidence about the Reformation?

3 a In what ways do Zwingli's 67 Theses (page 90) agree with, and in what ways do they differ from, Luther's 95-Point Theses (page 81)?

b How do you account for these similarities and differences?

4 Using these documents and your own knowledge gained from studying chapters 8 and 9, explain why many leading Protestant reformers regarded the Anabaptists and spiritualists as dangerous.

Further reading

G. R. Potter, 'Ulrich Zwingli' (Historical Association Pamphlet, 1989 revised edition) – a short and very useful introduction.

G. R. Potter, *Huldrych Zwingli* (Arnold, 1978) – by far the best biography; it also contains a good collection of documents.

T. A. Brady, *Turning Swiss. Cities and Empire, 1450–1550* (Cambridge University Press, 1985) – a thorough examination of the complexities of the Swiss Reformation.

T. Scott, *Thomas Müntzer: Theology and Revolution in the German Reformation* (Macmillan, 1989) – the standard work on Müntzer and his world.

M. G. Baylor (ed.), *The Radical Reformation* (Cambridge University Press, 1991) – offers some recent interpretations of the Anabaptist and spiritual sects.

10 Was Francis I of France an absolute monarch?

Time chart

1515: Francis I becomes king; he establishes a *parlement* at Rouen

1516: Concordat of Bologna signed between the Papacy and France confirms Gallican liberties

1517: Francis calls an Assembly of the Towns

1518: The Sorbonne ratifies the Concordat. Budé publishes *L'Institution du Prince*

1519: de Seyssel publishes *La Monarchie de France*

1523: The Duke of Bourbon is executed. Dijon *parlement* is established

1527: Baron of Semblançay found guilty of corruption and hanged. The Paris *parlement* is forbidden from modifying royal decrees. Assembly of Notables meets

1532: Brittany receives its charter

1534: **18 October** 'Day of the Placards'

1535: Trial and execution of Jean de Poncher, Treasurer of Languedoc

1537: Grenoble *parlement* is established

1540: The *gabelle* is extended to Vendée and Guyenne; Normandy *parlement* is suspended

1541: Philippe Chabot, Admiral of France, is executed

1542: Guyenne rebellion begins. France is divided into 16 financial areas

1543: Guillaume Poyet, Chancellor of France, is executed. The Sorbonne issues the first Index

1544: Lagny-sur-Marne is sacked by French troops

1545: Massacre of Waldensians in Aix-en-Provence

1547: Francis I dies; succeeded by his eldest son, Henry II

The aim of this chapter is to examine the historical controversy surrounding **Francis I** of France. First, read the two views overleaf.

Salic Law

The Salians were a fourth-century Frankish tribe. Their law-book contained a **Salic Law** which excluded females from dynastic succession – a practice observed in France and later in the kingdom of Aragon.

View 1: *Francis the absolutist*

In 1946 the French historian, Georges Pagès, claimed that 'Francis I and Henry II were as powerful as any other kings of France; it was at the beginning of the sixteenth century that the absolute monarchy triumphed'. Earlier historians – like Imbart de la Tour and Roger Doucet – made similar claims that the reign of Francis either exhibited or foreshadowed 'the absolute and centralised monarchy of the following centuries'. The principal modern historian who holds this view is Robert Knecht. He has consistently argued that while 'absolutism in practice has always fallen short of its theoretical completeness ... Francis would appear to have been about as absolute as any European monarch of his day could hope to be'.

View 2: *Limitations on Francis's power*

In 1925 Henri Prentout questioned this view claiming that 'absolute monarchy, if one must use this label, begins only with Louis XIV'. This view is endorsed by several modern historians – like J. H. Shennan, D. Parker and R. Mousnier. Two US historians, Robert Harding and J. Russell Major, have argued that the origins of French absolutism are to be found at the beginning of the seventeenth century. Harding contended that the civil war which haemorrhaged France after 1560, revealed the power and independence of the provincial governors; while Major has stressed the limitations of the French renaissance monarchs in general and Francis I in particular.

PROFILE: *Francis I*

Born at Cognac in 1494, son of Louise of Savoy and Charles of Angoulême, a younger branch of the Valois family, **Francis** only became king because his cousin Charles VIII (1483–98), had no children and Louis XII (1498–1515) had no sons. The **Salic Law** debarred females from succeeding to the throne. Six foot [1.8 m] tall, broad shouldered and very strong, Francis enjoyed hunting, womanising and war. Though he was intelligent and literate – he acquired an outstanding collection of books and established Fontainebleau as the artistic centre of France – he spent most of his money and much of his time fighting against Henry VIII and Charles V. Although he had some military successes, his defeats were more numerous and decisive. He failed to hold on to Milan after 1521, was captured at the Battle of Pavia in 1525 and lost Boulogne to the English in 1544. He died on 31 March 1547.

The nature of Francis's authority in respect of justice, administration, finance and the Church is examined in this chapter and, where appropriate, the views of Knecht and Major are cited. It should be remembered, however, that only by reading their works will you fully appreciate the reasons for their differing viewpoints. Facts are rarely in dispute; disagreements stem from their differing emphases and interpretations of the evidence and from their understanding of the term 'absolute'.

Justice

Major and Knecht both agree that medieval legal writers considered that the French monarchy was limited and absolute. John Fortescue in the 1470s claimed that France was a *dominium regale*, a 'Turkish despotism', whereby 'the King may rule his people by such laws as he makes himself', and 'he may set upon them such taxes and other impositions as he wishes, without their assent'. In 1518 Guillaume Budé, Francis's secretary, asserted that the King could exercise independent power according to the customary law. His contemporary, Claude de Seyssel, reminded the King that his theoretical absolutism was actually restricted by certain obligations. For instance, all French monarchs had a duty to provide justice for their subjects. Thus, at his coronation, Francis swore to uphold the fundamental and divine laws of the land. By this he confirmed that he was male, French, Catholic and legitimate, that he would reside in – and give away no part of – his kingdom, and that he would uphold the principles of God's law. In Seyssel's view: 'So long as the King respects the Christian religion he cannot act as a tyrant.' Should any subjects have recourse to justice against the King, they could always do so through the *parlements*, 'whose principal role is to bridle the absolute power which kings might seek to use'. Therefore, in theory, it was possible for an individual to prosecute the Crown. But it was a brave person who attempted it and none did so in Francis's reign.

Did Francis abide by the law? The answer appears to be 'only when it suited him'. He used his undefined prerogative to interfere in the affairs of the Paris *parlement*, to impose **arbitrary taxation**, to strengthen the Crown's authority in the towns and provinces, and to issue instant justice on anyone who crossed him. Special commissions, for instance, were appointed to try the accomplices of the Duke of Bourbon in 1523, Admiral Chabot in 1541 and Chancellor Poyet in 1543. The judges who tried Semblançay (*Général des finances*) and Jean de Poncher (*Trésorier-général*) of Languedoc were handpicked by the King and known to be their enemies. His treatment of Lagny-sur-Marne in the aftermath of a rebellion in 1544 was neither fair nor equitable. The town was sacked, its

KEY TERM:

Arbitrary taxation

This refers to the power of raising taxes from subjects without reference to any other authority. Thus Francis I resorted to taxing whenever he needed the money and without consulting the Assemblies or Estates.

inhabitants' right of appeal suspended and judges and *parlement* ordered not to investigate the case.

Thirty years later, Jean Bodin (1529–96), a deputy in the Estates-General, probably had Francis in mind when he wrote:

> *'sovereign majesty and absolute power lies principally in giving law to the subjects in general without their consent. Wherefore let this be the first and chief mark of a sovereign prince, to be of power to give laws to all his subjects in general, and to every one of them in particular without consent of any other greater, equal, or lesser than himself.'*

In Bodin's view, absolutism was perpetual and sovereign power, and as the state was perpetual and the monarchy exercised sovereignty, so the French monarchy was absolute. Theoretically, there was no clear understanding as to what the king could and could not do. In practice, Francis appears to have done as he liked.

Robert Knecht has suggested that Francis 'did not consider himself bound by tradition and believed that he had the right to depart from existing ordinances, institutions and methods of government'. He cites Francis's treatment of the *parlements*. At his accession there were four situated in Aix-en-Provence, Bordeaux, Toulouse and Paris, to which three more were added at Rouen (1515), Dijon (1523) and Grenoble (1537). Among their functions was the registration of royal edicts, the hearing of appeals and voicing of local grievances. As the guardians of the law, they could prevent undesirable royal policies, though the King had the power to overrule them if he felt a *parlement* was being deliberately obstructive. Knecht believes they were frequently bullied and intimidated by the Crown. In 1518 the Paris *parlement* was told to accept the terms of the Concordat of Bologna or it would lose its regular meeting place, and two of its delegates were warned that they should 'leave now or stay forever'. In 1527, following his release from prison in Madrid, Francis confronted the *parlement*, rounded on president Guillart's suggestion that he was subject to the law and forbade it from interfering in affairs of state or modifying future royal legislation. It was, Knecht suggests, 'a watershed in the relations between crown and *parlement*. The king had successfully checked the tendency towards a more limited monarchy, which his recent incapacity had encouraged.' Francis's treatment of the Rouen *parlement* was equally high-handed. For much of his reign he had a running battle with the Normandy deputies. In 1527 he threatened to dismiss them all and in 1540 suspended them. When it re-opened four months later, nine councillors were excluded and it was warned not to

KEY TERM:

Customary law

France had no single law code, but a variety of legal practices. Roman law was the prevailing system in the south; in the north each region followed its own customs, according to seigneurial and local tradition. The preservation of **customary laws** was a vital function of the provincial estates.

'contradict, discuss, deduce or allege anything against verification of the edicts'.

In contrast, Russell Major has argued that Francis ruled his country 'according to the law, not in defiance of it'. He believes that the rights and privileges of subjects were respected and that the creation of three new *parlements* indicates Francis's willingness to extend, not restrict, the provincial law courts. In 1523, for example, when Dombes was annexed to the Crown, a charter confirmed its existing privileges. Nine years later, Brittany received a similar charter. Major contends that the absence of any uniform judicial administration also worked against royal authority. There was much procedural confusion between the central, provincial and seigneurial courts, and the magistrates who toured the country, and the judges who heard appeals from inferior courts. In addition, French law varied from region to region. Common law was predominant in the north and centre, Roman law in the south, and throughout the country there were variants of **customary law**. Attempts at standardising the law had begun in 1497 but Major believes that, far from strengthening the Crown, reforms only served to reinforce regional differences.

Knecht disagrees. 'The unification of custom had to begin somewhere', he suggests, 'and if it failed to produce a nationwide French law, it facilitated centralisation by removing innumerable local discrepancies and clarifying customs hitherto vague and obscure.' He does, however, accept that the unpopular forest laws of 1516, the 1521 heresy laws and a proposed reform of the judicial system in 1539, were not consistently applied.

Finally, it should be remembered that Francis's legal authority did not extend throughout his kingdom. Control of Auvergne and Brittany only passed into his hands in 1522 and 1532 respectively, and the principalities of Dauphiné, Béarn and Navarre, the counties of Foix and Périgord, and the viscounties of Bigorre, Nebouzau and Soule, remained outside his jurisdiction.

Central and provincial administration

How far was central government consultative? Russell Major believes that the early years of the reign saw a 'large amount of consultation'. The King took advice from his *Conseil des Affaires*, comprising his *noblesse d'épée*, princes of the blood, household officers, clerics and lawyers. He called an Assembly of the Towns in 1517, an Assembly of Notables in 1527 and maintained regular correspondence with provincial towns. Major concedes that thereafter less use was made of consultative

KEY TERM:

Élus

The king's chief financial representative in each of the *élections* was the *élu*. As the term implies, these officials were elected by the Estates and originally imposed on the Crown. In French, *élire* means 'to elect'.

assemblies, though not because Francis was opposed to them in principle but because he found them 'time-consuming and useless'. Moreover, although he never convened an Estates-General, he had authorised his regent to do so in 1515 and 1523 when he was absent from France. In addition, claims Major, 'he accepted the existence of the provincial and local estates, recognised their right to give consent to taxation, and generally respected their privileges'. In 1519 when Languedoc and Guyenne protested at the introduction of *élus* and other royal officials, the King agreed to withdraw them:

'Neither we, nor our successors, will levy any taxes on the said pays (provinces) without assembling the Estates to seek their consent, as has been the custom in the past, including the acceptance of lists of grievances, requests and remonstrances which the said Estates care to offer towards remedies and provisions which are reasonably needed.'

Francis further promised not to levy taxes in Provence and Brittany without their consent, and totally failed to increase old taxes or introduce new ones into Burgundy. He never forgot that these were border provinces and had to be handled sensitively.

Knecht sees the Crown's relationship with representative assemblies rather differently.

'The fact that Francis I never called a meeting of the Estates-General shows that he regarded them as both useless and dangerous and never found himself in a sufficiently weak position to be compelled to call them.

'[The provincial estates] depended for their existence on the King. He called them, fixed the date and place of their meeting, appointed their president and determined their agenda. The estates frequently complained of some of the King's fiscal expedients, but seldom persuaded him to abandon them. It is a mistake to imagine that the King could not raise taxes within a pays d'état except with the consent of the people's representatives. In Languedoc the town's clergy and nobility were all subjected to impositions quite regardless of the estates.

'Under Francis the effectiveness of the estates was limited to matters of secondary importance to the Crown; where its financial interest was at stake, they were virtually powerless.'

R. Knecht, *Francis I* (1982).

Effective government rested upon the nobility, whose influence in their *pays* limited an expansion of royal power. The 11 provincial governors in early modern France (16 by 1547) exercised considerable authority as army commanders, political leaders and patrons. Each, moreover, was a leading aristocrat, royal relative or favourite. Part of their strength lay in their loosely defined duties and their distance from the court. As Francis encouraged the practice of hereditary appointments, so powerful families extended their patronage at a local level. It was in this way that the Montmorency family came to control Languedoc, the Condés Picardy, the Guises Burgundy and Champagne, and the Bourbons the south-west of France. If the monarch was strong, such governors complemented his power; if he was weak, then they presented a serious challenge. Knecht recognises the autonomy of these nobles but suggests that in seeking royal patronage they became increasingly dependent on the King's authority. As a result, he believes France became more centralised in the early sixteenth century. Major, on the other hand, sees these years as a period of decentralisation.

Finances

Knecht and Major have expressed fundamental differences over Francis's fiscal reforms. Knecht believes that by 1547 the 'three objectives of his financial reforms had been achieved: centralisation, uniformity and simplification'. In contrast, Major warns against exaggerating the importance of the fiscal innovations and suggests that Francis's experiment in centralisation failed. Both historians agree that in 1515 French government finances were chaotic and that subsequent periods of reform (1515–17, 1522–4 and 1542–4) were largely in response to military needs.

At Francis's accession, royal revenue totalled 4.9 million livres and fell well short of expenditure; debts were running at over 3 million livres. He managed to increase the main sources from rents, seigneurial dues, the *taille* (land tax), *aides* (sales tax) and *gabelle* (salt tax) to 7.1 million livres, but never eliminated several fundamental weaknesses. For instance, many sections of society – such as the nobility, clergy, royal servants and universities, and towns like Paris, Toulouse and Lyon – were exempt from the *taille*. *Aides* were not paid by everyone, and traditionally only the northern, central and south-eastern provinces paid the *gabelle*. Methods of assessment and collection were equally variable. In the *pays d'élections*, indirect taxes were assessed and collected by *élus* and **tax farmers**, who forwarded them to the *Généraux des Finances*; seigneurial and ground rents were collected by bailiffs who sent them to the *Trésoriers de France*.

KEY TERM:

Tax farmers

In return for a fee paid to the Crown, **tax farmers** were allowed to organise the collection of taxes. Some were probably directly involved in the collection, while others may have paid other people to do the actual tax-gathering.

The *pays d'états* paid taxes regularly, and the estates voted an annual sum which was collected by tax farmers. An attempt to investigate municipal finances foundered in 1515 due to self-interest. Between 1522 and 1524 a variety of expedients were introduced: government bonds – *rentes de l'hôtel de ville*, with an interest of 8.5 per cent guaranteed by the Paris city council – were set up, Crown and Church lands sold off, forced loans demanded, and administrative offices made available for sale. Finally, a central treasury (*Trésor de l'Epargne*) supervised the entire revenue administration.

If it was Francis's aim to centralise his system and build up money for his wars by securing a regular supply of cash in hand, then he failed. By the 1530s, only a quarter of all revenue was reaching the Treasury, and further reforms were needed. In 1542 Francis divided the country into 16 districts, each with its own treasurer who was told to reside in his *généralité*. Such changes have prompted Major to suggest that 'the financial system became more decentralised than before'. Knecht disagrees. Personal extravagance and demands of war obliged Francis to impose more expedients in the 1540s. For example, a tax was imposed on walled towns with more than 50,000 people and the salt tax was extended to the previously exempt provinces of Vendée and Guyenne. The result was a serious revolt which at its height in 1542 saw 10,000 men at arms. Francis did not have the means to suppress it militarily and agreed to remove the tax in exchange for a gift of 20,000 crowns. To Major this revolt exemplifies the King's limitations and confirms that 'the ability of Francis I to tax, like that of his predecessors, was dependent on public opinion'. Knecht disagrees. While accepting that 'the King's power over taxation was not absolute', he suggests that the provincial estates had no right 'to refuse the *taille* or even to negotiate about it; only increases and surtaxes were negotiable'.

The Church

As the 'Most Christian King', Francis exercised considerable power over the French Church, but was his authority diminished by the Concordat of Bologna negotiated with the Papacy in 1516? Major thinks so; Knecht does not. Since 1438, the King had elected all clerical officers and collected papal taxation. The Concordat gave him the right to nominate all priors, abbots and bishops, while the Pope was granted the power to confirm them and to receive taxation. Thus, Francis effectively controlled episcopal and monastic patronage, ecclesiastical property and taxation, all of which, in Knecht's opinion, 'helped to buttress royal absolutism'.

The Sorbonne and Paris *parlements* viewed the Concordat differently.

They believed that Francis had made important concessions to the Papacy, if only on paper, and so condemned it as an arbitrary royal act against the liberties of the French Church. Some limitations upon the King's authority certainly existed – royal nominees had to be 27 years old, university graduates and appointed within six months of a vacancy – but such restrictions were easily overcome. On balance, the Crown's authority does not appear to have been seriously affected by the Concordat.

In the first half of his reign, Francis clashed on several occasions with the Sorbonne as it resented his protection of humanists and Lutherans. From 1534, however, he took a less equivocal view towards heretics. On 18 October, 'the Day of the Placards', the Catholic faith was ridiculed in posters all over France. The King took action by ordering all heresy cases to be tried by lay courts so that death sentences could be passed. There was no right of appeal, and prosecution could be based on hearsay, oral or written evidence – which was defined as 'all words contrary to the Holy Catholic Faith and the Christian Religion'. Further measures followed in 1543: secular as well as church authorities were given the power to search and arrest heretics, the Sorbonne defined the 25 articles of the Catholic faith and published the first Index of 65 prohibited titles.

Yet, in spite of these laws, the reformed faith continued to be preached and in certain regions – like Guyenne, Normandy and Dauphiné – few prosecutions occurred. In reality, the heresy laws were only enforced when provincial estates chose to cooperate with the Church and Crown. When over 6,000 heretical Waldensians refused in 1545 to recant their faith, it was the Aix-en-Provence *parlement* which ordered their massacre. The King was never more powerful than when he had the nobility, Church and provincial estates behind him. Without their cooperation, his wishes could be effectively resisted.

Conclusion

What, then, are we to conclude about the controversy surrounding Francis I? Both Russell Major and Robert Knecht agree on a number of points, and have presented convincing arguments. Each recognises that 'absolutism' was an unattainable condition in the context of early modern France, that the absence of a uniform legal and financial system obstructed the growth of royal power, that Francis exercised considerable control over the Church in France but was not strong enough to challenge the military and political influence of the provincial nobility. They disagree, however, on the extent of Francis's control over the Church, the nobility and the provinces; whether the administration was centralised and the motives behind his reforms.

Major believes that Francis was a 'constitutional monarch' and that there were 'significant institutional, theoretical and/or practical limitations upon the authority of the king. A monarchy becomes absolute when these institutional and theoretical limitations are removed and the king has the necessary bureaucracy and army to impose his will.' Indeed, not until the seventeenth century would France, in keeping with other European states, acquire a large standing army. Knecht, in response, has argued that 'if constitutional labels are to mean anything at all they ought surely to take into account not only the realities of power but also the intentions of the ruler. Absolutism in the seventeenth-century sense of the word cannot be said to have been achieved in Francis's reign, but his actions and some of his pronouncements certainly pointed in that direction.'

Are Knecht and Major merely arguing over words or are they in disagreement about the interpretation of Francis's motives? In many respects 'absolutism' is an inappropriate term for the sixteenth century. In theory, Francis I could act outside the law, and occasionally did so, but he was well aware that his power was really limited. 'Autocratic' seems a more suitable description of his behaviour. He extended the power of the Crown at every opportunity, negotiating an agreement with the Papacy to give him greater control over the French clergy, increasing the numbers of paid civil servants and tax collectors, and taking the nobility into a political partnership. The nobility and the aristocrats were the sticking-point. Until he had enough revenue to rule independently, a standing army to enforce his will and a judicial and government administration that was subservient to the Crown, his authority would be limited. Major and Knecht appear to be arguing over more than semantics; they are disagreeing over Francis I's motives and how to interpret the events of his reign.

Task

1 Make a list of those features of Francis I's reign on which Knecht and Major **a** agree and **b** disagree.

2 Why should historians be cautious when applying the term 'absolutism' to states in the sixteenth century?

3 'Historians produce different interpretations of past events not because they directly contradict each other but because they study different aspects of the same problem.' How far does your study of the different views of Francis I's reign lead you to support this conclusion?

Further reading

J. R. Major, *Representative Institutions in Renaissance France, 1421–1559* (Wisconsin University Press, 1960).

J. R. Major, *Representative Government in Early Modern France* (Yale University Press, 1980).

R. J. Knecht, *Francis I and Absolute Monarchy* (Historical Association, 1969) – a short account of Francis's reign.

R. J. Knecht, *Francis I* (Cambridge University Press, 1982) – an outstanding biography unlikely to be surpassed.

R. J. Knecht, *French Renaissance Monarchy: Francis I and Henry II*, Seminar Studies in History (Addison Wesley Longman, 1984) – similar, if shorter, interpretation of Francis but contains a number of useful documents.

R. J. Knecht, *Renaissance Warrior and Patron: The Reign of Francis I* (Cambridge University Press, 1994) – his most recent work on this period.

D. Parker, *The Making of French Absolutism* (Arnold, 1983).

R. Mousnier, *The Institutions of France Under the Absolute Monarchy*, 2 vols. (University of Chicago Press, 1979).

R. R. Harding, *Anatomy of a Power Elite. The Provincial Governors of Early Modern France* (Yale University Press, 1978) – demonstrates the importance of the nobility in the provinces.

11 What issues were at stake in the Italian Wars, 1494–1559?

Time chart

1494: Charles VIII invades Naples

1495: Ferdinand sets up the League of Venice

1499: Louis invades Milan and Naples

1504: Treaty of Blois confirms Aragonese possession of Naples

1508: Julius II sets up the League of Cambrai against Venice

1509: France defeats Venice at Agnadello

1511: Julius II sets up the Holy League against France

1515: France invades Milan and defeats the Swiss at Marignano

1516: Treaty of Noyon secures French control of Milan

1521: Francis invades Navarre

1522: Spain recovers Milan after Battle of Bicocca

1525: Francis is captured after his defeat at Pavia

1527: Imperial troops destroy Rome. France invades Italy

1529: Imperial victory over France at Landriano; Treaty of Cambrai

1536: France occupies Savoy; Imperial troops invade Provence

1538: Truce of Nice is signed between Francis and Charles V

1542: Francis invades Nice

1544: Anglo-Imperial invasion of France. Franco-Imperial peace of Crépy

1552: France captures Metz, Toul and Verdun from Charles V

1556: Philip II signs Truce of Vaucelles with France

1557: Philip invades France and wins Battle of St Quentin

1559: Treaty of Câteau-Cambrésis ends Italian Wars

The Italian Wars, which began in 1494 and continued intermittently until 1559, had a profound effect on the leading states of Europe. War lasted so long because a number of issues had first to be resolved, and the powers concerned were reluctant to compromise and unwilling to admit defeat.

This chapter examines the principal events which, for convenience, have been divided into three phases: 1494–1516, 1516–29 and 1529–59. At the heart of the conflict lay the dynastic claims of France to the kingdom of Naples, Milan, Navarre and Burgundy. In response, the King of Aragon disputed Naples, Milan and Navarre, and the Austrian Habsburgs contested any challenge to Burgundy. War in Naples and Milan sparked off long-standing economic and political rivalry between the Italian states, which took generations to die down. The accession of a Habsburg – first as Duke of Burgundy, then as King of Spain, and finally as Holy Roman Emperor – extended the conflict and for the next 30 years, the personal rivalry between Charles V and Francis I, and to a lesser extent Henry VIII, dominated events. Significantly, the conflict ended when each of the main adversaries had died and none of the leading powers could afford to carry on fighting.

Origin of the wars

On 2 September 1494, Charles VIII of France crossed the Alps into Italy at the head of 29,000 troops and announced his claim to the throne of Naples. There can be no doubt that he was the aggressor. His declared wish to use Naples as a base in order to drive the Ottomans out of Europe and liberate Istanbul did little to strengthen his legal claim to the kingdom. In truth, he was motivated by self-glory and the prospect of spoils of war. Rich cities, portable works of art and vulnerable territories offered attractive rewards to the best heavy cavalry and light artillery in Europe. Indeed, it is difficult to agree with the Florentine historian, Francesco Guicciardini, writing in 1537–40, that Charles's invasion 'sprang from impulse rather than reason'. For two years he had been planning the operation, buying off potential rivals like Henry VII of England, Ferdinand and Maximilian, and enlisting the support of Genoa and Milan. The Cardinal of Genoa resented Pope Alexander VI, an ally of Naples, and urged Charles to depose him and start the long-awaited church reform. Even more valuable was the offer of assistance from Ludovico Sforza, regent of Milan. Ludovico had no intention of surrendering power to his nephew, Gian Galeazzo, and was aware that Gian's wife, Isabella, had complained to her uncle, Ferrante, King of Naples. Moreover, he knew that the new ruler of Florence, Piero de' Medici, supported Naples and relished the opportunity of attacking Milan. Ludovico urgently needed allies and, as his invitation in 1494 fitted neatly into Charles's dynastic plans, an agreement was struck and the Italian Wars began (see Figure 11.1).

Figure 11.1 *Italy, 1494–1559*

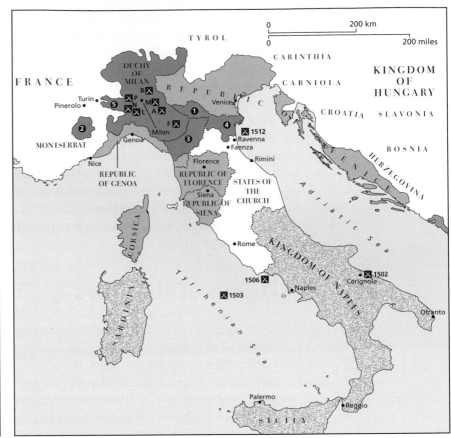

battles
F – Fornovo, 1495
A – Agnadello, 1509
N – Novara, 1513
M – Marignano, 1515
B – Bicocca, 1522
P – Pavia, 1525
L – Landriano, 1529

❶ Marq. of Mantua

❷ Marq. of Saluzzo

❸ Duchy of Modena

❹ Duchy of Ferrara

❺ Marq. of Milan

Events, 1494–1516

Within six months of Charles entering Italy, he was in Naples. He had encountered no serious opposition from either Florence, which turned against Piero and deposed him, or Alexander VI, whose army had melted away with the spring snows and led to the Pope barricading himself in his fortress of Sant Angelo. Naples itself was in turmoil. Its elderly king died as the French troops entered his kingdom and the country chose to capitulate rather than fight for his unpopular son, Alfonso. Charles's passage had been victorious but to date he had not fought a battle, and dark Aragonese war-clouds were gathering. Using the claim that Naples was subject to the Papacy and that the Pope's honour had been attacked, Ferdinand of Aragon constructed the League of Venice with the intention of expelling Charles and becoming the ruler of a united kingdom of Naples, Sicily and Aragon. Charles began to withdraw to France and though he won a battle at Fornovo, his garrison could not hold Naples. Federigo, Alfonso's brother, was installed as an Aragonese client-ruler in 1495. Charles had lost the campaign but not the war, and only his sudden death in 1498 prevented him from launching a second invasion. Italy was in disarray. Popular uprisings in Florence and Milan had seen the Medicis and Sforzas overthrown, and civil war raged between Pisa and Florence. Louis XII's accession further dimmed the prospect of peace.

Louis inherited the claim to Naples but his main objective was Milan. Urged on by Pope Alexander VI who, in Machiavelli's judgement, 'never did anything, or thought of anything, other than deceiving men', Louis invaded Milan in 1499. He quickly held the western half and gave the east to Venice, before marching south to Naples, which he agreed to share with Ferdinand. Machiavelli, writing in 1513, condemned Louis's decision to partition Milan and Naples: 'Whereas to start with he was master of Italy he now brought in a rival to whom the ambitious and the discontented might have recourse.' But diplomacy seemed a better option than force and Louis needed every ally he could find. Moreover, he was no more 'master of Italy' as a whole than Charles had been and Ferdinand had no intention of letting a French puppet rule Naples. By 1502 boundary disputes in Naples had spilled into war and the Spanish general, Cordoba, won decisive victories at Cerignola and Garigliano in 1503. By the Treaty of Blois, Louis yielded his right to Naples and the Pope's illegitimate son, Cesare Borgia, was given control of Perugia, Urbino and Pesaro. Here, Machiavelli believed, was a prince who could unite Italy against the barbarians. Unfortunately, Borgia died unexpectedly in 1508. Italy remained peaceful for four years though in practice rulers were preparing for the next round of battles.

The sudden death of Pope Alexander in 1503 brought Julius II – an even more unscrupulous and territorially ambitious man – into the fray. 'I was dreaming of an age that was really golden and isles that were happy', Erasmus recalled in 1512, 'when that Julian trumpet summoned all the world to arms.' In true papal style, Julius played the devil's advocate by encouraging foreigners to exploit Italian disunity so that he could gain Venetian lands. In 1508 he formed the League of Cambrai, comprising Maximilian, who was offered Padua and Verona, Ferdinand, who would be recognised as king of Naples, and Louis, who was promised eastern Milan. At the Battle of Agnadello in 1509, Venice was beaten; Spain and France agreed to share the republic and Julius took possession of Rimini and Faenza. However, news that Louis was going to call a general council of the Church encouraged the Pope to establish a Holy League in 1511, designed to weaken France. He attracted Ferdinand, who desired French Navarre, Henry VIII who wanted Gascony, and Venice who hoped to recover lost lands. Louis's infantry won at Ravenna in 1512 but defeat at Novara in the following year saw his hold on Milan, Venice and Navarre slip away.

Permanent peace seemed possible in 1514 as the foreign armies brought their siege trains to a halt and all sides welcomed the respite. Julius II had died and been replaced by Leo X, a less ambitious pope, and the Sforzas and Medicis had been returned to their republics of Milan and Florence. But peace proved illusory. Louis XII died in 1515 and his young successor, Francis I, was aggressive and vengeful. Convinced that his cause was just and equipped with 30,000 troops, Francis invaded Milan and at Marignano trounced the best mercenaries money could buy. It was the most decisive battle to date. Neither the dying Ferdinand nor the Sforzas could resist Francis's grip on Milan and only the Emperor, helped by English money, tried to raise fresh troops. By 1516, the principal combatants had withdrawn and peace was signed at Noyon. France controlled Milan and Genoa, Venice recovered everything lost since 1494, and Spain was confirmed as sovereign ruler of Naples.

Events, 1516–29

The death of Ferdinand brought Charles, Duke of Burgundy, to the throne of Spain and altered the balance of power in Europe. At 16 he had much to learn and was far from secure in his own kingdoms, but his inheritance of the Low Countries, Franche-Comté and Naples frightened France. Charles's power and Francis's vanity formed an explosive mixture, which was detonated when Charles was elected Holy Roman Emperor in 1519. This was a turning-point in the history of early modern Europe. As a result, the conflict in Italy would continue but now it was between the rival houses of Habsburg and Valois, and all the financial and military might they could muster. At first their attention remained fixed on Milan. The duchy was a crucial link in the Austrian–Spanish Habsburg line of communications, and as long as Charles had dreams of uniting Christendom under his leadership, France had to be removed from Milan and Genoa. The possibility of Habsburg encirclement may have been a myth but to Francis it seemed very real. Milan was his only route across the Alps to the lucrative trade of north Italy, and he had no intention of losing it by default.

Francis struck first in 1521 by invading Spanish Navarre, but he suffered a defeat at Pampeluna and an even greater setback at Bicocca when Spain seized Milan. Worse followed in 1525 when the French king was captured at the Battle of Pavia and taken prisoner to Madrid. When all seemed lost, Charles failed to follow up his victory and made the elementary mistake of believing Francis's promise that he would yield all claims to Burgundy and Italy in return for his release.

By 1526 it was clear that Francis would never willingly surrender Milan.

As Charles's imperial army once more marched into Florence and deposed the Medicis, his unpaid troops swarmed south into the Papal States and, in 1527, laid the city of Rome to waste. Francis responded by invading Lombardy and besieging Naples, but he could do little about the welfare of the Pope and even less about the desertion of his Genoese allies in 1528. By threatening France's north–south communications in Italy, Genoa tipped the scales of victory in favour of the Emperor. At Landriano in 1529, he took full advantage and inflicted a decisive defeat on the French army in Milan. The following treaties of Barcelona and Cambrai were the crowning glory of Charles's career. The Pope recognised him as King of Naples, the Medicis were restored to Florence and the Sforzas to Milan as Spanish clients, and Francis relinquished his claims to Milan, Naples, Genoa, Artois and Flanders. When Charles was officially crowned Holy Roman Emperor in 1530 and his brother made King of the Romans in 1531, it was clear that the Habsburgs were the effective rulers of Italy.

Events, 1529–59

Why did the Italian Wars not end in 1529? Francesco Vettori believed that Francis, after being taken prisoner and losing Milan, was 'so unused to experiencing humiliation, he could not accept it'. He would continue to fight until he had salvaged his pride and the nation's honour. Francis believed his cause was just, and God was on his side. Machiavelli also gauged his feelings correctly when he wrote in *The Prince*: 'A prudent ruler cannot, and must not honour his word when it places him at a disadvantage and when the reasons for which he made his promise no longer exist.'

French finances, however, were in a desperate condition, and herein lay the key to the prolongation of war. In 1499 the Marshal of France had reminded Louis XII that three things were needed for his invasion of Italy: 'money, more money, and still more money'. Francis I, in 1529, knew all too well that a military campaign could exhaust as much as 50 per cent of his annual revenue, and that his Treasury was empty. Charles V was financially better placed but had more commitments, and he too found it increasingly hard to raise enough capital to pay his troops. Only France and Spain had the wealth, fightpower and bureaucracy to sustain a long war, but financial constraints increasingly forced them to negotiate a truce: in 1538, 1546 and 1557 at the request of the Valois, and in 1534, 1544 and 1557 the Habsburgs.

Thus, once Francis had raised sufficient capital, he was ready to renew his quest. The death of Francesco Sforza, Duke of Milan, in 1535 presented him with his chance. In 1536 he invaded the duchy and occupied Savoy, while an unlikely ally, the Ottoman Turks, targeted Genoa. Charles was forced to play for time. By the Truce of Nice (1538) Francis held Savoy and for three years he was persuaded by his advisers that diplomacy could also bring him Milan. By 1542, he was tired of waiting and decided to renew his strategy of aggression. As the Ottomans sacked Reggio in Naples, he attempted to move into Nice but overreached himself by also laying claim to Artois, Brabant, Luxembourg, Milan and Roussillon.

Charles V was stung into retaliation. In conjunction with Henry VIII, a joint invasion of France occurred. Savoy and Boulogne were captured and even Paris was threatened. The treaties of Crépy (1544) and Ardres (1546), signed respectively with Charles and Henry, demonstrated that the focal-point of the Habsburg–Valois conflict had shifted away from Italy to north-west Europe. Though the death of Francis I in 1547 closed one chapter of the long-running saga, the accession of Henry II opened another. He had spent three years in a Madrid prison and had a personal score to settle with Charles V but he did not allow this to obscure his objectives. In this respect, Henry II was a far better statesman than his father. In 1550 he took advantage of England's ill-fated war with Scotland to recover Boulogne and then proceeded to exploit the Emperor's conflict with the Lutheran princes. At the Treaty of Chambord (1552), he promised them assistance in return for the bishoprics of Metz, Toul and Verdun, which gave him access to Germany via the Moselle.

The fate of the Habsburg Empire seemed to be in the balance between 1552 and 1555: German princes were disaffected, French troops occupied Metz, the Duke of Guise won a handful of victories in north Italy and was threatening Milan, and the Ottoman Turks were advancing along the north African coast. Charles was in the depth of a personal depression. In 1556 he handed over control of Spain to his son, Philip, who negotiated a truce with Henry in 1556. Both countries were again in dire financial straits, but not yet desperate enough to secure peace. The accession of the anti-Habsburg Pope Paul IV in 1555 once more encouraged France to invade Italy. For two years the Duke of Guise tried to recover Naples and Milan before being recalled to defend France from a Spanish invasion. From his base in the Netherlands, Philip had proved his manhood by defeating a small French army at St Quentin in 1557. Not until the following January did Henry II feel his honour had been vindicated when Guise seized England's last continental outpost of Calais. Neither country could afford to continue fighting. Peace was not just desirable, it was essential.

Results

The Treaty of Câteau-Cambrésis in April 1559 ended the Italian Wars. France gave up its claims to Naples and Milan but was allowed to keep a handful of towns, including Turin, Pinerolo and Saluzzo on the Italian side of the Alps – all valuable toeholds for future military excursions. In addition, France kept Calais and the former imperial towns of Metz, Toul and Verdun. After more than 60 years of fighting, Spain emerged as the dominant power in Italy though France had reduced the Habsburg threat of encirclement and gained some tangible rewards. Both countries were financially drained.

Italy, too, was exhausted, but more from the effects of marauding armies as they trekked through Milan, Florence, the Papal States to Naples and back again. Guicciardini's claim that after 1509 Italy 'saw nothing but scenes of infinite slaughter, plunder and destruction of multitudes of towns and cities, attended with the licentiousness of soldiers no less destruction to friends than foes', was overstated but it does contain some truth. Ravenna (1512), Fabiano (1519), Como (1521), Genoa (1522) and Pavia (1525) had all been pillaged. The Italian states had once again demonstrated their individual and collective inability to withstand an invader. Leagues had been formed and broken, victory for one had bred reaction in another, and old rivals showed an unwillingness to bury the hatchet – except in each other. Florence rejoiced at the defeat of Naples in 1502 and political revolutions in Florence and Milan delighted their enemies. Many privately celebrated the sack of Rome in 1527 for it seemed a poignant act of retribution for the numerous occasions when the Papacy had invited foreign armies into the peninsula.

Machiavelli was convinced that Italy's dependence on unreliable mercenaries had kept it divided and that the duplicity of the popes had prevented it from ever being governed by one ruler. Earlier Italian writers like Alighieri Dante and Leonardo Bruni had argued that without a single ruler peace would never prevail in Italy. Dante believed that only the intervention of a redeemer would impose political security upon the Italians; Bruni favoured increasing the authority of the state to preserve and extend its liberty. But neither solution proved feasible in the sixteenth century: the Valois lacked the strength to accomplish it and the Habsburgs were preoccupied with more pressing commitments. Instead, Italy became the anvil for western powers to hammer out their dynastic ambitions, a fate repeatedly re-enacted over the next 300 years.

Task: note-making

This chapter covers a lot of complicated events. The following is a note-making exercise which will help you sort out your ideas and improve your understanding of the Italian Wars.

Take six sheets of paper. Head five of them France, Spain, England, the Empire and the Papacy. Divide each in half horizontally. The top half is for their aims in 1494; the bottom half is for their gains/losses by 1559 (for example: land, war-debts, prestige, security).

Now try to get a summary of events concerning the country on to each half page. Look for: important dates; one-sentence summaries of situations; turning-points. You could colour-code different types of action; for instance, red for battles; blue for peace treaties; green for formation of a league; yellow for accession of a ruler, and so on – or make up your own code.

Keep space for a one-sentence explanation of events at the bottom of each page. Put a box round it.

Take the sixth sheet. Look at all the boxed statements on your notesheets. Write your own summary of how each country helped to prolong the war and of their overall gains/losses.

Discuss your sheets and your conclusions with other members of the class.

Further reading

J. R. Hale, *War and Society in Renaissance Europe, 1450–1520* (Fontana, 1985) – a good introduction to the Italian Wars.

M. E. Mallett, *Mercenaries and their Masters: Warfare in Renaissance Italy* (Oxford University Press, 1974).

M. Rodríguez-Salgado, 'The Habsburg–Valois Wars', *New Cambridge Modern History*, vol. 2, 2nd edn (Cambridge University Press, 1990) – the most recent account of the wars.

L. Martines, *Power and Imagination: City States in Renaissance Italy* (Knopf, 1979) – examines the intrigue and diplomatic rivalry.

F. Gilbert, *Machiavelli and Guicciardini: Politics and History in Sixteenth-Century Florence* (Princeton University Press, 1965) – discusses the views of two of the best known political commentators of this period.

Part Two   Religious wars and political turmoil, 1559–98

12 How do you account for Calvin's international appeal?

Time chart

1509: **Calvin** is born at Noyon, Picardy

1523: Studies theology at the Sorbonne

1531: Calvin returns to Paris on the death of his father

1534: Leaves France for Basel

1536: Arrives in Geneva; publishes the *Institutes of the Christian Religion*

1538: Calvin is expelled from Geneva; enters Strassburg

1541: Returns to Geneva; publishes *The Ecclesiastical Ordinances of Geneva*

1544: Sebastian Castellio is forced to leave Geneva

1547: Gruet is burned for blasphemy

1551: Bolsec is banished for criticising predestination

1553: Servetus is burned for denying the Trinity

1555: The Libertines are voted off the city council

1559: An academy opens in Geneva; national synod meets in Paris

1560: Scotland adopts Calvinism

1563: Frederick III proclaims the Heidelberg Catechism

1564: Calvin dies

1573: François Hotman publishes *Francogallia*

1574: Théodore de Bèze publishes the *Right of Magistrates*

1579: Philippe Du Plessis-Mornay publishes *The Defence of Liberty Against Tyrants*

Geneva: 1536–64

In 1536 the Geneva city council expelled its Catholic bishop and won political freedom from the Duke of Savoy. However, amid a wave of Protestant ideology, it was in danger of falling under the influence of the Zwinglian church of Berne.

Order and discipline were vital if Geneva were to retain its independence.

PROFILE: *John Calvin*

Born the son of a canon lawyer in 1509, **Calvin** studied theology at the Sorbonne in 1523 before changing to law at Orleans and Bourges universities. The death of his father in 1531 and his subsequent return to Paris caused him to turn away from Catholicism. Convinced that he was 'chosen by God to proclaim the truth', he most probably composed the Protestant address delivered by his friend, Nicolas Cop, the new rector of the Sorbonne in 1534. Such views were unwelcome and both men were forced to leave France. Between 1534 and 1536 Calvin travelled to Basel, Strassburg and Ferrara, before reaching Geneva. Having just published his *Institutes of the Christian Religion* – a 'small treatise containing a summary of the principal truths of the Christian religion' – he was persuaded by Farel, a French pastor, to stay and help implement a reformation. However, Calvin's strict code of conduct, compulsory confession of faith and insistence that the city council submit to clerical control proved unacceptable, and he was expelled from the city in 1538. For three years he lived in Strassburg, befriended Martin Bucer, married and wrote several theological works before being tempted back to Geneva in 1541 where he remained until his death in 1564.

In 1541 Calvin worked with the council to draw up *The Ecclesiastical Ordinances of Geneva* by which order would be restored and a reformed church established. For seven years, Geneva and Calvin enjoyed a period of tranquillity though he had to compromise many ideals and was subject to considerable personal abuse from a leading magistrate, Ami Perrin, and his faction known as the Libertines. They resented the influence of foreigners (not one pastor was a Genevan and the city was full of refugees), the strict regime and the inquisitorial conduct of the consistory (the ruling body of the Church). Calvin made no concessions to the rich and powerful. They, in turn, viewed him as arrogant and dictatorial even though he held no political office and was only one of many pastors, albeit the most important.

Matters came to a head in 1555. A financial crisis in the city made the presence of wealthy French aristocrats and merchants very desirable and when the Libertines voiced their objections, they were voted off the council. To the majority of citizens, Calvin was now indispensable. In 1559 he was granted the status of *bourgeois*, which entitled him to vote, and he opened an academy for the training of future leaders and missionaries. At his death in 1564, the academy had 1,500 students. Geneva was the model of the Reformed Church and the centre of an international movement.

Theology

Figure 12.2 A fifteenth-century woodcut of St Augustine

KEY TERMS:

Augustinianism

St Augustus was a fifth-century writer (see Figure 12.2), who viewed human history as a conflict between two societies – the heavenly kingdom of God and the earthly kingdom of Satan. He stressed man's sinfulness and dependence on God for his salvation.

Nominalism

This was a philosophical exercise in which general ideas were treated simply as names, and universal concepts were regarded as 'unreal'.

Transubstantiation

At the Last Supper, Christ first blessed and then ate bread and drank wine. To Catholics the act of consecrating the bread and wine at the Eucharist converts the whole substance of the bread into the substance of the body of Christ and the whole substance of the wine into the substance of His blood. This conversion is known as **transubstantiation**.

Calvin's principal ideas were originally set out in six chapters in a famous book *Institutes of the Christian Religion*, published in 1536. Thereafter, as he expanded and elaborated his beliefs, it was revised three times until the final edition in 1559 contained 80 chapters. Much of his thinking was an amalgam of **Augustinianism**, **nominalism** and Christian humanism. He was greatly influenced by Erasmus, Luther and Bucer, but not Zwingli, for whom he had little respect. Calvin did not have an original mind, but he knew how to avoid the theological confusion and complexities which surrounded the first generation of Protestant reformers. His great contribution to the Reformation was that, at a time of uncertainty concerning its leadership and doctrine, he synthesised the essential ideas of evangelicalism into a logical, coherent and intelligible theology.

Calvin, like Luther, denounced indulgences, celibacy and pilgrimages, and believed in only two sacraments, baptism and holy communion. Though he rejected **transubstantiation** in favour of a spiritual presence in the Eucharist, he wisely offered no clear definition confessing that he 'would rather experience it than understand it'. In fact, he attached less significance to the Eucharist than either Luther or Zwingli, perhaps because he was well aware of the theological disputes generated by this subject. More important to him was the doctrine of justification by faith. 'Man' was evil and insignificant. 'Man's' corruption could only be redeemed by the grace of God whose power was omniscient, which implied that 'man' would be saved not on account of his good works but because God had predestined him as one of the 'elect'. Those with faith would be sure of salvation (the doctrine known as single predestination); those without would be damned (double predestination). Of course, this would only be known after death and on earth everyone must try to live as good a life as possible. Calvin thus outlined his doctrine of predestination:

> 'As scripture, then, clearly shows we say that God once established by his eternal and unchangeable plan those whom he long before determined once for all to receive into salvation, and those whom, on the other hand, he would devote to destruction. We assert that, with respect to the elect, this plan was founded upon his freely given mercy, without regard to human worth; but by his just and irreprehensible but incomprehensible judgement he has barred the door of life to those whom he has given over to damnation.'

These ideas, which Calvin described as 'the principal article of the Christian religion', were only developed in the 1550s. They differed from Luther and Zwingli, who both placed more emphasis on salvation and did not accept the notion of double predestination. 'To know God by whom all men were created' became the centre of his creed and 'the chief end of human life'; and God's word would only be revealed by a careful study of and implicit belief in the Bible.

Geneva never became a theocracy though its organisation – which owed so much to Bucer's reformed church in Strassburg and reflected a strong clerical influence and Calvin's personality – made it seem like one. The four orders of the Church – elders, deacons, pastors and doctors – were annually elected by the Small Council of 25 male citizens, who in turn were elected by the Council of Two Hundred. Each order had a clearly defined function:

- The elders were 'to supervise every person's conduct'.

- The deacons were 'to care for the goods of the poor' and 'to look after the sick'.

■ The pastors were 'to proclaim the Word of God, to teach and to administer the sacraments'.

■ The doctors were 'to instruct the faithful in sound doctrine'.

Discipline was enforced by a consistory comprising 12 lay elders and six clerical pastors, who had the power to investigate and punish anyone. Sexual promiscuity, dancing, singing outside church, excessive drinking, gambling and wearing ostentatious clothing were all heavily censored. Though Calvin believed that the moral and political condition of the people should be determined by the Church, in practice punishments were sanctioned by the city council. These ranged from gentle rebukes to public confession, from exclusion from communion to excommunication, and, in extreme cases, exile and death. Among the more celebrated victims were Sebastian Castellio expelled for claiming that the biblical 'Song of Songs' was an erotic poem, Jacques Gruet burned (in 1547) for blasphemy, Jerome Bolsec banished for attacking predestination (1551) and Michael Servetus burned for denying the Trinity (1553). As a disciplinarian, Calvin upheld the principle of obedience to a magistrate and preached that rebellion was sinful. Though privately he modified his views, it was not until after his death that writers like Hotman, Bèze and Plessis-Mornay propounded the view that an unlawful ruler could be resisted and if necessary overthrown.

Calvinism's international appeal

Calvinism became the faith of many minority groups in the second half of the sixteenth century. The clear, logical exposition of the *Institutes* and accessible prose style, whether in Latin or French, appealed to literate urban groups such as skilled craftsmen, lawyers and merchants. Its attraction may have been due to its reverence for authority, order and discipline – both public and private – which enabled people to get on with their lives quietly and industriously.

Indeed, early twentieth-century historians like Max Weber and Richard Tawney believed that it became the faith of the middle classes for moral and economic reasons: rich bankers and merchants sought respectability, rejected the Papacy's criticism of **usury** and equated the acquisition of wealth (capitalism) with moral self-righteousness. The Protestant 'work ethic', argued Weber, was the logical result of identifying personal prosperity with a divine sign of being one of the elect. While some support for this theory remains among present-day Marxist historians, it is clear that Calvinism's appeal was not just to the middle classes.

KEY TERM:

Usury

The practice of lending money at unreasonably high interest rates is known as **usury**, since money has been put to use. The medieval scholastic view was that usury was unjust and a sin if it was the intention of the creditor to make a profit; on the other hand, charging interest on a loan to cover expenses or to compensate for risks involved in lending the money was considered lawful. The Papacy believed that 5 per cent interest was acceptable but Calvin held that the Scriptures did not forbid usury to all, only to Jews. Although Calvin was opposed to profiteering, his support for usury in principle opened the door for higher interest rates.

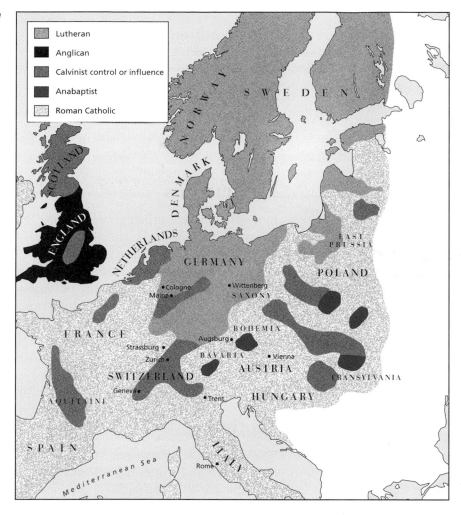

Figure 12.3 *Religious beliefs and adherents in Europe in the later sixteenth century*

The printing press was of great importance in turning Calvinism into an international movement. More than 30 printing houses operated in Geneva in the 1550s producing anti-Roman propaganda as well as Calvinist evangelical and theological tracts ready for export. As the city's reputation spread, so it attracted refugees and foreign immigrants. Between 1550 and 1562, perhaps as many as 10,000 entered Geneva, thereby doubling the city's population. By then, Calvinism had been accepted by the Swiss Confederation as its official faith and was beginning to establish itself internationally (see Figure 12.3).

France

In France, Calvinism appealed to all social groups, and particularly to urban workers and nobles. Between 1555 and 1562, some 88 Genevan missionaries had travelled to every part of the country and established themselves in cities such as Poitiers, Lyon, Paris and La Rochelle. There

Consistories

The **consistory** was the ruling body of the Calvinist Church. Comprising ministers and elders, it met once a week to implement the church discipline.

Colloquies

These were judicial and legislative courts, where judgements were spoken (*loqui* is Latin meaning 'I speak').

National synod

This was an assembly (*sunodos* is Greek for 'a meeting') where Calvinists representing district and provincial synods met to discuss national issues.

Huguenotism

Genevan Calvinists who settled in France were named after a burgomaster, Hugues, and were known as Huguenots. **Huguenotism** is therefore a term for French Protestantism.

they set up cellular systems in which local churches were organised into district **consistories**, regional **colloquies**, provincial assemblies and, by 1559, a **national synod**. In a wide-sweeping arc – stretching from the west coast south of the Loire to Perigord and the Dordogne, and east to Provence and Dauphiné – **Huguenotism** (as it was known in France) embraced perhaps 40 per cent of the nobles and hundreds of thousands of urban workers, though only a minority of peasants. It has been suggested that by 1600 perhaps as many as 10 per cent of the population was Huguenot.

Netherlands

In the Netherlands urban groups and the lesser nobility, especially among the southern provinces, and isolated peasant settlements in the north-east had adopted Calvinism. However, the rigidity of its principles, which failed to embrace the whole of the community, the extremism of some of its leaders which reminded many of Anabaptism, and its stern discipline made it at best a minority faith. Both Holland and Zealand experienced civil wars in the 1560s and Calvinist churches became paramilitary organisations setting up cadres on a local, provincial and national basis. The move from passive to active resistance was but a short step and even though a theory justifying rebellion was only worked out afterwards, it added to its appeal in many quarters.

Scotland

Scotland adopted Calvinism in 1560 as its national faith though it owed little to Calvin, theories of resistance or the presence of a middle class. In fact, the lairds, merchants, nobles and preachers simply rejected the prevailing Catholic faith and supplanted it with their own brand of presbyterianism because they were willing to change their faith and because ex-Genevan theologians like John Knox were able to exploit them.

German states and elsewhere in Europe

The Palatinate, Westphalia, Wesel, Nassau-Dillenburg, Brandenburg, Bremen, Anhalt and the Lower Rhenish duchies of Mark, Julich, Cleves and Berg were among 28 German states which converted to Calvinism. Some rulers, like Elector Frederick III of the Palatinate (1559–76), were genuine religious converts; others no doubt welcomed the increased control Calvinism gave them over their Church and their subjects' lives. Elsewhere in Germany, Lutheranism in the north and Zwinglianism in the far south proved difficult to displace. Scandinavia was already Lutheran and proved unreceptive to Calvinism but in eastern Europe – especially in Bohemia, Poland and Hungary – missionaries found the nobility a fertile seed-bed for their evangelism.

Task: work with sources

Read the following four sources and then answer the questions below.

Document A

Calvin writes about obedience to magistrates and kings.

'We are not only subject to the authority of princes who perform their tasks towards us uprightly and faithfully as they ought, but also to the authority of all those who, by whatever means have control of affairs, even though they perform only a minimum of the prince's office ... [God] says that those who rule for the public benefit are true patterns and evidence of His benevolence; and those who rule unjustly and incompetently have been raised up by Him to punish the wickedness of the people; that all equally have been endowed with that holy majesty with which He has invested lawful authority... But we must, in the meantime, be very careful not to despise or violate that authority of <u>magistrates</u>, full of venerable majesty, which God has established by the weightiest decrees, even though it may reside with their own wickedness. For, if the correction of unbridled despotism is the Lord's to avenge, let us not at once think that it is entrusted to us, to whom no command has been given except to obey and suffer.

'I am speaking all the while of private individuals. For if there are now any magistrates of the people, appointed to restrain the wilfulness of kings, I am so far from forbidding them to withstand, in accordance with their duty, the fierce licentiousness of kings, that, if they wink at kings who violently fall upon and assault the lowly common folk, I declare that their dissimulation involves nefarious perfidy, because they dishonestly betray the freedom of the people, of which they know that they have been appointed protectors by God's ordinance.'

Document B

In this letter to Coligny, dated 16 April 1561, Calvin renounces violence and his alleged support for the Huguenot Conspiracy of Amboise in 1560.

'Seven or eight months before the event, a certain person consulted me, whether it was not lawful to resist the tyranny by which the children of God were then oppressed ... I strove to demonstrate to him that he had no warrant for such conduct according to God; and that even in worldly terms such measures were ill-organised, presumptuous and could have no *successful outcome ... I admitted, it is true, that if the Princes of the Blood demanded to be maintained in their rights for the common good, and if the* Parlement *joined them in their quarrel, that it would then be lawful for all good subjects to lend them armed resistance.'*

Document C

From Bèze's *The Right of Magistrates*, published in 1574. Bèze was Calvin's lieutenant and his successor in Geneva, 1564–80.

'It is thus apparent that there is a mutual obligation between the king and the officers of a kingdom; that the government of the kingdom is not in the hands of the king in its entirety but only the sovereign degree; that each of the officers has a share in accord with his degree; and that there are definite conditions on either side. If these conditions are not observed by the inferior officers, it is the part of the sovereign to dismiss and punish them, but only for definite cause and according to the procedures prescribed by the law of the realm, and not otherwise, unless he is himself to violate the oath he took to exercise his office in conformity with law. If the king, hereditary or elective, clearly goes back on the conditions without which he would not have been recognised and acknowledged, can there be any doubt that the lesser magistrates of the kingdom, of the cities, and of the provinces, the administration of which they have received from the sovereignty itself, are free of their oath, at least to the extent that they are entitled to resist flagrant oppression of the realm which they swore to defend and protect according to their office and particular jurisdiction? ... On the other hand, it is by the sovereignty itself that lesser officers are charged with enforcing and maintaining law among those committed to their charge, to which duty they are further bound by oath ... Is it not then reasonable, by all law divine and human, that more should be permitted to these lesser magistrates, in view of their sworn duty to preserve the law, than to purely private persons without office? I say, therefore, that they are obliged, if reduced to that necessity, and by force of arms where that is possible, to offer resistance to flagrant tyranny, and to safeguard those within their care, until such time as the Estates, or whoever holds the legislative power of the kingdom or the empire, may by common deliberation make further and appropriate provision for the public welfare.'

Document D

From *The Defence of Liberty against Tyrants* by Philippe du Plessis-Mornay, a Huguenot gentleman, 1579.

'When kings were given to the people, this compact did not lapse but was instead confirmed and constantly renewed. We have said that at the coronation of a king a twofold covenant was made. The first was between God, the king, and the people. And its purpose was that the people should become God's people, that is that they should be God's Church ... Since it was dangerous to entrust the Church to a single, all-too-human individual, the Church was committed and entrusted to the people as a whole. The king, situated on a slippery height, could easily have fallen into irreligion. Hence, God wished to have the people intervene, so that the Church might not be ruined with the king ...'

1 Study documents A and B.
   a What did Calvin mean by the term 'magistrates'? *2 marks*
   b Under what circumstances, according to these two sources, might a king be resisted? *3 marks*

2 In what respects do Bèze's ideas (in Document C) differ from those of Mornay (in Document D)? Explain your reasons. *5 marks*

3 Study all four documents. Why did Bèze and Mornay support the use of violence but Calvin oppose it? *6 marks*

4 Study all four documents and use your own knowledge. How far do these four sources account for the international appeal of Calvinism? *9 marks*
   (You will find more information for your answer to this question in chapters 13, 18 and 26.)

Further reading

K. Randell, *Calvin and the Later Reformation* (Hodder and Stoughton, 1988) – a useful starting-point for students new to this topic.

T. H. L. Parker, *John Calvin* (Dent, 1975) – the most readable biography for A- and AS-Level students.

M. Greengrass, *The French Reformation* (Blackwell, 1987).

A. E. McGrath, *A Life of John Calvin* (Oxford University Press, 1990) – a detailed and academically rigorous study.

A. Duke, A. Pettegree and G. Lewis (eds), *Calvinism in Europe* (Manchester University Press, 1993) – a collection of scholarly essays on the impact of Calvinism in Europe.

M. Prestwich (ed.), *International Calvinism, 1541–1715* (Oxford University Press, 1985).

G. R. Potter and M. Greengrass (eds), *John Calvin* (Arnold, 1983) – contains a good variety of documents.

13 Why did the French Wars of Religion last so long?

Time chart

1559: Henry II dies; accession of Francis II

1560: Death of Francis II; accession of Charles IX

1562: Edict of January collapses. Massacre of Vassy begins the civil wars

1563: Edict of Amboise ends first war

1567: Second war begins

1568: March War ends by Edict of Longjumeau
August Third war begins

1570: War ends by Treaty of St Germain

1572: 18 August Margaret of Valois marries Henry of Navarre
24 August Massacre of St Bartholomew's Day. Fourth war begins

1573: Truce of La Rochelle ends the war

1574: Charles IX dies; accession of Henry III. Fifth war begins

1576: Peace of Monsieur ends war

1577: Sixth war begins; ends in September at Treaty of Bergerac

1578: Seventh war begins

1579: Treaty of Nérac ends war

1580: Eighth war begins; ends in November by Treaty of Fleix

1585: Ninth war begins – the 'War of the Three Henries'

1588: 12 May 'Day of the Barricades' – Henry III leaves Paris
23 December Assassination of Henry of Guise and the Cardinal of Lorraine

1589: 5 January Catherine de' Medici dies
1 August Assassination of Henry III; accession of Henry of Navarre

1593: Henry of Navarre is converted to Catholicism

1594: The coronation of Henry IV at Chartres

1598: Treaty of Vervins and the Edict of Nantes end the Wars of Religion

Figure 13.1 *France during the Wars of Religion*

Between 1562 and 1598, France suffered nine periods of warfare known as the 'Wars of Religion'. This chapter seeks not to recount the events but to examine the factors which prolonged the wars. In spite of numerous truces and 13 years of intermittent peace, the underlying issues which caused the civil conflict were too strong to achieve a permanent settlement. It will be argued, therefore, that only when these factors had been played out would the wars finally end (see Figure 13.1).

Factor 1: The Valois Monarchy

For 30 years the French monarchy epitomised the problems facing the country: it was weak, impoverished and divisive. The expected role of a king was to protect and lead his subjects in peace and war, to be the source of justice and patronage, and to symbolise the nation's unity. None of the Valois kings between 1559 and 1589 fulfilled these expectations. Francis II (1559–60) was 15 and his brother, Charles IX (1560–74), 10 when they ascended the throne. Both were weak in stature, periodically unwell and heavily dependent on their mother, Catherine de' Medici (see profile on page 131). Henry III (1574–89) at 22 was at least old enough to rule without a regent but he preferred the company of his dissolute 'mignons' and had neither the ability nor the temperament to assert himself authoritatively. Their problems were compounded by the intrigues of their youngest brother, Alençon, who attempted to murder Charles and Henry, and tried to draw France into a war with Spain. None of the Valois brothers produced any heirs and upon Alençon's death in 1584, a succession dispute brought the monarchy to its knees. Henry III could not prevent the Guise family from assuming control of Paris in 1588 and forcing him to recognise their claimant, Henry, Cardinal of Bourbon.

Seven months later, the King retaliated by arranging the murder of the leading Guises and arresting Bourbon. This act of violence, however, only convinced the surviving Guises that the King must be removed and a willing friar, Jacques Clement, assassinated him in August 1589. The accession of Henry of Navarre (1589–1610) – a proven soldier, statesman and legitimate claimant – gave France the leadership and authority it had so patently lacked. His most serious impediment – his Huguenotism – was overcome when he announced his conversion to Catholicism in 1593. In the following year he was crowned king.

Finances

The Valois monarchs also had serious financial difficulties. The Italian Wars had left the Crown with debts estimated at 41 million livres in 1560 but it also had peacetime costs running at four times the annual income. Inherent corruption, the Estates-General's refusal to reform the tax system and the continuation of civil war hindered attempts to raise revenue and reduce costs. The Crown's cash flow problems meant the nobility received inadequate patronage and provincial governors lacked the credit (both financial and political) with which to command obedience. The steady disbandment of the regular army – from 61 companies in 1562 to 21 in 1570 and 12 in 1585 – further increased the likelihood of violence as unpaid troops deserted and plundered crown revenues.

Factor 2: Catherine de' Medici

Traditionally, historians have charged **Catherine de' Medici** with keeping France divided while attempting to rule it. Constitutionally, she was entitled to be regent on behalf of Francis II and Charles IX but, if it was her intention to let them rule once they came of age, she found it hard not to interfere. At heart, Catherine was an astute stateswoman. She knew that her sons were likely to be exploited by powerful families like the Guises, whom she adjudged 'were used to playing the king'. She also believed that the Valois' survival depended upon her setting one faction against another. In 1561 she appointed the Huguenot Louis, Prince of Condé, as Governor of Catholic Picardy and in 1563 supported Gaspard de Coligny only to remove him when he became too powerful. Tragically for her, his death in 1572 triggered off the massacre of 11,000 Protestants on St Bartholomew's Eve, which French historians have customarily laid at her door. Today, they are inclined to believe her claim that all she wanted was to serve God and to maintain her authority – not for herself, but in order to preserve the kingdom for her sons. Responsibility for the massacre should not rest with Catherine, who was only guilty of conspiring to remove Coligny. It should rest instead with the King, the Guises and fanatical Catholics. Throughout these years, and especially between 1561 and 1571, Catherine de' Medici's position was too weak to achieve a durable peace. The nobility simply did not respect or trust her.

Certainly her religious objectives were at best naive and, in the opinion of most Catholics, indefensible. She appears to have favoured a policy of limited toleration whereby the Catholic majority would allow the co-existence of Huguenotism within a single church, and privately instructed royal officials not to enforce the heresy laws. Saulx-Tavannes wrote from Dijon that he had 'received different despatches from court: those from Guise said to kill them [the Huguenots] all; those from the queen said to save them all'.

PROFILE: *Catherine de' Medici*

The niece of Pope Clement VII and daughter of the Duke of Florence, **Catherine** married Henry, Duke of Orleans, Francis I's second son, in 1533 at the age of 14. In spite of her husband's liaison with Diane de Poitiers, she produced four sons and three daughters in the space of 11 years, and in 1552 assumed the regency of France in the absence of the King. On his death in 1559, Francis II took the throne but his sudden death in the following December enabled Catherine to resume the position of regent on behalf of Charles IX. Henry IV later expressed surprise that, given her universal unpopularity and persistent meddling, 'she never did worse'. Arguably Frenchmen would not rest easily until the queen mother had been removed from the political scene. On 5 January 1589, she achieved the rare distinction – for her family – of dying in her bed.

Factor 3: The nobility

The French nobility also took advantage of the ineffectual royal family. With time on their hands and retainers at their disposal, most were relieved to be free from the centralising ambitions of Francis I and Henry II. Perhaps as many as 40 per cent of nobles by 1562 had expressed their independence by converting to Huguenotism and, of course, many took their clients with them. The lesser nobles and their tenants increasingly attached themselves to leading aristocratic families rather than to the Crown.

The American historian, Robert Harding, was convinced in consequence that 'the fundamental cause [of the wars] was the crisis in the [aristocratic] clientage system that had become so dependent on brokerage [negotiation]'. Francis, Duke of Guise, and Louis, Prince of Condé, each commanded 500 noble retainers and Henry de Montmorency-Damville, Governor of Languedoc, exercised virtual independence for more than 30 years. Between 1564 and 1566 Catherine tried to rebuild bridges with the provincial landowners: the royal family toured the country, staged spectacular displays and dispensed patronage, but to little effect. In truth, political and military power rested with the leading aristocratic families: the Guises, Montmorencys and Bourbons.

In 1562 Francis, Duke of Guise, controlled the royal ordnance, and his brothers, Charles and Louis, monopolised the Church's patronage. None had any intention of relinquishing power to an Italian and her sons. The Montmorencys were led by Constable Anne who controlled the army and as Grand Master dominated the royal court. Less powerful, but well capable of driving a wedge between these factions, were the Bourbons. Anthony, Duke of Bourbon, had inherited the right to the throne of Navarre and in 1562 was the senior prince of the blood. His brother Louis, Prince of Condé, was politically more ambitious and unwilling to let the Guises throw their weight around. In this climate of unbridled tension, family feuds were bound to turn to bloodshed.

In 1560 Condé supported the Huguenot conspiracy at Amboise which clearly intended to kill the Duke of Guise, seize the King and put Bourbon in control of the government. When the Duke was murdered in 1563, Condé endorsed it. Coligny allegedly said that it was 'the best thing that could happen to this kingdom ... and it will be the means to pacify the realm'. In the short term, he was right and peace prevailed for four years. But the Guises vowed revenge. Condé was murdered in cold blood in 1569 and Coligny shot in the Paris massacre of 1572. Within ten years of the outset of the wars, most of the heads of noble families had been killed, but their surviving relatives thirsted for revenge and this helped to keep the wars going. Violence became a way of life for many young nobles in the south and west; this period became notable for the sharp increase in duelling. From their respective power-bases – the Guises in northern and eastern France and Brittany, the Montmorencys in the centre and the Bourbons in the south, south-west and Normandy – the nobility inflicted feudal anarchy upon a hapless monarchy. Civil conflict would only cease when a family's honour had been vindicated and survivors believed that peace was preferable to intermittent warfare.

Factor 4: Huguenotism

Though Huguenots constituted no more than 10 per cent of the population in 1562 and were arguably not much larger by 1598, they were a major factor in the prolongation of the wars. According to the Edict of Compiègne (1557), Huguenots were an illegal group but the lack of a strong government after 1559 encouraged Calvinist missionaries and the lower clergy to spread the word. Soon they had established district, provincial and national synods, and were training and arming volunteers. Calvin had once promised, 'Give me wood and I will send you arrows', and weapons were certainly transported from Geneva to France. At first, such *chevaliers du désordre*, as the Huguenots were called, confined their guerrilla activities to plotting against the Crown's 'evil advisers', the Guises, but once the wars began they resorted to the fiction that they were fighting for the King. By 1562 they controlled much of central, western and southern France in a broad crescent from Poitou to Dauphiné. Huguenotism owed much of its strength to the support received from nobles like Condé, Navarre, Coligny and Odet de Châtillon. Catherine's chancellor, Michel de l'Hôpital, believed that 'several [nobles] take shelter beneath the cloak of religion even though they have no God and are more atheistic than religious'. Though this was true of Condé and some of the Languedoc nobles, Coligny was a devout Protestant.

The Huguenots wanted religious and civil liberty. Such ideals seemed unattainable in an overwhelmingly Catholic country where the monarch took an oath to defend the faith from heretics. But the idea of limited toleration was supported by Catherine and Catholic writers like Postel, Bodin and Pasquieur. The Peace of Amboise allowed them to worship in specified towns, on nobles' estates and in their own homes, but the uneasy peace was broken in 1567 by the Huguenots' frustration at the unwillingness of pro-Catholic officials to implement the edict. Coligny believed that conditions were actually worse during peacetime than in open warfare.

Further rights were gained by the Peace of St Germain and a lasting peace seemed possible in 1572 when the houses of Valois and Bourbon were united in marriage, but this harmony was shattered by the Bartholomew massacre (see time chart and Figure 13.3). This hardened attitudes and deepened rivalries. Huguenots in the Midi, for example, swore 'never [to] trust those who have so often and so treacherously broken faith and the public peace; never [to] disarm as long as the enemy continues to oppose the true faith and those who profess it; and [to] sign no peace treaties that can be used to start massacres'. Huguenot writers, such as Hotman, Bèze, and du Plessis-Mornay, justified the right to bear arms and overthrow tyrannous monarchs (see chapter 12), and virtual republics were established in Languedoc, Poitou, Guyenne, Gascony and Dauphiné, where Huguenots levied their own taxes, customs duties, justice and militia, and prepared for a long campaign.

Huguenot success on the battlefield earned important concessions in the Treaty of Bergerac. Not only were the Huguenots allowed to control eight towns and have a church in every *bailliage* but the law courts, which were notoriously biased, also had to contain Huguenot as well as Catholic magistrates. This was a practical and necessary concession if the edicts of pacification were to be upheld.

Peace lasted for seven years until Henry III displayed his fickleness and yielded to the Guises by agreeing to repeal all existing Huguenot privileges. Once again, the Huguenots had to fight for their lives. Some were undoubtedly disturbed by Henry IV's conversion to Catholicism in 1593 but he commanded enough moral high ground to be able to establish a mutually acceptable peace settlement at Nantes in 1598. This edict gave the Huguenots full civil rights, entry to schools and universities, mixed law courts, religious liberty and control of 100 towns, though not Paris. It

Figure 13.3 Dutch engraving showing Paris during the Massacre of St Bartholomew's Day, 24 August 1572

was the best that they could hope for and, if its terms were 'by the grace of the King', Henry was determined that the letter as well as the spirit of the law would be enforced.

Factor 5: Catholic sectarianism

A principal obstacle to any lasting settlement was the extent of militant support for Catholicism: Catholic sectarianism. Devotion to the faith – which inspired many prominent nobles and clergy as well as ordinary French Catholics to resist the Huguenots – deepened in the course of the wars. **Fraternities** and pilgrimages were revived, miracles were reported and saints were revered as oaths bound local communities to defend their faith and commit sectarian murders. Angry Catholics, the *acharnés*, believed that Huguenots were no better than animals to be hunted and killed. In 1562, an entire Calvinist congregation in Sens was slaughtered and massacres occurred at Tours, Angers and Carcassonne.

Anti-Protestant prejudice was epitomised by the Guises who obstructed all peace initiatives and called upon all Catholics to exterminate Huguenotism. It was Duke Francis who first sparked off the wars in 1562 when he dispersed an illegal meeting at Vassy by murdering 70 and injuring 120 Huguenot worshippers. His brother, Cardinal Lorraine, spoke for the family when he informed Charles IX that they would 'neither approve nor suffer in his kingdom any diversity of religion'. Following Francis's murder, one of his clients swore 'to use all my strength in exterminating those of the new religion'. It was Lorraine – dubbed 'the tiger of France' by Hotman – who in the 1560s conspired to remove Condé, Coligny, d'Andelot and Esternay. It was his nephew, Henry, who helped set up a Catholic League after the Peace of Monsieur (1576) and turned Paris against the Crown.

After 1584 Henry III was no longer in control. The capital came to be ruled by the Council of Sixteen, a group of Catholic lawyers, merchants, clerics, officials and workers. On 13 May 1588 – the 'Day of the Barricades' – Parisians revealed their radicalism by preventing the King from entering the city and Catholics dressed in white shifts marched through the streets 'chanting in great devotion'. Priests like Jean Boucher, curé (priest) of St Benoît, called upon their congregations to assassinate the King. The Sorbonne declared that Frenchmen were no longer bound to the monarch and propagandists claimed that the Second Coming was at hand. Only when the Catholic League ran out of acceptable alternatives and Henry IV abjured his faith in 1593 would Paris be won over.

Throughout the wars, the French *parlements* undermined royal attempts

to protect the Huguenots. In 1562 the Paris *parlement* had reminded magistrates to enforce the death penalty for heretics and subsequently refused to register edicts of pacification in 1563, 1570, 1576 and 1598. Regional *parlements* were just as partisan. Judges from the Toulouse *parlement* urged the crowd to attack Protestants in 1562. At Guyenne they tried to convince the people that the governor's orders were not those of the King and the Rouen *parlement* delayed ratifying the Edict of Nantes until 1609. It is hard to disagree with the historian N. M. Sutherland who suggests, 'It would be untrue to say that the *parlements* caused the civil wars, but it is uncontestable that they prolonged them'.

Not all Catholics, of course, were fanatics and a more moderate view emerged in the 1570s, largely in response to the horrors perpetrated on St Bartholomew's Day. According to Montmorency-Damville, he and his *politique* sympathisers 'would rather the kingdom remained at peace without God than at war for him'. In spite of genuine efforts by Damville, Catherine and her son, Alençon, to persuade die-hard Catholics that co-existence was more preferable to civil war, the *politique* sentiment made slow progress. Not until the Guises had been silenced, the League conquered and Paris seduced by Henry IV, would these views prevail.

Factor 6: Foreign interference

The presence of foreign troops kept the wars alive and served to confuse those issues which had originally divided Frenchmen. The Huguenots received support from England and Germany but most came from the Netherlands. William of Orange pledged his support in August 1568 and took part in the siege of Poitiers. His brother, Louis, helped to defend La Rochelle (1569–70). After 1572, however, the Netherlands became embroiled in its own civil wars and could only offer occasional diversionary assistance.

In contrast, external help for the Catholic cause was more persistent and by its very presence more detrimental to domestic peace. As early as 1561 the 'triumvirate' of Guise, Montmorency and St André invited Spain to help exterminate the heretics, and Pius IV sought to draw Philip into a union of Catholic princes. At first Spain sent limited military aid but the formation of the Catholic League in 1584 and an invitation to Philip to defeat Navarre and enforce the bull of excommunication against him meant Spanish and Italian troops would occupy French towns for the next 14 years. Not until Paris experienced what a Spanish army of occupation was like, in 1590 and 1592, and Philip announced that his daughter had as good a claim to the French throne as anyone else, did most French Catholics concede that Spain and not the Huguenots was the real enemy. Henry IV's *raison d'être* and pedigree as the saviour of his nation was confirmed when he drove the Spanish troops out of France and concluded a satisfactory treaty at Vervins.

The French wars lasted so long because:

- no faction had been strong enough to secure outright victory;
- none was sufficiently weak to submit indefinitely;
- the Valois monarchs lacked the ability to lead and protect their people adequately.

By the 1590s, unwelcome foreign troops in northern France, popular disorder in Paris, economic discontent, and the realisation that too much blood had been shed in the name of religion, convinced most people that internal peace could only be achieved under Henry IV.

Task: class discussion

Discuss the following within the class or group.

1 Look at the factors in this chapter which historians have used to explain the length of the French wars.
  a Put the factors in order of importance, giving your reasons.
  b Do you think this list helps you to explain the precise timing of the French Wars of Religion? Explain your answer.
  c Six factors have been identified. Do you think that convincing explanations of the French wars need to stress how factors acted together, rather than separately? Explain your answer.

2 Do you think that the 'French Civil Wars' is a more appropriate description of this period than the 'French Wars of Religion'? Explain your answer.

3 What can you work out from this chapter about the kinds of evidence historians rely on when they try to explain why the French wars lasted so long?

Further reading

J. H. M. Salmon, *Society in Crisis: France in the Sixteenth Century* (Benn, 1975) – by far the best analysis of the wars.

R. J. Knecht, *The French Wars of Religion, 1559–1598*, Seminar Studies in History (Addison Wesley Longman, 1989) – a short and readable account with documents translated by the author.

N. M. Sutherland, *The Huguenot Struggle for Recognition* (Yale University Press, 1980) – this studies in depth the significance of Huguenotism.

B. Dienfendorf, *Beneath the Cross. Catholics and Huguenots in Sixteenth-Century Paris* (Oxford University Press, 1991) – examines sectarian violence.

R. M. Kingdom, *Myths about the St Bartholomew's Day Massacre* (Yale University Press, 1988) – considers the latest research on this complex event.

14 The printing press: an agent of change

Time chart

1453: Gutenberg prints 42-line Bible at Mainz

1474: Caxton prints (in Bruges) first book in English

1477: Publication of Italian–German dictionary

1481: Illustrated edition of Dante's *Divine Comedy* is printed in Florence

1494: Aldine Press begins in Venice

1520: Hans Lufft begins publishing Luther's works

1521: Lucas Cranach illustrates Melanchthon's *Passional Christi und Antichristi*

1532: Robert Estienne prints a Latin–English dictionary

1543: Vesalius publishes *De humani corporis fabrica*; Copernicus publishes *De Revolutionibus Orbium Coelestium*

1545: Spain issues its first index

1554: Julius III issues a Roman index

1559: Paul IV expands it

1564: Publication of the *Tridentine Index Librorum prohibitorum*

1569: Mercator prints the *Cosmographia* and navigational map of the world

1570: Ortelius publishes *Theatrum orbis terrarum* – the first modern atlas

1572: Henri Estienne publishes the first Greek lexicon

1587: Vatican press is established

1596: Revision of the Roman index

Early impact of the printing press

If any invention can be said to have ushered in a new age, unleashed latent forces and altered our understanding of the world, it is the printing press. At first, its impact was slow, conventional and in keeping with commercial trends. By 1500, most west European countries had a press: there were 73 in Italy, 64 in Germany, 45 in France and four in England. These continued to expand as businessmen realised the opportunities available to them, but conflicting politics and religion brought them mixed fortunes. In 1515 Lyon, France's principal business city, had over 100 presses, but from 1550 began to lose its trade in the face of Catholic pressure not to publish Calvinist material. Paris was similarly affected and suffered a severe blow when Robert Estienne, who published most of Calvin's works, emigrated to Geneva. By the 1560s some 40 presses operated in the Swiss city, centred upon a small group of French refugees. It soon captured the market for publishing Greek studies from Venice, Milan and Paris. Frankfurt-am-Main, Cologne, Nuremberg, Augsburg, Strassburg and Wittenberg became major publishing centres in Germany, and thrived on the religious controversies of the period. The Plantin family of Antwerp remained the principal printing and publishing company in the Netherlands throughout the sixteenth century, in part due to Philip II's patronage but also because of its diverse business contacts and quality of production.

The workshops of leading publishing firms – like those of Anton Koberger of Nuremberg and Aldus Manutius of Venice – soon became religious, cultural and commercial centres where client, printer, scholar, compiler, engraver and merchant could meet and exchange ideas. For instance, Lucas Cranach and his son, artists and engravers, worked in close collaboration with Luther at the press of Hans Lufft in Wittenberg between 1520 and 1546; and leading Protestant reformers like Servetus, Ochino and Oecolampadius received hospitality in the 1540s and 1550s at Oporinus's workshop in Basel. The German historian S. H. Steinberg believes such printers played an important role in spreading religious ideas although they probably recognised that the variety and growth of evangelical reform also ensured an expanding market.

As the number of presses increased, the type of literature produced became more varied. Small firms tended to meet local market needs, but the wealthy companies could risk publishing unknown authors or works of questionable appeal. The staple diet of most publishers was religious and devotional material like the Bible, catechisms, psalters, evangelical treatises, primers and schoolbooks. In Germany the number of new titles increased between 1519 and 1523 from 111 to 498, of which 418 dealt with religious issues. Thomas à Kempis's *Imitation of Christ* went through 99 editions before 1500. Genevan presses annually produced as many as 300,000 volumes of Calvinist material in the 1560s and it has been estimated that one million copies of Luther's German translation of the New Testament had been sold by 1600. Interest in theology had, of course, existed before the Reformation and it naturally quickened in the course of the sixteenth century. It should also be remembered that romances, ballads and tales of chivalry remained popular reading, and nothing served an author better than to find his literature classified as

Commonweal

To improve the 'weal', welfare or prosperity of the common people was the intention of several Christian groups in the early sixteenth century. One circle of English scholars and clerics, which included Thomas More, Hugh Latimer and Thomas Cromwell, called themselves the **commonweal**. They proposed social and economic reforms in aid of the poor.

forbidden reading. Sales of the *Amadís* romance, for instance, rapidly increased after the Spanish Cortes banned it in 1518.

The effect on literacy

How far did the printing press increase the levels of literacy? Historians have traditionally reached their conclusions by counting the number of people who could sign their name, but it is now evident that this is a very unreliable method as some people could sign a name but could not read or write. It seems likely that no more than 3 to 5 per cent of people in the more advanced countries could read and that the highest literacy levels were among the noble and merchant groups in urban centres, especially in northern Europe. The Netherlands had high literacy rates. More than 25 per cent of adult men in Amsterdam and Venice could probably read by the end of the sixteenth century but literacy levels in the countryside and for all females were invariably much lower. Existing ecclesiastical, university and trading centres probably experienced the greatest increase but once the clergy's monopoly of Latin and education ended – and the press was the principal reason for this development – lay authorities took control.

At first humanist Catholics and evangelical Protestants hoped that a laity versed in the scriptures would provide the basis of a new Christian **commonweal**. Recent studies of German and French cities suggest that the early Reformation owed a great deal to literate groups in urban areas. However, in the wake of popular radicalism in the 1520s and 1530s, it was realised that literacy could be a dangerous tool in the wrong hands. Luther himself saw the need to confine biblical reading to the clergy and lay authorities. Henry VIII took a similar stance. Such restrictions worked against a rapid expansion in literacy but of greater importance was the traditional practice of listening to, and looking at, written material.

Illustrations

In the fifteenth and sixteenth century, most people acquired knowledge by word of mouth. 'Printing was, in fact, an addition to, not a replacement for, oral communication', writes Robert Scribner. He sees the pictorial images produced by woodcuts as a more important source for conveying religious ideas among the people, at least until the mid sixteenth century. A woodcut block could produce over 3,000 copies before it started to deteriorate, whereas book editions averaged 1,000 copies. When woodcuts were combined with printing in the 1470s to produce the woodcut broadsheet, it provided a 'meeting-point between the illiterate, the semi-literate and the literate'.

In 1522 Luther explained why he had combined visual woodcuts with his text:

> *'I thought it good to put the old Passional with the little prayer book, above all for the sake of children and simple folk, who are more easily moved by pictures and images to recall divine history than through mere words or doctrines.'*

Luther was right, and herein lay much of his appeal. Theological issues could best be presented by the written word and through sermons but illustrative propaganda could teach the main ideas more effectively. To point the difference between evangelical and Catholic teaching, the woodcut by Georg Pencz entitled 'The Content of Two Sermons' (see Figure 14.1) contrasts one group steeped in Bible studies with another playing with their rosaries. Similarly, Lucas Cranach illustrated Melanchthon's *Passional Christi und Antichristi* (1521) with 13 pairs of woodcuts, each of which contrasted an aspect of Christ's life with the antichrist (see Figure 14.2). The *Passional* became one of the most popular

Figure 14.1 *Woodcut by George Pencz entitled 'The Content of Two Sermons', printed in Nuremberg in the 1520s*

Figure 14.2 Woodcut by Lucas Cranach entitled 'Passional Christi und Antichristi'

evangelical books and an effective means of suggesting to semi-literates that the Pope was antichrist. The production of cheaper paper enabled broadsheets, unlike books, to fall within the range of most literate people who were encouraged to read and pass on the contents orally. From the mid sixteenth century, however, publishers had a large enough literate market to begin to dispense with woodcuts and to print texts only, at least insofar as theological literature was concerned. Calvin appealed to an altogether more learned and sophisticated reader who was attracted to his style and lucidity of expression. Few of his works were accompanied by illustrations.

In the field of science, geography and mathematics, illustrations became increasingly important. Indeed, it may be argued that printing transformed religious images into words and scientific words into images. Printing from woodcut blocks and later copper-plates, scientific texts were illustrated with greater accuracy and clarity. Vesalius's *De humani corporis fabrica* (1543) contained finely drawn and labelled anatomical dissections which were of greater practical use in surgery than the texts alone (see Figure 14.3). In the sixteenth century, for the first time, printers employed skilled draughtsmen and illustrators to bring exactitude and realism to the writing just in case, as the German scientist Agricola explained, 'descriptions which are conveyed by words should either not be understood by the men of our times or should cause

---

Passional Christi

And while they beheld, he was taken up and a cloud received him out of their sight . . . this same Jesus, which is taken up from you into heaven, shall so come in like manner as ye have seen him go into heaven [*Acts 1:9, 11*]. And of his kingdom there shall be no end [*Luke 1:33*]. If any man serve me, let him follow me; and where I am, there shall also my servant be [*John 12:26*].

Passional Antichristi

And the beast was taken, and with him the false prophet that wrought miracles before him, with which he deceived them that had received the mark of the beast, and them that worshipped his image. These both were cast alive into a lake of fire burning with brimstone. And the remnant were slain with the sword of him that sat upon the horse, which sword proceeded out of his mouth [*Apocalypse 19:20–21*]. And then shall that Wicked be revealed, whom the Lord shall consume with the spirit of his mouth, and shall destroy with the brightness of his coming [*Thessalonians 2:8*].

---

difficulty to posterity'. Charts, maps, globes and books on architecture, botany, zoology and anatomy all benefited from the expertise of skilled artists and lithographers, who became an integral part of the printing profession.

Vernacular publishing

Figure 14.3 Woodcut from Andreas Vesalius's De Humani corporis fabrica, 1543. This was the first textbook to have systematic illustrations.

A major obstacle to widening literacy levels was the use of medieval Latin. Only a minority could read it and outside Italy few chose to speak it. Latin was the language of the professions – law, medicine and the Church – and remained so for a further 400 years, but it was also the medium of serious academic literature. Erasmus, Luther, Calvin, Loyola and Copernicus, for example, published most of their work in Latin because its vocabulary and syntax were precise and it was the only international language.

Gradually, the printing press highlighted the humanist emphasis on vernacular studies. An Italian–German dictionary printed in Venice in 1477 was the first dictionary of living languages. Erasmus revealed arcane areas of linguistic knowledge as well as the richness of the Greek, Hebrew and Latin languages. His *Adagia* sold 72,000 copies between 1500 and 1525. Readers became more literate, and literates more thirsty for material in their own language. The average yearly output of books in the German language rose from 40 in 1517, to 211 in 1521 and 498 in 1525.

Writing in 1542, Johann Sleidan in his *Address to the Estates of the Empire* claimed that printing had 'opened German eyes even as it is now bringing enlightenment to other countries. Each man became eager for knowledge, not without feeling a sense of amazement at his former blindness.' Luther addressed his people in German, Rabelais in French, and Ximénes in Spanish. Much of Calvin's popularity resulted from his alphabet manuals and textbooks which promoted literacy and his graceful style which commended his ideas to a reading public within and beyond the frontiers of France. In contrast, Luther's German was less refined and influenced fewer people outside Germany in the sixteenth century. One of the main reasons why Lutheranism stayed a predominantly Germanic movement was because 80 per cent of Luther's publications were written in German and only 4 per cent were translated into other European languages.

The effect on religion, science and the advancement of knowledge

It has already been noted that a distinguishing feature of the fifteenth- and sixteenth-century European Renaissance was its continuity and permanence (see chapter 4). The advent of the printing press secured the survival of single manuscripts, multiplied the number of extant texts and created opportunities to compare different editions of the same work. Scholars for the first time could build up their own library, rather than spend days travelling in search of manuscripts and then laboriously copying them out. Time and energy saved in having a set of nautical tables, a dictionary, a lexicon or a precisely drawn diagram enabled them to apply their creative talent more effectively. Printed material ended textual errors and inaccurate transliterations, which had bedevilled scribal literature. If mistakes did occur, publishers could issue an *erratum*. Certain disciplines – like architecture, geometry, natural science and geography – benefited in another way. In the course of making copies from the ancient Greek scholars, particularly Ptolemy, Vitruvius and Galen, original illustrations had become detached or wrongly positioned. Their restoration was only made possible after the script was replaced by print.

Religion and censorship

Some historians, like Elizabeth Eisenstein, believe printing played a prominent role in causing the Reformation. In 1515 the German humanist Jakob Wimfeling spoke of 'the noble art of printing, which makes it possible to propagate the correct doctrines of faith and morals throughout the world and in all languages'. Luther agreed. The printing press was, he contended, 'God's highest and extremest act of grace

'Sola fide'

Luther interpreted the passage 'by faith are ye saved' in the Book of Romans to mean 'by faith alone are ye saved'. The Latin phrase *sola fide* (by faith alone) became the essence of Luther's understanding of salvation.

Liturgies

A **liturgy** is a form of public worship. Although originally applied to the celebration of the Eucharist, Christian rituals such as baptism, confirmation and marriage also had their procedures detailed in a set of formularies, known as the liturgy.

Catechisms

To catechise is to instruct by asking and answering questions. A favoured method used by Lutherans and Calvinists was to present their ideas in a dialogue between the pastor and his student. A **catechism** was thus an elementary book of religious instruction.

whereby the business of the gospel is driven forward'. When Luther appealed to church doctrine, he could point to specific scriptural passages which his audience could read and judge for themselves. The scriptures were revealed as printed words which required no sacred mediation and were accessible to all believers. Once his translation of the New Testament had been printed, German people were able to see what Luther meant by '*sola fide*'. By 1534, 200,000 copies had been sold and he was a national hero.

If Luther was unequivocal about the importance of the press, the Papacy was alive to its disadvantages. The printing of sermons, prayers, **liturgies** and **catechisms** helped to standardise orthodox beliefs and played a significant part in propagating the reformed Catholic movement. That same press, however, also generated Protestant tracts and as there were fewer Catholic printers their books sold less enthusiastically. By the mid sixteenth century, Protestant works outnumbered them by 20 to one. Moreover, the Church found it increasingly difficult to censor printed material and quickly realised that the press was more of a curse than a blessing.

As early as 1479 the Papacy granted permission to Cologne University to extend its censorship to printed books and seven years later the Archbishop of Mainz began censoring undesirable publications in Frankfurt. In 1501 Alexander VI tried to extend clerical control over all literature but without success, and Leo X fared no better when he attempted to ban Luther's writings in 1520. A list of banned or 'proscribed' authors was first issued by the Sorbonne and Louvain universities in the 1520s. But unlike earlier heretics like Hus and Wyclif, the works of Luther, Zwingli, Bucer and Calvin could not be so readily suppressed. The sheer volume of publications and the keenness with which printers competed to publish outlawed tracts proved more than a match for civil and church authorities alike. Though printers were forced to emigrate – from Catholic Dutch provinces to the Calvinist north, from south to north Germany, from England to Strassburg, from France to Geneva – still the presses turned. The flow of Calvinist literature into France from Genevan emigré printers was so successful in stimulating Huguenot churches that a convert, Jean Morély, could describe the press as 'Truth's triumphal chariot'.

In response, lengthy indexes were issued and re-issued by the Sorbonne and Venice, Spain, the Netherlands, Florence and Rome, but evidence suggests that the more radical the lists became, the less effective was the censorship. Paul IV's Index of 1559 was particularly harsh and doubled the number of forbidden authors to over 500. Among them were Boccaccio, Castiglione, Erasmus, Rabelais, Machiavelli, and over 50 vernacular (native-language) editions of the Bible. The decrees of the Council of Trent in 1563 tried to censor the press by confining the reading of existing literature to the clergy, vetting new works and expurgating unacceptable ones, but its attempts were in vain. By the end of the century all indexes had been expanded. Spain's had been increased from 670 to over 2,500 titles. Not until 1587 did the Vatican establish its own press and by then it was clear to everyone that printing had done more to encourage heresy than orthodoxy.

Science

The press revolutionised the study of natural and pure science, and enabled philosophers to examine the world around them. Sixteenth-century scientists devoted much of their time to collecting, collating and understanding tenets of knowledge. As such, they tended to copy and confirm the long-established beliefs of ancient Greek writers like Ptolemy, Pliny, Galen and Aristotle. Paracelsus (1493–1541) recognised the limitations of slavishly repeating traditional truths and advocated **empiricism**. 'He who wishes to explore nature must tread her books with his feet', he declared. 'Writing is learned from letters. Nature however by travelling from land to land: one land, one page. This is the *Codex Naturae*, thus must its leaves be turned.'

By acquiring as much knowledge as possible and testing it against their own experiences, two of the greatest scientists coincidentally published their novel treatises in 1543. Vesalius (1514–64) printed a precisely illustrated anatomy of the human body and Copernicus (1473–1543) questioned whether the earth really was the centre of the universe. Copernicus had at his disposal more records, astronomical tables and data of Alexandrine and Islamic origin than any previous astronomer. Though he privately expressed his heliocentric theory as early as 1512, his fear of ridicule delayed publication of *De Revolutionibus Orbium Coelestium*.

The Danish scientist Tycho Brahe (1546–1601) continued Copernicus's work but from a more advanced baseline. He was interested in locating the stars accurately and predicting the position of planets. When a new star appeared in 1572 in the constellation of Cassiopeia, he realised that new data was needed. As a result, sine tables, trigonometry texts and star catalogues were printed, amended and recharted in works such as the *Progymnasinata*, which accurately plotted 777 fixed stars. Navigational science was also assisted by comparing ancient maps with recently printed and updated data. Gerardus Mercator first mastered Ptolemy's *Geographia* before constructing his own projection of the globe in 1569. Abraham Ortelius's *Theatrum* (1570), a collection of European maps, was regularly corrected and reprinted in the light of new discoveries. By 1598 some 28 editions had been published in five languages.

Conclusion

By the end of the century, maps were more accurate, stars more precisely charted, the workings of the human body better understood, mathematical knowledge more complete and each discipline delineated in greater detail and precision. The printing press had transformed humanism, split the universal Christian Church and radically changed human perception of ourselves and the world around us.

Task: visual sources

1 Study Figure 14.1. The evangelical preacher is on the left and the Catholic priest is on the right.
   a Describe what is shown in each scene.
   b Why do you think the engraver decided to put these two scenes side by side?
   c What are the reasons for combining visual images and written texts?

2 Study Figure 14.2.
   a In what ways are the two drawings similar?
   b Do you think that visual images of Christ ascending to Heaven and the Pope descending to Hell were an effective way of spreading the Gospel? Explain your answer.
   c Why was the *Passional* such a popular evangelical book in the early sixteenth century?

3 From the mid sixteenth century, books contained fewer illustrations and more texts. What does this suggest?
   a levels of literacy were rising
   b quality engravers were hard to find
   c publishers were cutting their costs.
   Explain your answer fully, referring to each of the possible explanations.

Further reading

R. Scribner, *For the Sake of Simple Folk: Popular Propaganda for the German Reformation* (Cambridge University Press, 1981) – emphasises the significance of oral history and contains several illustrations.

Elizabeth Eisenstein, *The Printing Revolution in Early Modern Europe* (Cambridge University Press, 1983) – it offers a rather laboured view of the importance of the press but is a useful starting-point for this topic.

R. A. Houston, *Literacy in Early Modern Europe* (Addison Wesley Longman, 1991) – provides the most recent discussion of literacy levels.

15 Counter-Reformation or Catholic Reformation?

Time chart

1500: Oratory is founded in Genoa

1512: Fifth Lateran Council opens (ends in 1517)

1517: Oratory of Divine Love begins in Rome

1524: Order of Theatines is established in Venice and Naples

1528: Capuchins (reformed Franciscans) founded in Umbria

1530: Barnabites founded in Milan

1534: Paul III (d.1549), first Counter-Reformation Pope

1535: Ursulines founded

1540: Ignatius Loyola (1491–1556) founds the Jesuits

1541: Colloquy of Regensburg

1542: Roman Inquisition begins

1545: Council of Trent begins first session (ends 1549)

1551: Council of Trent begins second session (ends 1552)

1559: Paul IV establishes *Roman Index*; accession of Pius IV (d.1565)

1562: Teresa of Avila (d.1582) founds Order of Discalced Carmelites; Council of Trent begins final session (ends 1563)

1564: Publication of the *Tridentine Index*

1566: Accession of Pius V (d.1572)

1572: Gregory XIII (d.1585) begins improvements to the city of Rome

1585: Sixtus V (d.1590) reorganises the papal Curia

1596: Publication of the *New Index*

Historians have always had difficulty defining historical periods and movements. The term 'Counter-Reformation' was first used by the German jurist Johann Stephan Pütter in 1776 to describe the reaction to Lutheranism in the years following 1517 when the Roman Catholic Church rallied its troops and waged war on the Protestants. It was argued that until the 1530s a corrupt Papacy lived in fear of a general Church council being called and secular rulers were more interested in dynasticism than spiritual reform; that the Catholic revival evident in the second half of the century owed very little to the Middle Ages and a great deal to Martin Luther.

Since the 1970s, some historians have revised this view of the Counter-Reformation. Geoffrey Dickens, for example, has highlighted evidence of a Catholic revival before the advent of Luther. Jean Delumeau has stressed the spiritual well-being among ordinary Catholics independent of any institutional reforms. John Bossy has also drawn attention to the strength of Catholicism in the fifteenth century. It was, he believes, the foundation of its later resurgence as it focused its thoughts and crystallised its aims in response to the Protestant Reformation. In their view, the Counter-Reformation did not begin and end in the sixteenth century but was a much longer, broader and altogether more continuous movement. In this chapter we will examine the nature of change and continuity, of novel and traditional ideas which shaped the Catholic Church in the sixteenth century.

Religious orders

In spite of these differences, historians agree that a prime feature of the Catholic revival was the diverse character of its religious orders. The Jesuits, founded by **Ignatius Loyola** in 1540, have been described as the 'shock-troops' of the Counter-Reformation who gave the movement its cutting edge. But it is important to remember that Loyola conceived his society as a crusading order ready to do battle with the Turkish Muslims rather than the Lutheran Protestants. The Jesuits were just one of several new and reformed orders though their track record subsequently proved more durable and better publicised.

PROFILE: *Ignatius Loyola*

Born into a noble Basque family in 1491, **Loyola** served as a soldier in the Spanish army until he was seriously wounded in 1521. During his convalescence, he had a vision and decided to devote his life to God. He went on a pilgrimage to Montserrat, then lived as a hermit in a cave at Manresa for nine months, before visiting the Holy Land in 1523. On his return he decided to study at Alcalá, then Salamanca and finally Paris universities between 1528 and 1535. In August 1534, he and six friends vowed to convert all Moslems to Christianity but war made it impossible to reach Jerusalem. Instead they went to Rome and pledged their lives in the service of the Pope. Loyola died in 1556.

The fifteenth century saw a wave of popular piety sweep across western Europe which affected secular and spiritual leaders and, in turn, ordinary Christians. This had many expressions:

- The Augustinian canons of Windesheim and the Brethren of the Common Life began the *devotio moderna* (see page 44) in the Netherlands and north Germany.
- A spiritual revival was implemented in Castile and Florence by Ximenes and Savonarola, respectively.
- Dominican and Franciscan orders encouraged missionaries.
- The Carthusians developed transcendental and mystical ideas.

All of which heralded the mainstream sixteenth-century movement.

In Italy, the Oratory of Divine Love – first in Genoa, then in Rome (see time chart) – led to the formation of new orders:

- the Theatines specialised in preaching and charitable work;
- the Capuchins were dedicated to a life of poverty, chastity and obedience;
- the Barnabites cared for the young and the poor;
- the Ursulines educated girls and worked with the poor and the sick.

Outside Italy, Catholic orders and individuals found inspiration in well-established ideas:

- the Dominicans followed the doctrine of the thirteenth-century scholar Thomas Aquinas (known as 'Thomism');
- the Franciscans followed the ideas of Duns Scotus, a thirteenth-century philosopher (developing 'Scotism');
- Ximenes, Erasmus and Colet were inspired by fifteenth-century humanism;
- Loyola was inspired by Carthusianism, an eleventh-century monastic order.

It is clear, then, that the sixteenth-century Catholic Reformation had its roots deeply embedded in medieval precedents.

The Jesuits

The new orders, however, were different from monks, nuns and friars who lived in religious houses. The new orders lived and worked with the people, devoted their lives to charity and preaching, and became noted for their rejection of material possessions. What set the Jesuits apart from their contemporaries was their distinctive training and privileges. Educated for at least 10 years in theology, philosophy, reasoning, logic and humanism, steeped in self-denial and charitable experience, their mind and body disciplined by Loyola's rigorous *Spiritual Exercises*, and pledged to serve God and the Papacy in all matters, only the very best novitiates (novices) completed their training. Less than a third of these were judged academically suitable to take a fourth vow of obedience to the Pope. This vow ordered them 'to perform whatsoever the reigning pontiff should command them, to go forth into all lands, among Turks, heathens or heretics, wherever he might please to send them, without hesitation or delay, as without question, condition or reward'. If the excellence of their education was admired by their enemies, their privileged status was resented by fellow Catholics, for the Papacy released them from restrictive practices like fasting, wearing a clerical habit and keeping the daily canonical routine, so that nothing would impede their vital work.

At first, Jesuit seminaries (training colleges for priests) were established to train the secular clergy in Spain, Portugal and Italy, but the strength of their teaching and academic reputation saw several universities – such as Cologne, Ingolstadt and Munich – establish their own colleges. At Mainz, Trier, Vienna and Würzburg, Jesuits came to staff entire departments and actually ran the universities in Rome, Prague, Osnabrück and Paderborn. Loyola called upon the Jesuits to convert 'persons of considerable importance'. Increasingly their students were sons of the rich and famous, who were well placed to advance the Catholic Reformation. In fact, Jesuit schools were so much in demand that sons of Protestants often sat alongside Catholic novices. By the early seventeenth century more than 3,000 schools, colleges and seminaries were in existence, spread across 32 provinces. The first generation of graduates blazed a well-documented trail as preachers, confessors, private tutors and above all as missionaries. Among the best known were Peter Canisius, who travelled to Austria, Switzerland, Bavaria and the Rhineland, covering 6,000 miles between 1555 and 1558; Francis Xavier who went to India, the East Indies and Japan; and Matteo Ricci who reached China.

The Jesuits were the most important new order but other groups also broke away from the traditional monastic rules and devoted their lives to helping the poor, sick and young in the world at large. The Roman Oratorians and the Spanish Discalced Carmelites (founded in the 1560s), the Camillians (1584), the Piarists (1597), the Visitandines (1610), the Lazarists (1625) and the Daughters of Charity (1633) are all examples of the developing spirit of the Catholic revival. They, like the Jesuits and their predecessors, were the product of their own Christian devotion and God's grace rather than a response to the Protestant Reformation. Yet they were so different from the religious orders of the Middle Ages that some historians feel they 'owed nothing to medieval tradition'.

The Papacy

The Papacy was a major obstacle to Catholic reform. The early sixteenth-century popes had been preoccupied with Italian politics and with the defence of the Papal States. Some pontiffs – like Alexander VI (1492–1503) and Julius II (1503–13) – actively encouraged warfare, while Leo X (1513–21), Hadrian VI (1522–3) and Clement VII (1523–34) were the victims of dynastic quarrels between Charles V and Francis I (see chapter 11). When not at war, papal interests generally settled on secular and artistic pursuits rather than questions of Church unity or clerical reform. Even the emergence of Luther failed to shake the Papacy out of its lethargy. Leo dismissed his challenge to scriptural and papal authority as inaccurate and inconsequential, issued the customary bull of excommunication and called upon the Emperor to enforce it. Perhaps there was little more that he could do under the circumstances.

Hubert Jedin has argued that if a general council of the Church had met in the 1520s it could have halted the growth of Protestantism. While it is impossible to prove this, Italy's unstable political condition and the rivalry between the Catholic Monarch and the Most Christian King did little to encourage reform. Michael Mullett has suggested that the Sack of Rome in 1527 was the event which 'initiated the Italian Catholic Reform as an active process' because it appeared to pious Italians as a 'divine punishment and warning'. Though this is feasible, the impetus for reform was evident before 1527 in the works of Bishop Giberti of Verona and Cardinals Cajetan, Lippomano, Caraffa and Sadoleto in Rome. Also, the threat to the Papal States themselves from the contagious growth of heresy in northern and central Italy played an important part in changing papal attitudes in the 1530s.

If Paul III (1534–49) can be described as the last of the Renaissance popes because of his materialistic and nepotistic tendencies, he was also the first of the Counter-Reformation popes. He set the machinery for reform in motion by commissioning a report on clerical abuses in 1537, licensing the Jesuits in 1540, establishing a Roman Inquisition in 1542 and, three years later, opening the Council of Trent. Little progress was made under his immediate successors, Julius III and Marcellus II, but Paul IV (1555–9) sentenced more than a hundred disreputable friars to the galleys and introduced the first Roman Index in 1559. Pius IV (1559–65) re-summoned the council and in 1563 put its findings into operation. The personal piety and militant Catholicism of Pius V (1566–72) were a potent combination which brought reforms to the Curia and called upon Spain and France to eliminate Dutch Calvinists, French Huguenots, English Protestants and Turkish Muslims. Both Gregory XIII (1572–85) and Sixtus V (1585–90) supported the Catholic armies in their wars of religion but also endorsed more peaceful measures to spread the orthodox faith.

Meanwhile, Rome underwent a major facelift. The city was purged of its many sorcerers, homosexuals and prostitutes, the buildings modernised and numerous seminaries founded. By the end of the sixteenth century, the Papacy had re-established its reputation as the moral and spiritual leader of the Catholic Church, a characteristic that had been so patently lacking in the formative years of the Protestant Reformation.

The Council of Trent

The traditional method of resolving theological and heretical problems was for the Papacy to convene a general council of cardinals, archbishops and bishops and await its verdict. However, the conciliar movement in the early fifteenth century had threatened papal supremacy and made later popes very nervous about calling another council. Lateran (papal) councils continued to be convened but, in spite of the need to reform clerical and administrative abuses and to clarify theological doctrine, the agenda consisted of items of marginal significance. The fifth Lateran Council of 1512, for example, advocated only one major reform: that simony should be prevented at papal elections. Similarly, no progress was made at conferences called by the Church between 1530 and 1541 either in healing the religious schism or resolving disputed theological points. Given the recent history of failure and indifference, especially after the optimistic opening to the Colloquy of Regensburg, observers would have justifiably scoffed at Bishop Bertrano's comment at the opening of the Council of Trent that 'if it will not help those already lost to the Church, it will at least help those still in danger of becoming lost'. Instead they would have agreed with Luther that if 'the remedy comes too late, it will not achieve its purpose'. If Luther had been alive in 1563 when the Tridentine Decrees (as those coming from the Council of Trent were called) were published, he would have been surprised by the Council's achievements.

The numerical dominance of Italian bishops and cardinals and the irrepressible influence of the Jesuits ensured that the Pope emerged supreme and the upper clergy retained their authority over priests. The traditional seven sacraments were reaffirmed and defined such that no compromise was offered to the Protestants. The mass was declared a sacrificial act, celebrated in bread only and sung in Latin. The Vulgate remained the official Bible and all liturgical documents were published in Latin which further served to distance the priest from his congregation. By emphasising the distinct qualities of the clergy and insisting upon a better trained, celibate and resident priesthood, and by transferring the practice of public penance into the private confessional, the Church skilfully combined medieval beliefs with modern requirements.

Finally, a more professional clergy were to be trained in diocesan seminaries, further evidence of the need to produce well-versed preachers and missionaries. Having set its own house in order and weathered potential attacks on its spiritual leadership, the Papacy called upon secular rulers to implement the Tridentine Decrees. No general council of the Catholic Church would be called for another 300 years.

The Inquisition and Index

Protestant writers have tended to give an exaggerated importance to two of the agents associated with the Catholic Reformation – the Roman Inquisition established in 1542, and the Roman Index set up in 1559. Both had medieval and Spanish precedents and fulfilled a repressive role in stamping out heretical beliefs and enforcing perceived standards of social morality. More than 50 per cent of the cases brought before the Roman Inquisition between 1560 and 1614 concerned offences connected with personal enjoyment and pleasure-seeking – like dancing on Sundays and boisterous behaviour during fiestas and carnivals. Like their Spanish counterparts, only a minority of cases investigated by the Italian tribunals dealt with heretics. Much of the inquisitors' time was spent in authorising the publication of books and censoring literature. The first Roman Index proscribed over 500 authors and publishers; five years later, it was replaced by the Tridentine Index and in 1596 by the New Index. It is hard to gauge whether the indexes effectively shielded Catholics from potentially harmful material. Henry Kamen's recent research suggests that the Spanish index had 'little impact on literature and even less on science'. Censorship in both Italy and France proved ineffective.

Mass appeal

A more positive method of countering Protestant literature and spreading Catholic beliefs was the printing press. By simplifying its faith in catechisms, prints, pictures, plays and songs, and by producing a vast amount of devotional material, the Church endeavoured to instruct its congregations and wean them away from their attachment to local religion. Catechisms were particularly important in offering a basic instruction in obedience and civility and in expounding prayers, the Creed and the Ten Commandments. The importance of visual culture, especially painting, must not be underscored. Jacopo Tintoretto's 'Last Supper' (1592), for example, celebrated the Eucharist, Titian's 'The Magdalen' (1532) reminded people of the divinity of the Blessed Virgin, and El Greco's 'St Jerome' (1590) revered martyrdom. Such works of art were just as eloquent and arguably more important than the printed word in transmitting the message of the reformed Catholic Church.

Missionaries and preachers worked hard to appeal to the laity and, recognising the popularity of confraternities, holy relics, saints, pilgrimages and religious processions, rescued them from the attacks of Protestant reformers. Inevitably, Catholic communities clung to their local religious customs and, it seems, successfully resisted attempts at unilateral conformity. Italians suffering from leprosy, for example, continued their practice of jumping into the sea on Easter Saturday to the sound of church bells; German peasants insisted on buying 'Xavier water' to protect their cattle from disease; and in 1644 villagers near Chamonix in France called upon their priest to perform an exorcism to stop an advancing glacier. Belief in the supernatural was deeply embedded in popular and spiritual culture.

Conclusion

The Catholic Church proved extraordinarily adept at seeing off its critics and at adapting to changing circumstances. However, it lacked the unity and resources to recover most of its sheep lost to Protestantism. Its major triumphs were in France, the Spanish Netherlands, Austria, Bavaria, Bohemia and Poland, all of which had wavered between Protestantism and Catholicism in the 1560s but by the mid seventeenth century were irreversibly Catholic. Yet in many cases these achievements were accomplished by the political and military authority of secular rulers rather than by the traditional agents of the Catholic Church. The Wittelsbachs of Bavaria illustrate this point most effectively. Duke Albrecht V (1550–79) started religious visitations in 1558, five years before the conclusion of the Council of Trent, and in 1570 established a College of Ecclesiastical Councillors to enforce the decrees. Maximilian I (1597–1651), a product of Ingolstadt University, went further. In 1629 he set up his own style of inquisition in Bavaria under his Jesuit confessor.

Some rulers refused to recognise the validity of the Tridentine Decrees (as in France and most German states) or enforced them partially or conditionally (as in Spain and Italy), and only a minority of countries (notably

Pluralism

Priests were in theory only allowed to hold one benefice or clerical appointment; **pluralism** is the unlawful practice of holding two or more clerical offices without a licence at any one time. As most benefices carried a low salary, pluralism was a widespread practice in the early sixteenth century.

Concubinage

A concubine is a woman who lives with a man that is not her husband. **Concubinage** is when a cleric, who has taken holy orders and a vow of chastity, cohabits with a woman. This was a common abuse in sixteenth-century Spain.

Portugal and Poland) put them into operation straight away. Moreover, if the overall quality and level of clerical conduct seems to have improved and complaints about absenteeism, **pluralism** and **concubinage** dried up in the course of the seventeenth century, not all dioceses had resident, chaste priests and a seminary. More than half the Italian dioceses, for instance, were without a seminary by 1630 and Paris only agreed to accept one in 1696. It is a salutary reminder that the Counter-Reformation was a slow, patchy and diverse process which owed more to its local teachers, preachers, missionaries and confessors than to institutional reform from Rome. Vincent de Paul in France, François de Sales in Geneva, Carlo Borromeo in Milan, Philip Neri in Rome and Teresa of Avila in Spain were the real inspiration behind the Church's new vitality.

A study of the Counter-Reformation reveals the intricate interplay of continuity and change. The beginnings of the Catholic revival came before the Protestant Reformation, which in turn occasioned certain features of a Counter-Reformation already evolving under its own spiritual regeneration. Countries were affected in varying degrees and at different times so that any attempt to define this movement or to compartmentalise its successes and failures presents the historian with considerable difficulties.

Tasks

Form into groups to discuss, and then write down in note form answers to the following questions.

1 Which do you consider was the most important influence on the revival of the Catholic Church in the sixteenth century:

- monastic orders
- the Jesuits
- the Papacy
- the Council of Trent
- the Index and the Inquisition
- devotional literature?

Explain your reasons, referring briefly to each.

2 Make a list of the reasons given in this chapter for suggesting that the Counter-Reformation was a movement which both preceded the Reformation and reacted to the Reformation.

3 In your view which is the more appropriate term to describe the Catholic revival: the Counter-Reformation or the Catholic Reformation? Explain your answer.

Further reading

K. Randell, *The Catholic and Counter Reformations* (Hodder and Stoughton, 1990) – provides a useful introduction for A- and AS-Level students.

M. Mullett, *The Counter-Reformation*, Lancaster Pamphlets (Methuen, 1984) – a short and readable booklet which sets out the main developments.

N. S. Davidson, *The Counter-Reformation* (Blackwell, 1987) – discusses the impact of the movement.

A. G. Dickens, *The Counter-Reformation* (Thames and Hudson, 1969) – in spite of its age, this book remains essential reading.

J. Delumeau, *Catholicism between Luther and Voltaire: A New View of the Counter-Reformation* (Burns and Oats, 1977) – a revisionist account which has now become a standard work on the Counter-Reformation.

J. Bossy, *Christianity in the West, 1400–1700*, (Oxford University Press, 1985) – scholarly and penetrating ideas.

A. D. Wright, *The Counter-Reformation in Catholic Europe and the Non-Christian World* (E. Mellen Press, 1982) – provides some very thoughtful insights.

M. Jones, *The Counter-Reformation* (Cambridge University Press, 1995) – the most recent work and more difficult.

16 Philip II's influence on Spanish internal affairs

Time chart

1556: Accession of Philip II

1557: Royal debt is rescheduled

1558: Mary Tudor (second wife) dies

1559: Philip arrives in Spain from the Netherlands

1560: Philip suspends interest payments. He marries Elizabeth of Valois (d.1568)

1561: Madrid becomes new capital

1564: Publication in Spain of the *Tridentine Decrees*

1568: Don Carlos dies. *Morisco* rebellion begins

1570: Philip marries Anne of Austria (d.1580)

1572: Appeals to Rome are prohibited

1573: Mateo Vázquez becomes royal secretary

1575: Second rescheduling of royal debt

1578: Murder of Escobedo. Prince Philip is born

1579: Dismissal of Alva. End of 'first' ministry

1583: Granvelle is replaced by 'second ministry' of Zúñiga, Idiáquez and Moura

1590: *Millones* tax. Aragon revolt begins

1596: Third rescheduling of debt

1598: Philip II dies

This chapter studies four key areas of Spanish domestic history in the reign of **Philip II** – government, finance, religion and justice – to discover how they were affected by the character of the King. In an age of personal monarchy Philip epitomised its strengths and weaknesses. More than any other European ruler, he assumed total responsibility for governing his subjects and saw it as his duty to God to fulfil this obligation. The task he set himself was far greater than it needed to be but his devotion to the Catholic faith and obedience to his father's wishes shaped the destiny of Spanish history.

PROFILE: *Philip II*

Born in 1527 in Valladolid, the eldest son of Charles V and Isabella of Portugal, **Philip** received a traditional education from Castilian scholars and theologians. At the age of 12 he attended council meetings, at 16 became Regent of Spain, and, when his father abdicated in 1556, became King. He married four times: in 1543 to Maria of Portugal, who died giving birth to Don Carlos; in 1554 to Mary of England; in 1560 to Elizabeth of France; and in 1570 to Anne of Austria, who provided him with five children. He died in 1598.

Government and administration

In 1543 Charles V had exhorted his son to 'depend on no one but yourself. Make sure of all but rely exclusively on none. In your perplexities trust always in your Maker. Have no care but for him.' Philip applied this advice with exactitude, developing a deep distrust for his ministers and never doubting that he alone should take all decisions in matters of government. A slow thinker and extremely cautious, Philip always preferred to administer by paper. It was, he believed, more discreet than listening to suggestions. However, it is more probable that he felt uneasy in councils, where he might have to make an instant decision. Finding it near impossible to delegate on significant matters, he lacked the political judgement to discriminate quickly between the important and the trivial.

As his reign progressed so the volume of administration multiplied: in 1571 he was reading and annotating an average of 40 memoranda a day and on one occasion he read over 400 papers. Gradually his health began to give way. 'Those devils, my papers' were reportedly giving him severe headaches and eye-strain in the 1570s and at times he despaired how he could continue. In 1577 he told his secretary, 'I have just been given this other packet of papers from you. I have neither the time nor the strength to look at it, and so I will not open it until tomorrow. It is already past 10 o'clock and I have not yet dined.'

In addition to the daily routine, petitions and letters required answering. Administration was a time-consuming business and before any decisions were taken, many intermediaries had to be consulted and secretaries spent hours with the King achieving the exact wording he required. The bureaucratic machinery turned over at its own measured pace. Men who knew Philip II, like Cardinal Granvelle, viewed him as someone who put

159

off decisions. He claimed that 'in all his affairs, his sole decision consisted in remaining eternally indecisive'.

In his defence, however, it should be remembered that the slowness of communications and the changing nature of international affairs encouraged caution. Moreover, Philip may appear to be prudent precisely because so many volumes of documentary material written by him have survived. Some councillors bypassed delays by taking decisions without obtaining royal assent, but this only added to the air of distrust. Once Philip suspected someone of deception he set out to trap them. It was apparent to Gonzalo Pérez in 1565 that 'His Majesty makes mistakes and will continue to make mistakes in many matters because he discusses them with different people, sometimes with one, sometimes with another, conceding something from one minister and revealing it to another'.

Philip was never short of advice. He almost certainly received too much and found it difficult to assess its relative value. Much of the routine administration was delegated to his more trustworthy officers, but ministries were short-lived and unsettled because he was eternally suspicious. One of the most spectacular dismissals was that of Cardinal Espinosa who, according to the King, was the most able of his servants but who nevertheless fell from power in 1572 when Philip believed he held too much responsibility. His fall paved the way for Mateo Vázquez to rise to prominence as the King's private secretary and confessor between 1573 and 1591. He provided the continuity of government which factional rivalry and Philip's intriguing did so much to frustrate. Vázquez suggested that he should read the King's private correspondence, memorials and *consultas*, and then draft the appropriate recommendations which Philip would approve. Vázquez's long tenure in office owed much to his skill at playing down his own importance in the administration and not giving any cause to suspect or distrust him. It was a singular achievement.

Three consistent traits are apparent in Philip's administration.

1 He generally preferred Castilians and only a few outside the charmed court circle received principal appointments and rewards. Men like Espinosa, Vázquez, Zúñiga; and the Guzmán, Mendoza, Enríquez and Toledo families dominated central government.

2 The King's desire to be well informed led to his ministers attending several councils whereby each acquired just enough knowledge to keep the others in check but never enough to be omnipotent. Francisco de Eraso, for instance, was secretary to six councils and a member of two

KEY TERM:

Consultas

Summaries of council meetings, drafted by royal secretaries, were known as *consultas*. They were drawn up for the King's consultation; if he approved, they received his authorisation.

more in 1559. Cardinal Espinosa served as inquisitor-general and as president of the councils of Castile and the Indies.

3 As the administration expanded and Philip sought to increase state control, so he required more lawyers (known as *letrados*) than grandees and nobles. This resulted in frequent quarrels between grandees and *letrados*, and ministers, secretaries and officials were always ready to cut the ground from under one another's feet. Rival factions characterised each ministry: in the 1560s between Eboli and Alva, in the 1570s Pérez and Alva, and for most of the 1580s and 1590s Idiáquez, Zúñiga, Moura and Chinchón.

Philip's decision to establish his capital in Madrid rather than in Toledo or Valladolid, taken in 1561, ensured he would be surrounded by his 14 councils. Each exercised executive, legislative and judicial power. No attempt was made to unify them but each was treated as a separate satellite responding to his command. In this way he hoped to know all aspects of a problem anywhere in his *monarquía* at any given moment. In practice, his knowledge was fragmentary and at times inaccurate. As he never travelled outside the peninsula after 1559, he had no ready way of validating what he had been told. From 1566 he resided most spring and summer months in the Escorial – part palace, part mausoleum and part monastery, it was his ultimate defence against an intrusive world (see Figure 16.2).

The administration of each of Philip's dominions largely depended upon viceroys, governors and royal servants, most of whom he never met and whose activities were watched over by permanent institutions such as the *audiencias* (courts of appeal). The system was one of checks and balances: the viceroy, for example, was monitored by the *audiencia*, the *audiencia* by the viceroy, and both were scrutinised by the council in Madrid which was answerable to the King. The Crown's principal servant in local government was the *corregidor*. Trained in the law and appointed by the councils in Madrid, some 66 *corregidores* presided over town councils and exercised considerable authority. Their main political function was to manage local councils and influence the election of the *procuradores* (local representatives) to the Cortes to ensure that they were willing servants of the Crown rather than tools of their constituents. This was never an easy task, as became evident in 1566. Philip instructed all *corregidores* to secure the return of deputies who were ready to grant taxation unconditionally. Most of the local councils strongly resisted this infringement of their customary rights and there was little the *corregidores* could do to stop them. They experienced similar difficulties in the 1580s when called upon to coerce town councils into providing more money, men and materials for the war effort. In 1588 Valladolid would not draw up a

SCENOGRAPHIA FABRICÆ ✝ S LAVRENTII IN ESCVRIAL

Figure 16.2 *The Escorial, near Madrid*

muster list; in 1590 Seville ignored requests to raise troops; and in Murcia unpopular crown nominees were rejected in favour of traditional captains. The Crown was powerless to act, and at times it appears that even the *corregidores* colluded with the local nobles to exercise as much independence as was mutually convenient. Loyalty to the Crown existed but it was not so compelling as the opportunities of self-advancement.

Finances

Charles V once advised his son to 'attend closely to finances and learn to understand the problems involved'. Philip, like a dutiful son, stuck at his task and earned a reputation for prudence. However, he never mastered the intricacies of the royal finances. Inheriting a debt of 36 million ducats, an annual deficit of 1 million, *asiento* repayments (loans) of 14 million and a system which was riddled with corruption, Philip became increasingly depressed by his failure to turn the ship of state around. His principal source of revenue remained the *alcabala* (a 10 per cent tax on sales which trebled in the course of his reign), customs duties, indirect taxes on silk, salt and sheep, and bullion from the New World. By 1598 ordinary revenue was in excess of 4 million ducats – three times as much as in 1556 – but still insufficient to meet his expenses. Every effort was therefore made to raise extra taxes from the Cortes and the Church, and expedients such as the selling of land, titles and offices. Economies were also made at Court where Philip exercised personal frugality though he could not resist filling his palaces with expensive artefacts, which have been valued at 7 million ducats, or building the Escorial at an estimated cost of 5.5 million ducats. Financing the army and navy was the greatest item of royal expenditure. At first annual military costs averaged less than 2 million ducats, but in the 1570s they had risen to 4 million and by 1598 exceeded 10 million ducats.

The only way Philip could bridge the gap between revenue and expenditure was to borrow money. Deficit financing was nothing new to continental countries but the scale of his commitments and the frequency of state bankruptcies were unprecedented. In 1557, 1560, 1575 and 1596 he suspended repayments and converted the floating debt into low-interest bonds in an attempt to break the stranglehold of his creditors.

Philip acknowledged his own lack of expertise: 'I have never been able to get this business of loans and interests into my head', he candidly informed his secretary in 1580. This criticism of the King is forgivable but not when he insisted on taking all financial decisions and all too readily succumbed to the advice of self-interested financiers. As a result, proposals to create a state bank, centralise the administration and reform the council of finance all made good economic sense but were hit on the head by those who had most to lose. By 1598 the national debt stood at 85 million ducats and carried interest payments which alone accounted for 40 per cent of Philip's total revenue. Although finance was his blind spot, he lacked the confidence to trust those who could have assisted him. He once confessed to Vázquez, 'I cannot tell a good memorial on the subject from a bad one and I do not wish to break my brains trying to comprehend something which I do not understand now nor have ever understood in all my days.' It was a sad but true admission.

Religion

Philip's devotion to the Catholic faith was legendary. Throughout his life, he attended mass daily, heard sermons weekly and received communion quarterly. Pious and orthodox, he endowed monasteries and shrines, kept religious books at his bedside and saw evidence of divine intervention in all affairs. God was omniscient; His cause was Philip's cause. In 1566 he reminded Pius V that 'rather than suffer the least damage to religion and the service of God, I would lose all my states and a hundred lives, if I had them; for I do not propose nor desire to be the ruler of heretics'. Behind this diplomatic statement lay a basic truism: Philip knew

KEY TERMS:

Autos de fe

Penitential ceremonies where judgement on heretics was passed, after which they were publicly burned at the stake.

Fifth-columnist activities

This term is used to describe a group of spies sympathising with, and working for, the enemy within a country. In the Spanish Civil War (1936–9), General Franco attacked Madrid with four armies and declared that a fifth group of sympathisers within the city was assisting the besiegers.

it was his duty as a Christian and as the Most Catholic King to eliminate all brands of heterodoxy from his dominions. Heresy was not a serious problem in Spain but the Inquisition remained eternally vigilant and received full support from the Crown. Philip actually presided over five *autos de fe* and appears to have enjoyed them. In 1574 he informed Espinosa, 'I shall always favour and assist the affairs of the Inquisition because I know the reasons and obligations which exist for doing so, and for me more than anyone'. It was, however, neither conceived nor used by him as an instrument of royal power. Only on one occasion, in 1591, when he was trying to silence Antonio Pérez, did he mobilise its machinery for a blatantly political purpose, and, significantly, it proved unsuccessful.

Mystics, humanists, Protestants, deviant Catholics, lapsed *Moriscos* and *Conversos* became the staple diet of the 15 tribunals in Spain. In all it has been estimated that the Inquisition dealt with about 40,000 cases, most of them involving ordinary Catholics accused of religious or moral deviation, though fewer than 250 were burned at the stake. The cases brought before each tribunal, however, varied considerably. In Castile, the Toledo Inquisition dealt mainly with cases concerning *Conversos*, blasphemy, sacrilege and sex outside marriage. The tribunals of Granada, Saragossa and Valencia, on the other hand, devoted most of their time to investigating *Moriscos*. Their growing number, their suspected **fifth-columnist activities** and their subsequent revolt in 1568–70 convinced Philip that they must be deported from Granada. Rather than agree to their total expulsion, however, he intermittently expelled and re-settled them in Castile, Valencia and Catalonia, thereby creating more work for these tribunals.

Philip's relationship with the Papacy was surprisingly cool. A devout Catholic he may have been but he viewed the Pope as another princely ruler whose spiritual, as well as secular, authority fell short of his own on the Iberian peninsula. Before publishing the Council of Trent's Decrees in 1564, Philip instructed his lawyers to ensure that they contained nothing that might alter or reduce his authority or the powers of the Spanish Inquisition. Three years later, when Pius V issued an edict banning bullfights and excommunicated all participants, Philip disregarded it. In 1572 he denied his subjects the right of appeal to Rome. Clashes also occurred over the authority exercised in Spain by Jesuits and the Curia's support for the Italian Aquaviva, general of the order, whom Philip tried unsuccessfully to remove in the 1590s. He further resented the Papacy's persistent hectoring over his foreign policy and responded by telling popes to mind their own business.

Justice

The prevailing view in the sixteenth century was that the Spanish monarchy was absolute. Royal pageantry and the mystical coronation ceremony hedged the King with a divinity that surpassed popular understanding and, as God's sovereign ruler, he was the supreme law-giver. It was his prerogative to take all decisions, to interpret and when necessary override the laws, which in theory rendered his authority '*ab solutus*', free from control of the laws. Such power was needed for those rare occasions when justice required his intervention, but this did not give him the right to flout the law. Like his subjects, Philip was under the rule of divine and natural law, but whereas they had to answer to the king's judges, he was answerable to God alone. Contemporary scholars and jurists like Luis de Molina and Francisco Suárez were generally agreed that all men, including the King, were subject to natural law, but if he acted outside the law or imposed unjust laws upon his subjects, it remained their duty to obey him.

The maintenance and enforcement of law and order was the prime duty of all monarchs; without justice, government was neither respected nor effective. Philip aimed to be resolute and fair, which was in line with his father's advice to impart justice 'in such a manner that the wicked find him terrible and the good find him benign'. He inherited a system of hierarchical law courts which appears to have operated impartially. The Council of Castile acted as the supreme court of law, dispensing justice, hearing appeals and making recommendations to the King. For his part, Philip did his best to ensure no favouritism was shown to members of the nobility. Indeed Castillo de Bobadilla claimed in 1597 that 'there is no judge now who cannot act against them and take their silver and horses'.

Contemporaries certainly regarded Philip as 'the justest of rulers'. If he felt that natural justice could be or had been perverted, then he was prepared to intervene. In 1593 he used his prerogative to dispense with the law when he insisted that Toledo convicts who were transferred from serving on galleys to the mercury mines at Almadén had to be released as soon as they had served their sentences. 'Although galley labour may be harder than the mine', said Philip, 'it is not my wish that they be harmed.'

Sometimes the Crown intervened for reasons which were far from equitable, and it is on account of these occasions that charges of tyranny have been laid against the King. It was commonplace in all countries for men to be arrested, held indefinitely without trial and tortured. Philip was not above the authorisation of state murders. His mentally unstable son, Don

Carlos, died in solitary confinement in 1568 amid suspicious circumstances. Baron Montigny, a Dutch envoy to Spain, was charged with treason and, after four years' imprisonment, strangled in Simancas Castle in 1570. Juan de Escobedo, a double-agent, was found murdered in a Madrid side street after he threatened to reveal state secrets in 1578. 'It is preferable that all take heed from the public punishment of the few', Philip once said, and anyone who betrayed his trust was dealt with summarily. The Justiciar of Aragon and two of his associates, for instance, were executed without trial in 1590 as a result of their complicity in a revolt which directly challenged Philip's authority.

Conclusion

Philip was an uncompromising king. Strongly principled and convinced that his judgement was infallible, he trusted few of his ministers and ruled autocratically. Shortly after his death in 1598, a grandee declared that the world 'would see what the Spanish were worth now that they have a free hand, and are no longer subject to a single brain that thought it knew all that could be known and treated everyone else as a blockhead'. Few sixteenth-century monarchs took their royal duties so seriously or were temperamentally so ill-suited to the task. He neither had a strong physique nor good health. By the time he was 50, his body had become rounded, his reddish hair and beard turned white and his eyes were bloodshot with fatigue. Nor could he be a popular king because he isolated himself from his subjects, restricted his public appearances and, following two attacks on his life in the early 1580s, travelled in a sealed coach. Respected, feared, but never loved by his people, Philip II possessed many of the qualities that Spaniards admired and many that his enemies despised. To Castilians, he was benevolent, dutiful, just, *El Prudente*; to his critics, he was arrogant, hypocritical, bigoted and tyrannical – the spider king, the weaver of plots.

Task: writing examination essays

Philip II is a popular A-Level topic for students and examiners alike. The significance of his character in shaping his ideas and policies has long been recognised by historians, and is still regarded as central to our understanding of his reign. Select one of the following questions which concern his domestic problems. If you wish to write an essay under test conditions, allow yourself about 45 minutes to complete it. Each essay is followed with some hints on how it might be tackled.

Question 1

'How far did the domestic problems faced by Philip II stem from his own character?'

Hints: this question is about Philip II's domestic *problems* rather than about his character. You will probably begin by identifying the various problems he faced in the course of his reign – this can best be achieved by examining his problems thematically. (If you take the alternative approach and tackle his problems chronologically, your essay will become a narrative of his reign, and fail to focus on the issues in question.) Look at the political, governmental, administrative, financial, economic, social and religious problems. In each case, consider how far Philip's character created or worsened the problems. Were other factors as important *(e.g.* his inheritance)? This topic covers a range of material so remember to keep your argument and examples under tight control. Practise writing to time; you are unlikely to master this skill first time round.

Question 2

'Was Philip II an absolute monarch?'

Hints: begin by suggesting what the term 'absolute' might mean. Then link it to Philip's personality, to his power in central government and in the regions, and to control over the Church, especially the Inquisition. Consider what limits there were to his authority *(e.g.* financial) and how effective was his rule over his kingdoms outside Castile. If you believe that he was not an 'absolute' monarch, then try to explain why some historians have argued that he was. Your conclusion should be your own, but should recognise that different views have been taken.

Question 3

'Does Philip II deserve to be remembered as a "prudent king"?'

Hints: what does the phrase 'prudent king' mean? Careful, cautious, hesitant, or slow perhaps? Examine different aspects of his administration to see whether this is a fair comment *(e.g.* look at his decisions taken in council, his handling of the Cortes, economic investments, religious reforms, budgeting of finances, and patronage of the arts). Reach a conclusion based on your own judgement.

Question 4

'Was Philip II a successful ruler of Spain?'

Hints: any question about Philip's 'success' requires you to measure his achievements against his aims. To do this, start by briefly outlining his aims in 1556, consider how he tried to implement them, the difficulties he had to overcome, and those areas in which he was successful and unsuccessful. Reasons for success need to be explained and, where appropriate, moments of significance commented upon. A brief comparison might be offered, either with any other Spanish ruler or with a contemporary such as Elizabeth I. Success is a subjective term: remember that contemporaries regarded Philip as a very successful king but modern historians have been less fulsome in their praise.

Question 5

'His sole motivation was religion.' Discuss.

Hints: questions which invite you to discuss a quotation are open-ended and present certain difficulties. As there is little tangible to get hold of in the title, you may struggle to get started unless you decide at the beginning what the question is about and plan your response carefully. Try rephrasing the quotation. In this case it implies that Philip was inspired by, and only interested in, the Catholic faith. Now although Catholicism was very important to him, he was motivated by additional influences. Economic, social and political affairs, for instance, were often pursued independently of his religion. Examine the significance of his faith, and then look at those features of his reign which were not affected by it. In this way you will achieve a balanced argument. As a discussion of the quotation is required, there will be no right or wrong answer. Remember, finally, that all questions which include 'absolute' phrases – 'sole motivation', 'entirely unsuccessful', 'no chance of success' *etc.* – are an open invitation to qualified disagreement. History essays should always show awareness of 'shades of grey'.

Further reading

G. H. Woodward, *Philip II*, Seminar Studies in History (Addison Wesley Longman, 1992) – offers the most recent assessment.

P. Pierson, *Philip II of Spain* (Thames and Hudson, 1975) – provides a reliable account of his life and times.

G. Parker, *Philip II* (Hutchinson, 1979) – an excellent biography written by an expert.

J. Lynch, *Spain, 1516–98: From Nation State to World Empire* (Blackwell, 1991) – sets Philip against his inherited problems.

I. A. A. Thompson, *War and Society in Habsburg Spain* (Athlone Press, 1992) – demonstrates how the administration coped with the difficulties of war.

H. Koenigsberger, 'The statecraft of Philip II' in *Politicians and Virtuosi: Essays in Early Modern History* (Hambledon, 1986) – considers Philip's character at work.

A. D. Wright, *Catholicism and Spanish Society under the Reign of Philip II, 1555–98, and Philip III, 1598–1621* (E. Mellen Press, 1991).

17 Philip II's foreign policy

Time chart

1556: Philip becomes King of Spain

1557: Battle of St Quentin

1559: Peace of Câteau-Cambrésis ends war with France

1565: Bayonne meeting. Relief of Malta

1566: The first Dutch Revolt begins

1568: Elizabeth seizes Genoese silver fleet

1571: Battle of Lepanto

1572: Second Dutch revolt begins at Brill and Flushing

1578: Sebastian I, King of Portugal, dies

1579: Spanish troops assist Munster rebellion

1580: Portugal is annexed. Turks sign treaty of peace

1584: Philip joins the Catholic League; signs the Treaty of Joinville

1585: Spain prepares for war with England

1587: Execution of Mary, Queen of Scots

1588: The Armada sails

1594: Henry of Navarre is crowned King of France

1595: Spain declares war on France

1598: Treaty of Vervins ends war with France. Philip dies

The aims and motives behind Philip's foreign policy have long perplexed historians, as they did most contemporaries. In 1559 the Venetian Ambassador, Michele Suriano, suggested that Philip did not intend 'to wage war so that he can add to his kingdoms but to wage peace so that he can keep the lands he has'. In Suriano's view, the King was a gamekeeper not a poacher. Thirty years later, Pope Sixtus V was not so sure. 'The King of Spain, as a temporal sovereign, is anxious above all to safeguard and to increase his dominions.' The papal nuncio (representative of the Pope) in Madrid wrote in a similar vein. 'He says he does not want the property of others, but the chances of the occasion, the penchant for domination which is innate in men, unforeseen incidents, could end in the establishment of a universal monarchy.'

The myth of the 'black legend' – the notion that Spain was destined to rule Europe if not the world – may have originated in Italy but it was widely believed by Catholics in France, Protestants in England and Philip's own subjects in the Netherlands. Modern historians are also divided on the subject. Four schools of thought predominate:

1 That Philip, the Most Catholic King, was inspired by his faith as the secular champion of the Counter-Reformation and that this was the mainspring of his foreign policy. This interpretation – first proffered by the German historian Leopold von Ranke in 1843 – has more recently been endorsed by Philip's biographer, Geoffrey Parker.

2 That Philip II was motivated by political ambition and wished to extend his *monarquía* over western Europe. Writing in 1937, R. Trevor Davies claimed:

> *'To Philip, no doubt, all his policy was consciously directed to the glory of God and the good of his Church; but these things were identical in his mind with the exaltation of the power of Spain ... Whenever political interest and religious zeal clashed, religious zeal almost invariably gave way.'*
>
> R. Trevor Davies, *The Golden Century of Spain, 1501–1621* (1937).

3 That he was intent upon defending Spain's reputation and security, preferably by peaceful diplomacy but if necessary by war. Robert Stradling believes this motive was inseparable from his religious goal.

> *'His prior and unquestioning task was to defend in arms the interests of God and His Church, to a degree which was, quite simply, absolute. It was the essence of the contract between the Habsburg rulers and their maker and benefactor, that they would unceasingly advance His cause, just as He automatically protected theirs. In terms of policy-making, therefore, spiritual and secular arguments were in the last analysis identical.'*
>
> R. A. Stradling, *Europe and the Decline of Spain. A Study of the Spanish System, 1580–1720* (1981).

4 That Philip was inspired by personal considerations which overrode religious and political issues and resulted in his behaving in an opportune and at times inconsistent manner. In this chapter, Philip's relations with four countries – France, Portugal, the Ottoman Empire and England – will be assessed before reaching a conclusion (see Figure 17.1).

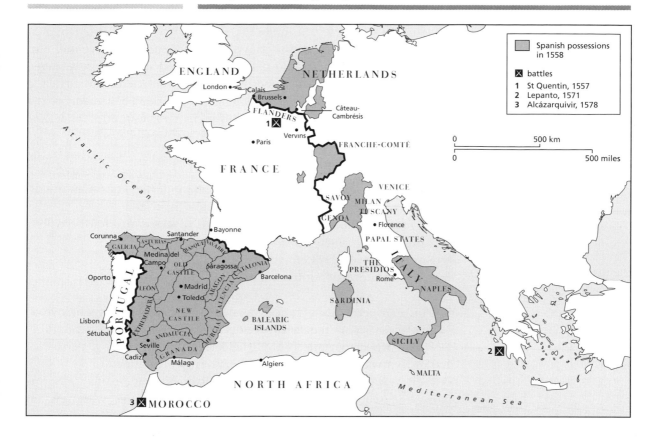

Figure 17.1 The monarquía of Philip II

France

Antonio Pérez once informed Philip, 'The heart of the Spanish Empire is France'. In 1556 and for much of his reign this was certainly true. Having first enlisted the support of England, Philip launched a 'blitzkrieg' on the preselected and vulnerable French town of St Quentin. The young Spanish King's triumph in 1557 not unexpectedly caused the old French king, Henry II, to retaliate by capturing Calais, an English fortress nominally under Philip's jurisdiction through his marriage to the English queen, Mary I. By 1559, neither France nor Spain could afford to carry on fighting and as each had gained a victory over the other, their reputations were safeguarded. At the peace of Câteau-Cambrésis, the fate of Savoy and Calais – the two key issues – was resolved. France gave up all claims to Italy, retained Calais and agreed to a double marriage between Philip and Elizabeth, Henry's daughter, and between the Duke of Savoy and Margaret, Henry's sister. Philip was delighted with the treaty: he had won his laurels on the international stage, he had a new wife and Italy would not again be contested by France.

Philip's policy towards France after 1559 was to keep it politically divided and religiously united. The outbreak of the civil wars assisted him in achieving the first aim but the growth of Huguenotism prevented him from accomplishing the second. For much of the 1560s he wisely stayed out of French affairs and confined himself to sending letters of advice to the queen mother, Catherine de' Medici. Much has been made of the secret meeting at Bayonne in 1565 between Alva, Catherine and King Charles IX. The Duke of Alva, a Spanish envoy, pressed Catherine to act against the French Huguenots, to join in an attack on the heretics in the Netherlands, and to consider further Habsburg–Valois marriages, but such discussions remained inconclusive except in fertile Protestant minds.

In fact, Franco-Spanish relations were about to take a turn for the worse.

1 Family ties were broken when Philip's French wife died in 1568 and he turned her sister down in favour of an Austrian princess.

2 Philip suspected that France was starting to probe his imperial weaknesses. In 1570 French Huguenots attacked Spanish Navarre and in 1571 he learned that one of their leaders, Admiral Coligny, persuaded Charles to invade the Netherlands. Apparently they aimed to partition it between France, England and the Holy Roman Empire but Catherine vetoed the scheme at the eleventh hour and Charles withdrew his support.

Philip was delighted when he heard of the massacre of St Bartholomew in 1572; Coligny was dead, some 12,000 Huguenots had been slaughtered and France was again at war with itself.

The defence of Navarre and the Netherlands was central to Philip's thinking after 1572. The rising star in the French galaxy was Henry Bourbon, King of Navarre, who – as well as having a claim to the throne of France and Spanish Navarre – was leader of the Huguenots. Of equal concern to Philip was the behaviour of Francis, Duke of Anjou (brother of Henry III). Anjou was restless for real power and aware that he was less than welcome at his elder brother's court. For six years he tried unsuccessfully to assist the Dutch rebels against Spain until he died in 1584.

His death made Henry of Navarre heir-presumptive and it was now in the mutual interests of Philip, French Catholics and the Guises to prevent him from becoming king of France. In September the Duke of Guise, his two brothers and two nobles formed a Catholic League to keep Navarre off the French throne. In December 1584 at Joinville, Philip joined them. 'In truth we have been moved to negotiate this because it seems to be the only way to remedy matters of religion in that kingdom', Philip wrote to Don Juan de Idiáquez. He committed troops and cash to the League, though in practice he exercised little control over the Guises, who seemed better at spending his money than advancing his cause. He had even less control over Henry III, who skilfully evaded Spanish requests for access to a deep-water Channel port for the Armada in 1588. The assassinations of Guise and his brother, and finally of Henry III, convinced Philip that he must intervene in France if he was to prevent Navarre's accession. Neither planned nor desired, the military option now became inevitable. 'The affairs of France are at this moment the principal thing', he informed General Parma. Three million ducats were sent to the surviving members of the Catholic League and Parma was ordered to invade France with his Army of Flanders.

In 1590 Spanish troops occupied Paris, Brittany and eastern France. Henry of Navarre's days appeared to be numbered. When his elderly uncle, the Cardinal of Bourbon, who had a claim to the French throne, died in May, Philip suggested that his own daughter, Isabella, should become the next monarch. Philip's motives are as hard to discern now as they were then. The French suspected he was seeking to extend his empire at their expense, though this seems unlikely. He knew that the Salic Law debarred a female from the French throne but of course he could always rule in Isabella's name. Pope Clement VIII believed that Philip wanted to establish a universal monarchy and rejected his claims to be the protector of French Catholics, but of course his Holiness's opinion was not without bias.

The death of Parma in December 1592 was a bitter blow to Spanish ambitions, and when Henry of Navarre declared his conversion to the Catholic faith, Philip's cause became hopeless. Foolishly, he persisted in challenging Henry's right to the throne even after the Catholic Church and French people had been won over. He announced that Isabella would be proclaimed Queen of France and would marry Ernst, heir-presumptive to the imperial throne; if the people preferred a French husband, then Charles, Duke of Guise, was acceptable to Philip. This piece of Spanish impertinence united the French nation far more effectively than anything Henry could have said or done.

In February 1594 Henry was crowned King Henry IV and less than a year later declared war on Spain. The wheel had come full circle. Philip was again fighting France but in less promising circumstances than in 1556. In spite of initial Spanish victories at Calais and Amiens, subsequent losses in 1597 and impending bankruptcy convinced Philip that peace must be concluded. The resulting Treaty of Vervins in 1598 enabled France to recover Calais, Brittany and Languedoc, and on balance to emerge as the victor.

Corsairs

These were pirates who attacked shipping and made inroads (Latin: *cursus*) at another's expense. The Barbary **corsairs** operated in the Mediterranean from their bases along the Barbary coast in the western part of north Africa.

Turkey

Most Spaniards regarded the Mediterranean as the true sphere of royal influence in the mid sixteenth century. In the 1550s the Turks threatened Spain's north African coastline and endangered its communications with Naples and Sicily. Not until 1559 was Philip freed from his northern commitments and able to devote his resources to the problem. The island of Djerba off the coast of Tripoli was the target of an expedition in 1560 but a surprise attack was routed by **corsairs**. Ten thousand troops and eight galleys were captured. Philip's reputation was hurt but he did not have a navy large enough to respond until 1564. Then he attacked Morocco and seized Peñón de Vélez.

The relief of Malta in 1565 by the Viceroy of Naples further enhanced Philip's prestige but he was not keen to follow up this success and only with great reluctance agreed to join a naval crusade against the Turks. Privately he had grave doubts about its chances of success and indicated that he would have withdrawn had he not believed that 'our prestige will certainly suffer if we do not provide what we promised'. Nevertheless, at Lepanto in 1571, the Ottoman fleet suffered an unexpected defeat. Though Philip only contributed 79 out of 208 ships, he enjoyed the kudos of victory. Titian was commissioned to paint on a particularly large canvas, 'Spain Coming to the Aid of Religion'.

From 1575 Philip sounded out the possibility of reaching a truce with the Sultan. Each had domestic troubles and reached the same pragmatic conclusion that neither could win the Mediterranean conflict. Moreover, each was willing to set aside religious goals in the face of political reality, and agreed to a treaty in 1580. When news broke, the Pope was mortified, the Venetians felt betrayed but Philip remained unmoved. Unlike his father, he was not a crusader; on the contrary, he believed it was his Christian duty to reach an honourable understanding with the Turks. The benefits were mutual. They could expand towards the Caspian Sea and engage the Persians in war; he could confidently turn his back on the Mediterranean and attend to Portugal and northern Europe.

Portugal

Portugal was ruled by Sebastian I until his ill-fated decision to lead a crusade against the Turks resulted in his disappearance and presumed death at Alcázarquivir in 1578. The heir was his great-uncle Henry, a deaf, half-blind, toothless, 66-year old cardinal who was far from well when he married the 13-year-old daughter of the Duchess of Bragança.

On 31 January 1580 Henry died and a succession dispute broke out. Philip was well prepared, having already set up a Portuguese committee to advance his claim. On paper he was the best male claimant on account of his Portuguese mother but he faced challenges from Don António and Catalina, Duchess of Bragança. Philip responded decisively. The Portuguese nobility, clergy and merchants were bribed, and opposition towns like Oporto, Lisbon and Sétubal forced to recognise him as their king.

The annexation of Portugal in 1580 can be regarded as a turning-point in Philip's foreign policy. For the first time since the Roman occupation the Iberian peninsula was under one Christian ruler and with a *monarquía* comprising more than 40 million people, he was the most powerful man in the world. The Portuguese Empire brought him much needed wealth, a stronger navy, and enormous prestige. However, above all, after years of financial difficulties, he now had a base from which he could launch expeditions to the Netherlands, England and France. After 1580 he had sufficient resources to pursue a more aggressive foreign policy. If Philip had ever harboured ambitions, particularly in relation to England, he could now put them into practice.

England

Philip shed few tears at the death of his second wife, Mary Tudor, in 1558 but he was concerned to retain Elizabeth's friendship and to offset the Guises' influence in Scotland and France. Early in 1559 he suggested that he might marry Elizabeth but his offer was primarily designed to impress the French negotiators at Câteau-Cambrésis. Privately, he was relieved when she turned him down and he was free to marry Elizabeth of Valois instead. Between 1559 and 1567 Anglo-Spanish relations were cordial but never rock-solid because they rested merely on mutual opposition to the Guises and personal ties, rather than on trade and family connections. Elizabeth I's Protestant religious settlement of 1559 disturbed Philip but he believed the time was not right to intervene in English affairs. He informed Feria, his ambassador in London: 'The evil that is taking place in that kingdom has caused me the anger and confusion I have mentioned ... but we must try to remedy it without involving me or any of my vassals in a declaration of war until we have enjoyed the benefits of peace.' In the 1560s, Philip personally persuaded the Papacy not to excommunicate Elizabeth. He was fearful that such action might trigger off an English Catholic revolt which France would exploit. Neither a minor trade war nor trouble in the Netherlands was allowed to disturb the Anglo-Spanish diplomatic harmony.

The turning-point in Philip's relationship with Elizabeth came in 1567 and the key to it lay in the Netherlands. Elizabeth was convinced by her councillors, Leicester and Walsingham, that if the Dutch revolt of 1566 was suppressed, Philip would try to regain England for the Catholic faith. In hindsight this seems highly unlikely since Philip was neither willing nor able to undertake such an enterprise in 1567, and there is no evidence in the Spanish archives to support their analysis of Philip's motives. Of course, if pricked, he would feel obliged to defend his honour as best he could. Over the next 18 years Elizabeth more than pricked him: she attempted to bleed him white. First, in 1568 she seized Genoese silver ships bound for the Netherlands; then in the 1570s she encouraged privateers to plunder the Spanish Main. In the 1580s she gave political asylum to Don António, the Portuguese pretender. Then, after many years of prevarication, she sent an army to the Netherlands in 1585. English troops had invaded his territory and challenged his sovereignty. They must be removed and his reputation avenged.

The breakdown in Anglo-Spanish relations was not entirely England's fault. Philip also acted provocatively. In 1571 he approved his council of state's recommendation to send an army to help Mary, Queen of Scots, secure the English throne. He informed the Duke of Alva: 'I am so keen to achieve the consummation of this enterprise, I am so attached to it in my heart, and I am so convinced that God our saviour must embrace it as his own cause that I cannot be dissuaded from putting it into operation.' Even so, it became increasingly obvious that this enterprise (known as the Ridolfi plot) was doomed to fail and Philip cancelled his orders. For 20 years he had questioned the wisdom of putting Mary Stuart on the English throne – it was neither practicable nor expedient – but after 1580 it became desirable. The Guises were no longer a threat, Turkey was preoccupied and Portugal was in the bag. If the Netherlands were still a nightmare, he had not been helped by Elizabeth's dishonesty and continued endorsement of Protestantism. In 1580 Philip stirred the Irish waters by encouraging an armed uprising there; three years later he was clearly involved in the Throckmorton plot to assassinate the Queen and start an English Catholic uprising in preparation for an invasion. By 1585 his patience was exhausted. As the Most Catholic King, it was time to teach Elizabeth a lesson.

Historians agree that Philip may have had several aims in sending the Armada of 1588 but that his prime objective was to stop England from interfering in the Netherlands. The English navy impeded his control of the sea and without it he would not recover the disobedient Dutch provinces. A projected attack on England would tie down Elizabeth's fleet and commit her to heavy defence. Perhaps Philip was mindful of the Venetian Ambassador's comment that 'vigorous preparations for war are the surest way to secure favourable terms of peace'. Ideally, Philip would have welcomed the conversion of England to Catholicism, and there is no reason to doubt that religion was a genuine motive, even if a secondary one, as he prepared the 'Great Enterprise'. After all, 180 clerics accompanied the fleet, 24 Jesuits waited in Flanders and Cardinal Allen, an English-born missionary, was ready to assume control of religious affairs in England. Philip instructed Parma in April 1588 that even if the invasion was only partially successful, he must demand toleration for Catholics. The King explained:

> 'With regard to the free exercise of Catholicism, you may point out to them that since freedom of worship is allowed to the Huguenots in France, there will be no sacrifice of dignity in allowing the same privilege to Catholics in England.'

Philip was a realist not a visionary; the Armada was not primarily a religious crusade. He doubted the strength of English Catholics to rise up in support of an armed invasion, and there is no evidence that he intended the complete conquest of England or even believed that it was possible. At best he hoped to secure the south-east between Margate and London as a bargaining counter to accomplish his more pragmatic objectives of peace, compensation and toleration for Catholics.

Mary Stuart's execution in February 1587 played no decisive part in determining Philip's course of action. By then he had already decided to attack England. However, as he explained to the Marquis de Olivares in a letter which predated her death:

> 'Failing the Queen of Scotland, the right to the English crown falls to me.
> My claim, as you are aware rests upon my descent from the House of
> Lancaster, and upon the will made by the Queen of Scotland, and
> mentioned in a letter from her of which the copy is enclosed herewith.
> I cannot undertake a war in England for the purpose merely of placing
> upon that throne a young heretic like the King of Scotland who, indeed, is
> by his heresy incapacitated to succeed.'

Did Philip seriously consider laying claim to England? It seems likely although Mendoza was instructed to reassure the Pope that it was Philip's intention to settle the crown upon his daughter, the Infanta. The Armada's failure destroyed all of Philip's English schemes but after re-assessing the situation, he set about rebuilding his fleet. Two further armadas set sail in 1596 and 1597 only to be destroyed by severe gales.

Indeed, the war continued through the 1590s as both Philip and Elizabeth were too proud to admit they could not win it or bring themselves to reach a compromise. It required new leaders and a fresh appraisal of their countries' affairs before peace would result in 1604.

Conclusion

Was Philip motivated by religious or political objectives? If he regarded them as inextricable, then such a question is historically inappropriate. But is this the case? Most historians acknowledge that his prime aim was to defend his dominions and his Catholic faith, and not to act aggressively. If provoked, he would respond as far as his commitments allowed. In the first half of his reign, financial limitations, the Dutch Revolt and the defence of his Mediterranean possessions from the Turks tied his hands. Peace with the Sultan and the annexation of Portugal in 1580 gave him the resources to assume the initiative. Contemporaries were convinced that his ambition to rule over a universal monarchy was now revealed, as he laid claims to the crowns of England and France. Was this the behaviour of an imperialist, the secular leader of the Counter-Reformation or of an opportunist in danger of overreaching himself? The English Puritan, Sir Edwyn Sandys, was in no doubt. Writing in 1599, he claimed that Spain was 'a nation that aimeth so apparently at the Monarchy of the whole west'. The truth appears to have been more complex. 'Honour' and 'reputation' were the underlying principles of his foreign policy in the 1560s, and remained so throughout his reign. They meant more to him than acquiring lands, fighting wars or creating a universal monarchy. Of course, we can never be totally sure of Philip's intentions. Not all that he said was intended, and much of what he desired was never documented. Such unresolved ambiguities continue to make Philip II's foreign policy a controversial subject.

Task: making sense of a historical controversy

1 Is Geoffrey Parker's view (page 170), that Philip was motivated by his faith, confirmed by Philip's domestic policies? (See chapter 16.) Explain your reasons.

2 According to Trevor Davies, Philip desired 'the exaltation of the power of Spain' (page 170). What do you think he meant by this phrase?

3 Does Robert Stradling's view, that Philip aimed to defend Spain's reputation and security, conflict with or support the views of Parker and Davies? Explain your answer.

4 Peter Pierson's view, that Philip responded to opportunities and reacted to events, suggests that the king had an inconsistent foreign policy. Do you agree? Explain your reasons.

5 Do these four views, taken together, suggest that modern historians are no nearer to understanding Philip's motives than were his contemporaries? Explain your answer. What is your own interpretation of this controversy?

6 Philip ruled Spain for 42 years, during which time his policies and the motives underlying them will most certainly have changed. Can you suggest when and why changes may have occurred? What resulted from these changes? Explain your reasons.

Further reading

J. Lynch, *Spain, 1516–98: From Nation State to World Empire* (Blackwell, 1991) – puts foreign affairs in the wider context of the sixteenth century.

M. J. Rodríguez-Salgado, *The Changing Face of Empire: Charles V, Philip II and Habsburg Authority, 1551–9* (Cambridge University Press, 1988) – although a detailed account of the 1550s, it offers perceptive comments on Philip's later years.

F. Fernández-Armesto, *The Spanish Armada* (Oxford University Press, 1988) – provides a very readable background to this event.

C. Martin and G. Parker, *The Spanish Armada* (Penguin, 1988) – excellent illustrations in keeping with the commentaries on the latest research.

18 Why did a revolt break out in the Netherlands in 1572?

Time chart

1555: Spain formally takes possession of the 17 provinces

1559: Philip leaves the Netherlands; Margaret becomes governess-general

1561: Spanish troops embark for the Mediterranean. Church reforms begin; Granvelle becomes Archbishop of Mechlin

1563: Orange, Egmont and Hornes withdraw from the Council of State

1564: Dismissal of Granvelle; religious reforms are abandoned

1565: October 'Letters from the Segovia Woods'
December 'Compromise of the Nobility'

1566: Montigny and Bergen go to Madrid; first revolt begins

1567: May Revolt ends
August Alva's troops arrive and the Council of Troubles is set up
September Margaret ceases to be governess-general

1568: Execution of Egmont, Hornes and Brederode

1569: States-General agree to pay a Hundredth Penny tax

1571: Twentieth and Tenth Penny taxes rejected by the States-General

1572: Sea Beggars seize Brill and Flushing; the second revolt begins

The 17 provinces constituting the Netherlands were the most recent acquisition of the Spanish Habsburgs (see Figure 18.1). Created in 1548, they remained under imperial rule until 1555 when Charles V transferred them to Philip as heir to the Spanish throne. Philip stayed in Brussels between 1555 and 1559, leaving only to visit his English wife, Mary, and to campaign against Henry II in France. During these years the wealth and prosperity of the Dutch greatly impressed him but he was increasingly worried by their religious and political ideas. Over the next few years, a number of factors combined to present Philip with serious difficulties. His decision to send an army to the Netherlands in 1567 sparked off a revolt which no one wanted or planned, but behind the immediate causes of war there was a smouldering discontent.

Figure 18.1 The Netherlands in the reign of Philip II

legend:
------- frontier as in 1609
▨ Bishopric of Liège

North sea

Groningen •
GRONINGEN
FRIESLAND
DRENTHE
Alkmaar •
Amsterdam •
OVERIJSSEL
UTRECHT
Leiden •
GELDERLAND
HOLLAND
Brill •
Flushing •
Middelburg •
Breda •
ZEELAND
Antwerp •
Dunkirk •
• Ghent
FLANDERS
Brussels •
BRABANT
• Tournai
ARTOIS
Mons •
Arras •
• Valenciennes
Cambrai •
LUXEMBOURG
HAINAULT
F R A N C E

0   50 km
0   50 miles

Constitutional problems

From the outset, Philip intended increasing royal control over the Dutch; the States-General, their representative assembly, intended resisting him. In 1556 they refused his request for a 1 per cent tax on property and a 2 per cent tax on goods, claiming that they had already contributed over 7 million Flemish pounds towards his wars in north Italy and France. Only after 17 months of wrangling did they approve a reduced grant, and then on condition that they supervised its collection and distribution. When Philip recalled them one month later, in August 1557, to demand another subsidy, there was uproar. Brabant led the opposition but other provinces demanded a review of their tax quotas and responded by stalling and vetoing proposals. Not until January 1559 did the assembly vote a 'Nine

181

Years' Aid' of 3,600,000 ducats, and then they made it conditional on their controlling its administration. This was an unpleasant experience for the new King.

Philip was convinced that the Dutch nobles needed firmer handling. He was prepared to conciliate them by increasing their authority, but if his power was not to be eroded, then a strong regent was essential. Emmanuel Philibert, Duke of Savoy, had been his lieutenant-general since 1555, but a more sensitive and reliable representative was required. He settled upon his half-sister, Margaret of Parma, although she was not his ideal choice. She possessed little administrative or diplomatic experience and, in his opinion, even less intelligence. However she had been born in the Netherlands but had no close contact with the nobles. Above all, Philip knew her limitations and so detailed her duties before he left for Spain: he would give her a garrison of 3,000 troops and appoint her advisers but decisions on all significant matters would be taken by him alone.

Religion

Religion was not a major issue in the Netherlands in 1556, but by 1559 it was fast becoming one. Charles V's imperial commitments and the unwillingness of several civil authorities to cooperate with the Inquisition encouraged a steady growth in the number of Lutherans, Calvinists and Anabaptists. Such tolerance was unacceptable to Philip, who in 1557 instructed the inquisitor in Delft to step up the rate of arrests. When in 1559 the King expressed his intention of restructuring the Dutch dioceses and introducing more inquisitors there was an immediate outcry from the States-General. On leaving the Netherlands, Philip sought to appease his subjects by promising to treat them favourably and to return as soon as possible. That he never came back and proceeded to implement unpalatable policies goes a long way towards explaining why within 10 years he was facing a serious rebellion.

Philip's policy

Philip pursued consistent aims in his rule of the Netherlands. He wanted to establish greater religious conformity, subordinate the States-General and the grandees and ensure that his Dutch subjects remained peaceful and prosperous so that they would continue to fund his *monarquía*. Although he may have wanted to achieve a more centralised government by gaining greater control of the government and the Church it is unlikely that he intended establishing an absolute rule, as the Dutch later proclaimed. He knew all too well that they had experienced immense financial hardship in the 1550s and were in urgent need of peace. It was not his wish to disturb their tranquillity nor to push them into revolt. Moreover, the end of Habsburg–Valois hostilities in 1559 and growing attacks by the Turks in north Africa shifted Philip's priorities to the Mediterranean; for the next 20 years, no matter what happened in the Netherlands, he would always keep one eye firmly focused on the Turks. If this emphasis was quite intelligible to all Spaniards, the Netherlanders saw it as a dereliction of duty. Historians have subsequently argued that it was a serious miscalculation.

Orange, Egmont, Berlaymont, Viglius, Glajon and Perrenot were appointed Margaret's major advisers in 1559. Principal among these councillors was Antoine Perrenot, Bishop of Arras (from 1561 Cardinal Granvelle), who was responsible for keeping the King fully informed. Greedy, haughty and nepotistic, Granvelle sought to accelerate the persecution of heretics, increase the King's authority over the States-General, and further his own career at the expense of the Dutch grandees. By putting his trust in Granvelle and allowing him in effect to run the government of the Netherlands, Philip committed another serious error of judgement. Grandees like Lamoral, Count of Egmont, and Philippe de Montmorency, Count Hornes, were outraged by the Cardinal's high-handed behaviour and virtual monopoly of royal patronage.

Another councillor, William, Prince of Orange, expected more political power in Philip's absence. After all, had not the ailing Charles rested on his shoulder at the abdication ceremony in 1555? As well as being the most recent Knight of the Order of the Golden Fleece, was William not also the foremost landowner in the country? William suspected Granvelle of undermining his reputation at the court in Madrid by insinuating that he wanted to gain control of the government. To an extent this was true, but then Granvelle equally wished to monopolise political patronage.

Philip could ill afford to divert his attention from the increasing Turkish threat to his lands. Consequently, between 1559 and 1564, he began to make concessions. In 1560 he planned to garrison 3,000 troops along the southern border of the Netherlands, allegedly to defend it from a possible French attack, but the municipal authorities refused to release any funds to pay the soldiers. Tension rose as unpaid Spanish troops clashed with the local militia. Margaret pleaded with Philip to remove the troops, and in spite of Granvelle's perceptive warning that 'there will be trouble here sooner or later on some other pretext', the King agreed. On 10 January 1561 the troops embarked from Zeeland.

A more important concession was made in July 1561, at least as far as Granvelle was concerned: Philip abandoned his plan to appoint more Spanish nobles to the Council of State and, taking the lead from Orange and Egmont, increased the number of native stadholders. Orange, in particular, benefited: he was confirmed in his stadholdership of Holland, Zeeland and Utrecht, and in the following year became stadholder of Franche-Comté.

Church reform

Perhaps more than any other episode, the hostile reception that greeted Philip's programme of episcopal reforms announced in 1561 demonstrated the strength of the anti-Granvelle faction. In May 1559 Philip and the Pope had agreed to reform the ecclesiastical administration of the Netherlands: 14 new bishoprics and 3 archbishoprics controlled by a primate (the most senior of the three)would reduce the influence of foreign bishops and combat heresy more effectively. Each bishop would be university trained, have two inquisitors as assistants and be financed out of local abbeys. Such proposals, however well-intentioned, proved extremely provocative: the abbots resented the new abbot-bishops, the grandees suspected their political power would be reduced and the nobles believed their younger sons would find successful ecclesiastical careers closed to them since they were unlikely to gain the necessary university qualifications. Above all, everyone feared that an enlarged Inquisition would result in a Spanish invasion of personal and spiritual life. In 1562 alone there were some 600 prosecutions. It certainly looks as if Philip intended reducing the power of the abbots and nobles, especially those of Brabant, which was the staunchest defender of Dutch liberties and whose boundaries fell within the new archbishopric of Mechlin. When it was announced that Granvelle would hold this office, there was a howl of protest. The Cardinal was later to confide to a friend, 'Would to God the creation of these bishoprics had never been thought of'. But it was too late.

In March 1563 Orange, Egmont and Hornes sent an ultimatum to Philip: they would resign from the Council of State if Granvelle was not dismissed. The States of Brabant put further pressure on Margaret by refusing to collect taxes. She informed Philip and he began to receive reports from his agents in Brussels that Granvelle was treating heretics leniently. As Turkish problems multiplied and the possibility emerged that the French civil war might spill into his lands, Philip knew that Granvelle must be sacrificed. It was a view shared by the Cardinal's enemies in Madrid. In January 1564 Philip informed him, 'I deem it best that you should leave the Low Countries for some days and go to

Burgundy to see your mother, with the consent of the duchess of Parma. In this way, both my authority and your reputation will be preserved.' Two months later Granvelle resigned and in July Philip dropped his entire ecclesiastical reform programme.

In spite (or perhaps because) of these concessions, the King had no intention of letting the Dutch nobility control policy-making. From his perspective in Madrid, their desire to restore the traditional style of administration smacked of insubordination and threatened his central-isation plans. Moreover, their links with the Huguenots and factious nobles in France began to worry him – the Hornes and Egmonts were related to the Montmorencies and Montigny's cousin was the Constable of France. As the grandees began to tighten their grip on the Council of State, Philip came to suspect that Margaret sympathised with them and so would have great difficulty refusing their demands for a relaxation of the heresy laws. This was confirmed in February 1565 when Egmont unexpectedly arrived in Madrid to ask for religious concessions and more political power for the nobles. The King was greatly embarrassed. He kept Egmont waiting for six weeks before giving him the guarded reply that although he would not stop the punishment of heretics he was prepared to exam-ine the 'methods' of persecution. Upon returning to Brussels, Egmont encouraged the Council of State to modify the heresy laws but was per-plexed when in June further letters arrived from Madrid rebutting his interpretation of the meeting. Margaret asked for clarification but Philip demurred until he had more reassuring news from the Mediterranean. Repeated 'headaches' stayed his hand until 17 October when, having heard of the relief of Malta, he sent six documents known as the 'Letters from the Segovia Woods', categorically rejecting Egmont's proposals.

Four hundred lesser nobles – led by Philip of Marnix, Nicholas de Hames, Louis of Nassau and Henry de Brederode – responded by drawing up a petition known as the 'Compromise of the Nobility' in which they pledged themselves to resist the Inquisition and disobey Philip's orders. Four months later, on 5 April 1566, armed confederates led by Brederode forced Margaret to repeal the heresy laws and ban the Inquisition's activities. The grandees conveniently withdrew to their estates; they would neither condone the lesser nobility's actions nor support the Crown in enforcing the heresy edicts. Margaret was therefore forced to make further concessions and allow the Baron of Montigny and the Marquis of Bergen to visit Madrid to obtain Philip's approval. From his position of weakness the King agreed on 31 July 1566 to remove the Inquisition and pardon the rebels. However, he claimed later that he was not obliged to honour the agreement because he signed under duress and his signature was witnessed only by an official.

While Margaret and the Council of State awaited his reply, which did not arrive until 3 October, popular disturbances broke out in the southern and western provinces. Calvinist preachers like Sem Jansz of Monnikendam in Holland proclaimed that 'those who attack images and shatter them are doing God's will'. More than 400 churches were sacked in Flanders alone. In August and September, Margaret permitted limited toleration in an attempt to subdue the religious violence and, with the support of the grandees, she slowly restored public order. But her succession of alarmist letters, which spoke of 200,000 in open revolt, convinced Philip that the situation could only be remedied by despatching a large Spanish army. The decision was probably taken after a crucial council debate on 29 October 1566 when Philip accepted that the situation was too volatile for him to visit the Netherlands and that instead the Duke of Alva should be sent with a large army. Arguably, he overreacted to a situation which Margaret was beginning to get under control. Indeed, by May 1567, following successes at Tournai, Oosterweel and Valenciennes, the first revolt had been suppressed. However, the King did not know this nor could he have acted differently, claims Professor Koenigsberger, 'when faced with the double opposition of the high nobility ... and a revolutionary religious movement with a military organisation'.

Military intervention

The Duke of Alva entered Brussels at the head of 10,000 seasoned troops on 22 August 1567 and at once took control, even though Margaret remained regent. She strongly disapproved of his billeting of Spanish troops in loyalist towns and the creation of a special 'Council of Troubles'. This was set up to overcome ineffectual law courts and to prosecute leading trouble-makers. On 8 September, three days after the arrest of Egmont and Hornes, Margaret resigned. Alva assumed control as governor-general and regent. He was the first regent not to be a prince of the blood, a point of protocol not lost on the Dutch nobles. It was Alva's intention to cow 'the men of butter', and the Council of Troubles certainly did this. Between 1567 and 1573, more than 12,000 people were arrested, at least 9,000 had their goods confiscated and over 1,000 were executed in what most contemporaries claimed, and many historians have confirmed, was a reign of terror. Among the more celebrated victims were Brederode, Egmont and Hornes. Even Montigny, who was still in Spain, did not escape. He was arrested in 1567 and in October 1570 strangled in Simancas Castle on the King's orders. William of Orange had fortuitously evaded Alva's clutches by fleeing to Germany but his Dutch estates were seized and his son arrested.

By endorsing Alva's strong-arm methods, Philip had irredeemably alienated his Catholic and aristocratic subjects – the very people who had stood by him in 1566. Tales of Spanish outrages and news that Alva was beginning to implement the postponed ecclesiastical reforms reached Orange in his German exile. He organised an invasion in 1568. Calling upon the Netherlanders to take up arms not as 'rebels' but as 'liberators', he returned to his country only to find that not a single town supported him. In November, Orange was again in exile, this time in France. His abortive uprising should have heralded the end of Dutch resistance but in fact it was a new beginning.

Orange learned from his mistakes and saw the necessity of acquiring foreign aid. Meanwhile, Alva persuaded Philip not to visit the Netherlands. While domestic circumstances may have convinced the King that he should not go in 1568, he would never again have a better opportunity. The postponement may well have cost Spain the Netherlands. In addition, keeping such a large army in the field had to be financed and Philip made it clear this would fall on the Netherlanders. The States-General's response was to vote a non-permanent tax of 1 per cent and 4 million florins spread over two years, but it flatly refused Alva's request for a permanent Twentieth Penny (5 per cent) tax on the sales of landed property and a Tenth Penny (10 per cent) tax on all other sales. For two years Alva bided his time, but on 31 July 1571 he declared that he would collect the two new taxes with or without the States-General's consent. Predictably a tax strike ensued and Artois, Flanders, Hainault and Brabant sent a deputation to protest to the King. Philip was unimpressed and failed to see that Alva had brought the Netherlands to the brink of another revolt.

When, in April 1572, de la Marck and his 'Sea Beggars' sailed into Brill and Flushing harbours and seized control of the towns, they caught everyone by surprise. Instantly a wave of insurrections broke out in the west and north while Orange took his opportunity to invade from the east. Unlike 1566, this second revolt against Spain proved more difficult to suppress.

Task: class discussion

Work on the causes of the Dutch Revolt lends itself to a class debate. Trouble between Spain and the Netherlands had been near the surface since Philip's accession; riots broke out in 1566 before the main revolt started in 1572. Each side blamed the other for causing the revolt. This debate is about who was responsible.

Divide your class into four groups, each one representing people with different views about what caused the revolt in 1572. Each group has to use the evidence of this chapter to defend itself against allegations that it was responsible. You should not only seek to justify your own involvement but also throw light upon the conduct and responsibility of others.

a Philip, King of Spain
b Margaret, governess-general (1559–67)
c Alva, governor-general (1567–73)
d William of Orange, Dutch stadholder

Further reading

M. Rady, *The Netherlands: Revolt and Independence, 1550–1650* (Arnold, 1987) – a sound general introduction to this topic.

P. R. Limm, *The Dutch Revolt, 1559–1648*, Seminar Studies in History (Addison Wesley Longman, 1989) – contains perceptive comments and useful documents.

A. Duke, 'The Origins of the Revolt of the Netherlands: The Crisis of 1566', *History Review*, 18 (1994) – an article written for A-Level students.

G. Parker, *The Dutch Revolt* (2nd edn, Penguin, 1985) – remains the most authoritative account of the revolt.

A. Duke, *Reformation and Revolt in the Low Countries* (Hambledon, 1990) – offers a revisionist explanation.

H. G. Koenigsberger, *Estates and Revolutions* (Yale University Press, 1971) – contains several useful essays on the nature and origin of the revolt.

19 What was William the Silent's contribution to the Dutch revolt?

Time chart

1555: Philip assumes control of the Netherlands

1559: Orange becomes stadholder of Holland, Zeeland and Utrecht

1561: Grandees revolt against Margaret's regency

1563: Orange withdraws from the Council of State

1564: Cardinal Granvelle falls from power

1566: Revolt of Brederode and the Confederates

1567: Orange goes into exile. Alva arrives in the Netherlands

1568: Execution of Hornes, Egmont and Brederode. Orange's abortive uprising

1572: Revolt of the 'Sea Beggars'; Orange returns from France and remains stadholder of Holland, Zeeland and Utrecht

1573: Requesens replaces Alva as Governor-General. Orange becomes a Calvinist. Siege of Alkmaar

1574: Relief of Leiden

1576: Requesens dies. Sack of Antwerp. Pacification of Ghent

1577: Don John imposes the Perpetual Edict. Orange becomes Governor of Brabant

1578: Death of Don John; Philip appoints Parma as Governor-General

1579: Union of Arras and Union of Utrecht

1580: Philip declares Orange an outlaw; Orange replies with the *Apology*

1584: Death of Orange

In 1609 – 37 years after the 'Sea Beggars' had inadvertently triggered off the Revolt of the Netherlands – Philip III of Spain called a halt to the war and effectively conceded defeat to the seven northern provinces. Retrospectively, it is not difficult to see why they had won:

■ the inspiration of Calvinism

■ strategical and political mistakes made by Philip II and his advisers

PROFILE: *William of Orange*

Born in 1533 into a small German noble family with property in the county of Nassau, **William** unexpectedly inherited estates in 1544 in Brabant, Holland, Luxembourg and Burgundy belonging to the French house of Orange. As a stadholder of three provinces and a councillor of state in Brussels in the 1550s, he exercised considerable influence. He actively campaigned in 1561 to get Granvelle dismissed and the Inquisition removed from the Netherlands (see chapter 18). The arrival of Alva's army in 1567 turned him from a loyal into a disobedient subject and marked the beginning of his anti-Spanish propaganda campaign. Orange's opponents viewed him as an embittered and disillusioned politician driven by personal ambition and revenge. In many ways they were right: he never forgave Granvelle and Alva, nor trusted Philip's governors Requesens, Don John and Parma. But most of all, he publicly condemned the King, who correctly identified Orange as the principal source of Dutch resistance. William of Orange was assassinated in 1584.

- topographical conditions exploited by the rebel farmers and fishermen
- the determination of the Dutch to defend their freedom from Spanish oppression
- Spain's commitments elsewhere
- assistance from England and France.

Above all, historians recognise the importance of **William of Orange**. This chapter seeks to assess his contribution, first by outlining his qualities of leadership, and then by setting such an assessment against a selection of primary and secondary evidence.

Orange's leadership

At first Orange showed little aptitude for leading a rebellion: in 1566 he rejected the Calvinist call to arms, fled to Germany in 1567, and a year later failed ingloriously to dislodge Alva's army from the Netherlands. Yet in these darkest of hours, he refused to submit but continued to condemn the Spanish administration, trying to enlist foreign support and financing resistance out of his family funds.

Document A

In 1568 Orange encourages the Dutch to resist Alva and Spain.

'Open your eyes and consider the present situation more closely. If you sift out all the deeds and acts of one party and the other, you shall undoubtedly find the truth to be that all the vices with which those tyrants attempt to slander and traverse the holy, reasonable and necessary enterprise of those who for the true service of God, the King and the fatherland and the deliverance of you all, courageously endanger their lives, property and wealth, are in fact their own vices. It is they who must be blamed for deeds by which they openly disgrace themselves. You well know that by the King's own proper consent you are freely released from the oath of obedience you owe him, if he or others in his name infringe the promises and conditions on which you have accepted and received him, until finally every right has been restored. I also remind you that according to your privileges you are permitted to close your towns and to resist by force not only the servants of your prince but also the prince himself, in person, whenever he attempts to proceed by force of arms.'

The deaths of Egmont, Hornes and Brederode in 1568 left the Dutch without a leader and, by degrees, Orange came to convince himself that he and he alone could save his people. In May 1572, in response to the Sea Beggars' attack on Brill, he once more returned to the Netherlands. Writing to his brother, John, he declared, 'I am bent on going to Holland and Zeeland, to maintain the cause there as far as that may be possible, having decided to make my grave there'.

The legend that Orange dedicated his life to serve his people has its origins at this time and for the next 12 years he was its main propagator.

Document B

In June 1572, William wrote this 'open' letter.

'I pray you once again, because of the loyalty which you and I owe to our dearest fatherland, that with my help you rescue, take back and protect what you do not want to lose for ever. If you do not do so, then I assert most solemnly that it will not be my fault if severer measures are taken. But if you take my admonition to heart (and I sincerely hope you will do this for your own sake) then swear allegiance firstly to Christ the only God our Saviour, next to the King who takes delight in the sworn laws, finally to me as patron of the fatherland and champion of freedom.'

Unquestionably, he and his family made great sacrifices and enabled the rebels to survive. Orange helped to defend the besieged towns of Alkmaar (1573) and Leiden (1574). He consistently refused to accept Spanish offers of compromise and in 1584 paid the ultimate price of resistance at the hands of an assassin. Three of his brothers died fighting, a fourth heavily financed the rebels, and his son, Maurice, led them to eventual victory.

Not everyone, however, saw Orange as the 'Father of the Fatherland'. As early as 1563, Granvelle had warned the King:

> *'The Prince of Orange is a dangerous man, sly, full of ruses professing to stand by the people, to champion their interests, but seeking only the favour of the populace; appearing sometimes as a Catholic, sometimes as a Calvinist and sometimes Lutheran. He is capable of any underhand deed that might be inspired by an unlimited ambition.'*

Political aims

In June 1572 Orange outlined his objectives. Without denying Philip his right to rule over the Netherlands, he raised questions as to where sovereignty actually resided – with the monarch or with the Sates-General?

> ### Document C
>
> *'I have only the following objectives in this war:*
>
> *That with full respect for the King's sovereign power, all decrees contrary to conscience and to the laws, shall be annulled and that every one who so wishes shall be free to adopt the teaching of the prophets, of Christ and the apostles which the Churches have taught until now and that those who reject these doctrines may do so without any injury to their goods as long as they are willing to behave peacefully and can show that they did so in the past.*
> *That the name of the Inquisition shall be erased for ever ...*
> *That those who have no right at all to be in this country and, of course, are not allowed to oppress the soul of our humble people by force of arms, shall be banished.*
> *That people be given back their houses, possessions, hereditary estates, their good name, their freedoms, privileges and laws, by which liberty is maintained.*

> *That state affairs shall be discussed in the States of the provinces in accordance with the custom of our ancestors.*
> *That political matters will be dealt with by the King himself and by the States which are chosen in every province and not dispatched secretly by hired foreigners through whose faithlessness and greed the present troubles have come about.'*
>
> William of Orange, June 1572.

Having raised the question of sovereignty, William attempted to play down any suspicion concerning his own political ambitions. In July 1572, his spokesman, Philip Marnix, outlined Orange's proposals for a provisional government:

Document D

'They [the Estates of Holland] shall discuss and ordain the best and most suitable means of restoring and re-establishing in their old form and full vigour all the old privileges, rights and usages of the towns, which may have been suppressed and taken away by Alva's tyranny ... His Grace [Orange] has no other purpose than to see that, under the lawful and worthy government of the King of Spain, the power, authority and prestige of the Estates may be restored to their former state, in accordance with the privileges and rights which the King has sworn to maintain in these countries. And without the estates, His Grace shall not endeavour to do or command anything that concerns the provinces or that may be harmful to them ... His Grace binds himself to undertake or command nothing without the advice or consent of the estates or at least the majority of them, and without consulting these estates and countries if and when they desire this. To this end, the estates and the delegates of the towns shall swear to His Grace to be faithful to him for ever and not to desert him, but to assist him in every possible way.'

Many were unconvinced. They saw the prince's 'silent' disposition as evidence of his deviousness. The Estates resented any suggestion that they should surrender their privileges to him as their stadholder. For his part, he believed that their particularism could lose them the war, especially after the separation of the northern and southern provinces in 1579. When he again spoke to the representatives of Holland and Zeeland, in January 1580, he reminded them that their survival depended upon subduing political and religious extremism within their own towns and working together in a common cause (see Document E).

Document E

'Your first and foremost mistake is that as yet neither you nor your masters, the provincial States, have established any assembly or council on behalf of the States which has the power to take decisions beneficial to the whole of the country. Everyone in his own province or town acts as he thinks is beneficial to himself and his particular affairs without realising that when some town or province is under attack, it may be useful not to help it for the time being so that in the end the whole country, including these towns and provinces, may be saved.

'We meet often enough and deliberate long enough, but are as negligent in implementing our decisions as we are diligent in deliberating at length.'

In December he went even further, and rejected Philip's authority. In the *Apology*, he declared:

Document F

'This name of King is not allowed of by me. Let him be a King in Castile, in Aragon, at Naples, among the Indians, and in every place he commands at his pleasure: yes let him be a King if he will, in Jerusalem, and a peaceable governor in Asia and Africa, yet for all that I will not acknowledge him in this country for any more than a duke and a count, whose power is limited according to our privileges, which he swore to observe.'

Belief in national unity

Some historians, like Pieter Geyl, believe that Orange's greatest legacy was his ability to keep the States united and to convince others that, if they became divided, then they would fall.

Document G

'In a crisis caused by the abuse of monarchical authority, Orange's greatness as a leader of the Netherlands people lay precisely in his unsurpassed talent for cooperating with the States assemblies which ... had been impelled to go beyond their appointed places in that people's

ancient constitutions. Persuasion was what he excelled in. Many were the long memoranda which he wrote to refute objections to his views; in the council-chamber he was clear and firm, but also resourceful and patient. Thus it was that under his auspices the new oligarchy had been able to form itself into a real ruling class, in which, owing to the defection of so many nobles, the town element had become predominant. Several who were too firmly fixed in the government of their provinces not to see everything primarily from a provincial standpoint had yet, by the circumstances which demanded the weightiest decisions from both provincial States and town governments, been taught to grapple with problems of general policy. Moreover, in close intercourse with Orange, there had arisen from out their midst, in the States-General and in the Councils, a group of truly national statesmen of a different character from the official, noble, mostly non-Dutch class which the monarchy had reared.'

Pieter Geyl, *The Revolt of the Netherlands 1559–1609* (1958).

Professor Koenigsberger is not so sure. 'Even so,' he writes, 'the insistence of the towns on withholding from their deputies full powers in financial matters still led to much friction with the prince. In practice, it was the prince's skill in handling the estates which overcame the inherent difficulties of the system.'

Religious tolerance

Orange's religious beliefs also caused some ambivalence. Brought up as a Catholic, in 1561 he had married the niece of the Lutheran Elector of Saxony and by 1564 was advocating religious toleration. A startled Council of State heard him declare, 'However strongly I am attached to the Catholic religion, I cannot approve of princes attempting to rule the consciences of their subjects and wanting to rob them of the liberty of faith'. Orange may have genuinely believed that political unity depended upon religious harmony but his own conversion to Calvinism in 1573, arguably for reasons of state, lost him considerable support among Catholic families throughout the Netherlands. Nevertheless, in an age notorious for its persecution, his tolerance was applauded by the historian Veronica Wedgwood (see Document H).

Document H

'He belonged in spirit to an earlier, a more generous and more cultured age than this of narrowness and authority, and thin, sectarian hatred. But he belonged also to a later age; his deep and genuine interest in the people he ruled, his faith in their development, his toleration, his convinced belief in government by consent – all these reach out from the medieval world towards a wider time. Few statesmen in any period, none in his own, cared so deeply for the ordinary comfort and the trivial happiness of the thousands of individuals who are 'the people'. He neither idealised nor overestimated them and he knew that they were often wrong, for what political education had they yet had? But he believed in them, not merely as a theoretical concept, but as individuals, as men. Therein lay the secret of the profound and enduring love between him and them.'

Veronica Wedgwood, *William the Silent* (1944).

Many contemporaries, however, doubted William's sincerity. His motives were further distrusted when he allowed Calvinist-led town councils to deny Catholic inhabitants, often in a majority, to have freedom of worship.

Statesmanship

Most historians agree that it was Orange's affable nature and shrewd statecraft which transformed a domestic revolt into an international rebellion. 'While it is not to be contested that the Low Countries were, and remained, his principal concern', writes N. M. Sutherland, 'it is because they became the political hub of western Europe that William's life and role should be placed in a broader context.' More than any other Dutch leader, he saw the importance of keeping the revolt on the political agenda of Spain's enemies and remained ever hopeful of enlisting foreign aid. His willingness to accept as sovereign rulers of the Netherlands, the Austrian Catholic Archduke Matthias, and the French Catholic Duke of Anjou, and to work with the mercenary German Calvinist Elector Palatine, John Casimir, financed by England, lays him open to suggestions of inconsistency and opportunism. But desperate times called for desperate measures. In September 1579, Marnix reported Orange's views about acquiring an external patron:

Document I

'His Excellency [Orange] answers that unless peace is offered by the deputies of the King on terms favourable to the fatherland as well as to religion, and assurances are given that there shall not be the slightest reason for suspicion that on the pretext of peace the King and his servants should want to tyrannise once more over the country and exterminate religion, the provinces may want to choose a prince as their protector. All things considered His Excellency thinks that in that case no lord or prince could be found whose authority and means are of greater importance and consequence than those of the kingdom of England or the Duke of Anjou ... But if the provinces think it more advisable not to elect a prince as their protector, His Excellency will comply with their discretion and counsel. In that case too he promises to serve and assist them as much as he can in all matters that they may consider advisable for the benefit and prosperity of these countries.'

Ironically, it was Orange's death rather than the contributions of foreign patrons when he was alive which convinced Elizabeth that England must intervene with military assistance in 1585, but by then he had given the seven northern provinces a life-line and pointed the way to eventual salvation. The Dutch historian, K. W. Swart, was in no doubt wherein lay Orange's greatness (see Document J).

Document J

'Orange was not a doctrinaire revolutionary intent on founding a new political and social order but a prudent, highly practical and occasionally unscrupulous statesman. As the almost perfect incorporation of the sixteenth-century idea of a politique, he readily changed his political and religious affiliations when it suited his purposes. Yet there was one cause which he embraced with grim determination and to which he remained wholeheartedly committed until the end of his life: the struggle against the King of Spain in order to ensure that justice be done to himself and other victims of Spanish tyranny. It was on this issue that he rejected any idea of compromise and felt more strongly than almost any of his supporters.

'In the unequal conflict with his powerful opponent Orange suffered one defeat after another. Yet in spite of his numerous failures he was one of the most effective statesmen of his time. Although not a leader who was ever in perfect control of the course of events, he was one of those rare individuals of whom it can be said that their actions were decisive at a critical stage of history. Orange played this role mainly during the darkest

> *hour of the revolt when Holland and Zeeland were fighting their lonely battle against the Spanish armies. At this highly critical phase of the struggle against Spain, the revolt would have come to an early end – with all the effects that this would have had on the later course of Dutch and European history – if it had not been for the superior leadership provided by Orange. In this period there was absolutely no one else available who had the abilities which were needed for the task of effectively organising the resistance of a small, internally divided population.'*
>
> K. W. Swart, 'William the Silent and the Revolt of the Netherlands' (1978).

Tasks: evaluating sources

1 Study documents A, B, C, D, E, F and I. What evidence is there that Orange was motivated more by personal ambition than by love for his country?

2 To what extent and why might these documents be considered unreliable sources of evidence?

3 In what respects might Geyl, Wedgwood and Swart (documents G, H and J) be accused of being biased in their views on Orange's statesmanship?

4 How far are the views expressed in documents G, H and J supported by evidence contained in the primary sources in documents A, B, C, D, E, F and I?

Further reading

P. Limm, *The Dutch Revolt, 1559–1648*, Seminar Studies in History (Addison Wesley Longman, 1989) – a fine introduction with useful commentaries on documents.

G. Parker, *The Dutch Revolt* (Penguin, 1985 edn) – remains the classic account.

P. Geyl, *The Revolt of the Netherlands, 1559–1609* (Benn, 1958) – a little dated but still a useful account.

K. W. Swart, 'William the Silent and the Revolt of the Netherlands', (Historical Association pamphlet, 1978) – a short and informed assessment by a leading Dutch historian.

H. G. Koenigsberger, *Estates and Revolutions* (Cornell University Press, 1971) – contains several valuable essays on William and the revolt.

A. C. Duke, *Reformation and Revolt in the Low Countries* (Hambledon, 1990) – demonstrates the unifying and divisive forces of Calvinism at work in the revolt.

N. M. Sutherland, *Princes, Politics and Religion, 1547–89* (Hambledon, 1984).

20 What factors promoted economic change in sixteenth-century Europe?

Time chart

1492: Columbus reaches the West Indies

1493: Treaty of Tordesillas divides the New World between Spain and Portugal

1497: Vasco da Gama reaches Calicut (India)

1499: Antwerp is granted the Portuguese pepper market

1511: Malacca becomes a Portuguese base

1519: Cortés sails from Cuba to Mexico

1522: Magellan's expedition circumnavigates the globe

1531: Pizarro begins the conquest of Brazil

1545: Potosí silver mine is discovered in Peru

1557: Spain and France suspend their interest payments on debts

1566: Iconoclasts disrupt trade in the Netherlands

1568: Jean Bodin publishes his theories on price inflation

1572: Dutch Revolt begins; river Scheldt is blocked

1576: Spanish troops mutiny in Antwerp

1583: French troops mutiny in Antwerp

1585–8: Plague ravages France

1593: Revolt of the Croquants in France

Most historians believe that the sixteenth century was a period of rapid economic change, although they disagree over the reasons. They do, of course, acknowledge that changes did not begin suddenly, and recognise that cause and effect were often cyclical. Rates of growth also varied enormously from country to country, region to region, as well as at different times and in different types of economic activity. Some elements also remained largely unchanged. Transport was poor, financial institutions were primitive, and only limited improvements occurred in agricultural and industrial techniques. Indeed to suggest that the sixteenth century was an era of 'proto-industrialisation', as some historians have done, is to look at this period from a nineteenth-century perspective. Nevertheless, changes were occurring: patterns of trade altered, commercial activities expanded, population levels rose and the cost of living increased. The economy of Europe in 1600 was profoundly different from that of 1500. Four themes will be considered in this chapter: population trends, European expansion, government initiatives and the impact of the Reformation.

1 Population trends

As far as it is possible to draw conclusions from insubstantial and unreliable figures, Europe's population (excluding Russia, the Ottoman Empire and Hungary) rose from about 62 million in 1500 to 78 million in 1600. Growth began in the final quarter of the fifteenth century and by the 1550s it was commonly held that countries were 'full of people'. The largest increases were in Germany (12 to 20 million) and France (10 to 16 million). Large towns and cities mushroomed: in 1500 there were 154 towns of more than 10,000 inhabitants; by 1600 there were at least 220. In 1500 only Paris, Naples, Venice, Milan and Istanbul had more than 100,000 people; a century later, they had been joined by London, Lisbon, Rome, Palermo, Messina and Seville. The overall rise was probably due to a combination of early marriages, good harvests and declining plague epidemics, so that for much of the century birth rates outstripped mortality. Only in the final decades were there indications of population levels falling in some towns.

An outbreak of pestilence or a harvest failure could dramatically affect the economy of a town or region. Five serious outbreaks of plague occurred across the continent – in 1522, 1564, 1580, 1586 and 1599 – as well as several localised epidemics (for example, 47,000 people died in Venice in 1575–6, 18 per cent of Milan in 1576–7 and 33 per cent of Uelzen in Lower Saxony in 1597). On average, harvests failed every four or five years. If there was a run of bad harvests – as in the Papal States 1578–96, Sicily 1575–7 and villages near Paris 1594–7 – famine and death resulted. There is also some evidence to suggest that the half-century after 1550 saw climatic changes which amounted to a 'little ice age'. Springs were cooler, summers wetter and winters very severe, which affected food supplies and led to a slowing of population growth. Between 1591 and 1598, the south of France suffered eight consecutive heavy frosts, cool summers and prolonged periods of rain; corn prices were higher in 1591–2 than at any time between 1500 and 1700.

The increase in population created a demand for food and clothing, which led to a rise in the price of grain and wool. For instance, the price of wheat in Castile rose by over 300 per cent, in Poland by 400 per cent and in France by 650 per cent. East of the river Elbe, landowners exploited the large supply of labour to pay low wages, raise rents and entry fines, and so force many tenants to become landless serfs. Those peasants who had unsuccessfully sought employment in the towns returned to suffer even heavier labour services. In western Europe agrarian conditions were more variable but in general agricultural wages were less than prices. In Portugal, Aragon, Catalonia, Sicily and Naples, peasants were exploited by the landowners; in northern France in the last decades of the century, debt-ridden peasants were subdividing and selling off their holdings to better-off landowners. In contrast, peasants in the west and south of Germany and in the Low Countries were more prosperous at the start of the century and better placed to defend their economic position.

Sixteenth-century agriculture remained largely unchanged: the low crop yields and the limited amount of fertile land under cultivation meant that food production could not satisfy the demand. By 1580 most countries had to import wheat: Spain did so from Sicily, Venice from Egypt and Rome from the Baltic. Even the Netherlands with its own dairy products, horticulture, hops, livestock and wheat supplies had to import 14 per cent of its grain from Poland to feed its dense population. Industrial activity flourished in a minority of towns like Barcelona (shipping), Venice (silk and shipping), Milan (armaments) and Antwerp (cloth). However, the availability of cheap labour, because of the population rise, ensured that most owners were content to make a profit not through innovations and greater efficiency but by keeping wages low. **Guilds** were a further obstacle to industrial expansion. By controlling the size and wages of a workforce, the quality and price of a product, and by protecting trades and crafts from competition, they erred on the side of conservatism.

A rising population and limited employment opportunities led to serious urban problems as people migrated to the towns in search of food and work. As early as the 1520s cities had begun to supervise poor relief: Nuremberg in 1522, Strassburg in 1523, Zurich, Mons and Ypres in 1525, Venice in 1528–9, and Lyon, Rome and Geneva followed in the 1530s. Poor laws were introduced in the Netherlands in 1531, France in 1536 and Brandenburg in 1540. In Spain, the town councils of Toledo, Madrid, Valladolid and Seville established charitable institutions, hospitals and workhouses. In Italy new hospitals were built in Florence, Modena and Venice at the end of the century to cope with the rising number of sick, poor and orphans. Among Rome's 80,000 people in the 1590s were 4,000 migrants who had allegedly arrived one night looking for food.

KEY TERM:

Guilds

These were a medieval form of trade union, which safeguarded the wages and working conditions of craftsmen and regulated the quality and output of their trades.

2 European expansion

If population growth was the soul-mate of social distress, it was not the only cause at work. A dramatic rise in inflation, new trade routes and commercial activity on an unprecedented scale changed the economic outlook of most countries and brought western Europe to the threshold of its later and more celebrated industrial revolution. The spur behind this movement was the overseas expansion of Portugal and Spain. By 1515 Portugal had established commercial bases in Africa, India and the East Indies, and for the next 50 years controlled the lucrative spice trade with the Far East. In South America, Portuguese sailors had discovered Brazil in 1500, colonised it by the 1530s and established a slave trade with Angola (in south-west Africa). The trading posts, however, were never easy to defend and Portuguese merchants' preference for large, cargo-carrying carracks meant heavy losses when they foundered. Between 1550 and 1600, 20 per cent of its shipping never returned. The long-haul pepper trade particularly suffered at the hands of the Arabs, Indians and Turks and, at the turn of the century, from rival English (1600), French (1602) and Dutch (1604) East India chartered companies.

Of greater significance and durability was the Spanish overseas empire. Magellan's expedition proved in 1522 that the earth could be circum-navigated; the *conquistadores*, Hermann Cortés and Francisco Pizarro dis-covered the wealth of the Aztec, Inca and Maya empires and the globe was opened up to European trade. In 1504, transatlantic trade totalled 300 tons. By 1545 it exceeded 20,000 and, at its peak in 1605, 59,000 tons. Though there were occasional years of depression in the 1550s and 1560s, this rapid growth had a profound effect on every European coun-try. At first sight the principal beneficiary appears to have been Spain. Having received the monopoly of all Spanish–American trade and com-merce, Seville emerged in the sixteenth century like a Castilian meteor. Its streets thronged with foreign merchants, financiers and brokers; its population doubled to 100,000 by 1600, and its new administrative buildings reflected its wealth (see Figure 20.1). American pearls, silver and gold arrived in the summer, and manufactured goods, luxuries, wine, oil and corn left for the colonies. However, most exports passing through Seville were supplied by Portuguese, German and Genoese mer-chants. Similarly, very little American bullion entered Castile's money supply but went instead to meet Spain's military costs and to pay off royal loans. In 1570–71, for example, over 7 million ducats in silver entered and left Seville.

The greatest volume of silver arrived in the second half of the century as new mines were discovered and the process of refining silver from the

Figure 20.1 Sixteenth-century Seville – detail from a painting by Alonso Sanchez Coello

ore was improved. The mere 86 metric tons of silver entering Spain in the 1530s rose to 2,707 tons in the 1590s. The historian Geoffrey Elton has described the influx of American silver into Europe as 'the most important economic feature of the age'. The Spanish kings, who were entitled to one-fifth each year, used it to lubricate their government machinery: officials were paid, debts honoured, trade fairs kept from closing and troops from mutinying. The injection of so much silver after long periods of stable prices and bullion shortages had a potent effect. The production of Bohemian and Hungarian silver had already triggered off price inflation in the 1480s and Portuguese gold sustained it between 1500 and 1520, but the impact of Spanish bullion after 1560 traumatised the European economies: manufactured goods doubled in price and food and drink showed a fivefold increase.

Rates of inflation, however, had complex regional and national causes. Spain's main increase of 2.8 per cent occurred between 1501 and 1562. It dropped to 1.3 per cent between 1562 and 1600, when bullion imports were at their height. In fact, for much of the century, Spain suffered from a silver shortage, and price inflation owed more to changing population patterns, the volume of goods in circulation and the popularity of *juros* and *censos*. Italy had its steepest price rise between 1550 and 1570 when it was recovering from declining trade, falling population and the ravages of war. It owed little, if anything, to American bullion. The French writer Jean Bodin acknowledged the relative significance of silver injection into a stable economy but saw population, trade, currency debasement and public spending as more important influences. In short, the influx of silver accelerated existing inflationary trends and in some respects speeded up economic changes.

The increase in cash supplies encouraged commercial activity and generated a demand for goods. Money rarely changed hands except when supplementing bills of exchange or IOUs at the international fairs. Antwerp became the *entrepôt* of western Europe. Situated on the river Scheldt in a densely populated area, it had received the sales of Portuguese pepper and ginger since 1499, became the main market for English and Spanish wool and cloth, and attracted international financiers to its quarterly fairs. As the city prospered and its population doubled to 100,000 in the 1580s, the Netherlands emerged as the richest trading nation in Europe.

Its wealth rested on the carrying trade. None of the great maritime powers – Venice, Spain or Portugal – had sufficient ships to conduct their trade, and the Dutch filled this vacuum. When herring shoals deserted the fishing grounds in the Baltic for the North Sea, they designed a new fast ship, the *ventjager*, to transport the fish from the fleet to the ports. Their *fluyt*, a proto-container ship, could be adapted for shallow or deeper water (see page 263) and Dutch marine owners were able to undercut competitors by paying lower wages to their crews and offering low insurance rates to their customers. In these ways, they cornered the market in transporting Baltic grain, fish, textiles and timber to Spain and the Mediterranean in return for carrying Castilian wool, soap, salt, wine, and goods from the Portuguese Empire to northern and western Europe.

Antwerp's gain was Lübeck's loss. As the principal Baltic city-state in the Hanseatic League, Lübeck suffered from the diminishing revenue from the Saxon and Bohemian mines and resented the rivalry from German, Scandinavian and Dutch merchants. Between 1533 and 1536 it failed to gain control of Copenhagen and was then powerless to prevent Danzig and other ports from seizing its own Polish and Baltic trade. Between 1557 and 1585 more than half the recorded traffic sailing through the Danish Sound came from Danzig.

The emergence of the Atlantic trade and policies of the Spanish

KEY TERM:

Hinterland

The area behind that lying along the coast. In this instance, Venice's **hinterland** stretched from the Adriatic to the Alps and embraced the cities of Vicenza, Verona, Udine, Treviso, Padua, Belluno, Brescia, Este and Bergamo.

Habsburgs had a major effect on Mediterranean commerce. Aragon, Valencia and Catalonia were denied a share in the transatlantic trade and struggled to survive attacks from the Barbary corsairs and Turks. Indeed, the Mediterranean economies were damaged as much by the westward expansion of the Turks as by the rising importance of the Atlantic and North Sea coasts.

Perhaps Philip II, cushioned by his American silver, could afford to turn his back on the declining west Mediterranean trade, but Genoa and Venice could not. Once the Turks captured Genoa's Black Sea and Aegean bases, Genoese merchants turned to Spain and supplied Charles V with ships and financial loans in return for commercial privileges and first call on the New World bullion. Venice responded differently. It lacked the ships to ward off competitors in the Indian Ocean and west Mediterranean and instead concentrated on the Adriatic and Levantine trade. It expanded its **hinterland**, developing its own broadcloth industry and speculating on several international exchanges. A decision in 1537 to increase the number of galleys, soldiers and the amount of money spent on the navy, undoubtedly enabled Venice to continue its trading in the Mediterranean in times of war as well as peace and so remain Italy's principal commercial city-state throughout the century. By 1600, however, the new port of Livorno in Tuscany was beginning to challenge its merchants for north Italian commerce, and Dutch and English ships were threatening its pepper trade.

3 Government policies: peace and war

A constant problem facing governments was how to raise enough money to administer their lands, defend their subjects and fight their enemies. Various strategies were applied:

- new and increased taxation
- debasement of the coinage
- secularisation of church property
- sale of land, titles, monopolies, annuities and bonds
- borrowing from merchants and reneging on the repayments.

Whatever they tried, the same fate awaited the monarchs of Spain, France, Portugal and, to a lesser extent, England: permanent debts, rising interest payments and the collapse of their creditors. The Fuggers, Europe's wealthiest financial house, claimed that they never recovered from Philip II's suspension of debt repayments in 1557. When he repeated it in 1575 and 1596, several leading bankers went to the wall.

The Lyon financiers, Bonvisi and Kleberger, were similarly bankrupted in 1557 when Henry II reneged on his loans, and between 1551 and 1584 five major Venetian banks collapsed.

The principal cause of this financial insecurity was war. Most west European countries experienced prolonged periods of warfare in the sixteenth century and although few wars were fought primarily for economic reasons, it was the most dynamic of all agents of economic change. War could have positive and negative effects: it stimulated the armaments and provisions trade, generated shipbuilding and mining, gave employment to professional administrators and soldiers, and enabled military supply contractors, mercenary captains and the urban nobility to make sizeable profits.

For the vast majority of people, however, the only dividends were disease, destruction and death. With the exception of Venice, much of the Italian peninsula was devastated by foreign armies between 1494 and 1559. Milan's art houses were looted, Florence's trade was disrupted and Rome sacked. In Germany, the Knights' and Peasants' War damaged the economy of towns such as Nuremberg, Augsburg and Strassburg; and religious conflict resulted in the 'confessional migration' of Protestants to Bremen, Hamburg and Hanover, and of Catholics to Bonn, Trier and Mainz.

The Dutch Revolt saw a similar flood of religious refugees: 7,000 Walloons and Dutch Calvinists fled to the north or to Germany. The presence of troops in the Netherlands from 1567 had a devastating effect on its commerce. In the north, the influx of southern refugees, high prices and growing unemployment led to food shortages and riots, though some towns like Leiden and Middelburg benefited from the arrival of skilled Flemish textile and craft workers. In the south, armies of occupation pillaged towns and lived off the land. Brabant's population fell by 25 per cent between 1575 and 1586. Antwerp suffered irreparably from three 'sackings' at the hands of Calvinists (1566), Spanish mutineers (1576) and French deserters (1583). Its commerce had already been hit by the loss of the Portuguese pepper monopoly in 1549 and by the blockading of the river Scheldt from 1572 by anti-Spanish rebels. As a result, Antwerp's population fell from 80,000 in 1568 to 42,000 in 1589. Amsterdam took over as the premier city of commerce.

The French economy suffered the full rigours of war in the last third of the century. Its population fell from 18 to 16 million between 1560 and 1600 after rising from 10 million in 1500. Inept government financial policies and recurring civil war shook the confidence of investors in Lyon. In 1545 Lyon had 41 banks; by 1592 there were only four. Trade declined

KEY TERM:

Tenant farmers

Tenant farmers did not own their own land. They rented it from landowners and were responsible for keeping it productive. The tenant farmer paid an agreed sum for a lease from the landlord which gave him the right to farm the land.

in the 1580s in Amiens, the main weaving town, and Rouen, a major port. From 1589 to 1594, it was Paris's turn to suffer the full effects of fighting, food crisis and plague – an era appropriately termed *les années terribles*. War against Spain between 1596 and 1598 completed the agony in Burgundy and parts of Brittany, while in the south-west the *Croquants* (country yokels) rose up in revolt against war taxation and noble repression.

4 The Reformation

Marxist historians once claimed that the Reformation produced a new class, the bourgeoisie, which rose on the backs of the **tenant farmers** and day labourers, and displaced the traditional nobility in western Europe in the sixteenth century. Some sociologists also contended that the Reformation produced Protestants who believed that economic activity and profiteering was blessed by God, and so generated a 'spirit of capitalism'. Today, few historians accept these interpretations. If we take 'capitalism' to mean monetary investments, usury and profit-making, it is clear that such activities existed well before the Reformation. Indeed, in the 1540s an interest rate of 5 per cent was acceptable to both the Catholic and Reformed churches provided it covered business costs and expenses. The sixteenth century was not an 'age of capitalism'. Wealth was confined to a minority of urban groups who preferred to invest in land and trade; the vast majority of people lived on the land, received wages in kind and were in no position to invest in trade and industry.

It is, of course, true that there was a greater availability of silver for investment in commerce, as well as easier credit transactions. There was increasing speculation on exchange rates and the creation of joint stock companies and attractive government bonds provided investment opportunities. More banks existed at the end of the century. However, it was an era notable for the absence of any intrinsic 'capitalist spirit'. Luther and Calvin unreservedly condemned usury and not until the nineteenth century did Calvinists propound the godliness of making profits. Though many social and economic changes occurred in the course of the sixteenth century, the Reformation was not responsible for creating a proto-industrialised society. This was the creation of dialectically and ideologically inspired historians whose theses have been overthrown in the last quarter-century.

Task: analysis of factors

Interpreting economic changes over a long period of time and for many countries is a difficult, if not impossible, task. Indeed, insufficient evidence exists for a comparative assessment of every European country, but the following exercise will help you to understand when and why six areas of Europe experienced economic changes in the course of the sixteenth century.

Take a sheet of paper. Divide it into six horizontal sections and three vertical columns. The horizontal sections represent: Portugal; Spain; France; the Empire; Italian states; and Eastern Europe. The vertical columns represent: population trends and natural disasters; European overseas expansion; government initiatives.

Read the chapter again. Whenever a country, region or town is mentioned, put the information in note form into the appropriate square on your paper. When you have completed the analysis, you should be able to see when and why each area's economy changed. Summarise these changes in one-sentence explanations at the bottom of each square and compare your findings with other students.

Further reading

E. E. Rich and C. H. Wilson (eds), *The Cambridge Economic History of Europe*, vol. iv (Cambridge University Press, 1967) – provides a good starting-point for this theme.

C. R. Boxer, *The Portuguese Seaborne Empire, 1415–1825* (Hutchinson, 1969).

J. H. Parry, *The Spanish Seaborne Empire* (Hutchinson, 1966) – still a valuable source of information on Spain's overseas possessions.

D. O'Sullivan, *The Age of Discovery, 1400–1550* (Addison Wesley Longman, 1984).

H. Kamen, *European Society, 1500–1700* (Hutchinson, 1984) – contains a mine of information.

R. Mackenney, *Sixteenth Century Europe: Expansion and Conflict* (Macmillan, 1993) – is an excellent recent study covering far more than economic themes.

F. Braudel, *The Mediterranean and the Mediterranean World in the Age of Philip II* (2nd edn Fontana, 1975) – an outstanding work unlikely to be surpassed.

21 Did Spain experience a 'decade of crisis' in the 1590s?

Time chart

1580s: Regular imports of wheat into Spain

1585: War against England begins

1588–91: Plague in Valencia, Catalonia, Galicia and Murcia

1590s: Valladolid, Toledo, Ciudad Real and Córdoba record a decline in births

1590: Demonstrations in Madrid over the introduction of the *Millones*

1594: Dutch merchants begin voyages to the Caribbean

1596: *Sisa* tax is introduced. Indies fleet delivers 5.7 million ducats. War against France begins third state bankruptcy. Plague in Old Castile and Portugal

1598: State debt stands at 85 million ducats. War with France ends

1600: Cellorigo publishes his *Memorial*

In the previous chapter we saw how changing economic and social trends affected different European countries in the course of the sixteenth century. Some states responded positively, others were perplexed and failed to take advantage of them. Much of western Europe had been disrupted by wars, which served to accelerate the forces of change and create an increasingly unstable society. The last decade of the century saw many countries experience serious difficulties which some historians have suggested amounted to a 'crisis'. This chapter examines Spain in the 1590s to see how far it may be said to have experienced a 'decade of crisis'.

Peter Clark has defined the term 'crisis' as 'short-term, interrelated economic, social and political upheavals precipitating longer-term structural changes in society'. Difficulties arise when we begin to consider the evidence: variations clearly existed between regions but are these variations simply a reflection of the uneven quality of surviving evidence? Overall trends could be exaggerated and of course local conditions were not necessarily repeated in other parts of a country. If a town experienced a commercial decline because of a fall in demand for its products but

KEY TERM:

Arbitristas

Arbitristas were Spanish writers who drew up *arbitrios* or recommendations for economic and political reform. Many of these were more idealistic rather than practical solutions to Spain's domestic problems.

increased its agricultural output to satisfy a rise in population, can it be said to have suffered a crisis? Peasants' wages rose and urban workers' wages fell according to demand, so there were constant fluctuations in wages, prices and patterns of employment. It is likely that in many cases potential 'crises' were overcome by self-regulating triggers. For example, if a city's population fell as a result of plague there was less pressure on resources, wages began to rise, people tended to marry earlier and a recovery followed. Similarly, long-term forces for stability could counter-act short-term problems, though to contemporaries these problems might appear symptomatic of a real decline.

The Spanish *arbitristas* in particular complained about economic problems and tried to present a case in favour of their particular reform programme.

The evidence

For much of the 1590s Spain experienced a combination of plague, famine, war, rising poverty and unemployment. Spain suffered two visitations of the 'pest' (plague), in 1588–91 and 1596–1602. The east coast of Valencia and Catalonia and the northern provinces of Galicia and Asturias were first affected though the rate of mortality was far higher in the second epidemic which hit the northern and southern coastal areas, much of Old Castile and Portugal. In Santander in 1599 four-fifths of its 3,000 inhabitants died and in Valladolid 6,500 (one-sixth of its total) died. Running in tandem with these outbreaks of plague were food crises, caused principally by bad weather. Long spells of heavy rain followed by prolonged drought seriously affected the harvests in Valencia and Murcia between 1589 and 1598, Galicia in 1589–91 and 1597, and led to a general grain crisis.

In Andalucía, the price of corn more than doubled between 1595 and 1598, and in central Spain more people died from starvation than from plague. Historians continue to argue about the preconditions of the plague of 1599. They warn against automatically linking disease with subsistence, but it seems likely that successive years of malnutrition did reduce the immunity of unprivileged masses of people and left them vulnerable to the bubonic epidemic. As a consequence, over 600,000 (one-tenth of Spain's population) had died by 1602. Two notable results followed:

1 Towns and villages in northern Castile, especially Galicia, witnessed a migration of unemployed, impoverished starving people to the richer south, which served to accentuate existing urban problems there.

2 Reports of deserted villages and depopulated towns convinced contemporaries that Spain was facing an imminent demographic crisis. Valladolid, Toledo, Cáceres, Burgos and Córdoba had falling populations and lent weight to the Cortes's claim in 1594 that 'the kingdom is wasted and destroyed, for there is hardly a man in it that enjoys any fortune or credit'. Although this report was gloomy, the sentiments were sincere.

Agriculture

Spain experienced an agrarian depression in the 1590s. Declining animal herds and poor arable farming led to a fall in production, which in turn forced food prices to rise above wages and landlords to increase their ground rents. The peasantry suffered most. Many were forced to negotiate *censos*; some failed to sustain their payments and were forced to sell their freehold and move to the towns or became tenant farmers. The Castilian Cortes asserted in 1598 that 'everything tends towards the destruction of the poor peasantry and the increase in property, authority and power of the rich'. Martin González de Cellorigo, writing two years later, pinpointed what he believed was the cause:

> 'Censos *are the plague and ruin of Spain. For the sweetness of the sure profit from* censos *the merchant leaves his trading, the artisan his employment, the peasant his farming, the shepherd his flock; and the noble sells his lands so as to exchange the one hundred they bring in for the five hundred the* juro *[annuity] brings.'*

Trade

Merchants, tradesmen and craftsmen also suffered in the 1590s. A shortage of raw materials and a failure to develop domestic manufactures meant that for much of the sixteenth century there was an adverse balance of trade. In the last decade this became a recession. Exports had been falling since the 1580s in the cloth-producing towns of Córdoba, Segovia, Cuenca and Burgos. One of the most important commercial towns, Medina del Campo, had been declining since the 1570s, when the Crown suspended interest payments for the second time. A third state bankruptcy decree in 1596 dealt a body blow to the confidence of merchant bankers, and many local families were ruined.

A handful of industries like the iron foundries in Vizcaya, shipbuilding in Barcelona and silk trade in Granada continued to flourish; the value of goods entering and leaving the port of Seville, which handled all trade with America, reached its maximum in the years 1596 to 1601; however, these examples of economic activity belied underlying weaknesses. Most domestic trade was already controlled by Genoese and Flemish merchants, and it was Dutch shipping which conveyed most Baltic grain supplies to the Mediterranean. In addition, from 1594 the Dutch were making regular voyages to the Caribbean. Together with the English, they were threatening Spain's transatlantic commercial monopoly. Moreover, Mexico and Peru were producing their own goods and beginning to look beyond Spain for their trade.

Government finances

Between 1591 and 1600 the silver mines of Potosí produced more ore than at any subsequent period; in 1595 the Indies fleet brought in its highest ever load of bullion worth 5.7 million ducats, but most of it left Seville via foreign bankers or was earmarked for war. Only a small amount was invested in trade and industry, and by the end of the decade *arbitristas* like Cellorigo were issuing doom-laden forecasts. 'Henceforward, we can only expect shortages of everything because of the lack of people to work in the fields and in all the manufactures the kingdom needs.'

To offset rising government expenditure, taxation was increased and as the clergy and nobility were exempt it was the towns that bore the brunt. The principal tax, the *alcabala*, had tripled between 1559 and 1577. Town authorities, responsible for its collection and payment, borrowed money to meet its charges. Though there was only a 30 per cent increase between 1577 and 1600, several town councils became impoverished in the 1590s.

Matters worsened in 1590 when the Castilian Cortes begrudgingly consented to a new indirect tax, the *millones*, on meat, wine, oil and vinegar. Though it was a once-only tax designed to raise 8 million ducats spread over six years, it was very unpopular because it affected basic foods. There were more complaints in 1596 when a *sisa* tax was introduced on other foodstuffs. Several town councils, led by Avila and Burgos, refused to collect it.

Unrest

Few cities were like Toledo which had its own poorhouse for 600 inmates. Most towns depended on private and clerical charity, hospitals and granaries in times of famine, but it is clear from the number of complaints voiced by the *procuradores* (representatives elected to the Cortes) between 1592 and 1598 that this system of poor relief was breaking down. Popular disturbances occurred in Madrid, Saragossa, Toledo and Seville; banditry was apparently increasing in Valencia, Catalonia and Murcia, and riots broke out between lords and vassals in Ribagorza. Yet, as in most European countries, there were no large-scale revolts. The historian Clifford Davies has suggested that as social and economic tension heightened, every effort was made by all groups to contain the problem. Town authorities appear to have learned from how to defuse potential flashpoints – emigration to America was encouraged and no attempt was made to push a heavily taxed population too far. For their part, the urban poor and peasantry desisted from acts of open rebellion as they had no wish to lose their land tenures to the nobility.

War and defeat

Some historians have attributed the main source of Spain's ills to her military commitments, which by the 1590s had exhausted the country financially, physically and psychologically. Wars against the Netherlands (1568–1609), England (1585–1604) and France (1596–8) had seen annual military expenses rise from 2 to 10 million ducats between the 1560s and 1590s. The Cortes complained in 1591, 'Our wars only suffice to make us poorer and our enemies richer'. One *procurador* asked, 'Was the war really necessary? Could Castile continue to afford it?' The inevitable corollary to this unprecedented scale of warfare was an ever-spiralling national debt. In 1596 Philip II was forced to issue a decree of bankruptcy and two years later the state debt stood at 85 million ducats, with interest payments accounting for 40 per cent of total income.

To meet the needs of a maritime and land war, the Spanish nation had been put on a war footing. Recruiting, billeting, supplies and the levying of contributions tended to fall on the same geographical areas (Andalucía, Extramadura and Galicia) and on the same social groups (urban workers and rural peasants). This accelerated existing trends, namely the abandonment of land, migration to towns and an increase in **seigneurialisation**. Central and local administration in particular was put under severe pressure. The royal council acknowledged that the only sure way of victualling the troops, supplying arms and equipping the fleets was to assign regular revenues to finance specific aspects of naval and military expenditure. This process was known as *consignación*. However, giving local grandees and military contractors the authority to make on-the-spot decisions also caused tension as war secretaries and military governors clashed with town councillors over the implementation of orders.

For the first time since the acquisition of their empire, the 1590s brought

KEY TERM:

Seigneurialisation

'Lordships' or *señoríos* were areas of land over which a lord or señor exercised considerable rights. As peasants moved to towns in search of work, landlords acquired more property and enhanced their control over remaining tenants – the process known as **seigneurialisation**.

home to Spaniards the unpalatable taste of defeat. The defeat of the Armada in 1588 was not seen as an irredeemable disaster but the failure of two subsequent armadas in 1596 and 1597 and the sight of English privateers attacking the Spanish mainland were humiliating experiences. In 1589 Francis Drake and Sir John Norris sailed into Corunna and Lisbon; in 1596 Charles Howard and the Earl of Essex sacked Cadiz. Philip retaliated in kind but a decisive victory eluded him.

War against the Dutch also lost its sense of direction in the 1590s once Philip had ordered Parma to invade France. The general's death in 1592 was a serious blow and reports of persistent mutinies in the Army of Flanders convinced the King that a military solution was no longer feasible. The appointment of Isabella and Albert as regents in 1598, both advocates of peace, indicated that Spain had overreached itself. Philip now felt the same about his ill-advised attempts to deny Henry of Navarre the French throne, and the resulting Treaty of Vervins punctuated a chapter of military failures.

This unbroken sequence of national defeats had a depressing effect at all levels. Esteban de Ibarra, Secretary of War, declared in August 1597, 'Everything is in such a state that it takes away one's will to work and serve just to see the way things are going'. The King no longer had his hand on the tiller and the 'ship of state' appeared to be drifting. At his death in 1598, Spain urgently needed peace and clear-sighted leadership: it received neither. Philip III opened his reign with a flourish of militarism. Troops were sent to Ireland, a greater effort demanded from the Army of Flanders and an expedition planned against the north African Muslims. Defeat at Nieuwpoort (Flanders) in 1600, Kinsale (Ireland) in 1601 and repeated mauling of Murcian villages by Barbary corsairs intensified the feeling of *desengaño* (disappointment). *Don Quixote*, written in 1605, captured this sense of fatalism.

Were the 1590s an abnormal decade?

Historians have been wary of reading too much into fragmentary statistics and drawing conclusions about the effects of a single mortality crisis. In 1963 J. H. Elliott warned against placing too much emphasis on studies covering only 10 years and suggested longer periods of history might prove more rewarding. Recent studies of the population of Castilian towns reveal the long-term effects of Philip's decision to move his capital to Madrid in 1561. Thirty years later, its population had more than doubled but in doing so had drained the nearby towns and villages of their agricultural and commercial livelihood. As crop yields fell, infant death rates rose. Once an area became impoverished, it was more vulnerable to epidemics and subsistence crises, which in turn increased the incidence of mortality. Thus, in the 1590s, Valladolid, Toledo and Ciudad Real all showed a fall in the number of births and the once-flourishing town of Puente de Duero was semi-deserted.

Yet this decade was not a demographic turning-point. In each case, underlying trends can be traced back to the 1560s and 1570s when their population levels began to fall. It is generally accepted that populations are capable of recovering remarkably quickly from short-run epidemics and a marital boom often follows hard upon a demographic crisis. Córdoba, for instance, had a falling population in the 1590s yet experienced a sharp rise in marriages in the early seventeenth century. Pérez Moreda has suggested that what really mattered was the effect the mortality crisis had on the most fertile adult age-groups; in this respect, the 1590s was not an exceptional decade. As a result, population levels in many towns recovered in the reign of Philip III.

Similarly, rural debt, the movement from freehold to leasehold, and the urbanisation of the peasantry were features of Spanish society well before the end of the century. In the 1570s, Valencian farmers had complained of falling food production and growing poverty. Many, like their peasant counterparts in the north-east and south-west of France, had been forced to subdivide their smallholdings, sell them off and return to *métayage* (sharecropping). In the 1580s, Spain experienced serious grain shortages which could only be redressed by regular wheat imports. Trade and commerce fared little better, and again the underlying explanation can be found in long-term trends. Powerful town guilds had consistently resisted state intervention to regulate or change traditional trades, and only in a few industries like paper, printing, soap, armaments, glass and ship-building was there any significant modernisation. As native manufactures declined, foreign imports increased with any deficit being covered by the lucrative American silver bullion. In this respect the 1590s were not a turning-point. James Casey writes, 'Rather it [the decade] reinforced the structures of a traditional Spain. But Spain's peculiar failure was an inability to complete the transition to a more urbanised economy.' It was this weakness which bedevilled it throughout the seventeenth century.

However, one major change was taking place. The 1590s saw the high-water mark in Spanish-American commerce. After 1600 Seville received less silver and conducted less trade to and from America; at the same time, foreign competition stiffened. In the opinion of Professor Elliott, 'the economies of Spain and of its American possessions began to move apart, while Dutch and English interlopers were squeezing themselves into a widening gap'. This trend would also become more pronounced in the early years of the seventeenth century.

Conclusion

The 1590s may not have been a watershed in Spanish history but it was a critical decade and contemporaries sensed it was more than just a national disillusionment. Of course, Spain was not alone in experiencing severe famine, widespread poverty, rising unemployment, epidemics and high mortality. Moreover, though it was spared the effects of armies invading the peninsula and religious conflict which so bedevilled France, it was still a nation at war. The years of crisis had long-term as well as immediate causes, and if structurally Spain's administration, economy and society continued essentially unchanged into the seventeenth century, existing weaknesses intensified and made future recovery, innovation and development all the more difficult.

Task: historical interpretation of events

a What are the advantages and limitations of using Peter Clark's definition of a 'crisis'? (page 209)

b Why are historians generally wary of linking the spread of diseases with subsistence conditions? (page 210)

c According to Cellorigo, what damage did *censos* do to the economy? (page 211)

d What evidence is there that trade and industry were in decline in the 1590s? (pages 211–12)

e Why, according to Clifford Davies, did Spain not see any rebellions in the 1590s? (page 213)

f In your opinion, how far was the government to blame for (i) the country's economic condition and (ii) its military defeats?

g Why have some historians questioned whether the 1590s really was a 'decade of crisis' in Spain?

Further reading

P. Clark (ed.), *The European Crisis of the 1590s* (Allen and Unwin, 1983) – contains an excellent introduction and several comparative studies.

T. Aston (ed.), *Crisis in Europe, 1560–1660* (Past and Present, 1965) – a series of essays which challenge the notion that there was a 'crisis'.

I. A. A. Thompson, *War and Government in Habsburg Spain, 1560–1620* (Athlone Press, 1960) – examines the effects of war upon Spain's infrastructure.

L. Martz, *Poverty and Welfare in Habsburg Spain: the Example of Toledo* (Cambridge University Press, 1983) – discusses social and economic problems.

M. Grice-Hutchinson, *Early Economic Thought in Spain, 1177–1740* (Allen and Unwin, 1978) – looks at the underlying philosophies behind economic ideas during this period.

Part Three Towards a new order, 1598–1648

22 Spain, 1598–1648: a period of recovery or decline?

Time chart

1598: Death of Philip II; accession of Philip III

1599: *Vellón* currency is introduced. Lerma becomes the *valido* (favourite)

1604: Treaty of London ends Anglo-Spanish war; relief of Ostend by Spínola

1607: Crown debts suspended

1609: Truce of Antwerp is signed. Expulsion of *Moriscos* from Valencia

1615: Franco-Spanish marriage treaties

1618: Lerma resigns

1619: Spanish troops assist Austria in Bohemia

1620: Spínola captures Heidelberg

1621: Death of Philip III; accession of Philip IV. Renewal of Dutch war

1622: Death of Zúñiga; Olivares becomes the *valido*

1624: *Almirantazgo* project begins. Union of Arms. Valtelline war begins

1626: Valtelline war ends

1627: Suspension of crown debts

1628: Spanish bullion fleet is seized by Dutch at Matanzas Bay

1629: Mantua-Montferrat succession dispute begins

1631: France captures Pinerolo; Treaty of Cherasco ends Mantuan war

1634: Spanish-Imperial army defeats Sweden at Nördlingen

1635: Start of the Franco-Spanish war

1636: Spain captures Corbie

1639: Spanish armadas fail to recover Brazil; Tromp wins Battle of the Downs

1640: Battle of Pernambuco. Revolts in Catalonia and Portugal

1643: Olivares falls from office. Battle of Rocroi

1647: Luis de Haro becomes the *valido*. Revolts in Naples and Sicily. Suspension of crown debts

1648: Peace of Münster ends Dutch war. Battle of Lens. Treaty of Westphalia

In October 1648 the Treaty of Münster ended the Eighty Years' War between Spain and the United Provinces. It was Spain's first official acknowledgement of failure in a decade of disasters. The hitherto invincible *tercios* (infantry) suffered major reverses at Rocroi, Dunkirk (1646) and Lens (1648); the navy was well beaten by the Dutch at the Downs and at Pernambuco near Brazil; revolts had broken out in Catalonia (1640–52), Portugal (1640–68) and Naples (1647–8), and the Crown was declared bankrupt (1647) for the third time in the seventeenth century.

As the war against France continued, the question facing King Philip IV was whether he could halt Spain's international decline or was it irreversible and terminal? Traditionally historians have accepted that Spain was in decline after the 'Golden Age' of Philip II. More recently some have questioned whether it could decline since, in their view, it had never been a great economic power; and a few have argued that to speak of a *declinación* before 1648 is anachronistic as Spain remained a major power well into the reign of Charles II. This chapter compares the reigns of Philip III and Philip IV, and their *validos* (favourites), the Duke of Lerma and Count-Duke Olivares. It examines domestic and foreign policies, and it seeks to discover how far and why Spain changed between 1598 and 1648.

The reign of Philip III (1598–1621)

The legacy which Philip III inherited from his father contained enough problems to defeat the most able and industrious administration. Unfortunately neither the King and his favourite, the Duke of Lerma who controlled the household and royal patronage, nor his principal adviser Juan de Idiáquez who dominated the Council of State, were equal to the task. The King at 20 had limited governmental experience yet showed an initial enthusiasm for reform. He dispensed with his father's *Junta de Noche* and his secretaries of state and instead restored the councils of state, war and finance, and in his most significant policy change made them answerable to the *valido*. Yet problems remained.

1 The King continued to display his preference for hunting, religious devotion and travelling around his kingdom, leaving policy-making to the Council of State and to the Duke of Lerma. The *valido* rewarded himself and his family most handsomely, and the expanding secretariat became top-heavy and riddled with corruption.

2 The Cortes preserved its financial privileges, resisted any increase in indirect taxation and failed to tackle any of the Crown's economic problems. Instead of fundamental tax reforms, which might have narrowed the budget deficit and reduced Castile's massive contribution, short-term expedients were advanced. A copper currency (known as *vellón*) was introduced for the first time in 1599, and further debasements in 1603, 1618 and 1621 caused inflation; government offices were sold off, the *alcabala* trebled and a number of indirect taxes increased. The burden of taxation, however, still fell on Castile yet its economy was showing signs of decay: the number of sheep in the Mesta fell from 4 to 2 million, imports of food and manufactured goods continued to rise, and the bubonic plague and famine of 1596–1602 left villages deserted. In Seville alone more than 8,000 had died in 1599. Financially, the Crown's position seemed desperate: 50 per cent of its revenue – some 5 million ducats – went on annual interest payments to service the inherited debt of 85 million ducats. In 1607 they could no longer be met and not for the last time, repayments were suspended. Most ominously, American bullion imports were beginning to fall after peaking in the five years 1601 to 1605.

Undoubtedly this continuing economic crisis was worsened by Philip's reluctance to concede to his disobedient Dutch subjects. Though he wisely ended his inherited and largely unwelcome war with England in August 1604, his commitment to defeating the Netherlands was as sincere as it was misguided. Early defeats at Nieuwpoort, Rheinberg and Sluys were countered by General Spínola's relief of Ostend and subsequent successes between 1604 and 1606 as the Army of Flanders swept into the heart of the United Provinces. Prospects of victory, however, ended in 1607 when financial reserves ran dry. Archduke Albert and General Spínola were both ready for peace but the Dutch struck such a hard bargain that it took considerable strength of will by Philip to agree to a 12-year truce in 1609. Spain recognised Dutch independence and permitted their merchants to remain in the East Indies; while the Dutch refused to guarantee the safety of Roman Catholics in the republic and continued to blockade the river Scheldt.

To offset popular reaction to the truce, an antidote was required. On 9 April 1609, the same day that the Truce of Antwerp was signed, Philip took the decision to deport 300,000 *Moriscos*, first from Valencia and in 1614 from all remaining areas of Spain. Historians generally agree on the adverse impact of the expulsion. Most believe the textile and farming industries in Andalucía and Valencia were seriously affected, although James Casey has raised doubts about the *Moriscos'* overall contribution to the national economy in the early seventeenth century. Henry Kamen has stressed that, while Valencia and Aragon suffered an 'immediate economic catastrophe', the expulsion was not complete. Whether the motive for this 'ethnic cleansing' was religious, racial or national security, the news was popularly received in Castile. So, too, were reports of the successful expeditions against the Turks in Malta (1611) and the Barbary pirates in Tunis (1612) and Morocco (1614), which was further proof that Spain was now paying more attention to north Africa and Italy.

Lerma's aims

Each of the major political decisions in the first half of Philip III's reign bears the mark of the Duke of Lerma: peace with England, truce with the Dutch and the expulsion of the *Moriscos*. His long-term goal was to preserve the Spanish dominions by diplomacy not war, by dynastic alliances not confrontations. In the short term, he wanted to disengage Spain from the problems of northern Europe and once more make the Mediterranean the axis of foreign policy. The death of Henry IV in 1610 spared Spain a major war over Cleves-Julich between the Habsburg-backed Catholic League and the Franco-Dutch endorsed Evangelical Union. This gave Lerma his chance. A treaty of friendship was signed between Spain and France in 1612, cemented by a double marriage three years later between Louis XIII and Philip III's daughter Anne, and between Elizabeth of France and Philip III's son, Philip. France's minority rule, England's pacific king and the German Empire's unstable emperors helped to buttress an image of Spanish power while active diplomats like Gondomar, Zúñiga and Oñate maintained Spain's international profile.

Lerma strongly urged Philip against intervention in the Bohemia crisis. Once committed, he claimed, 'it would be impossible to find a way out'. But the former ambassador to the Empire, Don Baltasar de Zúñiga, was convinced that the Italian possessions were at risk. Archduke Albert believed the Dutch would be more likely to negotiate a favourable settlement in the face of an active Spanish foreign policy, and the King himself declared, 'Germany simply cannot be lost'. Finding his peace policy out of favour in October 1618, Lerma quietly withdrew from public life and Philip assumed a more personal direction of affairs.

Philip's direction

Two vital decisions were taken between 1619 and 1621.

1 The government committed itself to providing 100,000 ducats a month for the imperial armies in Bohemia and Austria, and despatched another 100,000 ducats to Spínola to invade the Lower Palatinate, the centre of European Calvinism. By the end of 1620, the Austrian Habsburgs had captured Bohemia, forced Frederick of the Palatinate into exile and Spanish troops had seized his capital of Heidelberg.

2 The hawks in Madrid, Brussels, Vienna and Naples convinced the King that as the Twelve Years' Truce neared its expiry, a renewal of war with the Netherlands was preferable to a prolongation of peace. Dutch merchants, it was argued, had exploited the armistice to interlope in west Africa, India, Indonesia and South America. They had tightened their grip on commercial and maritime trade in Europe and were uncompromising in their peace negotiations. Undoubtedly, Dutch trade had expanded considerably since 1609. According to Francesco de Rétama, some 820 Dutch ships were visiting Iberian and south Italian ports each year and controlled 80 per cent of all Baltic trade. Spain's reputation was at stake.

The death of Philip III on 31 March 1621, nine days before the end of the truce, left the declaration of war to his successor. Forgotten were the complaints of the *arbitristas*, those harbingers of doom who for the past 20 years had lamented Spain's economic and social ills. Deleted from the political agenda was the Council of Castile's *Memorial* of 1619 urging the Crown to implement a fairer tax system, reduce royal patronage and raise the level of morality at the court. Instead, optimism replaced pessimism as a new age dawned and Spain prepared to embark on the next chapter of its imperial destiny.

The accession of Philip IV (1621–65)

The accession of Philip IV – a sensuous, cultured, fatalistic 16-year-old – did not bode well for Spain. Admittedly, in later life he became more administratively conscientious but at first he depended heavily on his valido, **Count-Duke of Olivares**.

Spain and France

Helping the Austrian Habsburgs was, in Olivares's view, crucial to the survival of the Spanish Empire for if Germany were to fall, then so would Italy, 'after Italy, Flanders, then the Indies, Naples and Sicily'. To maintain a regular supply of men, money and weapons along the 'Spanish Road' from Milan to the Netherlands and Empire, he saw how vital it was to safeguard the Valtelline, an alpine valley between Milan and the Empire, inhabited by Catholics and ruled by Protestant Grisons (see Figure 24.2 on page 244). In 1620 Spanish troops secured its control but four years later France attempted to dislodge them. Though they failed and agreed to withdraw in 1626, the threat remained.

Olivares's perceived fear of destabilisation in north Italy prompted him to intervene in the Mantua-Montferrat succession dispute in 1628. It was

PROFILE: *Count-Duke of Olivares*

Gaspar de Guzmán, Count-Duke of Olivares, was born in 1587. As the nephew of Zúñiga, Olivares was well schooled in court intrigue, first acquiring offices in the royal household and then removing Lerma's principal clients and successors. When his uncle died in 1622, Olivares was ready to continue the aggressive foreign policy in the Holy Roman Empire and the Netherlands in defence of Spain's reputation. He would remain the King's *valido* until 1643. Strong in physique and temperament, hard-working and mentally agile, Olivares charted the course of the 'ship of state', letting his captain rule while he governed the country. The King's readiness to endorse Olivares's lead mirrored Louis XIII's partnership with Richelieu, and their contemporary careers make an interesting comparison. Olivares died in 1645.

his most serious error. In trying to prevent the legitimate French claimant, the Duke of Nevers, from taking the duchy, Olivares believed he would be strengthening Spanish communications between Genoa, Milan and the Valtelline, but in practice he needled Louis XIII into sending assistance to Nevers. French troops promptly invaded Savoy, Spain's ally, and seized Pinerolo for themselves and Mantua for the French duke. When the war ended in 1631, it was apparent who had won. Olivares had spent 10 million ducats, his domestic reforms had been shelved and Spain was one step nearer to open warfare with France.

Yet it is hard to see how he could have avoided war with the Bourbons since it was Richelieu's avowed aim to probe the sensitive points of the Spanish Habsburgs – the Valtelline, Flanders, the Rhineland and the Pyrenees – and to form anti-Habsburg alliances with Protestant states. Certainly, Spain's seizure of Trier in 1635 forced France into declaring war, as Olivares knew it would. It is possible that having heard of the imperial success over the Swedes at Nördlingen he believed a short and decisive war was there for the taking. At first, it seemed he was right. In 1636 the Cardinal-Infante, Philip's brother, captured Corbie on the river Somme, just 80 miles from Paris, but the success was not followed up. Worse, Richelieu's offer of a truce was rejected out of hand and the chance to end the conflict on his own terms never recurred. Thereafter Olivares witnessed a series of defeats, the most devastating of which was the fall of Breisach in the Rhineland in 1638, resulting in the permanent severance of the 'Spanish Road'.

Spain and the Netherlands

War against the Dutch was renewed in August 1621 and was central to Olivares's foreign policy throughout the 1620s. Spínola's defeat at Bergen-op-Zoom in 1622, with the loss of 9,000, men, was countered by victory at Breda three years later but it was clear to Olivares that drawn-out sieges did not favour Spain. It took 11 months to capture Breda and its fortress needed more troops to garrison than the number of inhabitants in the town. Moreover, he could not see where the 14 million ducats needed for the following year's campaign would come from.

A new initiative was required. When peace terms were again rejected by the Dutch, Olivares implemented his most far-sighted strategy to date: he intended imposing a naval blockade on Dutch ports, putting an embargo on their goods, using Dunkirk as a centre for scuttling the North Sea fisheries and, in conjunction with the imperial army, establishing a north German trading base to capture their Baltic trade. An offensive by sea would replace the offensive by land. This **Almirantazgo** (or Admiralty) project of 1624–5 was designed not only to hit the Dutch where it hurt but to bring the imperial forces into Spain's theatre of operations.

For four years the strategy was very effective but its success endangered Sweden's livelihood. Once it entered the conflict in 1629, the Baltic was soon cleared of Spanish ships and imperial troops; the economic blockade was relaxed and finally lifted. The tide had turned against Spain. Already, failure to honour interest payments in 1627 and the seizure by Dutch privateers of a treasure fleet at Matanzas off the Cuban coast in 1628 added to the Treasury's problems, which were not helped by Olivares's decision to involve Spain in the Mantua-Montferrat succession dispute.

As the Dutch resumed the offensive, capturing Wesel and 's Hertogenbosch in 1629, Maastricht and Limburg in 1631, and three more towns by 1632, the Spanish Army of Flanders was in disarray. The death of Spínola in 1630 left it without an experienced leader and, reduced to one-third its usual size due to imperial commitments, outnumbered. More poignantly, it was the Dutch who held the whiphand and between 1629 and 1632 their States-General, led by the Zeeland and Gröningen regents, scuppered Spanish-initiated peace talks. Richelieu's clandestine activities in the 1630s obliged Olivares to concentrate his forces on Germany and assume the offensive against France. Though this strategy was widely supported, it remained a gamble which ultimately played into Dutch hands. In 1637 the Dutch recaptured Breda and two years later Admiral Tromp's navy sank 32 Spanish ships at the Downs, effectively ending Spanish hopes of defeating the Franco-Dutch alliance. Though 90,000 troops remained in Flanders in 1640, their invincibility was exposed at Rocroi in 1643; by then Olivares had fallen from power.

Domestic policy

Olivares, like Richelieu, subordinated his domestic policies to foreign affairs. But whereas the Cardinal refrained from committing his country to an active strategy until France was internally secure, Olivares set in motion long overdue domestic reforms alongside heavy imperial commitments. The combination proved fatal. Olivares knew that to sustain a forward policy he had to reduce the economic and military burden on Castile, but at every step his fiscal policy was baulked by vested interests and indifference. The Cortes opposed his idea of a national bank in 1622 and refused to abolish the *alcabala* and *millones* in place of a single, consolidated tax. Instead he sought to raise revenue by forced loans, sale of offices and royal villages, taxes on salt, paper and playing cards, the introduction of excise duties and a stamp tax, and by reluctantly doubling the *millones* from 2 to 4 million ducats in 1626. To cut inflation the *vellón* currency was withdrawn in 1626 but declining silver and gold reserves, falling American imports and rising imperial expenditure forced him to rethink his strategy. Without warning, and reminiscent of Philip II in 1575, Olivares suspended repayments to his creditors in 1627 and debased the currency by 50 per cent in 1628.

Further expedients followed in the 1630s: *juros* payments were confiscated, Crown lands sold off and another copper coinage issued in 1636. One way or another – through loans, sales, taxation, bullion imports and currency manipulation – enough money was found to lubricate the war machine but Olivares was scraping the barrel.

Like Thomas Wentworth in England, Olivares believed that an extravagant court lifestyle corrupted social values and discouraged economic investment. Spanish nobles were ordered to spend no more than 30 days at Court and to desist from wearing ostentatious clothes. Latin was only taught to selected boys to discourage them from entering the unproductive professions rather than going into trades and industry. In an attempt to counter falling population levels, bachelors were taxed, married persons received rebates, emigration licences were restricted and vagrants severely sentenced. Such measures were welcomed by the *arbitristas* but they made little impact on Spain's falling economic growth rate. The inequitable tax system, corrupt administration, absence of native trading companies, and limited industrial base remained unchanged and were no longer masked by American silver imports. In the late 1640s official figures suggest that an average of 3 million ducats entered Seville.

Even if this figure is too low (Dutch public gazettes reveal an average of 12 million), more than 75 per cent was earmarked for foreign bankers. After allowance is made for peculation (fraudulent practices), the Crown only received about 14 per cent. The gross tonnage of transatlantic trade also showed a downward trend totalling 121,308 tons between 1646 and 1650, a fall of 60 per cent since 1606–10; the number of sailings had fallen from 965 to 366.

Administration

Philip IV – like Charles I in England and Louis XIII in France – believed that a more centralised and unitary state would be administratively more efficient, financially more frugal and politically more effective. In theory this was correct. Spain's administration was decentralised, power resting with town oligarchs and local nobles, but in practice Olivares's reforms met so much resistance that the Crown's control actually decreased. Particularism (*i.e.* separatism) ran deep in Aragon, Catalonia, Granada and Portugal and regional practices were too well protected by the Cortes for Olivares to make any significant progress: his persistence in the face of adversity is a reflection of his flawed statesmanship and largely explains his fall from power.

In 1624 he issued the Union of Arms, designed to establish a national reservist army of 140,000 troops. Each province was expected to contribute towards it though Castile would, as usual, shoulder most of the burden. Philip played down the unitary idea and stressed the state of the nation instead, but it is clear from Olivares's *Great Memorial* of December 1624 what lay behind the reform. He urged the King to 'reduce these kingdoms of which Spain is composed, to the style and laws of Castile, with no difference whatsoever'. His hopes were the kingdom's fears. Valencia agreed to a small annual financial contribution of 70,000 ducats spread over 10 years; Aragon offered twice as much but refused to send any troops; and Catalonia rejected the proposition outright. In their view the Union would not pave the way for greater equality between the provinces but seek instead to Castilianise them. Though the proposal was dropped by 1626, their suspicions were borne out in the 1630s as Peru, Mexico, Franche-Comté and Spain's Mediterranean possessions made increasing contributions. Taxation in the Spanish Netherlands trebled in the 1620s and Naples and Sicily were annually drained of 4 million ducats and 6,000 men between 1630 and 1650.

To make central government more responsive to Olivares, **juntas** replaced councils in Madrid in 1634 and Castilian councillors and bishops were sent to Portugal. Their failure to observe the customary Con-

KEY TERM:

Juntas

A *junta* was a small committee of advisers to the King set up in 1585. The most important committee was the *Junta de Noche*, which met in the evening, until it was superseded by the *Junta de Gobierno*.

226

stitutions of Tomar was insensitive but proposals to abolish the Cortes and enlist Portuguese nobles into the Castilian army was very foolish. Flames of discontent, fanned by French agents, turned into open rebellion and in December 1640 the Duke of Bragança declared himself King John IV. Disturbances also broke out in Catalonia where the viceroy was killed and French troops occupied Barcelona. The Catalans rejected Olivares's plan to billet 9,000 Castilian troops on them and instead called for his resignation. These revolts, which would continue until Portugal gained its independence in 1668 and Catalonia was subdued in 1652, left Castilian councillors and grandees looking for a scapegoat.

In January 1643 Olivares was dismissed. He had seriously misjudged his country's capacity to sustain a war with France and the Netherlands, failing to see that victories could only be gained by reaching a compromise. Above all, his supreme self-confidence blinded him to political reality. In the opinion of Matías de Novoa, the death of Olivares in 1645 was 'the cause of universal satisfaction', but Spain fared little better with Philip IV at the helm. Assisted by a new *valido*, Don Luis de Haro, Olivares's nephew, there was no perceptible change in policy nor in the result. Military and naval defeats combined with fresh revolts in Naples, Sicily and Aragon, and an outbreak of bubonic plague in 1647–8, to rock the monarchy on its heels. After two years of negotiations, Philip reached a permanent peace with the Dutch in January 1648 but he refused to consider ending the conflict with France as long as French troops remained in Barcelona.

The half-century following 1598 had shown that war and reform were incompatible. Philip III and Lerma understood this maxim; Philip IV and Olivares did not. Looking back over his reign, it was apparent to Philip IV that in 1629 'my monarchy began, as everyone agrees, to decline'. Not all historians accept this judgement. Certainly, Spain was far stronger in 1621 than in either 1598 or 1648, but it can be argued that while the 1640s was a decade of unrelieved disasters, there was more cause for optimism in the 1650s. The year 1652, for instance, saw the recovery of Barcelona, Dunkirk and Casale, and has been rightly termed an *annus mirabilis*. Whether the 'ship of state' was heading for the rocks is a debatable point, but that the ship itself was basically unseaworthy is incontestable. No matter who was at the helm, Spain and its *monarquía* were unlikely to survive inclement conditions in the second half of the century.

Task: note-making

This exercise is designed to show that presenting information visually can help you sort out your ideas when you are planning an essay. The title is: 'Did Spain experience a period of recovery or decline between 1598 and 1648?'

Take a sheet of paper and divide it into four columns. The left-hand column need only be the width of a margin; the other columns should be evenly divided. Head these columns: Spain in 1598; Spain in 1621; Spain in 1648. The left-hand margin should be divided into seven sections and headed:

1 character of the ruler

2 policies of the valido

3 central administration

4 finances

5 economy

6 domestic rebellions

7 international relations.

Now read the chapter again carefully and summarise within each square the important events, developments and dates which will help you explain any changes or continuity in Spanish history during these years. Look for the key episodes or turning-points and circle or colour-code them. Remember to make use of the time chart.

Further reading

J. Elliott, *The Count-Duke of Olivares* (Yale University Press, 1986) – the standard biography of this important statesman.

J. Elliott, *Spain and its World, 1500–1700* (Yale University Press, 1989) – a collection of his most informative essays.

R. Stradling, *Philip IV and the Government of Spain, 1621–65* (Cambridge University Press, 1988) – a detailed and revisionist study of Philip IV.

R. Stradling, *Spain's Struggle For Europe in the Seventeenth Century* (Hambledon, 1993) – a fine evaluation of international relations.

J. Lynch, *The Hispanic World in Crisis and Change, 1598–1700* (Blackwell, 1992) – an update on his earlier work *Spain Under the Habsburgs* (Oxford University Press, 1985).

G. Darby, *Spain in the Seventeenth Century*, Seminar Studies in History (Addison Wesley Longman, 1994) – a short and highly readable study that reassesses Lerma.

23 Strengths and weaknesses of the French monarchy in 1648

Time chart

1598: Edict of Nantes. Sully is appointed Superintendent of Finance

1601: France gains Gex, Bresse, Valromey and Bugey from Savoy

1602: Biron conspiracy

1604: Introduction of the *Paulette* (see key term, page 232)

1609: Henry IV supports the Protestant claimant to Cleves-Jülich

1610: Death of Henry IV; accession of Louis XIII. Regency of Maria de' Medici; dismissal of Sully; emergence of Concini

1614: Estates-General is convened. Maria's regency ends

1616: Louis XIII marries Anne of Austria

1617: Louis assumes control; royal favourite Luynes replaces Concini

1621: Huguenot revolt. Death of Luynes

1622: Richelieu becomes a councillor and cardinal

1624: Richelieu becomes *principal ministre*. Valtelline crisis

1625: Final Huguenot revolt starts

1627: War with England begins

1628: France backs Nevers' claim to Mantua-Montferrat

1629: Marillac proposes the *Code Michaud*. Huguenot revolt ends at Peace of Alais

1630: 10 November The Day of Dupes

1631: *Chambre de l'arsenal* set up. Treaty of Bärwalde is signed with Sweden

1635: Declaration of war on Spain

1639: Jean Va-nu-pieds revolt in Normandy

1642: Cinq-Mars conspiracy. Death of Richelieu

1643: Death of Louis XIII; accession of Louis XIV. Regency of Anne of Austria. Mazarin becomes *principal ministre*. *Les Importants* plot fails

1644: *Toisé* tax on houses outside Paris

1648: Treaty of Westphalia. The Fronde begins in July

The strength of the monarchy in France, as in all other European countries, depended on the age and ability of its ruler. The recurrence of civil war, which had torn the country apart in the second half of the sixteenth century, was always a possibility as the minorities of Louis XIII and Louis XIV revealed. The presence of foreign female regents, Maria de' Medici (1610–14) and Anne of Austria (1643–51) and their upstart favourites, was a potent mixture guaranteed to stir up noble and princely factions. If nothing else, the periods of royal minority served to remind the French how much they needed a strong adult king. Charles Loyseau's *Traité des Seigneuries* (1614) and Cardin Le Bret's *De La Souveraineté du Roy* (1632) suggested that an absolute monarch was the best defence against discontented nobles. The clergy and the nobility, anxious to safeguard their privileges, and the peasantry and bourgeoisie, eager to protect their rights, would have most probably agreed. Nevertheless, princes of the blood and disaffected aristocrats were always capable of destabilising the royal administration during this period. This chapter examines the condition of France in the first half of the seventeenth century in the light of these tensions.

The nobility

It is often forgotten that even the most popular of French kings, Henry IV (1589–1610), had to spend 24 million livres buying off potential enemies, that he rebuffed numerous aristocratic plots, and faced 19 attempts on his life before falling to an assassin's dagger (see Figure 23.1). The frailty of his achievements in restoring royal power were laid bare after his death when leading nobles forced Maria de' Medici to convene an Estates-General in 1614 and then raised rebellion with dissatisfied Huguenots. A degree of stability was achieved in 1617 when Louis XIII (1610–43) began to rule personally, but until he had a son in 1638, the succession remained uncertain. His principal minister, **Cardinal Richelieu,** was the target of palace and council coups. Though he remained one step ahead of his enemies, his position and at times his life was far from secure. The Day of Dupes (10 November 1630) is often cited as a turning-point in Richelieu's career since the King supported him in the face of considerable pressure from his mother, brother and Marillac to dismiss him. The Cardinal knew, however, that in spite of his victory royal favourites like Baradat and Cinq-Mars could always be found to challenge his position.

Richelieu responded by strengthening royal power and attacking anyone who proved obstructive, thereby identifying his survival with the Crown's well-being. Louis recognised the mutual benefits and stood by him. Richelieu banned duelling in 1624, ordered non-strategic castles to

Figure 23.1 *The assassination of Henry IV in 1610. The assassin, Ravaillac, having just stabbed the king, is being detained by La Force. The king's hat has fallen off as he slumps back.*

PROFILE: *Cardinal Richelieu*

Born in 1585, the third son of a minor noble family, **Armand Jean du Plessis Richelieu** became Bishop of Luçon, which was in the family gift, at the age of 22. In 1614 he was chosen by the clergy to give an address to the Crown in the Estates-General and caught the attention of Maria de' Medici who gave him a minor post in the royal council. In 1622 he was rewarded with a cardinal's hat and two years later became a regular member of the council. From 1624 until his death in 1642, Richelieu remained the *principal ministre*, administering the Crown's domestic affairs and assisting the King in his foreign policy. Like all ministers of the Crown, Richelieu tried to make himself indispensable and, in his case, to a great extent succeeded.

be destroyed in 1626 and, over the next 16 years, executed five dukes, four counts and a marquis for political misdemeanours. Though the Cardinal always acted according to the law, his creation of the *chambre de l'arsenal* in 1631 (a tribunal with tame judges) showed how the law could be manipulated in the name of the King. Powerful nobles, however, outlived Richelieu and from 1643 to 1648 began to exert pressure, first on the ailing King and then on his widow and regent Anne of Austria. All but one of the governors dismissed by Richelieu received a royal pardon. But some, like Vendôme and Longueville, were still dissatisfied; along with Condé and Châteauneuf, they were willing to unleash a civil war on France. Most nobles drew back from an armed conflict in 1648 but the young King Louis XIV, if not the monarchy itself, was in a perilous condition.

Finance and administration

Serious financial problems were largely responsible for the recurrent political crises during this period. Insufficient revenue, unfair taxation, and an inefficient and corrupt administration proved insuperable obstacles in spite of able treasurers and *surintendants des finances*. By not attempting to tax the nobility, clergy and *robins* (the legal and political class), most of the burden of taxation fell on those least able to pay. The main direct tax, the *taille*, and the indirect tax on salt, the *gabelle*, provided most of the Crown's revenue, which rose from 20 to 120 million livres between 1600 and 1648. Tax expedients were applied to all sections of society: office-holders, who had paid a **paulette** from 1604 to secure tenure for their family, had to renegotiate the fee every nine years; investors in government stock, the *rentes*, had their rates intermittently manipulated; and town-dwellers were obliged to pay a forced loan in 1636–7. Louis XIII's *surintendants*, Bullion and Bouthillier, created and sold new offices, raised loans at high interest, introduced a 5 per cent sales tax, debased the currency and imposed new taxes on houses in and outside Paris, in a desperate effort to raise more money.

Part of their problem was the antiquated administrative system; it was unsystematic, and riddled with bribery and self-interest. No serious attempt was made to streamline the multilayered structure which spawned pensions, annuities and fees at every administrative level. The Duke of Sully, Henry IV's financial adviser from 1598, reduced the number of tax farmers and rejected 40,000 claims for exemption from the *taille*. In 1642 Richelieu granted the *surintendants des finances* power to assess and collect the *taille*. Nevertheless, favouritism and corruption, practised by 3,000 *élus* and **trésoriers**, ensured that no more than one-quarter of the *gabelle* and one-sixth of the *taille* ever reached the Treasury.

Marillac's *Code Michaud* of 1629, which proposed many legal and fiscal reforms, was too doctrinaire for the pragmatic Cardinal and had no chance of being implemented once he set France on a war footing. In fact, the level of expenditure between 1598 and 1620 was kept under control precisely because serious military commitments at home or abroad were avoided. Sully reduced an inherited debt by more than 100 million livres and built up a reserve of about 20 million livres by 1611. From 1621 onwards military costs rose from an average annual outlay of 5 million to 48 million livres in the 1640s in the wake of the Huguenot troubles and the declaration of war on Spain. The overall expenditure increased from 108 million livres in 1636 to some 220 million in July 1648, leading to bankruptcy.

The expansion of commerce was one area of government policy which showed signs of bearing fruit. Henry IV encouraged the foundation of the East India and New France companies and investments in luxury industries like silk, carpets and glass. Laffemas, his Controller-General of Commerce, favoured a protectionist policy to restrict the export of raw materials and precious metals and the import of goods manufactured by French industries. Sully, however, took less interest except in new drainage techniques in agriculture, reforestation and the construction of better roads, bridges and canals.

Richelieu was more committed to commercial projects. Guilds proliferated, more overseas trading companies were founded, the Saône-Loire canal was completed in 1640 and maritime trade expanded as the French government took control of the entire coastline in 1626, rebuilt dockyards and created a royal navy. As Superintendent of Commerce and Navigation, Richelieu assumed responsibility for France's economic progress. However, apart from the West Indies, where a colony was successfully established, the English and Dutch merchants had a firm grip on colonial and mercantile trade in Europe, west Africa and America.

How effective was royal administration by 1648? Henry IV and Louis XIII received advice from a handful of experienced councillors and secretaries. They in turn sat on other councils so that ministers invariably fulfilled more than one function. From 1636 the Secretary of State for War – Sublet de Noyers (1636–43) and Le Tellier (1643–77) – became increasingly important; though, as Richelieu and his successor Cardinal Mazarin demonstrated, it was the councillor who controlled foreign affairs and had the support of the King who became the *principal ministre*. The total number of royal councillors steadily grew under Louis XIII, from 31 in 1624 to 63 in 1640. They became even more unwieldy during the minority of Louis XIV, when Anne of Austria increased it to 122 in 1644.

Local particularism

Though Henry IV never called a meeting of the Estates-General, and only one met in Louis XIII's reign, the nobles and clergy were regularly consulted on an informal basis. As long as the Crown respected customary laws and privileges, the provincial estates remained content but they had to be handled sensitively and they resisted royal attempts to encroach upon their legal and administrative affairs. Henry IV had been able to stop the Guyenne and Périgord Estates from meeting and undermined that of Dauphiné, but it was Richelieu in his drive to raise more revenue who really attacked their privileges.

1 He tried to turn the *pays d'états* into *pays d'élections*, and so extend taxation to more Frenchmen. Burgundy, Provence and Languedoc handed over large cash payments to retain their independence, the Estates of Brittany (1626) and Languedoc (1632) had their powers reduced, Dauphiné (1628), Guyenne (1635) and Normandy (1638–43) had their meetings suspended, and Provence (1639) was replaced by an assembly.

2 The traditional guardians of provincial privileges, the *parlements*, had their objections overruled by a decree in 1631 and by a *lit de justice* in 1641 which obliged them to register all laws without discussion. Though recalcitrant members were brought before the *chambre de l'arsenal*, most felt compromised by the *paulette* as they wished to preserve their hereditary offices. Significantly, it was Mazarin's attempt to renegotiate the *paulette* by making it conditional on a forced loan that led to **the Fronde** in 1648.

In the late sixteenth century, the provincial governors had been a source of trouble to the Crown. They controlled the infantry in peacetime and commanded regiments during war and, as most were nobles, they built up powerful ties of clientage. As the size of the standing army grew under Louis XIII from 50,000 to 150,000, Richelieu continued Henry's policy of appointing military and provincial *intendants* to watch over the governors.

In 1643 Mazarin even gave them control of the troops marching across France to their wartime billets. Before 1630 there were few *intendants* and their function had been to troubleshoot urban and provincial problems. Richelieu extended their role to include police as well as finance and justice, appointed them for three years and increased their numbers so that by 1642 each province and *généralité* had one *intendant* and larger provinces had two. Social and political relations between governors and

KEY TERMS:

The Fronde

A **fronde** was a sling used by children to throw mud at nobles' coaches. In 1648 the term was applied to two anti-government movements: the *Fronde parlementaire* (1648–9), principally centred upon attempts by the Paris *parlement* to remove Mazarin and the Regent from power; and the *Fronde des princes* (1649–53), which was a reaction to the government by members of the upper nobility and princes of the blood.

Intendants and *généralités*

At first the *intendant* was an itinerant inspector acting for the central government; under Richelieu, *intendants* became more settled and their powers were extended. Among their new duties was the supervision of the *trésoriers* (see key term, page 232) in a *généralité* (area of financial administration).

generals, nobles and towns, and *trésoriers* and *élus*, were exacerbated by the all-powerful *intendants* in the 1640s. Everybody seemed to resent them. Urban and peasant rebellions had been common in France in the first half of the seventeenth century but worsened during the war years after 1635. Usually they were inspired by rising taxation, debts and the presence of royal officials. In the Jean Va-nu-pieds revolt in Normandy (1639), *officiers* allied with peasants and lesser nobles to voice their grievances, a practice which became widespread in the 1640s. It fell to the *intendants* to use troops to collect taxes, dispel rumours of tax remissions and put down riots. As Richelieu and Mazarin discovered, the urban and provincial response to heavy war taxation and state interference was indignation and rebellion.

Religion

In two important respects – in religion and war – the French monarchy was inherently strong. As *le roi très chrétien*, the King could count on the support of his Catholic subjects provided he courted no ideas of toleration towards Huguenots. Henry IV never cleared himself of the stain of the Edict of Nantes which had granted Huguenots religious, civil and military privileges. In spite of his reconciliation with the Jesuits and the Papacy, he was regarded by many as a *politique* and given little credit for encouraging the Catholic revival in France.

Louis XIII, in contrast, supported the Jesuits, monastic and secular orders, and won much respect for his devotion to the Catholic faith. His conquest and catholicisation of Béarn in 1620 was welcomed by *dévots* and Gallicans alike, and he totally endorsed Richelieu's dictum that 'diversity in a state was dangerous'. Huguenot revolts in 1615–16, 1621–2 and 1625–9 in the west and south-west of France were ample proof of their disloyalty, claimed Catholics, though in most cases these uprisings were protests at the failure of Catholic magistrates to enforce the terms of Nantes. The Huguenot defeat at La Rochelle in 1629 saw them lose all but their religious privileges and these were only held 'by grace of the King'. Nevertheless, in spite of persistent discrimination against them, they remained loyal and obedient servants of the Crown, a fitting response to Richelieu's statesmanship.

Foreign wars

Henry IV believed that France could not be secure or strong until the Habsburgs had been weakened and he took a personal interest in planning their demise. He strengthened France's eastern border in 1601 by acquiring Gex, Bresse, Valromey and Bugey from Savoy, and enhanced his reputation as a strong ruler by resisting Habsburg claims to Cleves-Jülich in 1609. Though historians continue to argue whether his conduct was provocative or pacific, his death in 1610 certainly eased Franco-Spanish tension. It paved the way for a family compact in 1614 and Louis's subsequent marriage to Anne of Austria.

The accession of Philip IV in 1621 and the appointment of Olivares put France on her mettle. Though French *dévots* pressed Louis XIII to maintain a pro-Catholic foreign policy, he and Richelieu were convinced that the Spanish and Austrian Habsburgs were once again on the march. No chance should be missed to disrupt their lines of communication, finance their enemies or foment trouble on their borders. France's intervention in the Valtelline (1624–6), support for Nevers' claim to Mantua-Montferrat (1628–31), war by proxy in Germany, and declaration of war on Spain and Austria in 1635, could all be justified as defending *la patrie*.

Once committed to war, it was impossible for Richelieu and Mazarin to conceive of anything but outright victory as they became locked in a death or glory struggle. Increasing domestic criticism and suggestions that Mazarin was protracting the war by attempting to extract too high a peace bargain finally forced him to sign an agreement with the Emperor at Westphalia in 1648. France acquired Casale and Pinerolo in Savoy, Breisach and Sundgau in Alsace, Philippsburg in the Rhineland, Artois in the Netherlands and Roussillon in the Pyrenees. Territorially France was much stronger than in 1635 but peace with the Emperor had been a long time coming and the war against Spain showed no sign of ending. As political and financial problems once more threatened to rip the nation apart, most Frenchmen believed that their only salvation lay in the hands of the monarchy, but in 1648 Louis XIV was only five years old.

Task: source interpretation

In 1643 the province of Languedoc was served by two *intendants*: Jean Baltazar, a hard-nosed, uncompromising official; and François Bosquet, a native of the province and temperamentally more moderate. In this letter, dated 22 June 1643, Bosquet informs Pierre Séguier, Chancellor of France, of the situation in Languedoc. Read it and, in the light of information contained in this chapter, answer the questions that follow.

'Monseigneur, two matters have occurred in the province which I must report to you so that you may be in a position to give whatever orders are necessary.

'First, Monseigneur, a decree has been issued by the parlement of Toulouse, a copy of which I am attaching to this letter. Mischief-makers have made this a pretext to stir up the people in various places and to persuade them to refuse payment of taxes, chiefly in upper Languedoc from where those who have the task of collecting taxes by virtue of extraordinary warrants now suspended by this decree, have withdrawn, bringing their complaints to me and asking me to ensure the safeguarding and protection of their persons. It has even been reported to me that a tax collector has been killed in Toulouse by the enraged people and the same thing has very nearly happened at Lavaur. Current rumours have made of the decree far more than its actual terms justify and the people cannot be disabused of the idea that according to this decree they are only obliged to pay the ancient royal taille, that all extraordinary commissions, including those of the intendants, have been revoked and that henceforth they will only be bound by orders emanating from the parlement. I am trying to dispel all these false rumours and up to this moment I do not believe that any great harm has been done but what may follow is to be feared to this extent that I understand that under the pretext of preserving public well-being, the bishops in some dioceses, where they have absolute control, are not doing all that they could to persuade the people of where their duty lies. I gave this as my opinion shortly after the Cardinal's death foreseeing then at an exclusively clerical assembly held in the diocese of Narbonne, that individuals were not so disposed to be obedient as they had been in the past. I took action, issued a writ and had the matter taken before the council. I have written about it to M. d'Hémery to have a decree issued confirming my orders; that procedure was approved yet I am still awaiting the decree three to four months later. I have seen sedition beginning to break out in Guyenne and although I am aware of the difference in the people's attitude and of the difference in governorship in this province and know likewise that at the moment there is no need to fear a similar situation here, nevertheless there is no doubt that if the two sovereign companies of this province are not kept in order and if the prelates are not exhorted to see that the orders of the council are executed, in a short time the people will be in revolt, not from any spontaneous movement, because they are incapable of that in this province, but as a result of the bad example which they will have received.'

1 Explain these terms: *parlement, taille, intendant*.

2 Who were the Cardinal (line 24) and M. d'Hémery (line 28)? Explain your answer.

3 According to Bosquet, what had provoked disturbances in Guyenne?

4 How did Bosquet believe similar disturbances could best be avoided in Languedoc?

5 What evidence is there in this letter that Bosquet was overreacting to rumours of unrest? Explain your answer.

6 a Write down a list of possible reasons why Bosquet decided to write to the Chancellor.

b Which do you think was the most important reason? Explain your answer.

Further reading

R. Bonney, *Political Change in France under Richelieu and Mazarin, 1624–1661* (Oxford University Press, 1978) – an indispensable study of early seventeenth-century French government.

M. Greengrass, *France in the Age of Henry IV: the Struggle for Stability* (2nd edn, Addison Wesley Longman, 1994) – the most recent assessment of the early years of this period.

R. Briggs, *Early Modern France* (Oxford University Press, 1977) – provides a good introduction to France, Richelieu and Mazarin.

R. J. Knecht, *Richelieu* (Addison Wesley Longman, 1991) – is a detailed and balanced biography.

G. Treasure, *Mazarin* (Routledge, 1994).

R. J. Knecht, *The Fronde* (Historical Association, 1986 edn) – a succinct introduction and explanation of this event.

24 Motives of the main participants in the Thirty Years' War

Time chart

1617: Election of Ferdinand of Styria to the kingdom of Bohemia

1618: Defenestration of Ferdinand's governors in Prague

1619: Bohemian estates depose Ferdinand as king and elect Frederick V of the Palatinate. Ferdinand is elected Emperor Ferdinand II

1620: Battle of the White Mountain and defeat of the Bohemian rebels

1621: Renewal of the Spanish-Dutch war

1623: Maximilian is granted the Upper Palatinate; Saxony given Lusatia

1624: Valtelline war begins. *Almirantazgo* plan is put into operation

1625: Wallenstein becomes 'generalissimo' of the imperial army. Christian IV of Denmark enters the war

1626: Danish army loses at Lutter

1627: Ferdinand imposes a new constitution on Bohemia

1628: Mantua-Montferrat succession dispute starts. Wallenstein acquires Mecklenburg, is appointed Imperial Admiral and besieges Stralsund in Pomerania

1629: Denmark withdraws from the war at the Treaty of Lübeck. Ferdinand issues the Edict of Restitution. Truce of Altmark between Sweden and Poland

1630: Dismissal of Wallenstein. Gustavus lands in Pomerania

1631: Treaty of Bärwalde between United Provinces and Sweden. Gustavus announces the *Norma Futurarum Actionum*. Wallenstein is recalled

1632: Battle of Lützen and death of Gustavus

1633: Oxenstierna forms the League of Heilbronn

1634: Murder of Wallenstein. Sweden is defeated at Nördlingen. Collapse of the Heilbronn League

1635: Spain attacks Trier; France declares war on Spain. Peace of Prague

1637: Election of Emperor Ferdinand III

1638: Bernard of Saxe-Weimar captures Breisach

1640: Frederick William, the Great Elector, enters the war

1648: Treaty of Westphalia ends hostilities

On 23 May 1618 two imperial Catholic governors, Martinitz and Slavata, were thrown out of a window in the Hradschin Castle in Prague. This was a symbolic act of defiance by a minority of Calvinists (known as the 'Defenestration of Prague'). It has traditionally been seen as the start of the Thirty Years' War (1618–48), though it was not until the rebels created a new constitution, deposed their designate-king Ferdinand and elected Frederick of the Palatinate in his place on 22 August 1619, that a war between Austria and Bohemia began. Few could have predicted that it would escalate from a local affair into a lengthy international conflict. In this chapter we shall be analysing the aims and motives of the leading participants in the Thirty Years' War. The consequences of the war are examined in chapters 25 and 28.

The Austrian Habsburgs

Ferdinand of Styria was unanimously elected Holy Roman Emperor six days after his deposition as King of Bohemia. His immediate aims were to recover his kingdom, avenge Frederick (the leading German Calvinist prince) and suppress sympathetic Protestant uprisings in his family lands. Ferdinand, a staunch Catholic, was strongly influenced by his Jesuit confessor, Lamormaini. He had no intention of letting Bohemia – which was not only an electoral state but also part of the Habsburg's traditional lands – fall into the hands of a heretic, whether Frederick had been constitutionally elected or not.

Once Frederick had been defeated at the Battle of the White Mountain, the uprisings suppressed and Bohemia absorbed into the Habsburg fold, Ferdinand II was ready to advance his religious and political designs. It seems that his main aims were to:

■ eliminate Protestantism from the Empire

■ regain land secularised since 1552

■ restore the status of the Emperor over the German princes.

According to his Edict of Restitution (1629), the Peace of Augsburg (which had established Lutheranism in 1555) would be cancelled and Calvinism outlawed; some 30 free cities, and 13 bishoprics and Calvinist states would be returned to Catholicism. Though this should have appealed to Catholic

PROFILE: *Albrecht von Wallenstein*

Born into a family of the Bohemian Brethren in 1583, **Wallenstein** was educated by Jesuits and, when his parents died, became a Catholic. He married Lucretia von Wishkow who left him a fortune when she died shortly afterwards. He entered the Emperor's service and assumed command of his army in Moravia in 1618 before becoming military governor of Prague. He then profited from the debased currency, speculated heavily on the land market and became the richest landowner in Bohemia and Friedland. This self-made millionaire was a mercenary entrepreneur. His role should have been to serve his paymaster, Emperor Ferdinand II, but as he steadily enriched himself out of the war many suspected that he desired an electorate, even the kingdom of Bohemia. Wallenstein publicly denounced such rumours and repeatedly told Arnim, the Saxon field-marshal, 'I have no more burning desire than to found a lasting peace in the Empire'. Few believed him. As the war progressed, he demonstrated his military ability and ambition, commanding the largest and most successful army which by 1630 numbered 130,000 troops. He was dismissed as 'generalissimo' in August 1630, but was reinstated in December 1631. In January 1634 he was dismissed a second time, and died shortly afterwards.

rulers, even they were alarmed at the resurgence of imperial power and noted that no diet had been convened to authorise the Edict. Ferdinand, however, decreed that he had the right to interpret acts of the diet without consultation. Unabashed by the lack of support he received from leading Catholic bishops and princes, he persisted and was still dictating terms at Prague (1635), offering only limited privileges to Lutherans and none to Calvinists.

The Emperor's son and successor, Ferdinand III (1637–57), was more pragmatic. He recognised that he could not hope to revive the imperialist dream of a united Christendom nor eliminate the inroads achieved by the Protestant faiths. Instead, he decided to concentrate on keeping firm control of his family lands, expelling foreign armies from Germany and winning a favourable peace.

Abrecht von Wallenstein

The war produced an extremely complex character in **Wallenstein** who became 'generalissimo' of the imperial army in 1625. At times he spoke of reshaping the Empire, leading a Turkish crusade, liberating his native land of Bohemia and establishing religious toleration, but Wallenstein was a confused man, as much influenced by astrological signs as by realism, and in later years developed a consuming fatalism. Ferdinand and his allies distrusted him, and with good reason. He proved unwilling to help Spain establish a fleet in the Baltic, refused to assist Olivares in the Mantuan crisis in 1628, applied the Edict of Restitution with great reluctance and ignored orders to help protect Bavaria in 1632. When he entered secret negotiations with Saxony, France and Sweden, Ferdinand was convinced that Wallenstein was only interested in his own gains. In January 1634, as his own officers questioned his conduct and some doubted his sanity, General Piccolomini, under imperial orders, murdered him.

Maximilian of Bavaria

In 1618 Maximilian was one of the most powerful German princes. Since becoming Duke of Bavaria in 1597, he had built up a strong state, funded a Catholic League with its own army in 1609 (reformed without the Habsburgs in 1617) and, more than any other ruler, led the Catholic revival in the Empire. At first he was a natural ally of Ferdinand and put his army at his disposal to oust Frederick from Bohemia and the Upper Palatinate. His reward was the much coveted title of Elector Palatine granted in 1623.

Always aware of the Emperor's absolutist motives, Maximilian was particularly aggrieved at the publication of the Edict of Restitution. He responded by supporting the Catholic opposition at Regensburg (1630), which refused to recognise Ferdinand's son as King of the Romans and forced the dismissal of Wallenstein. It was a notable victory and ensured, at least for the time being, that Maximilian's army was the principal force at the Emperor's disposal. Yet he never trusted the Habsburgs and from 1630 began cultivating the diplomatic support of France as an insurance policy against Sweden. Not surprisingly, as Maximilian fluctuated between toeing the imperial line, professing neutrality and secretly pocketing French bribes, he was rightly regarded as a selfish, fair-weather ally.

Bohemia

Josef Polišenský, the Czech historian, once claimed that the Bohemian revolt of 1618 resulted from the Austrian Habsburgs' attempt to impose Catholic absolutism on a socially and religiously liberated bourgeois society. Unfortunately, this explanation does not readily fit the facts, for the revolt was not a nationalist uprising but a constitutional protest led by a socially narrow section of Calvinist nobles who had no support from the Lutheran peasant majority. The nobles' aims were first to uphold the liberal 'Letter of Majesty' – granted by Emperor Rudolf in 1609 and confirmed by Ferdinand in 1617 – that allowed them religious and political freedom; and second, to regain their own control. Together with

Moravia, Hungary and Silesia, Bohemia hoped to secede from Austrian rule but within a few years they were all beaten into submission and in 1627 absorbed into the Austrian-Habsburg dominions.

The Palatinate

Frederick V, Elector of the Palatinate, was motivated by a mixture of dynastic ambition and religious fervour. As the leading Calvinist prince and Director of the Protestant Union between 1608 and 1618, he saw himself as the defender of German Protestant liberties. He justified his decision to accept the Bohemian throne as a 'divine calling which I must not disobey. My only aim is to serve God and His Church.' No one doubted his sincerity but few agreed with the wisdom of challenging the Austrian Habsburgs. After his defeat at the White Mountain in 1620, he left Bohemia to fight for his homeland. The invasion of the Lower Palatinate by Spain and the Upper Palatinate by Bavaria forced him into exile in the Netherlands where he died in 1632. His son, Charles Louis, continued to fight to recover the whole of the Palatinate but was always dependent on Dutch, French and Swedish aid and, in the final analysis, was likely to be sacrificed on the altar of diplomatic and military expediency.

Spain

In August 1619, Count Solms, Frederick of the Palatinate's ambassador at Frankfurt, remarked that 'the Spaniards would rather lose the Netherlands than allow their House to lose control of Bohemia so disgracefully and so outrageously'. If he was wrong about the Spanish order of priorities, he was right about their commitment to assisting their Austrian cousins. In 1618 Zúñiga had assumed control of foreign affairs in Madrid and a year later persuaded Philip III to send 17,000 troops and 600,000 ducats to Germany. From the outset, Spain's intentions were not altruistic. Under the guise of assisting the Emperor, their aim was to be well placed to renew the war with the United Provinces when the Twelve Years' Truce expired in 1621. Spain's occupation of the Lower Palatinate in September 1620 therefore provided a most useful base from which to mount military operations. Equally important, it secured the vital line of communications between Italy and the Netherlands, known as the 'Spanish Road' (see Figure 24.2). Though most of this route passed through Habsburg lands, there were several sensitive spots which Spain's enemies tried to exploit. Venice, Mantua, Modena and Parma bordered Milan and each was anxious to reduce Habsburg influence in north Italy. In the 1620s they supported French attempts to block the Valtelline, backed a French claimant to Mantua-Montferrat in 1628, and allied with France, Sweden and the United Provinces in 1635 against Spain. Charles Emmanuel of Savoy was equally anxious to undermine Habsburg

Map legend:
- Holy Roman Empire in 1648
- route of Gustavus Adolphus 1630–32
- the Spanish Road
- ☒ battles
1 White Mountain, 1620
2 Lutter, 1626
3 Regensburg, 1630
4 Lützen, 1632
5 Heidelberg, 1634
6 Nördlingen, 1634
7 Philippsburg, 1635

Figure 24.2 Sites associated with the Thirty Years' War

predominance: in 1618 he sent Frederick 2,000 mercenaries and opposed Spain's claim to Montferrat.

Olivares, Philip IV's principal adviser from 1622, believed that assisting Ferdinand to restore control was essential to the Spanish *monarquía*. It also opened up the possibility of weakening the Dutch. In 1624 he initiated his *Almirantazgo* plan, whereby a Spanish-Imperial fleet of 40 ships would wrest control of Baltic trade from the Netherlands and shut out all Dutch exports and manufactures. Its initial success was impressive, reducing the Dutch share of Baltic trade from 80 to 70 per cent by 1629, but the presence of Wallenstein's troops and

Olivares's ships also brought Sweden into the war, which was the last thing Spain wanted.

Several historians have highlighted the aggressive behaviour of Spain before, during and after the Thirty Years' War. Yet this only becomes intelligible when seen against a backdrop of continuing French provocation. It was, for instance, France's relief of Heidelberg in December 1634 that prompted Spain to attack Trier in 1635, which in turn forced Louis XIII to declare war on Spain. Neither country wanted the fighting to escalate as each realised the additional commitment that a war on two fronts would bring to their already overstretched treasuries. Nevertheless, from May 1635 Spain and France were once again locked in armed conflict.

The United Provinces

Dutch historians regard the years 1618–48 as the final stage of their Eighty Years' War (1568–1648) against Spain. As such, they see the German conflict as a peripheral part of a broader struggle against growing Catholic Habsburg absolutism. Like Spain, the United Provinces was alert to the danger signals coming from Prague in 1618–19. The government sent Frederick financial assistance, allied with England and France in 1624, and subsidised Denmark and Sweden in 1625 and 1631 respectively. But domestic strife weakened the Dutch commitment: though Calvinists supported the Orange family's aim of refusing to accommodate Spanish peace overtures and broadening the war fronts, the Dutch regents representing their States pointed to rising taxation and declining trade as good reasons for ending the war as soon as possible (see chapter 26).

Denmark

Christian IV entered the war against the Emperor in 1625. As a Lutheran, he sympathised with Frederick of the Palatinate and Elizabeth, his niece, and was concerned at the presence of Spanish troops in the Lower Palatinate. As he was King of Norway and Denmark, he wished to maintain his Scandinavian supremacy over Sweden and stem its economic and military expansion in the eastern Baltic. As Duke of Holstein and director of the **Lower Saxon Circle**, he had ambitions to seize one or more of the north German bishoprics, such as Bremen or Verden, for his younger son Frederick. Success would give him control over the Weser and lower Elbe rivers and strengthen his authority in the Baltic. With the United Provinces already at war, Sweden preoccupied with Poland, and England showing no signs of activity, the vain and well-off Danish king could not pass over the chance of putting himself forward as the saviour of German liberty and Protestant leader of Europe. Significantly, he made no mention of liberating Bohemia. His defeat at Lutter in 1626 was the prelude to an imperial invasion of Jutland, reconciliation with Sweden

KEY TERM:

Lower Saxon Circle

The Holy Roman Empire was divided into 10 administrative regional councils known as 'circles'. Each had a 'director' or spokesperson who exercised nominal control over financial and military matters within their boundaries and could, if they so wished, act as a brake on the Emperor's activities. The **Lower Saxon Circle** oversaw the north-western states of the Empire and entitled Christian of Denmark to intervene in German affairs.

and, finally in 1629, withdrawal from the war. Denmark's involvement was short, sharp but far from sweet.

Sweden

From the moment Gustavus Adolphus, King of Sweden, set foot on German soil in July 1630, historians have argued about his war aims. He informed the Electoral Duke of Brandenburg that 'I seek not my own advantage in this war, nor any gain save the security of my kingdom'. The Elector was not alone in disbelieving him. Wallenstein's siege of Stralsund in 1628 and his occupation of Pomerania, Mecklenburg and the mainland of Denmark in 1629 had certainly threatened Baltic trade and indirectly Swedish security, but as a Lutheran Gustavus was equally concerned about the advancing Catholic Reformation. As early as 1620 he had proposed a plan to lead Protestant forces against the Emperor but his high financial demands and professed priority of defeating Poland were less appealing to the German Protestants than Denmark's cut-price strategy. However, Christian's defeat and Gustavus's six-year truce with Poland in 1629 enabled him to enter the German war. For diplomatic reasons, Salvius, Sweden's official agent of propaganda, claimed in 1630 that the liberation of German land was his country's only motive. No mention was made of religion nor of the removal of the Habsburg fleet from German ports, and *assecuratio* (security) and *satisfactio* (compensation) remained secret war aims.

Unexpected success in 1630–31 saw Gustavus's horizon expand: in the *Norma Futurarum Actionum* he repeated his plan for a league of Protestant princes headed by himself. In June 1632 he announced that he wished to retain lands between the rivers Vistula and Elbe, that Calvinism and Lutheranism should be tolerated in the Empire and that all states seized since 1618 should be returned. Maurice Ashley suspects that Gustavus's real ambition was 'to make himself the master of northern Germany and thus convert his kingdom into the mightiest Baltic power'. However, this seems unlikely given Sweden's limited natural resources, the unpredictability of political alliances and Germany's distaste for foreign interlopers. When Gustavus marched into the Rhineland, Bavaria and Bohemia in 1632, he was a long way from home and had militarily and financially overreached himself (see Figure 24.2). Whether he ever hoped to destroy both Spain and Austria remains conjectural, however, for his death at Lützen in November put his chancellor, Oxenstierna, in charge of war operations. Oxenstierna initially toyed with the idea of resurrecting a Protestant league in 1633 but its failure and Sweden's defeat at Nördlingen in September 1634 saw him revert to the fundamental aims of security, compensation and the recognition of Calvinism under the protective wing of France (see chapter 27).

France

Throughout the sixteenth and early seventeenth century, French monarchs adhered to the dictum, 'Protestant abroad, Catholic at home'. It was not a deliberate policy but one which served their political ends most successfully. As Richelieu explained in 1629, 'France's only thought must be to strengthen herself and to open doors so that she may enter the states of all her neighbours to protect them from Spain's oppression when the opportunities to do so arise'. Preoccupied with domestic problems, he had confined his activities to financing the Dutch and Danes, supporting the Protestant Grisons in the Valtelline and the Duke of Nevers' claim to Mantua-Montferrat. A divided Germany would weaken the Habsburgs, keep Spain busy and increase French hopes of building territorial bridgeheads in the Rhineland and north Italy. He was not averse to allying with Lutheran Sweden and Catholic Bavaria in 1631 if it would sap the strength of the Habsburgs. Yet as long as France was officially sidelined, her ability to direct affairs remained uncertain.

Gustavus proved an unwilling servant and Maximilian an unreliable ally. The imperial army's seizure of Philippsburg in January 1635 alarmed Richelieu but it was the capture of Trier, a French protectorate, by Spanish troops in March which wounded the nation's pride. Open warfare against Spain had been a long time coming but was always probable once the Spanish-Dutch war began. Indeed it was arguably inevitable once a French army had gone to the relief of Heidelberg in December 1634. Richelieu and his successor Mazarin, like the Danes and Swedes before them, claimed that they were defending German liberties but this excuse thinly veiled their true objective: to counter the Habsburg ring of power that had threatened the safety of France for more than a century. As a result the Franco-Spanish war exceeded the limits of the German conflict and was not concluded until 1659 (see chapter 23).

German princes

German Catholic princes, prince-bishops and electors endeavoured to stay out of the war. Though they feared the prospect of Bohemia having a Calvinist king or the Emperor being a Protestant, and supported the restoration of all church lands unlawfully secularised, they had no wish to enhance Habsburg power in Germany. Their anxiety grew in the late 1620s and explains their opposition to Ferdinand at the Diet of Regensburg in 1630. The electors of Mainz, Trier and Cologne, supported by the bishops of Bamberg and Würzburg, forced the Emperor to reduce the size of the imperial army, dismiss his commander Wallenstein and temper his high-handed behaviour. By 1635, and the Peace of Prague, their opposition had produced a more conciliatory Emperor.

The two leading Protestant states, Saxony and Brandenburg, were more equivocal in their allegiance. John George of Saxony, a Lutheran elector, supported the Emperor in 1619 because he saw the opportunity to exploit the crisis: his reward was the Austrian province of Lusatia in 1623. He remained neutral until 1631 when his opposition to the Swedish invaders led him to produce the 'Leipzig Manifesto', a plan to create a German Protestant army. The sack of Magdeburg in May frightened him into allying with Sweden from 1631 to 1633 though he was anxious to make his peace with the Emperor at the earliest opportunity, and did so at Prague.

George William of Brandenburg was a Calvinist elector but had no sympathy for his co-religionist, Frederick, whom he regarded as a misguided rebel. Brandenburg remained neutral until Gustavus forced his hand in 1631 but he was not a willing ally and accepted imperial peace terms at Prague. His son, Frederick William (1640–88), held a more belligerent stance. He disassociated himself from the Prague agreement, made a truce with Sweden and entered the war. It was a gamble that worked, and at Westphalia he made considerable gains (see chapter 28).

Some Protestant rulers – like Anhalt, Baden and Brunswick – tried to enhance their power at the Emperor's expense in 1619 and paid the price of defeat. Others bided their time. William, Landgrave of Hesse-Cassel, for example, waited until 1631 before declaring his support for Sweden. An uncompromising Calvinist, he hoped to abolish the three ecclesiastical electorates and to secure a permanent Protestant majority in the imperial college. It remained but a dream. Bernard of Saxe-Weimar, on the other hand, was more pragmatic. He entered the war in 1631 under the tutelage of Gustavus, assumed the military leadership of the Protestant cause after the King's death and, motivated by the prospect of gaining land, held the Alsatian fortresses of Breisach, Neueburg and Freiburg, with every intention of keeping them. His death in 1639 removed one of the most enterprising characters of the war.

The problems of motivation

Historians, like detectives and psychologists, spend much of their time attempting to explain human behaviour. Where events have been recorded and contemporary views documented, it is possible to identify the motives which shaped the conduct of a diplomat, soldier or king. But in many cases, the surviving evidence is contradictory, incomplete or biased and secretly held ambitions underlie openly stated aims. This is the problem facing the historian of the Thirty Years' War. Religious zeal, dynastic ambition, *raison d'état*, German liberation, national security, commercial expansion and self-advancement have all been offered as plausible explanations for the participants' motives. Contemporaries and many historians have stressed the importance of religion. 'The Thirty Years' War was a religious conflict', writes Gerhard Benecke, 'if only because that is how the majority of people living through the period regarded the matter.' Steinberg disagrees, suggesting that 'it is anachronistic and unprofitable to isolate "religion" as a determining factor' since contemporaries saw 'no division between their religious convictions, their political aspirations, their economic theory and practice'. In his view, 'all decisions of consequence were taken in the cool light of what at the time became known as *raison d'état*'. The diversity of confessional alliances for political reasons would seem to bear out this thesis, yet Michael Roberts considers it unwise to put religion and politics into 'watertight compartments' for, in the seventeenth century, 'politics were to a large degree influenced by religion; the cause of religion was sustained by political weapons'. Thomas Munck concurs, suggesting that 'even the most cynical statesman or leader needed to pay lip service to religious justifications in order to win broader ideological support amongst subjects and allies'.

It should also be borne in mind that as events unfolded and initial objectives were accomplished or modified, pragmatic statesmen narrowed or broadened their sights accordingly. Those operating with larger budgets could afford to indulge in grand strategies; the majority responded to the circumstances of the moment. It is the variety of aims of the leading participants in the Thirty Years' War which largely accounts for the enduring complexity and fascination of this topic.

Tasks

1 What difficulties face the historian when trying to explain the motives of participants in the Thirty Years' War?

2 What evidence is there to support Benecke's view that the Thirty Years' War was principally a 'religious conflict'?

3 Which evidence in this chapter could Steinberg draw upon to support his opinions of the war?

4 In what respects do Roberts and Munck agree in their interpretations of the issues at stake in the war?

5 Which historian do you think offers the most convincing explanation of the participants' motives?

6 Do you believe that economic factors are just as important as religion or politics? Explain your reasons.

Further reading

P. Limm, *The Thirty Years' War*, Seminar Studies in History (Addison Wesley Longman, 1984) – provides a useful introduction and documents.

G. Parker, *The Thirty Years' War* (Routledge and Kegan Paul, 1984) – contains a series of very informative essays.

P. Brightwell, 'Spain and Bohemia: the Decision to Intervene, 1619', *European Studies Review* (1982) – re-appraises several important issues.

R. A. Stradling, 'Olivares and the origins of the Franco-Spanish war, 1627–35', *English Historical Review*, 101 (1986).

D. A. Parrott, 'The causes of the Franco-Spanish war of 1635–59' in J. Black (ed.), *The Origins of War in Early Modern Europe* (Cambridge University Press, 1987).

M. P. Gutmann, 'The Origins of the Thirty Years' War', *Journal of Interdisciplinary History*, XVIII:4 (1988).

25 What were the social and economic effects of the Thirty Years' War in Germany?

For over 100 years historians have argued about the effects of the Thirty Years' War upon Germany's economy and society. In its simplest form, the debate has revolved around two theses:

1 The traditional view was that Germany was an economically prosperous and thriving society in 1618 until war ruined its agriculture and industry, halved its population and destroyed thousands of towns and villages throughout the country.

2 Germany's economy was declining before 1618 and, though this trend for the most part continued, the damage caused by the war has been greatly exaggerated.

The traditional view owed much to Gustav Freytag's *Pictures from the German Past* (published between 1859 and 1862), which depicted 30 years of unrelenting 'devastation and death'. It largely endorsed the seventeenth-century accounts of Samuel Pufendorf and Christopher von Grimmelshausen. Pufendorf deliberately exaggerated stories of distress and destruction. This was partly to highlight Brandenburg's recovery under his patron, the Great Elector, and partly to put the blame for the worsening plight of the Prussian peasantry on the war rather than to exploitation by the Junkers. Grimmelshausen's novel *Der Abentheurliche Simplicissimus* painted vivid images of horror and mayhem perpetrated by marauding armies and peasants (see Figure 25.1). In spite of several local and regional studies suggesting that parts of Germany were unaffected by the war and that some examples of economic decline predated the start of the war, the traditional 'disastrous war' theory has held the consensus.

In the aftermath of the Second World War, the debate took a new twist. This was largely due to the extensive damage inflicted by modern warfare and the capacity of European states to recover from it. Steinberg, writing in 1947, claimed that seventeenth-century writers deliberately exaggerated the war damage, that many areas of Germany were comparatively

Figure 25.1 *Etching by Franck of violence committed on villagers by marauding soldiers*

untouched and some even benefited. He believed that economic and social activity of a town or region recovered quite quickly, and, where there was evidence of decline, it often preceded the war or could be explained by factors peculiar to a locality, unconnected with the war itself. Most historians found Steinberg's counter-thesis too radical to be accepted uncritically yet were hard-pressed to dismiss it totally. They certainly acknowledged the dangers of making categorical statements based on generalisations and were aware of the conflicting conclusions reached by local research.

Thus the debate gathered pace. F. L. Carsten in 1956 warned that Germany was neither an economic nor a political unit and any attempt to treat it as such was to create an artificial concept. T. K. Rabb agreed with Steinberg that 'the war's harmful effects have been exaggerated and its benefits rarely noticed', but still concluded that 'at best the Thirty Years' War started a general decline that had not previously existed; at worst, it replaced prosperity with disaster'. H. Kamen, in 1968, largely confirmed this picture of material devastation but warned against trying to categorise prewar and wartime decline and emphasised the variety of economies in Germany. He drew attention to the relative decline of certain areas, 'some of which may have suffered from long-term factors of decay, while others were directly and physically annihilated by war'.

A cautionary note was also struck by G. Benecke in 1972. His study of the county of Lippe in north-west Germany highlighted the danger of accepting evidence of war damage at its face value. He showed that many records of war damage were actually false claims made by officials attempting to avoid heavy taxation and that in reality the economic life of a community often continued in spite of the damaging effect of war. In contrast, Polišenský and other Marxist historians stressed the structural social changes brought about by the war which, at a time of economic stagnation, accelerated the movement from feudalism to capitalism. More recently, historians have agreed that western Europe experienced an economic contraction in the early seventeenth century and that the impact upon Germany was most pronounced. However, they still argue over the precise moment when its economy (or economies) began to falter. Kellenbenz, for instance, suggests that the war ended any demographic, agricultural or industrial expansion apparent in 1618; while Friedrichs believes that contemporaries inflated the effects of the war on an already declining economy.

This debate presents many problems for the historian.

1 We are confronted with different definitions of terms such as 'progress', 'recession' and 'decline', and need to be aware that an area like 'Germany' did not form an economic or social unit.

2 Parish registers, tax returns, customs and port tolls, private diaries, newsletters and personal accounts – which make up much of the surviving evidence – are fragmentary and unreliable, and must be interpreted carefully.

3 The mass of historical material is located in state, regional and municipal archives and libraries, throughout western and central Europe and requires a variety of linguistic skills if it is to be interpreted correctly.

The task facing the modern historian is gigantic and inevitably any attempt to form a conclusion on the basis of local or regional research is likely to stimulate discussion and prolong the controversy rather than provide a solution.

The state of the debate

Population

The claims made by Günther Franz and Roger Mols in the 1930s that the war destroyed between 30 and 40 per cent of Germany's population, or the suggestions made by Steinberg in the 1960s that the population actually increased can no longer be accepted. Overall, it probably fell from about 20 to 16 million between 1618 and 1648. Understandably, losses were heaviest in the war zones in Pomerania, Mecklenburg, Brandenburg, Württemberg, Bavaria and the Rhineland, which lost more than half their inhabitants. Rural areas suffered most of all. Marauding armies carried diseases, destroyed farm animals, crops and buildings, and drove peasants off their land. Rothenburg, for example, in south-west Franconia had some 100 villages with 1,503 taxable peasant households in 1618; in 1641 it only had 447 households. The county of Lippe in east Westphalia similarly suffered a population decline from 40,000 to 26,000.

Generalisation, however, is dangerous. In the neighbouring county of Schaumburg, no village 'disappeared' and deserted settlements were re-occupied by the end of the war; in Lower Saxony, also in the north-west, losses were under 10 per cent. In several areas, such as the Palatinate and the Neckar valley, falling population levels predated the outbreak of hostilities. Nevertheless, armies could and did bring considerable damage to towns and villages alike. Though exceptional in its destruction, few forgot the 'sack' of Magdeburg by Tilly's army in 1631 or the occupation of Leipzig (1631–3, 1642–50) and Nuremberg (1621–2, 1629–34, 1646–8) by imperial and Swedish troops. According to Langer, the Swedish army seriously ruined 1,500 towns, 2,000 castles and 18,000 villages in the course of the war. Most families came to terms as best they could with the war.

A cobbler from Weidenstetten, Hans Heberle, recorded in his diary how he and his family regularly migrated to the comparative safety of nearby Ulm before returning to the village to resume their lives when the troops had moved on. Ulm was not unique. Towns and cities throughout Germany bulged with refugees. Magdeburg had as many as 35,000 during its siege in 1631 (see Figure 25.2) and Leipzig more than 4,000 in addition to its 12,000 inhabitants. Walled towns could be more easily defended from ravaging armies but not from disease, and some became death-traps. Plague raged from 1634 to 1639 and accounted for nearly 7,000 deaths in Frankfurt (1634) and more than 17,000 in Augsburg between 1632 and 1635. By the end of the war, several cities – like Stuttgart, Augsburg and Nuremberg – had birth rates below that of 1618 due mainly to typhus, influenza and dysentery epidemics which decimated communities.

Nördlingen did not recover its prewar population level until the eighteenth century, though in this case the slow rate of recovery was probably due partly to an official policy which discouraged immigration and partly to the town's limited attractions. Yet population levels could

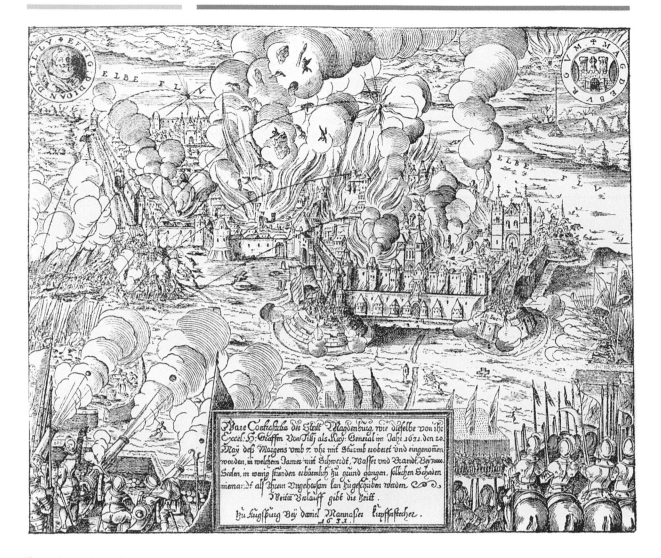

Figure 25.2 *Siege of Magdeburg, 1631*

recover quickly. Magdeburg, having lost 96 per cent of its inhabitants and most of its buildings in 1631, rose from 394 households in 1635 to 2,464 in 1644, and within a generation the town was entirely rebuilt. War accelerated existing demographic trends: on balance, population levels were adversely affected but where areas suffered, communities appear to have been redistributed rather than destroyed.

Agriculture

Historians now believe that the Thirty Years' War accentuated an agricultural recession. Between 1600 and 1620 grain prices were falling in western Europe but thereafter rose, principally due to rising inflation caused by the *Kipperzeit* (debased currencies). Mühlhausen wheat prices, for example, tripled in the early 1620s, and food prices in general continued to rise until the 1640s. Agricultural wages rose too and held their level in the 1640s, but the migration of peasants to the towns gave landowners the chance to buy up vacant farms and properties at bargain prices.

At the end of the war, the new owners controlled the demand for labour as well as many peasant dwellings in a village, and started practising commercial feudalised farming. This trend was particularly evident to the east of the Elbe in Mecklenburg, Pomerania and East Prussia. At Stargard, for example, in Mecklenburg, over 70 per cent of peasant holdings fell to the nobles. In Brandenburg-Prussia, landowners increased their control over the serfs in collaboration with the government, while in Swedish Pomerania the nobles extended serfdom contrary to state policy. Elsewhere, peasant conditions do not appear to have deteriorated. In Silesia, most peasants remained free landowners and in Anhalt and Lower Saxony noble–peasant relations were largely unchanged. In Bavaria a labour shortage accentuated the continuing decline of serfdom, and in Alsace the state policy after 1648 enabled peasants to recover lost lands.

Trade and industry

German trade and industry appears to have been affected in three ways.

1 The war reduced the volume of mercantile traffic entering the Baltic and North Sea ports and enabled Scandinavian and Dutch competitors to increase their share of the market. The Spanish-Dutch war of 1621–48 led to the imposition of embargoes on Baltic trade which were only effectively lifted with Sweden's defence of the Baltic in 1630. Rostock, Wismar and Stralsund – already suffering from the diminishing Hansa trade – further declined and Elbing experienced a double blow when first Swedish troops occupied it between 1626 and 1635 and then England transferred its trading company to Danzig. Traffic along the main German arterial rivers continued, however, and ports like Danzig and Lübeck prospered. Neutral Hamburg similarly expanded and by the end of the war had become Germany's wealthiest city.

2 The war affected industrial activity. Manufacturing grew in towns like Essen, Leipzig and Nuremberg, where there was a demand for armaments and textiles, and local industries flourished in Bremen (linen), Cologne (silk) and Aachen (brass). Leipzig, in fact, was occupied by Swedish troops from 1642 to 1650 but still emerged from the war as a prosperous centre of commerce. However, the impact of persistent fighting could drain a town of its economic life especially if levels of production were already falling. Silver mining at Marienberg and iron at Regensburg continued to decline, and Augsburg, which reached its height of commercial prosperity in 1618, could not arrest its slide. Small towns all over Germany were dislocated by occupying armies, and unemployment in one town soon affected neighbouring villages. The pastor of Calw, a textile town in Württemberg, which employed 243 local men (64 from nearby settlements), and on whom a further 1,200 men and over 1,200 women spinners depended for their livelihood, summed up the effects of war on his community: 'When Calw starves, most of the region around it starves too.'

3 Urban centres were hard hit by war taxation and tributes levied on them. Though most towns probably recouped much of their lost income by charging troops high prices for food and beer, and by drawing compensation for any disorderly behaviour, many municipal administrations ran up heavy debts by borrowing excessively to meet their costs. Nuremberg's debt in 1648 was 7.4 million gulden, a fourfold increase on 1618; Schwäbisch Hall claimed it lost 3.6 million gulden as a result of the war.

Nevertheless, care must be exercised when assessing a town's claim for war damages. Gerhard Benecke has shown that some councils deliberately submitted high claims in order to receive tax relief. When Lemgo in Lippe put in an 'unrealistic' claim, it provoked a spate of similar returns from embittered local towns.

Conclusion

At present the verdict of historical judgement remains open though closer to Steinberg's 'early decline' thesis than to the 'war devastation' school. As historians learn from comparative studies of war-ridden societies and as local research produces ever more data for analysis, it remains to be seen whether there will be a future reaction to, or confirmation of, this revisionism.

Task

This chapter has shown how modern historians have revised their views of the social and economic effects of the Thirty Years' War on Germany. Revisionism is an important part of the historical process. It results from the historian looking again at an event, person, period or place, and, in the light of fresh evidence, new skills or a different approach, revising a traditional interpretation. It is not enough for a revisionist to attack or demolish an orthodoxy; an alternative and convincing explanation must be supplied if it is to be taken seriously. Of course, not all revisionist judgements are considered correct. Many evaporate upon close scrutiny and most are modified in the course of time. The following questions concern the controversy discussed in this chapter and the role of revisionism.

1 Explain in your own words what the controversy is about.

2 a What is Steinberg's thesis?

b It was first published in 1947. Why has it, with only minor modifications, stood the test of time so successfully?

3 What difficulties face the historian in studying the economic development of a German town or village during the Thirty Years' War?

4 What evidence is there in this chapter that the German economy declined solely as a result of the war? Refer in your answer specifically to trends in population, agriculture, trade and industry.

5 Historians have disagreed about this topic for a number of reasons:

- they have argued over the definition of terms
- they have discovered new evidence and argued about its importance
- they have viewed the evidence differently (*e.g.* empirically or didactically)
- they have favoured particular interpretations.

Which is the most likely explanation for future revisionism of this topic?

Further reading

T. K. Rabb, 'The Effects of the Thirty Years' War on the German Economy', *Journal of Modern History*, 34 (1962) – reviews the historiographical debate and is a good starting-point for this topic.

S. H. Steinberg, *The Thirty Years' War and the conflict for European Hegemony, 1600–1660* (Arnold, 1966) – his major work (in English) on the war which challenges several traditional views.

G. Benecke, *Germany in the Thirty Years' War* (Arnold, 1978) – contains commentaries on more than 70 documents.

C. R. Friedrichs, 'The war and German society' in G. Parker (ed.), *The Thirty Years' War* (Routledge Kegan Paul, 1984) – one of many valuable essays on the logistics of the war.

S. Lee, *The Thirty Years' War* (Routledge, 1991) – a short introduction to the war.

J. V. Polišenský, *War and Society in Europe, 1618–48* (Cambridge University Press, 1978) – explains some of the difficulties facing the historian researching Bohemia.

26 What were the reasons behind 'The Golden Age of the United Provinces'?

Time chart

1584: Death of William of Orange

1602: Foundation of the East India Company

1604: Jacobus Arminius presents his theses on predestination

1605: Siege of Malacca. Amboyna, Tidora and Ternate captured from Portugal

1607: Archduke Albert authorises a ceasefire between Spain and the Dutch

1609: Twelve Years' Truce. Foundation of the Bank of Amsterdam

1610: Counter-Remonstrant movement begins against Arminianism (see key term, page 262)

1611: Amsterdam Stock Exchange is established

1614: English Cockayne project. Defence pact with Sweden

1619: Synod of Dort condemns Arminianism. Death of Oldenbarneveldt

1621: Renewal of war with Spain. West India Company founded

1623: Massacre of English merchants at Amboyna

1624: Bahía, capital of Brazil, is captured

1625: Death of Maurice of Orange. Eviction of Dutch from Bahía. Spain captures Breda. Dunkirk privateers attack Dutch shipping

1628: Piet Heyn seizes Spanish silver fleet at Matanzas Bay

1630: Franco-Dutch subsidy. Dutch capture Pernambuco in north Brazil

1632: Danish-Spanish treaty against the Dutch

1634: France renews its subsidy with the United Provinces

1637: Breda is recovered

1639: Admiral Tromp defeats a Spanish fleet at the Downs

1640: Spanish armada loses at Pernambuco. Swedish-Dutch treaty

1641: Truce with Portugal. Capture of Malacca and Luanda

1645: Denmark lowers Dutch tolls. Uprising of Portuguese settlers in Brazil

1647: Death of Frederick Henry. Ceasefire with Spain. Treaty with Denmark

1648: Spain grants the United Provinces independence

1650: Death of William, son of Frederick Henry

The rise of the United Provinces to world economic supremacy was one of the wonders of the seventeenth century. In spite of limitations – a small population (less than 3 million), most of its land at or below sea level, riven by internal divisions and ravaged by an Eighty Years' War with Spain – it became Europe's leading economic and cultural community. Its people enjoyed Europe's highest standard of living. Many urban families possessed a range of furniture, silverware, porcelain, clocks, mirrors, several sets of clothes and, in some cases, paintings by Rembrandt, Hals and van Goyen. Such artists embodied in their work a sophisticated and self-confident style, typifying the spirit of Dutch enterprise and freedom. This chapter examines how this economic 'miracle' occurred.

Political organisation

Politically the United Provinces was unique. Each of the seven states (see Figure 26.1) – Holland, Zeeland, Utrecht, Groningen, Friesland, Overijessel and Gelderland – was autonomous. Each held provincial assemblies, elected delegates to a national States-General at the Hague and appointed a stadholder as its political and military executive. Holland was the most powerful state: it contributed more than half the States-General's budget, held six votes and was traditionally represented by the Grand Pensionary, the most influential member of the States-General. Amsterdam, its wealthiest city, was controlled by four burgomasters drawn from a small number of 'regents' or ruling families. Other provinces viewed Holland with envy. Friesland, largely governed by peasants, consistently opposed its policies and leaders; Zeeland was pathologically suspicious about Amsterdam's aspirations to supremacy; and Groningen and Overijessel, both Catholic provinces and comparatively poor, resented its capitalist and Calvinist-driven policies. Voting in the States-General had to be unanimous which often presented difficulties that had to be resolved by behind-the-scenes bargaining. The *vroedschappen* (delegates) had a personal interest in the survival and prosperity of the republic, which resulted in a close alignment of political and economic decisions in a manner foreshadowing eighteenth-century **mercantilism**. The States-General, for example, endorsed Zeeland's demand that the river Scheldt should remain closed. It effectively ruined the

KEY TERM:

Mercantilism

Mercantilism was a term invented in the eighteenth century to describe the 'mercantile system' of the previous century. The mercantilist sought to increase the wealth of his country by exploiting natural resources and by accumulating supplies of precious metals. The economic system could then be used to strengthen the military and political power of the state.

Figure 26.1 United Provinces in the seventeenth century

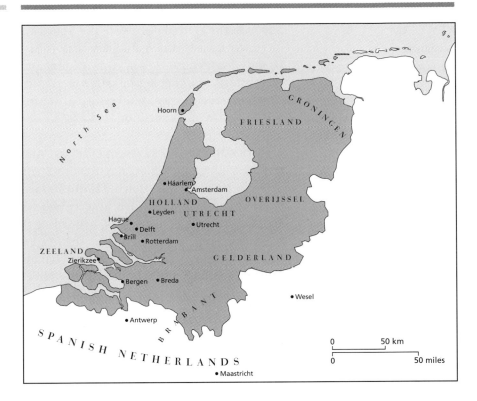

English Cockayne project in 1614, forced Denmark to keep the Sound open and its tolls low, supported the activities of overseas trading companies, imposed naval blockades on the Spanish Netherlands in the 1620s and negotiated war treaties with England, France and Sweden. The States-General monitored all commercial and banking activities, upheld trading standards and regulated the guilds' control of manufactures, thereby providing the stability that foreign merchants found so attractive.

The role of the House of Orange in the development of the United Provinces was ambivalent. Since the outset of the Eighty Years' War in 1568, first William, then his sons Maurice and Frederick Henry, as stadholders and captains-general, guided the 'disobedient' provinces to victory. Maurice held five stadholderships and his brother six, but Friesland consistently denied the Orange family absolute military leadership. The states, including Holland, suspected they wanted to be monarchs and were not prepared to jeopardise their republicanism. However, as long as Spain refused to recognise the independence of the United Provinces or concede sovereignty over the ten southern provinces, the Orange family was seen as a saviour.

Maurice was overtly ambitious and uncompromising. He welcomed the renewal of war in 1621 as much as he had opposed the earlier truce. He rounded on Amsterdammers for objecting to tax increases in the 1620s

Arminians

Jacobus Arminius was a Dutch Calvinist who became professor of theology at Leyden in 1602. He suggested that as God was merciful, man could be predestined to hell – an interpretation which was altogether too liberal for orthodox Calvinists. In the years following his death in 1609, his followers – known as **Arminians** – continued to strive for a broad-based Church in the United Provinces.

and won the eternal distrust of the States-General when he was involved in peace talks with Spain between 1621 and 1624. He despised the Grand Pensionary, Johan van Oldenbarneveldt, for siding with the **Arminians** in a theological controversy, finally resolved in 1618. When Oldenbarneveldt was found guilty of raising troops unlawfully, Maurice refused to stay his execution.

Frederick Henry was more conciliatory. An accomplished soldier, he was always willing to hold a dialogue with Spain if a satisfactory peace could be won. Nevertheless, Calvinists questioned his alliances with Lutheran Sweden and Catholic France, and republicans expressed anxiety when he adopted the title of 'Highness' instead of the traditional 'Excellency' in 1636. His son, William, craved the trappings of kingship even more patently but in vain. Nevertheless, whatever their shortcomings, the princes of Orange provided a unifying force at the most critical moments in the history of the Dutch Republic.

Religious toleration

In religious affairs, the United Provinces was the most tolerant country in Europe. Dissenters were allowed to worship privately throughout the provinces, whether in the predominantly Calvinist states of Holland and Zeeland, or in the Catholic states of Utrecht, Groningen and Overijessel. Portuguese, German and Polish Jews, English Puritans, French Huguenots, German Lutherans, as well as Catholics from the Spanish Netherlands, settled there and made vital contributions to the Dutch economy. The view that the country's economic welfare would be prejudiced by religious persecution was both original and enlightened and overrode the protests of the Reformed Church. In fact, it was not its democratic freedom and Calvinist determinism which gave the United Provinces its strength but its political and religious tolerance which bred a spirit of enterprise and individuality.

The basis of its economic success

The success of the Dutch economy rested on its control of European shipping. As the Hansa continued to decline – only 11 towns attended its diet in 1628 – and both Denmark and Sweden failed to fill the vacuum, so the Netherlands' share of Baltic trade increased to 60 per cent by 1648. Polish rye and wheat, Scandinavian naval supplies of timber, rope, tar and pitch reached Amsterdam, and ships returned with French wine, Spanish salt and Dutch 'new draperies'. The increasing dependence of Spanish and Italian states on imported food and manufactured goods

KEY TERM:

Fluytships

Fluytships were container ships made of cheap pine which were stripped of armaments and unnecessary rigging. Thus a ship of 200 tons only needed a two-man crew, compared with 30 men on a similar size English vessel. The *fluytship* was longer, broader and slower than conventional designs.

allowed Dutch merchants to widen their foothold in the Mediterranean after 1600, and to maintain their trading contracts with the Turks and Venetians. It was ironic that without basic supplies acquired from Amsterdam through its London and Lisbon factors, Spain would not have been able to sustain its war against the Dutch after 1621.

Of particular significance to the Dutch were their *fluytships*, built in the 1590s (see Figure 26.2 on page 266). *Fluytships* could carry more goods, and oak prows could easily be fitted to turn them into ocean-going ships. As well as constructing specialised ships like the fast *jacht*, shipwrights built a *buiz*. This was a decked fishing ship that enabled North Sea fishermen to trawl, salt and pack herrings ready for market on their return to port, and so steal a march on their competitors.

The foundation of joint-stock companies, chartered by the States-General, allowed thousands of shareholders from a wide social and geographical distribution to benefit from overseas trade. The East India Company, known as the VOC (*De Verenigde Oostindische Compagnie*), was established in 1602. It was divided into six chambers to share the profits and avoid interstate rivalry. Holland and Zeeland nevertheless dominated its affairs, and some of the leading politicians, notably Oldenbarneveldt, were principal shareholders. The VOC aimed to control the carrying trade east of Good Hope and west of the Magellan Straits, and in so doing set up bases in India, Ceylon, Java, Sumatra, Borneo, the Spice Islands, Formosa and south Africa. By 1620 it possessed a fleet of 68 ships and 10,000 troops well capable of deterring interlopers or removing undesirable competition, as it demonstrated in 1623 by massacring English settlers at Amboyna in the Moluccas. Such acts of aggression became hallmarks of a cold-war strategy pursued in the South China Sea and Indian Ocean by its governors-general, Jan Pieters Coen and Antonie van Diemen.

In contrast, the West India Company (WIC), founded in 1621, was more diverse in its membership. Eleven of its 19 directors represented the chambers of Zeeland, Maas, Groningen and the North Quarter, and were town merchants, burgomasters, nobles and office-holders. Unlike the VOC, some of its major contributors were inland towns such as Dordrecht, Deventer, Leiden and Utrecht. The company set out to ruin the colonial and maritime trade of Spain and Portugal by plundering silver ships and establishing bases in the Caribbean, Guiana, Mexico and Brazil. The seizure at Matanzas Bay in 1628 of a bullion ship carrying treasure and goods valued at over 11 million guilders was exceptional. Dividends were generally much lower than those of the East India Company. More normal were the large debts incurred in the 1630s resulting from high running costs and differences of opinion between directors as to whether to pursue a course of colonial trading or privateering activity. Their decision to concentrate on the Brazilian sugar trade proved to be a serious mistake. The Dutch–Portuguese truce of 1641 saw the WIC reduce its military and naval expenditure, and a revolt against the Dutch Sephardi Jews by Portuguese settlers in 1645 led to a sharp fall in investments in Amsterdam. Significantly, it was the West India Company's directors who consistently opposed peace talks with Spain in the belief that a continuation of war in the Indies would bring a reversal in their fortunes. In this respect, as in others, the economic prosperity of the WIC would be sacrificed in 1648 by the politically more influential VOC.

The benefits of trading success

The Dutch Republic benefited on two counts from their trade monopoly:

1 Raw materials brought industries such as silk, lens grinding and diamond cutting to Amsterdam, china to Delft, whale-oil and sugar refining to Rotterdam, salt refining to Goes, Dordrecht and Zierikzee, and shipbuilding to Zoandam and Hoorn. Each of these industries in turn generated more employment and further wealth. The import of bulk goods and rich trades complemented native linen and woollen cloth industries to provide a well-developed industrial base.

2 Amsterdam became the *entrepôt* of world trade. Unlike Antwerp, Lisbon or London, it bought its goods directly from the markets in Africa, Asia, America and Europe, and stored them ready for distribution. With a merchant marine fleet in 1650 in excess of 450,000 tons – three times the size of England's – it could offer low insurance premiums, reliable delivery dates and low operating costs, and so undercut its rivals. Profits were then available for further investment in native industries or for international and domestic loans. A national bank was established in Amsterdam in 1609 and a Stock Exchange in 1611, where interest rates of 2.5 to 4 per cent were half those of their rivals. Resultant market forces ensured that gold and silver reserves steadily accumulated and, in an age of insolvent governments, the Amsterdam bank never reneged on its loans. The wealth of the country was thus based on a healthy trade balance and, as most people lived in towns, thousands of families became prosperous even if the principal fortunes were reserved for the leading oligarchs.

Agriculture was of no small importance to the Dutch economy: Groningen and Overijessel produced livestock, Zeeland flax, Gelderland hops and horticulture, and Friesland and Holland dairy products. Though the country was not self-sufficient, relying on imported wheat, salt and wine, it continued to bring more land under cultivation, reclaiming 200,000 acres from the sea by 1640. Fertilisers and crop rotation were introduced, and greater efficiency was developed by using wind-driven sawmills and cranes instead of human labour.

By 1648 the Dutch maritime empire was supreme. During the Twelve Years' Truce, its merchants had exploited the vulnerability of the Spanish–Portuguese colonies, captured Iberian and Italian trade, and won control of 80 per cent of all Baltic commerce. Significantly, from 1621 and for much of the 1630s and 1640s, there was a strong peace lobby from those provinces which derived their wealth from the trade of continental Europe. Holland was consistently divided between war and peace, but Zeeland was opposed to anything less than a total economic and political victory over Spain. Dutch wealth and prosperity were based on trade not colonisation, on economic competition not conquest.

The renewal of war severely shook the republic's foundations. Spanish embargoes, Dunkirk privateers and the *armada de Flandes*, which sank more than 3,000 ships between 1629 and 1638, tested the United Provinces' resilience. War costs rose from 8.8 to 18.8 million florins between 1607 and 1640, taxation increased by more than 50 per cent in the 1620s alone, and fertile lands in the East were regularly devastated by invading armies. But the republic refused to surrender, and in 1648 finally won independence. Their sovereignty assured, merchants and citizens alike could sing the praises of their liberal and tolerant society. It was, however, the economic collaboration between inland cities, fishing villages, agricultural and industrial towns which had provided the foundations of their 'golden age'.

Tasks: interpreting sources

Study documents A to D below, and answer the questions which follow.

Document A

An extract from Jonathan Israel's *Dutch Primacy in World Trade, 1585–1740* (1989)

'Dutch world-trade primacy was built on an unprecendently broad foundation of shipping, fishing, and industrial resources, the bulk of which were based outside Amsterdam and which were dispersed right across the country, albeit weighted towards the maritime zone. In this

unique situation, so different from the past hegemonies of Venice, Antwerp and Genoa, Amsterdam was merely the hub of a large clustering of thriving towns, all of which directly participated in the process of Dutch penetration of foreign markets. The federal machinery of the Dutch state, by linking the many towns, waterways and outports which collectively constituted the Dutch entrepôt, *provided a context of continuous political and economic collaboration.*

'It was a system which encouraged investment in overseas trade in all parts of the country and which enabled the various secondary centres to participate in the framing of maritime, foreign and colonial policy. The Dutch federal machinery prevented Amsterdam from controlling Dutch foreign policy, limited Amsterdam's influence over the supervision of shipping, trade and fisheries, and precluded Amsterdam from dominating the VOC and WIC to anything like the extent that would have been the case had investment in the colonial companies not been federated into regional chambers.'

Document B

Figure 26.2
Painting of a typical Dutch fluyt
by M. J. Barton

Document C

'[The Netherlands] are a general sea-land, the great Bog of Europe. There is not such another marsh in the world that's flat. They are an universal quagmire: epitomis'd, A green cheese in pickle. There is in them an equilibrium of mud and water ... They are the ingredients of a black-pudding ... Even their dwelling is a miracle. They live lower than the fishes, in the very lap of the floods, and encircled in their watery arms. The waters wall them in, and if they set open their sluices, shall drown up their enemies.'

Owen Feltham, *A Brief Character of the Low Countries* (1648).

Document D

'For it seems a wonder to the world that such a small country, not fully so big as two of our best shires, having little natural wealth, victuals, timber or other necessary ammunitions, either for war or peace, should notwithstanding possess them all in such extraordinary plenty that besides their own wants (which are very great) they can and do likewise serve and sell to other princes, ships, ordnance, cordage, corn, powder, shot and what not, which by their industrious trading they gather from all the quarters of the world: in which courses they are not less injurious to supplant others (especially the English) than they are careful to strengthen themselves.'

Thomas Mun, *England's Treasure by Forraign Trade* (1622).

1 According to document A, why was Amsterdam unable to dominate the political and economic life of the United Provinces?　　　　　*5 marks*

2 Study document B. What are the advantages and limitations to historians of using a painting as a source of evidence?　　　　　*5 marks*

3 In the light of documents C and D, how valuable are foreign opinions of the United Provinces to the historian?　　　　　*7 marks*

4 How far do these four sources explain the rise to economic supremacy of the United Provinces? (You should recall that this type of question can only be tackled satisfactorily if you make relevant use of your own knowledge.)　　　　　*8 marks*

Further reading

J. I. Israel, *The Dutch Republic and the Hispanic World, 1606–1661* (Oxford University Press, 1982) – this has replaced earlier books as the standard work on the empire of the Dutch Republic.

J. I. Israel, *Dutch Primacy in World Trade, 1585–1740* (Oxford University Press, 1989) – an excellent study of the seventeenth-century Dutch economy.

H. H. Rowen, *The Princes of Orange* (Cambridge University Press, 1988) – looks at the contribution of the Orange family in Dutch history.

S. Schama, *The Embarrassment of Riches: An Interpretation of Dutch Culture in the Golden Age* (Fontana, rep. 1988) – a brilliant survey by an outstanding historian.

27 How and why did Sweden emerge as the leading Baltic power in 1648?

Time chart

1600: The *riksdag* deposes Sigismund III; accession of Charles IX

1604: Charles IX is crowned King

1611: Accession of Gustavus Adolphus. Kalmar war between Denmark and Sweden

1612: The Charter is presented to the King by the nobles

1613: Peace of Knäred ends war between Sweden and Denmark

1617: Peace of Stolbova ends war between Sweden and Russia

1618: Reforms to Treasury and Chancery

1621: Swedish forces capture Riga from Poland

1624: Denmark concedes Sound Dues to Sweden at Treaty of Sjöaryd

1626: Swedish-Polish war begins; Livonia is secured

1628: Joint Danish-Swedish expedition saves Stralsund

1629: Truce of Altmark is concluded between Sweden and Prussia

1630: Gustavus enters Thirty Years' War

1631: Treaty of Bärwalde between France and Sweden. Battle of Breitenfeld

1632: Gustavus dies at Battle of Lützen; accession of Christina

1634: Swedish army's defeat at Nördlingen. The 'Form of Government' is announced

1635: Sweden and Poland sign a 26 years' truce

1642: Swedish army wins second Battle of Breitenfeld

1643: Swedish-Danish war begins

1645: Peace of Brömsebro ends war between Sweden and Denmark

1648: Treaty of Osnabrück grants German lands to Sweden

At the beginning of the seventeenth century Sweden was a third-rate power. Small in population, with little trade or industry, administratively underdeveloped and politically divided, its prospects were not promising.

The nobility hoped to recover their power at the expense of a monarchy which was held in little respect. In 1600 the *riksdag* (assembly) had deposed King Sigismund III, a Catholic Pole in favour of Charles Vasa, a Lutheran Swede. But Charles lacked the ability to win the nobility's support, displayed no military prowess in his wars against Poland and Denmark, and came close to losing Ingria and Finland to Russia.

Fifty years later, a remarkable change had taken place. Sweden was now the leading Baltic power; it had a respected army, a navy better than Denmark's and an administration admired by everyone. Its empire stretched from Kexholm in Finland to Bremen in north-west Germany, and included most of the south Baltic coast, the offshore islands of Ösel, Bornholm and Gotland, and the Norwegian provinces of Jämtland and Härjedalen. Only Scania lay outside its control and, as Denmark no longer exercised a monopoly of the Sound tolls, it seemed inevitable that soon the entire mainland would fall under Swedish control (see Figure 27.1). This chapter seeks to explain this unprecedented transformation.

1 The decline of rivals

Part of the explanation for Sweden's rise to power was the relative decline of Denmark, Russia and Poland, the continuing demise of the Hanseatic League and the Order of Teutonic Knights, and the inability of any north German state to fill the vacuum. The Baltic states were riddled with internal weaknesses and traditional rivalries, which prevented a single power from exercising total control.

The Danish threat

Neither Finland under Swedish rule nor Norway under Danish control posed a threat to Sweden, but Denmark most certainly did. Christian IV (1588–1648) inherited the belief in Danish supremacy of the Baltic, regarded the Sound between Copenhagen and Scania as his maritime highway, and levied tolls on all shipping and goods. The ease with which he blockaded and captured Älvsborg in the Kalmar war (see time chart) was a clear reminder that until Sweden had a better navy, it would never command a port outside the confines of the Baltic. Älvsborg's importance to Sweden as a commercial outpost was evident from the speed with which one million riksdalers ransom was raised for its recovery in 1619. Fortunately for Sweden, Christian was contemplating entering the Thirty Years' War and needed money more than the fortresses guarding Halland. His subsequent crushing defeat at the hands of Wallenstein's imperial army at Lutter was a devastating blow and by 1629 it was clear that, as Catholic troops overran the Danish mainland, he would have to

Figure 27.1 *Swedish territorial gains by 1648*

withdraw from the war if he was to restore his credibility with his nobles and council.

Sweden's entry, under Gustavus Adolphus (see profile, page 273), irked Christian but there was nothing he could do about it. The tide had turned against Denmark. Already, at the Treaty of Sjöaryd (1624), Christian had reluctantly conceded his monopoly of the Sound dues and when he attempted to re-impose them on ships in Swedish-held ports in 1643, Sweden declared war on him. It was a disastrous time for Christian. Sweden captured two Norwegian border provinces, the islands of Ösel and Gotland – which gave it security from Finland – and overran Halland, Scania and Jutland. At the Peace of Brömsebro in 1645, Denmark only recovered Scania and Jutland in return for confirming Sweden's exemption from all Sound dues. Denmark was a broken reed and, thanks largely to Sweden, gained nothing from the Treaty of Westphalia at the end of the Thirty Years' War.

Russia's problems

Russia was another of Sweden's traditional enemies but it, too, faced internal problems during this critical period. Between 1604 and 1613 a disputed succession was played out during Russia's 'Time of Troubles' which gave Gustavus Adolphus the chance to seize Gdov and Novgorod, before exchanging them at Stolbova in 1617 for Ingria, Karelia, Ingermannland and Kexholm. Now Estonia and Finland were secure and Sweden's monopoly of east Baltic trade would be unchallenged as long as Tsar Michael Romanov devoted his energies to military reforms, securing his dynasty and defending his country against Poland.

Poland's threat to Swedish stability

Sigismund III, King of Poland from 1587 to 1631, was a serious threat to Swedish stability. Since his deposition in 1600 he had contested Charles IX's right to the Swedish throne but his Catholicism and arrogance won him few friends. In 1621 Gustavus's navy captured Riga in Lithuania, a victory which marked the emergence of Sweden as a Baltic power. Riga was held for a hundred years, initially as further security over Estonia, but from 1626 as a springboard for expansion into Livonia. Poland's preoccupation with Russia and Turkey gave Gustavus the chance to turn on the rich Prussian ports of Pillau, Elbing and Danzig. Though Sweden was not yet at war with Emperor Ferdinand II, this war against Catholic Poland weakened one of his allies and presented Gustavus with an excellent vantage-point from which to observe the German conflict. The Truce of Altmark in 1629 gave Sweden Livonia, Courland and control of Baltic ports from Kalmar to Danzig for six years. Gustavus was poised to enter the Thirty Years' War, his army having proved itself against the Poles and his finances made buoyant from valuable Prussian port dues. The accession of Ladislas IV to the throne of Poland in 1631 further benefited Sweden as he preferred to concentrate upon recovering lands lost to Russia and contesting the nobles' threats to his own authority.

Other opponents

None of the remaining Baltic states was in a position to impede Sweden's entry into the Thirty Years' War in 1630. Pomerania's elderly and heirless duke was unable to resist. Given the presence of Wallenstein, he was prepared to welcome Gustavus as a liberator rather than as an invader.

George William, Duke of Brandenburg, lacked the resources and courage to deter Swedish troops and preferred a position of neutrality, but his son, the Great Elector, was more adventurous and wisely chose to support Swedish activities in Germany. If the north German states were too weak or preoccupied to withstand Sweden's emergence in the Baltic, the Papacy, United Provinces and France positively encouraged it. Their motives were unquestionably selfish (see chapter 24), but it suited Sweden to receive their diplomatic and financial support, especially in the later stages of the war. After Gustavus's death in 1632 and the heavy defeat of Sweden's best troops at Nördlingen two years later, Chancellor Oxenstierna's objective was to gain financial compensation and territorial security. Victories at Wittstock in 1636 and Breitenfeld in 1642 strengthened his hand at the peace Treaty of Westphalia. Sweden's gains made it undisputed master of the Baltic, securing western Pomerania, including the valuable ports of Stralsund and Stettin, Wismar in Mecklenburg, the islands of Rügen, Usedom and Wollin, the imperial bishoprics of Bremen and Verden, and an indemnity of 5 million riksdalers.

2 Gustavus Adolphus and Oxenstierna

It is indisputable that Sweden's rise to prominence in the first half of the century would not have occurred without the inspiration of **Gustavus Adolphus** and Axel Oxenstierna (1611–54). Gustavus was the archetype soldier-king, cast in the mould of Saladin and Henry V. Brave, intelligent, resourceful and charismatic, he combined a love of fighting with a shrewd pragmatism; he led his troops in battle, shared their hardships and, above all, was very successful. Oxenstierna, the leading noble and head of the *riksdag*, complemented him perfectly. He administered the country, implemented Gustavus's ideas and led the government in the King's numerous absences. Their mutual trust was essential, and it was the chancellor who continued to guide the state during the potentially

---

PROFILE: *Gustavus Adolphus*

Son of Charles IX and Christina of Holstein, **Gustavus** was 17 years old when he succeeded his father in 1611. Educated by Johan Skytte and Johan Bureus, he developed a strong interest in political and religious affairs, a capacity for hard work and a driving ambition to be a successful king. A skilled linguist, a student of history and trained in the art of war, Gustavus gained his military experience on the battlefield but was not recognised for his expertise until the second half of his reign. He died in battle in 1632.

difficult years following the death of Gustavus and the regency of Queen Christina (1632–44).

In 1611 the 17-year-old Gustavus faced a serious political crisis. The nobility were reacting against Charles IX's autocratic rule and demanded a share in the responsibility and benefits of government. In the Charter of 1612 they forced the King to grant them their own legal status, their exemption from taxation and a monopoly of government offices. In return, Gustavus managed to harness their administrative and military talents, and won their impassioned loyalty in a partnership that was to unite the nation and run the empire for the rest of his reign.

Having resolved the constitutional problems and survived wars against Denmark, Poland and Russia, the decade following 1617 saw several fundamental administrative reforms without which, in the opinion of Michael Roberts, 'the emergence of Sweden as a great power could hardly have taken place'. At the centre of the administration was the Chancery, reformed in 1618 and run by Oxenstierna. He and the Council of State assumed control in the absence of the King and proved invaluable during Gustavus's future Polish and German campaigns. The nobility provided the bureaucracy of permanent departments of state (*collegia*), established in Stockholm in 1626, comprising foreign affairs, finance, justice and the armed forces. Earlier reforms created central law courts (1614), equal representation of the four estates in the *riksdag* (1617), a modernised treasury (1618) and 23 royal governors to supervise local bailiffs and to eliminate fiscal and judicial abuses (1624).

On the eve of Gustavus's entry into the German war, Sweden had an efficient centralised administration, features of which were admired by later European rulers like Louis XIV and Peter the Great. To staff the expanding bureaucracy, gymnasia (grammar schools) were set up in 1623 and Uppsala University was patronised by the Crown though the number of students in full-time education only increased in the 1650s. The Lutheran Church also put its weight behind the monarch's anti-Catholic foreign policy and domestic reforms. The government was therefore confident that it could carry the support of the people, even in the face of expensive military expeditions, principally because its reforms had satisfied most subjects. The 1634 'Form of Government', which confirmed that the 'King and Estates together constitute the sovereign authority of the realm', was more than mere rhetoric. Arguably Sweden was politically and socially the most united country in Europe.

3 An effective army and navy

The navy

Without an effective army and navy, Sweden would have remained a minor Baltic power. In 1631 Oxenstierna reminded Gustavus that 'it is essential that your Majesty should above all things labour to create a powerful fleet at sea ... so that you may be master of every nook and cranny of the Baltic'. Improvements had come slowly since Charles IX's time when Sweden possessed 100 small and mainly unseaworthy vessels. By 1648 the number was no larger but they were more powerful, faster and better equipped. In 1621 the navy blockaded and captured Riga; in the war against Poland, it countered a fleet based in Danzig, and thwarted Wallenstein in the relief of Stralsund. In 1630, it transported 14,000 troops to Pomerania, blockaded enemy ships and, between 1643 and 1645, demonstrated its power by capturing Danish Ösel, Bornholm and Gotland. Many of the improvements were attributed to Klas Fleming who supervised changes to the navy's administrative personnel and structure. In the long run, Sweden would not be able to police the entire Baltic coastline in the face of English, Dutch and French interlopers, but in the short term, its modest navy was more than a match for its competitors.

The army

Few monarchs knew as much about gunnery, military tactics and strategy as Gustavus, nor were they prepared to endure the hardships and dangers of warfare. In 1611 Swedish troops had a poor track record against their neighbours. The cavalry was no match for the Poles, its infantry struggled against the Russians and its navy was well beaten by the Danes. Gustavus, however, was a fast learner. He knew that his country's survival depended on improving the army and in 1620 began by issuing the 'Ordinance for Military Personnel'. All 15 to 44-year-old males were made eligible for conscription, infantry units were standardised at 408 men, drawn from local districts to create greater loyalty, and then quartered in peacetime on farms where they earned their keep. The light cavalry were noble volunteers. They were equipped with swords as well as pistols though Gustavus, like Maurice of Nassau, attached greater importance to the deployment of musketeers, pikemen and field artillery (see chapter 29). The musketeers, stationed in serried ranks six deep (not the conventional ten), had greater manoeuvrability. They fired a lighter weapon in short blasts or 'salvos' to break up enemy defences. The pikemen fought alongside them and were used both defensively and offensively. The artillery supported the infantry and cavalry by applying its 'regiment-piece', a three-pound ball-shot that could be manoeuvred by one horse wherever it was most needed. At Breitenfeld in 1631, for instance, the three newly created regiments of infantry, cavalry and artillery collaborated for the first time and overwhelmed Wallenstein's unbeaten imperial army; and at Lützen a year later, the cavalry was supported by the movable artillery to achieve another victory.

By 1632, the Swedish army was the most feared in Europe, numbering some 149,000 troops at its height. Though 80 per cent were mercenaries, it was the best paid and disciplined army in the war partly because Gustavus employed a higher ratio of NCOs and officers. His strategy was also unconventional. Whereas most generals sought to avoid defeat and rarely took risks, Gustavus abandoned caution and endeavoured to annihilate his opposition. The cavalry's victory over the Poles at Wallhof (1626), the infantry's defeat of Tilly at the Lech (1632) and the artillery's success at Janków (1645) were fitting testimonies to Gustavus's military reforms and to their importance in his country's rise to greatness.

4 Finances

'If we cannot say war will pay for itself, then I see no good outcome to all the work we have set our hand to', wrote Gustavus in 1628. Sweden was the first modern European state geared to war but how to pay, feed and equip over 100,000 troops remained a serious problem. Crown revenue was never very substantial: the Vasas gave away too much land to the nobles and hedged at attempting to tax them. In the 1620s a series of expedients were employed. Crown rents were farmed out since most taxes were in kind; land was sold, and new taxes imposed on stock, land and mills. But two sources gave Sweden a lifeline during the difficult period between 1626 and 1631:

1 A rich copper seam was discovered at Falun in 1619 at a time when the demand for minting coins and making armaments was growing. At Bergsladen, iron mines developed by Amsterdam and Liège entrepreneurs produced bar-iron and cannons.

2 Between 1626 and 1635, Sweden collected the Prussian tolls which in a good year – 1630, for example – yielded 758,000 riksdalers.

Nevertheless, variable Baltic dues and diminishing copper exports proved insufficient to finance a large standing army and alternative sources were required. Too much importance has been attached to the 400,000 riksdalers provided annually by France between 1631 and 1636 and from 1638 to 1648. Though it was useful, especially in the later years of the war, it was quite small in relation to the voluntary contributions and forced demands extracted from the occupied German lands. For example, Saxony paid protection money totalling 483,000 riksdalers, Brandenburg 360,000 and Pomerania 200,000 in 1630–31. The town of Erfurt contributed 600,000 towards the upkeep of the Swedish army in 1631–2 and, if much of this money found its way back into the town's economy, this was not always the case. In practice Gustavus, like Wallenstein, systematically exploited his German hosts. There was no other way that Sweden could finance an army which in all probability cost in excess of 20 million riksdalers a year. As the German states discovered, freedom was an expensive commodity.

Conclusion

Few could have forecast the advances made by Sweden between 1600 and 1648. It had progressed through an early period of survival and restoration to enjoy a golden age of military success and expansion. The monarchy emerged stronger and was respected by its subjects; its administration was modernised under the talented Oxenstierna; its army became one of the most respected in Europe and its navy patrolled an empire stretching from the Weser to the Neva.

Yet it was also evident in 1648 that the country faced many serious problems. Gustavus's wars and Oxenstierna's refusal to withdraw from the Thirty Years' War until Sweden had gained security and compensation took their toll. A small population, which felt it had already contributed enough in war taxation, demanded smaller armies and navies. But the recently acquired maritime empire with its lengthy north German coastline required permanent garrisons and more ships to defend it from predators. Moreover, Sweden's economy was flawed. The Falun mine was close to exhaustion, only 5 per cent of the population lived in towns, the Baltic tolls proved disappointingly low and most of Sweden's minerals were exported. Socially, superficial cracks concealed deeper divisions created by Oxenstierna's administration. Having received crown lands and titles and pocketed revenue collected from their peasant freeholders, the privileged nobility were weakening the unity of the kingdom. The *riksdag* sympathised with the overburdened burghers and peasantry and refused to meet the shortfall in royal revenue by increasing indirect taxes. Sweden's empire was real enough but its foundations were far from secure.

Was the reign of Gustavus a mixed blessing? As Anthony Upton suggests: 'Gustav Adolf is one of the most exciting and interesting figures in the history of seventeenth-century Europe, but it is still possible to think that for Sweden in particular and Northern Europe in general, it might have been better if he had never lived.' The 'Lion of the North' certainly left Sweden with as many problems as he had inherited and whether Christina and her beleaguered country were equal to the challenge remained to be seen. The signs, however, were ominous.

Task: historical assessment

1 Can you discover any common factors to explain the decline of Sweden's Baltic neighbours? Explain your reasons.

2 Assess the contribution of Oxenstierna to the development of Sweden **a** before 1632, **b** after 1632.

3 What was the importance of Sweden's army and navy in her rise to prominence?

4 'Sweden's limited human and economic resources meant that she would always struggle to hold on to her Baltic Empire.' Do you agree?

5 Do you agree with Anthony Upton that 'for Sweden in particular and Northern Europe in general, it might have been better if he [Gustavus Adolphus] had never lived'? Explain your reasons.

Further reading

M. Roberts, *Sweden as a Great Power, 1611–97* (Arnold, 1968) – contains commentaries and documents on this period.

M. Roberts, *Gustavus Adolphus and the Rise of Sweden* (English University Press, 1973) – deals with the rise to power of Sweden in the seventeenth century.

M. Roberts, *Gustavus Adolphus*, Profiles in Power (Addison Wesley Longman, 1992) – an excellent biography.

G. Masson, *Queen Christina* (Cardinal, 1968) – offers a useful biography on an extraordinary monarch.

A. Stiles, *Sweden and the Baltic, 1523–1721* (Hodder and Stoughton, 1993) – provides a basic study for this topic.

D. Kirby, *Northern Europe in the Early Modern Period* (Addison Wesley Longman, 1990) – a detailed study of international relations in the Baltic.

S. Oakley, 'War in the Baltic, 1550–1790' in J. Black (ed.), *The Origins of War in Early Modern Europe* (Cambridge University Press, 1987) – stresses the multicausal nature of conflict in Scandinavia.

28 The Treaty of Westphalia, 1648

When the terms of the Treaty of Westphalia (signed at Münster between the Emperor and France and at Osnabrück between the Emperor and Sweden) were published, contemporaries greeted the news with mixed feelings. Publicly, there was an enormous sense of relief that the long war and protracted peace talks should be finally over. Indeed, it was only the multiple disasters which confronted the leading participants in 1647–8 that brought seven years of negotiations to a conclusion. Spain was experiencing domestic revolts, financial crises, military defeats and a major plague epidemic. Philip IV was desperate to end his conflict with the United Provinces (though not with France) and, by signing a truce with the Dutch in June 1647, precipitated the other parties to reach a settlement.

Cardinal Mazarin needed little persuasion. France was financially exhausted although still at war with Spain. His attempts to raise new sources of taxation put his career in danger, through the outbreak of the Fronde (see chapter 23). Christina of Sweden, at heart a pacifist, instructed her representatives to reduce their demands. She, more than her principal adviser Oxenstierna, was aware of her country's worsening political and social problems. Emperor Ferdinand III (1637–57) also recognised that the game was up. Swedish troops were sweeping through Bohemia, the Catholic League's army had been routed at Zusmarshausen in Bavaria, and unless he called a halt to the fighting, he would have less to bargain with. Above all, he believed that he could gain more by skilful negotiation than by continuing the war. And so it proved.

The terms

France, Sweden and Austria were the principal guarantors of Westphalia, and they and their allies gained most (see Figure 28.1).

France

Mazarin expressed dissatisfaction at the French terms though he had little reason to complain. Pinerolo in north Italy (seized in 1630), Breisach, Philippsburg and the Sundgau in Alsace (acquired when Bernard of Saxe-Weimar died heirless in 1639), and Metz, Toul and Verdun (first won in

Figure 28.1 *The Treaty of Westphalia, 1648*

Territorial gains:

by Brandenburg

by Saxony

by Bavaria

by Sweden

by France

— Holy Roman Empire

1552) were useful gateways into Lombardy and Germany. If he was disappointed at not receiving Strassburg, Mazarin knew that France had a good chance of exploiting its sovereignty over Upper and Lower Alsace, and the Duke of Nevers, a French client, was recognised as ruler of Mantua, Montferrat and Casale. Mazarin achieved a further diplomatic coup by insisting on the exclusion of Spain from the peace congress. The decks were cleared for him to deal with the Fronde before turning to the Spanish war.

Sweden

Sweden's negotiating position in 1648 was confusing. Since the death of Gustavus Adolphus, Oxenstierna had assumed responsibility for determining his country's war and peace objectives. His profound distrust of Mazarin worsened Franco-Swedish relations in the 1640s and led him to strike a hard bargain, demanding the whole of Pomerania, Mecklenburg, Magdeburg, Halberstadt, Bremen and Verden, confirmation of the Treaty of Brömsebro (1645) and an indemnity of 20 million riksdalers. Queen Christina since her majority in 1644 had confidentially authorised her representative, Adler Salvius, to gain France's support, accept fewer territories and less compensation. In December 1646 she informed him: 'I put my entire confidence in you, that you will not allow yourself to be turned aside by anything, and by this I recommend to you very expressly the advancement of the peace.' Meanwhile Swedish generals were similarly divided into two camps: Field-Marshal Wrangel favoured a continuation of hostilities; Field-Marshal Torstensson a cessation. Inevitably a compromise was reached and it proved more satisfactory to Christina than to Oxenstierna.

Sweden was given western Pomerania, including Stralsund and Stettin at the mouth of the Oder, the port of Wismar in Mecklenburg, the bishoprics of Bremen and Verden which controlled the Weser and Elbe, confirmation of its islands and territories won from Denmark at Brömsebro, and 5 million riksdalers. Writing half a century after Westphalia, Samuel Pufendorf, a German jurist, could not see the value of Pomerania and Bremen. In his view, these lands were 'at a great distance from Sweden' and were 'very hard to be defended' but ''tis evident that as long as the Swedes are masters of Wismar and have a firm footing in Pomeren, they need never fear an invasion from the German side: besides ... they may be very serviceable for the attacking of Denmark on the side of Germany'.

Oxenstierna did not have the benefit of hindsight. In 1648 he regarded western Pomerania as 'a rope round the King of Denmark's neck' and the imperial bishoprics of Bremen and Verden were, in his view, economically and politically valuable. In practice, Denmark never forgave Sweden for seizing these lands. Having gained nothing from the peace treaty, Denmark intended slipping the Swedish noose at the earliest opportunity. Furthermore, having three representatives in the imperial diet was of no real advantage to Sweden; the Baltic and north German trade proved less lucrative than was at first anticipated; and patrolling a maritime empire that stretched from Finland to the North Sea brought more commitments than assets. Brandenburg felt cheated, Denmark and Poland aggrieved, and Russia was eager to gain access to the Gulf of Finland. Worse, the financial compensation was inadequate payment for the mutinous Swedish troops and the maintenance of peacetime garrisons. If the Swedish *riksdag* was unwilling to vote any new taxes, Christina was likely to exploit the social discontent in order to reduce Oxenstierna's authority. Like Mazarin, he returned home a worried man.

The Holy Roman Empire

The Emperor was represented at the talks by Maximilian von Trautmannsdorf. He skilfully conceded lands which were of limited value to Austria, held on to strategically vital territories, avoided paying any indemnity, and managed to satisfy both his enemies and allies. Pomerania, several north German bishoprics, Lusatia, Alsace and Breisach were therefore lost but Silesia, Breisgau, and the Rhenish fortresses of Laufenburg and Rheinfelden were retained. As Emperor, Ferdinand III was also ready to make political and religious concessions in return for territorial gains for the Austrian Habsburgs. He formally withdrew the Edict of Restitution and Peace of Prague, granted Calvinism official status and agreed that church lands should uphold their religious identity from the 'standard year' of 1624. The Ecclesiastical Reservation of 1555 was to apply to both Catholic and Protestant church lands. All future disputes would be settled by compromises rather than by the imperial diet's resolution. Constitutionally, the Emperor could no longer declare war and make peace; this became the right of the imperial diet. Never again would an Austrian Habsburg Emperor claim universal authority or attempt to establish unity within the Empire by enforcing Catholicism on hostile Protestants.

Ferdinand II would not have yielded so much political and theological ground; Ferdinand III did, but his outlook was altogether more liberal and pragmatic. In return, his lands in Bohemia, Hungary, Moravia and Silesia were declared hereditary, which had not been the case in 1619, and he was now able to extend his plans for centralisation and establish greater unity within his Empire. The 'new' constitutions for Austria (1625), Bohemia (1627) and Moravia (1628), which enforced the German language and annulled the existence of political estates (assemblies) and provincial diets, were confirmed. Religious toleration did not have to be applied, which further strengthened the Emperor's hand. No one spoke up for Bohemia which lost its privileges embodied in the 1609 Letter of Majesty and its Czech language and culture. It is hard not to disagree with Comenius who wrote from his exile in Poland, 'they have sacrificed us at the treaties of Osnabrück'. Moreover, Ferdinand could now concentrate on combating Turkish threats between the Danube and Drava.

Mazarin, as ever, had his finger on the pulse. He declared that though the terms were 'quite harsh' on the Emperor, they were also 'very advantageous'. At one time, it seemed as if the Emperor might lose many fortified towns and have to pay an indemnity but 'since he has now deflected such a blow and has got his breath back somewhat, he is ready at any time to take up the war again, whenever he chooses'. In fact, Ferdinand would be preoccupied with the Turks and domestic reform, but the point was clear: Austria had not been seriously weakened by the treaty and, like a pruned tree, the loss of its German and Spanish obligations may have even made it stronger.

German states

Brandenburg did particularly well out of the war despite its belated involvement and limited military successes. This was principally because Frederick William convinced Mazarin that Sweden needed to be neutralised in the Baltic, and the Dutch agreed as they were eager to consolidate their hold on Baltic trade. As a result, Brandenburg received eastern Pomerania – a large, barren dukedom – the bishoprics of Kammin, Minden and Halberstadt, and the right of succession to the rich archbishopric of Magdeburg (effected in 1680). As the Elector was confirmed in his possession of Mark, Cleves and Ravensburg (granted at Xanten in 1614) and east Prussia (granted in 1618), he was far stronger than his fellow Protestant electors.

Saxony got its just desserts – very little. Granted Lusatia by Austria in 1623, Lutheran John George had sat on the fence for much of the war, changed sides when it suited him and found that no one took much notice of him at Westphalia.

Bavaria fared much better but then the wily Maximilian had no intention of losing out at the peace talks having played such a durable role for most of the war. As an ally of both France and the Emperor, he was not short of friends though Ferdinand had to be persuaded to keep his promise to let Maximilian have the Upper Palatinate and turn it into an electorate. Ferdinand was more amenable to granting him the right of presentation to the secularised bishoprics of Osnabrück and Paderborn. They were a long way from the Austrian heartlands and of little significance to him. Nor was he unduly perturbed about dividing the Palatinate and letting Frederick V's son, Charles Louis, become an elector of the Lower Palatinate. Charles vented his feelings at losing the Upper Palatinate by having a medal struck inscribed with the words '*Cedendo non Cedo*', but to no effect.

Other leading German states whose lands had been invaded, with the exception of Pomerania (whose duke had died without a male heir in 1637), were restored to their rulers. Equally significant were the announcements that each of the 343 imperial states could make their own alliances as long as they were not against the Emperor, and that, as every prince was accorded equal status, the electoral princes would lose their 'pre-eminence'. The principle of *cuius regio eius religio*, won at Augsburg in 1555, still existed, though in practice princes were not inclined to force their faith on their subjects, and of course Calvinism was now permitted. German liberties, both political and religious, which had been a key issue for both Protestant and Catholic rulers, had therefore been achieved. A major drawback for most rulers, however, was having to meet the bill for the war indemnities while at the same time attempting to recover from the damaging effects of such a long conflict.

Switzerland and the United Provinces

Switzerland and the United Provinces, technically part of the Holy Roman Empire in 1618, were granted formal independence by the Emperor. In Switzerland's case, it was a statement of affairs that had existed since 1500. The United Provinces, on the other hand, were seen by the Habsburgs as rebels in arms and only Spain's admission in January 1648 that they should be recognised as 'free and sovereign states' forced the Emperor's hand. He acknowledged their gains in Brabant, Limburg and part of Flanders, and granted Calvinists the right not to extend religious toleration to Catholic minorities.

Ferdinand's readiness to make concessions like this compromised his integrity and earned him the wrath of the Papacy. To Pope Innocent X, the Peace of Westphalia was 'null and void, invalid, iniquitous, unjust, condemned, rejected, frivolous, without force or effect, and no one is to observe them, even when they be ratified by oath'. He had much to complain about: the recognition of Calvinism, the creation of an eighth electorate (and for a heretic to boot), the setting of the base-date for resolving ecclesiastical accessions at 1624 rather than 1552 and, most galling of all, the fact that he had not been invited to the talks. It was a nice irony since it was Urban VIII in 1634 who first suggested a multi-national peace congress, but a telling comment on the Papacy's declining status as an international force. No one listened to the complaints of the papal nuncio, Chigi, as he flitted from Münster to Osnabrück in search of a hearing in 1648, and the leading negotiators officially condemned the papal bull 'Zelo Domus Dei'.

Historical controversy

Historians continue to argue over the importance of Westphalia. Veronica Wedgwood, writing on the eve of the Second World War, took a jaundiced view of the Thirty Years' War, which in her view was 'futile and meaningless'. She was equally disparaging about the work of the peacemakers because the treaty:

'which had settled the disputes of Germany with comparative success because passions had cooled, was totally ineffectual in settling the problems of Europe. The inconclusive and highly unpopular cession of

Alsace led direct to war; the seizure of half Pomerania by the Swedish Crown was palpably too weak to hold it. The insidious growth of Bourbon influence on the Rhine, and Mazarin's deliberate policy of seizing good strategic points on the frontier, vitiated the settlement. The Peace of Westphalia was like most peace treaties, a rearrangement of the European map ready for the next war.'

Veronica Wedgwood, *The Thirty Years' War* (1938).

Georges Pagès disagreed. He believed the treaty had more positive features and marked a new era in European history.

'With the Thirty Years' War there came to an end the crisis which brought modern out of medieval Europe ... Instead of the unity of the Christian world, the Peace of Westphalia substituted – without saying so openly – the idea of a system of independent states, a kind of international society. It was a society which concerned itself neither with the type of government within its component States – monarchies, principalities, or republics – nor with the religious confessions which prevailed in them. Europe thus became a secular system (at the international level) of independent States. We are at the dawn of the principle of nationalities.'

Georges Pagès, *The Thirty Years' War* (1939).

S. Steinberg broke new ground in 1966 when he suggested that the Treaty of Westphalia:

'finally settled the constitutional and religious problems which had for centuries beset the German Empire; and it settled them within a European framework ... Although all the religious clauses were hedged in on every side by conditions, reservations and exceptions, they marked a definite step towards the separation of politics and religion. Politics became secularised, religion was to be left to the conscience of the individual.'

S. Steinberg, *The 'Thirty Years' War' and the conflict for European Hegemony, 1600–1660* (1966).

The Marxist historian, Josef Polišenský, writing in 1971, also saw the peace as a watershed in European history.

> *'Only the passage of time has revealed that the Thirty Years' War meant the completion of one stage in the process of world history, and that Westphalia inaugurated an era where this history becomes effectively a unitary one involving the whole continent of Europe and the overseas dependencies of the maritime powers ... It did so primarily because the war changed the structure of European society, a society which under pressure of events during the conflict for the first time became aware of its existence and its essential unity.'*
>
> Josef Polišenský, *The Thirty Years' War* (1971).

Peter Limm also saw 1648 as an important turning-point in European relations because 'when the essentially German peace of Westphalia had been negotiated it is significant that the remaining conflicts lacked the potency to renew the general European war'.

Conclusion

Though peace prevailed in northern Europe for less than five years and war between Spain and France continued until 1659, Westphalia was not designed to end all future wars and it would be wrong to make excessive claims to this effect. However, as a treaty settling long-standing German issues, it was more durable and would not be redundant until 1815 and the Treaty of Vienna. In this respect, Stephen Lee is right when he suggests that Westphalia is 'one of the definitive treaties of modern history'.

Task: interpreting source material

1 Veronica Wedgwood (page 284) sees Westphalia as 'totally ineffectual in settling the problems of Europe'. Do you agree with her? Do you think her judgement is too severe?

2 Why does Georges Pagès believe that the treaty marked a new era in European history?

3 In what respects does S. Steinberg's view differ from that of Wedgwood and Pagès?

4 Why do you think Josef Polišenský believes that 'the war changed the structure of European society'?

5 Stephen Lee claims that Westphalia was 'one of the definitive treaties of modern history'. Do you agree? Can you think of any other treaty of similar status? Explain your reasons.

Further reading

C. V. Wedgwood, *The Thirty Years' War* (Cape, 1938).

G. Pagès, *The Thirty Years' War* (A. and C. Black, 1939, rep. 1970).

S. H. Steinberg, *The 'Thirty Years' War' and the conflict for European Hegemony, 1600–1660* (Arnold, 1966).

J. V. Polišenský, *The Thirty Years' War* (Batsford, 1971).

P. Limm, *The Thirty Years' War*, Seminar Studies in History (Addison Wesley Longman, 1984).

S. J. Lee, *The Thirty Years' War* (Routledge, 1991).

29 Was there a military revolution in early modern Europe?

Time chart

1482: The first use of siege-trains in the Granada Wars

1494: Italian Wars begin. *Trace italiennes* are built in Italy

1525: Battle of Pavia

1534: Reduction in size of the *tercio* (infantry)

1550s: Spanish armies integrate musketeers and pikemen

1559: End of the Italian Wars

1568: Start of the Dutch Revolt

1590s: Maurice introduces reforms to the Dutch infantry. Philip uses private military contractors

1599: Dutch standardise their weaponry

1618: Thirty Years' War begins

1620s: Gustavus introduces reforms to his infantry, artillery and cavalry

1648: Treaty of Westphalia ends the Thirty Years' War

1659: Peace of Pyrenees ends the Habsburg–Bourbon war

In 1955 historian Michael Roberts claimed that between 1560 and 1660 changes in tactics, strategy and the size of armies, with attendant social and political effects, were so fundamental as to warrant the term 'military revolution'. This period, he believed, 'stands like a great divide separating medieval society from the modern world'. For more than 20 years his views remained unchallenged until Geoffrey Parker questioned several premises, especially the starting date. Yet, having made some modifications to the thesis, he confirmed that the early modern period had indeed witnessed a 'military revolution'.

The past 15 years have seen a two-pronged assault on Roberts' interpretation. On the one hand, Renaissance scholars have drawn attention to the major changes which occurred in the century before 1560 and the comparative conservatism in military developments thereafter. In contrast, a second school of historians has stressed important changes in the late seventeenth and early eighteenth centuries, so much so that Jeremy Black has suggested that 'it is far from clear that any military revolution occurred in the early modern period'. This chapter explores this debate before inviting you to form your own opinion.

Roberts' thesis

Roberts claimed that the four areas of military change which characterised the period 1560–1660 reflected the pioneering reforms of the Dutch prince Maurice of Nassau in the 1590s and the innovations of the Swedish king Gustavus Adolphus in the 1620s and 1630s.

Area no. 1: tactics

> 'In place of the massive, deep, unwieldy squares of the Spanish tercio, or the still larger but more irregular blocks of the Swiss column, they [Maurice and Gustavus] relied upon a multiplicity of small units ranged in two or three lines, and so disposed and armed as to permit the full exploitation of all types of weapons.'
>
> Michael Roberts, *The Military Revolution* (1956).

Maurice reduced the size of companies from 250 to 120, and introduced battalions of 580 troops instead of regiments of 2,000. In place of the slow-moving squares of pikemen flanked by eight rows of 'rotational' musketeers, he introduced ten rows in linear formation which could fire simultaneously across a broad front and, upon discharging their shot, retreat to the rear of the line to reload. Through greater practice and discipline, Gustavus was able to adapt this tactic to achieve six ranks of musketeers, 50 abreast; instead of retreating to reload, they advanced ten paces through stationary reloaders before firing, thereby turning the Dutch defensive strategy into an offensive movement.

From 1599 Maurice had begun to standardise the calibre of Dutch weapons, but it was Gustavus who built on this feature to revolutionise the artillery. He formed small field regiments instead of companies of gunners, and equipped each with light three- and four-pound field-pieces. This increase in flexibility enabled the artillery to be used either in conjunction with the infantry and cavalry, or as an independent unit. Gustavus also changed the tactic known as the 'caracole' (after successive battle charges and firing of pistols the cavalry retreated to the rear of the unit); instead the cavalry was equipped with swords and adopted a more aggressive full-charge. Roberts suggests that these 'fundamental changes' could not have been accomplished without hours of training and practice: 'drill for the first time in modern history became the precondition of military success'. Moreover, Dutch officers attended military colleges where they studied maps and training manuals, and acquired technical firearm competence and knowledge of the latest scientific advances.

Area no. 2: strategy

Roberts made significant claims on behalf of Gustavus's strategic thinking which, he suggested, 'seems a whole dimension bigger than any that had preceded it'. In his view the Swedish general 'successfully combines two types of strategy: on the one hand, a resolute offensive strategy designed to annihilate the enemy in battle . . . , on the other a wholly new gradualist strategy, designed to conquer Germany by the occupation and methodical consolidation of successive base-areas'.

Area no. 3: size

As a result of these tactical and strategic reforms, the size of armies and scale of warfare increased dramatically. In the 1630s, for example, the French army was three times larger than it was in the 1550s, the Spanish forces had doubled in size to 300,000 and Sweden's army increased from 15,000 in the 1590s to 120,000 in 1630. The balance of all armies in the seventeenth century remained mercenary but their retention over the winter for drilling and exercising led to the establishment of standing armies. In the case of Sweden, a conscript national militia was introduced – 'the first truly national European army,' claimed Roberts.

Area no. 4: socio-political effects

Roberts also stressed the social and political effects of these military changes. The expansion of armies opened up the prospect of successful careers in the armed forces. The military ranks of captain, colonel, major and general were established and, as the role of the cavalry declined, so the difference between nobles and commoners became blurred and insignificant. The new armies were, in his view, 'the social escalators of the age'. The state also began to recognise the political advantage of gaining control over the supply of men and raw material, which enhanced the power of the ruler and led to improved levels of administration and discipline. According to Roberts, these political and military reforms laid the foundations of the modern state, such that he could confidently conclude:

> *'By 1660 the modern art of war had come to birth. Mass armies, strict discipline, the control of the state, the submergence of the individual, had already arrived; the conjoint ascendancy of financial power and applied science was already established in all its malignity; the use of propaganda, psychological warfare, and terrorism as military weapons was already familiar to theorists, as well as to commanders in the field.'*

Michael Roberts, *The Military Revolution* (1956).

Parker's modifications

'The choice of the year 1560 as the starting-point of the military revolution was unfortunate', claimed Geoffrey Parker.

> *'Many of the developments described by Roberts also characterised warfare in Renaissance Italy: professional standing armies, regularly mustered, organised into small units of standard size with uniform armament and sometimes uniform dress, quartered sometimes in specially constructed barracks, were maintained by many Italian states in the fifteenth century.'*

Geoffrey Parker, 'The Military Revolution – a Myth?' (1976).

Yet while Parker agreed that both Maurice and William-Louis of Nassau made 'important tactical innovations in the army of the Dutch Republic', he pointed to the military changes in the Spanish army which predated the Dutch reforms. In 1534, for example, the *tercio* (infantry) was reduced from 3,000 to 1,500–2,000 men to achieve maximum firepower and greater flexibility while retaining its defensive strength. In the 1550s the Duke of Alva 'pioneered the introduction of musketeers into every company', and the Austrian Habsburgs had established permanent armies before the end of the century.

Parker also raised doubts about Gustavus's changes in strategic thinking. He questioned whether the Thirty Years' War was so different from earlier wars, arguing that set battles were rare and most of the fighting entailed lengthy sieges. In his opinion the invention of gunpowder and the creation of powerful siege-guns in the second half of the fifteenth century 'revolutionised the defensive and offensive pattern of warfare'. The Granada and Italian Wars of the 1480s and 1490s amply demonstrated the firepower of the siege-guns and obliged fortresses to be

Arquebus

Also known as an 'harquebus' (or hook-gun), the **arquebus** was a portable gun, supported on a tripod by a hook or a forked rest.

redesigned. High, rounded fortress walls gave way to lower, angular walls with perimeter ditches, redoubts and earthworks (known as *trace italienne*), which could only be captured after lengthy sieges and the deployment of large numbers of men. However, these designs were only found on the borders of eastern Europe in Poland, Hungary and Russia, where greater reliance was placed on the cavalry; because of their expense, they were something of a rarity in western Europe before the seventeenth century.

Of equal significance to Parker was the development of the **arquebus** and musket which by 1550 had replaced the medieval broadsword, halberd, crossbow and longbow in all continental armies. Arquebusiers needed no training, musketeers could pierce armour plating at 100 metres and the role of pikemen changed from protecting the cavalry to guarding the musketeers from attack. These new tactical arrangements were accompanied by a massive increase in the size of armies. The armies of the 1620s and 1630s were double those at the disposal of Charles V and Henry II in the 1550s. In Parker's view, the 'prodigious increase in the scale of warfare alone merits the title of "military revolution"', though he concedes that all armies still relied heavily on mercenaries. Indeed, when Gustavus invaded Germany in 1630, half his army was comprised of mercenaries, and by 1632 they made up 80 per cent. It was with some justification, therefore, that Parker questioned the claim that Gustavus commanded the first truly national army.

The state's attempt to harness its human and natural resources led to larger and more centralised bureaucracies. The capacity to pay one's troops was crucial in a prolonged war but only the Dutch developed techniques of war finance whereby they could sustain an army in excess of 50,000 without incurring a single mutiny. Other countries performed less creditably. The Spanish Army of Flanders faced logistical and financial difficulties resulting in 45 mutinies between 1572 and 1609. At the end of his reign, Philip II was hiring private contractors to raise and pay troops, supply food and ammunition and administer regiments – a practice that became commonplace in the early seventeenth century. In Germany during the Thirty Years' War, some 400 military 'enterprisers' supplied mercenaries though none rivalled Wallenstein's entrepreneurial vision in demanding contributions and *Brandschatzung* (fire-money) from the lands under occupation. Without these, he claimed, no more than 20,000 out of 100,000 troops could have been supported. The financial resources of the state clearly affected the size of European armies and revealed the limitations of governments when faced with funding and administering a prolonged war.

Finally, in his most recent study Parker has added to Roberts' thesis by stressing the changes in naval warfare, the logistics of war supplies and the global might of the military revolution in the seventeenth century, all of which enabled European powers to impose their will over Amerindians, Africans, Asians and Muslims.

Revisionist views

Several modern historians – such as John Hale, Michael Duffy and Jeremy Black – have questioned the ideas of Roberts and Parker on two separate counts.

1 They believe that Roberts has overemphasised the Dutch and Swedish innovations and underplayed earlier military changes evident in other countries.

2 Parker based his views principally on his studies of Spain and the Netherlands and, while he acknowledged that several changes preceded 1560, he was incorrect in terming such reforms 'revolutionary'.

Historians of the Renaissance have suggested that there was more continuity than change during this period and that the most significant developments occurred before 1560. In their view, if there was a revolution, it took place between 1480 and 1520 when the potential of siege-guns, arquebuses and muskets first began to be realised in the Granadan Wars (1482–92) and in the early Italian Wars (1494–1516). After witnessing the destruction of medieval fortresses by the latest siege-guns, Machiavelli declared in his *Discourses* (1516) that 'if there ever was a time when they [fortresses] were useless, it is now on account of the artillery'. Towns hastily invested in improved designs: Verona rebuilt its walls entirely, Marseilles and Pavia strengthened their existing defences, and Civitavecchia and Castel San Angelo in Rome constructed angular bastions, the *trace italienne*.

Strengthened fortifications resulted in prolonged stalemates and sieges, which in turn led to an increase in the numbers of troops and artillery and a reduction in the role of the cavalry. The French army which invaded Italy in 1494, for example, comprised 13,000 cavalry and 15,000 infantry but 30 years later at Pavia it consisted of 5,000 cavalry and 23,000 infantry, and at Metz in 1552, 6,000 and 32,000 respectively. The heavy and expensive cavalryman, armed with a lance, sword and mace, steadily declined in the face of pike and shot, though the lancers were still used in raids.

By 1560 most infantrymen were armed with either pikes or firearms.

They outnumbered the cavalry and were mainly used to assist the artillery in maintaining sieges and garrisoning towns. Set battles were few and far between, and a pattern of attritional warfare was established which would not change for more than a century.

Jeremy Black agrees that the period before 1560 saw more changes than the following century which, he suggests, was a time of 'relative stagnation'. In his view, Spain's extensive *monarquía* provoked dynastic rivalry and so required more and more resources to defend it. As a result, military tactics and strategy during the Dutch Revolt, the Thirty Years' War and the Habsburg-Bourbon War (1635–1659), were neither revolutionary nor successful. Moreover, he believes historians have devoted too much attention to the size of armies. Black warns against relying too heavily on official figures since army sizes varied according to the type of unit (regular, auxiliary, garrison or militia). He suggests that numbers were regularly inflated for purposes of fraud and propaganda. The average size of field armies in the 1620s was between 20,000 and 25,000, which was no larger than the army that Charles VIII took with him to Italy in 1494. Armies greater than 30,000, as at Breitenfeld in 1631, were exceptional. If Gustavus and Wallenstein commanded more than 100,000 men in 1630, most of them were detailed to garrison towns across the length and breadth of Germany. In 1626, for instance, the Army of Flanders employed 31,000 out of 50,000 in garrison duties and at least 17,000 troops were required in the siege of Leucate in 1637.

Black also questions the originality, extent and success of the Dutch and Swedish battle tactics. He argues that Henry IV reduced his infantry units to 500 and was flexible enough to fight in linear or stepped formation in anticipation of Gustavus's alleged innovations, that Saxe-Weimar spurned the novel methods in 1638 by using heavy cavalry to win the Battle of Rheinfelden, and that armies which employed the new Dutch infantry tactics at Dessau, Lutter and Breitenfeld all lost. In practice, generals were ultra-cautious, spent most of their time securing their position and supplies before advancing, and only applied untried tactics out of desperation. This is what happened at Wittstock when Banér split his army in two, at Rocroi when the French cavalry outflanked Spanish *tercios*, and at Janków when Torstensson combined his cavalry and artillery. Drawn battles were commonplace in the Thirty Years' War. When victory was gained – as at the White Mountain, Lutter and Nördlingen – it went to the larger and more experienced army. Gustavus was certainly more adventurous and his strategy more expansive, but at the end of the day he was not successful. In Black's view, this suggests that 'the "revolution" discerned by Roberts had not solved the basic military problem of securing decisive victory'.

Moreover, he argues that the seventeenth-century state was not strengthened as a result of military developments. Though the ruler was presented with opportunities to increase his power over his subjects either by force of arms, increased taxation or an enlarged bureaucracy, in practice the pressures of war exposed his limitations, it increased tension within the state and forced him into a policy of decentralisation.

Black believes that insofar as there was a military revolution, it occurred in the years following 1660. 'This is certainly true', he claims, 'with regard to the size of the armies of a number of the leading powers, Austria, Britain, France, Prussia and Russia.' It was in the second half of Louis XIV's reign when the musket and bayonet finally replaced the pike, when rapid-firing flintlocks took over from unreliable matchlock muskets and when ring and socket bayonets displaced plug bayonets. For the first time large armies were sustained, campaigns were more professionally directed, battle lines became larger and thinner to achieve greater firepower, and battles were more decisive.

Conclusion

'Whenever a situation of permanent or semi-permanent war existed . . . one finds, not surprisingly, standing armies, greater professionalism among the troops, improvements in military organisation, and certain tactical innovations,' wrote Parker. His emphasis upon the continuity of military processes is an apt reminder from an advocate of the 'military revolution' school that it is dangerous to generalise from the particular. Arguably he has concentrated too much on the dominance of the Spanish Army of Flanders, in much the same way as Roberts overstated Gustavus Adolphus's reforms.

The period from 1560 to 1660 did see significant military changes and innovations were made by Spanish, Dutch and Swedish generals, but do these developments merit the term 'revolutionary'? Much depends on the extent to which such changes can be interpreted as either innovatory, permanent or significant. Revisionist historians have challenged the orthodox view on several counts. Some see more continuity than change in the years 1480–1650, arguing that changes when they occurred were slow and haphazard. Others have questioned how far army sizes stimulated the growth of bureaucracy and doubt whether the military reforms were either sustained or systematic.

War stimulated growth. It presented a ruler with the opportunity to enhance his power over his subjects although in practice the pressures of war usually robbed him of the power to carry these out. Whether the development of an efficient bureaucracy was a precondition for the growth in army sizes or whether the latter stimulated the growth in bureaucracies remains an open verdict. To a great extent, the two evolved together but this progression was neither planned nor lineal before 1648. If war dictated the pace and necessity of change, it seems that states responded differently according to their particular circumstances. And in most cases, survival necessitated decentralisation. Only in the second half of the century would the administrations of France, Austria, Sweden, Brandenburg-Prussia and Britain begin to harness their resources more professionally.

Task: making sense of a historical controversy

1 What are the essential arguments in Michael Roberts' thesis?

2 a In what respects has Geoffrey Parker modified Roberts' thesis?
  b Do you find Parker's explanations more or less convincing than Roberts'?

3 Why have Renaissance historians (like John Hale) argued that, if there was a military revolution during this period, then it occurred before 1560?

4 What arguments does Jeremy Black advance for discounting the Parker–Roberts thesis?

5 'Historians produce different interpretations of past events not because they directly contradict each other but because they cannot agree on their terms of reference.' Does your study of the different views of the so-called 'military revolution' lead you to support this conclusion?

Further reading

M. Roberts, *The Military Revolution* (Belfast, 1956) reprinted in *Essays in Swedish History* (Weidenfeld and Nicolson, 1967).

G. Parker, 'The Military Revolution – a Myth?', *Journal of Military History*, 48 (1976).

G. Parker, *The Military Revolution* (Cambridge University Press, 1988) – a detailed assessment of the principal military changes.

J. Black, *A Military Revolution? Military Change and European Society, 1550–1800* (Macmillan, 1991) – sets the controversy in a broader context.

B. H. Nickle, *The Military Reforms of Prince Maurice of Orange* (Michigan University Press, 1984) – argues the case in favour of Orange's novel military reforms.

J. Hale, *Renaissance War Studies* (Hambledon, 1983) – looks at the main military developments during the Renaissance.

F. Tallett, *War and Society in Early Modern Europe* (Routledge, 1992) – provides a useful commentary on the debate.

J. A. Lynn, 'The *trace italienne* and the growth of armies', *Journal of Military History*, 55 (1991).

30 Why was there a witch-hunt in Europe, 1580–1640?

Time chart

1468: The Papacy declares witchcraft a *crimen exceptum*

1484: Witchcraft is denounced as heretical

1486: Heinrich Krämer and Jakob Sprenger publish the *Malleus Maleficarum*

1532: Charles V issues the *Carolina*, a revised criminal code

1563: Johann Weyer publishes *de Praestigiis Daemonum*, a criticism of witchcraft

1567: Genevan trials begin

1577: Chambery persecutions

1580: Jean Bodin writes *Demonomania of Sorcerers*

1584: Reginald Scot publishes *Discoverie of Witchcraft*

1587: Archbishop Johann von Schöneburg begins purges in Trier

1595: Nicholas Rémy publishes *Daemonolatrie*

1597: James VI publishes *Demonologie*

1602: Henri Boguet publishes *Examen des sorciers*

1608: Guazzo publishes his *Compendium Maleficarum*

1609: Pays de Labourd witch-hunt begins

1611: Witch-hunts at Ellwangen and Aix-en-Provence start

1612: Alonso de Salazar investigates Navarre

1623: Bamberg trials begin

1630: Last witch-trial in Luxembourg

1631: Friedrich von Spee writes *Cautio Criminalis*

1633: Louvais convent is investigated

1634: Persecution of Ursuline nuns at Loudun

Belief in witches was a widespread phenomenon in the medieval and early modern period. 'White' witches produced harmless spells, 'black' witches practised 'maleficia' or harmful activities, and it was believed that some witches were capable of consorting with the Devil. Between the fifteenth and eighteenth century, witches were persecuted throughout Europe and at the height of these witch-hunts, between 1580 and 1640, an estimated 110,000 witches were put on trial and some 60,000 executed. Sometimes the search lasted years and entailed hundreds of arrests; more typically, hunts were over in a few months and confined to a single community. This chapter seeks to explain the conditions which gave rise to this period of witch-hunting and to examine several related questions.

- Why did some areas of Europe experience epidemics but others only sporadic outbreaks?

- Why did the persecution reach a climax between 1580 and 1640?

- How important were wars and natural disasters, confessional strife and social tensions in causing panics?

- Why were the victims mainly poor peasants and elderly women?

- Among which social groups did pressure for persecution originate?

- How significant were ecclesiastical and secular institutions in encouraging or staunching levels of popular hysteria?

Geographical extent

The worst affected countries were Germany, France and Switzerland. According to Erik Midelfort, there were more than 3,229 executions in south-western Germany between 1561 and 1670; Lotharingia witnessed over 1,000 burnings, Westphalia 800, Würzburg 900, Ellwangen nearly 400 and Bamberg 300, mainly in the 1620s. Eichstätt in Bavaria saw 274 victims, Würzburg 160 and Coblenz 24 in 1627–9. In Luxembourg, the main years of crisis were 1580–1600 and 1615–30, and in nearby Franche-Comté, 1628–9 and 1657–9. France had its worst spells between 1580 and 1610 and 1628–30. According to the Catholic lawyer and witch-hunter, Nicholas Rémy, 3,000 trials occurred in Lorraine alone. Some of the more notorious outbreaks concerned the convents at Aix-en-Provence (1611), Loudun (1634) and Louvais (1633–44). At Loudun, for instance, the Ursuline nuns claimed to have been possessed by the Devil in the comely shape of a Jesuit priest. Switzerland may also have seen as many as 5,000 executions before 1620, especially in the frontier regions around Geneva. In the Pays de Vaud near Berne more than 2,000 witch-trials occurred between 1530 and 1680, and an execution rate of 90 per cent was not unusual.

In contrast, some countries experienced very few outbreaks. In Spain they were largely confined to the mountainous Basque provinces before

1610, and to Aragon and Catalonia intermittently thereafter. The only reported cases in Italy came from the north east near Venice and Naples, and in the United Provinces, where there were very few witch-hunts, the last trial took place in 1610. In eastern and northern Europe, witch-hunting rarely occurred before 1650, and such cases fall outside the scope of this study. Poland, Transylvania, Hungary, Austria, Russia and Scandinavia experienced witch-scares but none had a witch-hunt during this period.

One difficulty which faces modern historians is the defective nature of much of the evidence. Legal papers were sometimes burned with the witch, the verdict of a case is often unknown, and witches were regularly lynched without any surviving documentation. Where records have survived, some witch-hunters appear to have grossly inflated the figures to heighten popular alarm and to justify their own activities. The chief justice of Burgundy, Henri Boguet, claimed he condemned 600 witches between 1598 and 1616 but judicial records suggest that the figure was nearer to 80. It seems likely that Nicholas Rémy made similarly exaggerated claims for the numbers he executed in Lorraine. Even allowing for these errors, however, the fact remains that thousands of innocent people lost their lives between 1580 and 1640. How can this witch-hunt be explained?

1 Confessional explanation

In 1967 Hugh Trevor-Roper argued that the witch-craze (he used this term rather than witch-hunt) was a direct consequence of the confessional conflict between orthodox Catholics and reforming Protestants, as each sought to win the bodies and souls of half-pagan, half-Christian communities in post-Reformation Europe. 'It was', he claimed, 'the social consequence of renewed ideological war and the accompanying climate of fear.' Even though the Catholic Church's emphasis on the sacraments discouraged belief in magic, it recognised its hold over the people's imagination. In the course of the fifteenth century, the Dominicans pressurised the Papacy into declaring in 1484 that witchcraft was a heresy because it involved the renunciation of God and the worship of the Devil. '*Maleficium* was a purely secondary activity,' writes Keith Thomas, 'a by-product of this false religion. Whether or not the witch injured other people she deserved to die for her disloyalty to God.' Though there was a significant absence of witchcraft persecutions between 1520 and 1550 when the Reformation was in full flood, thereafter Catholic theologians came to oppose it with the same intensity as any other heterogeneous belief. Jesuit missionaries like Peter Canisius preached against witchcraft; court preachers like Jerome Drexel urged Maximilian of Bavaria to extirpate it from his lands; and Catholic lawyers such as de L'Ancre, Rémy and Boguet searched French Huguenot villages looking for traces of demonism.

Some of the worst excesses in France occurred during the peaceful interludes in the wars of religion, especially in the aftermath of St Bartholomew's Day (1572) when pockets of Protestantism in Orléans and Languedoc were purged and in the 1590s when Catholics refused to acknowledge religious toleration. In Germany, prince-bishops and abbots wreaked destruction. The Catholic archbishop-elector of Trier burned 368 witches between 1587 and 1593; the prince-abbot of Fulda in 1602 encouraged his minister to conduct an inquisition of his Protestant subjects, which resulted in the death of 250 by 1605. Between 1623 and 1633 the prince-bishop of Bamberg, known as the *Hexenbischof* (witch-bishop), burned some 300 witches including five burgomasters accused of attending a 'witches' sabbat' and a judge for being unduly lenient (see Figure 30.1).

Figure 30.1 *Woodcut of the witch trials in Bamberg, Germany*

Some Protestant rulers retaliated in kind. In the 1560s Lutheran preachers brought the witch-hunt to Brandenburg, Württemberg, Baden and Mecklenburg; and in the 1590s it was Brunswick, Westphalia and Pomerania that saw Lutheran purges. Northern Lutheran states, however, appear to have held fewer witch-trials than the central and south German territories. The first Calvinist Elector Palatine, Frederick III, prohibited witch-trials in his lands, which clearly indicates the significance of individual rulers in determining the existence of witch-hunts.

Some of the worst confessional clashes took place in Switzerland where Berne Protestants repeatedly attacked Catholic villages in the Pays de Vaud, an area with a long tradition of heresy. Protestant reformers turned to the Bible for support. They stressed the literal presence of Satan, demons and evil spirits in the world and emphasised man's vulnerability in the face of the Devil. 'God expressly commands that all witches and enchantresses shall be put to death, and this law of God is an universal law,' declared Calvin, paraphrasing *Exodus 22:18*. 'Thou shalt not suffer a witch to live.' Luther had no doubt that witches existed. They were, he claimed in 1522, 'Devil's whores who steal milk, raise storms, ride on goats or broomsticks, lame or maim people, torture babies in their cradles, change things into different shapes.'

All Christian sects raised popular awareness of diabolical activity and, in urging the destruction of the Devil's agents, accused one another of harnessing its powers of evil. Robert Muchembled has shown that in the region of Cambrésis in the Low Countries, priests encouraged their congregations to transfer feelings of guilt and moral unworthiness onto witches in their community. In the Jura, William Monter has demonstrated that witches willingly confessed out of a deep sense of sin and guilt. The belief among many congregations that their sins could only be expiated by the execution of witches, and that they were doing God's work, goes some way towards explaining the European witch-hunt. 'A population needed to be confessionally conditioned and partially (but not totally) literate, as well as poor, before a witch-craze could get under way,' writes Geoffrey Parker. This was certainly the case in most west European countries by 1580 as the Reformation and Counter-Reformation troops drew up their battle lines.

Yet there are enough examples of witch-hunts that were not confessionally motivated to suggest that this explanation cannot be universally applied. Sectarianism, though important in accounting for the high level of murders in France and Germany during the religious wars, does not explain the wave of judicial witch-burnings at other times and in other countries. In Germany in the 1620s Catholic witch-hunters were most active in Catholic communities, and both Lutheran and Catholic villages are known to have cooperated against witchcraft. This is not surprising since witchcraft was perceived as a threat to the entire community and surpassed different religious beliefs. It is also apparent that the European witch-hunt actually preceded the Reformation and there were relatively few witchcraft trials during the years 1520–50. The total number of executions in Orthodox Christendom was also extremely low, except for Poland in the 1680s, and there were very few witch-hunts in Catholic Spain, Portugal, Italy and Lutheran Scandinavia.

2 Economic causes

An alternative explanation of the European witch-hunt is that economic and social conditions of many peasant communities declined sharply in the second half of the sixteenth century and that inflation, food shortages, outbreaks of plague, rising poverty and recurrent war caused villagers to turn against each other. Many saw the work of the Devil in their own misfortune which galvanised their drive to wipe out the servants of Satan. 'In every country the most intensive outbreaks of persecution were in times of disaster,' writes Henry Kamen, and instances can certainly be found linking witch hysteria to natural catastrophes. Plague spread by 'magical grease' led to witch-hunts in Geneva, Chambery and at Ellwangen. A series of bad harvests at Trier accounted for epidemics of witch-hunting in the 1580s and 1590s, and in Lorraine and south-west Germany in the 1590s crop losses coincided with peaks of witch-hunting. A hailstorm, which suddenly destroyed crops at Wiesensteig in Germany in 1562, sparked off a local witch-hunt.

Regions beset by rebellion and war were also prone to outbreaks of witch persecutions. To many magistrates and theologians, witches were seeking to turn the world upside down and had to be purged if order was to be preserved. Rebels were frequently accused of satanism – did the Bible not proclaim that 'Rebellion is as the sin of witchcraft'? Areas affected by civil disturbances and warfare, such as north-eastern France in the 1590s, 1630s and 1640s, saw their communal life disrupted, and many communities blamed witchcraft. A madman from Arcée, for example, toured Flavigny near Dijon in 1644 identifying witches and sorcerers whom the assembled villagers put to death as they searched in vain for a scapegoat.

The Spanish Inquisition was well aware of the importance of social and economic conditions to rural communities and as early as 1538 was ordering priests to instruct people not to identify crop failures, thunderstorms and bad weather with the Devil. Clearly some communities attributed unnatural disasters and their own sufferings to the Devil, and in times of crisis turned upon minority groups. Yet there are many examples of witch persecutions in France where there were no local catastrophes, and in Franche-Comté, Lorraine and the Rhineland bishoprics, the process of witch-hunting was well under way in the 1620s in advance of any war devastation, popular rebellions or economic depression. Finally, it should be remembered that often regions which saw the most fervent persecutions experienced stable economic conditions.

3 Social changes

Some social historians have suggested that a marked decline in Christian almsgiving during this period worsened the plight of the poor, especially elderly women living alone, which increased communal ill-feeling towards them. William Monter has shown that in the Genevan trials of 1571–2 the median age of the accused was 60, and at Neuchâtel 44 per cent were widows. In an age of increasing numbers of young people whose average life expectancy was below 30 years, elderly people were readily identified and judged to be superfluous to their community. It has been suggested that between 10 and 20 per cent of women never married, that those who did stayed married for less than 20 years, and that old and poor widows were less likely to remarry. As a result, old spinsters and widows found themselves socially marginalised, often living on the edge of a village, and forced in some cases to resort to practising magic in order to survive. Nicholas Rémy claimed in 1595 that witches were 'for the most part beggars who support life on the alms they receive'. Some no doubt frightened neighbours in order to command respect or to be left alone; some probably cursed people out of frustration when they were ostracised; a few dabbled in demonology and, as the distinction between 'white' and 'black' magic became blurred, were suspected of invoking the Devil.

Though we should be wary of accepting stereotypical judgements and recall that in many early witchcraft trials male victims were more numerous than female, historians acknowledge that a commonplace male perception of females in the sixteenth century was not fictitious. Women were regarded as cantankerous, fickle, weak and passionate; they generally served as healers, cooks and midwives, which made them vulnerable to accusations of sorcery, and many men feared their alleged sexual prowess. 'All witchcraft comes from carnal lust, which is in women insatiable,' declared the *Malleus Maleficarum*, the witch-hunters' bible. In a patriarchal and intolerant society, elderly women and spinsters were often judged to be a burden, particularly during economic depressions. Though some men were misogynists (women-haters), the personal circumstances of particular women and the role of male theologians, magistrates and local councillors probably explains why female victims exceeded 75 per cent in most regions of Europe. In the words of Johann Weyer, a contemporary critic, 'Witches are poor ignorant creatures, old and powerless'.

4 Legal reforms

Between the fourteenth and sixteenth century most continental states introduced changes in their legal procedures which had a profound effect on the process of witch-hunting.

1 The customary practice of accusatorial justice was gradually replaced by an inquisitorial system of criminal procedure. As a result, the state assumed the role of prosecutor, acted on oral and circumstantial evidence, and encouraged witnesses to come forward. Hitherto **plaintiffs** had to prove that a crime had been committed and provide witnesses who were themselves open to prosecution if the accused was acquitted. This legal change was particularly significant in cases of witchcraft and certainly contributed to an increase in the number of trials in the second half of the sixteenth century.

2 From the beginning of witch-hunts in the fourteenth century, secular courts had participated in witch-hunting but by the sixteenth century they had eclipsed the ecclesiastical courts in most European countries in the belief that *maleficium* was a secular crime. Christina Larner has suggested that the drive to eliminate witchcraft reflected a general feeling among some magistrates that the Church was failing in its duty to correct people's morals. A perceived rise in the incidence of incest, infanticide, sodomy and adultery among peasant and marginal groups was proof that they were bedevilled, and it was the state's responsibility to regulate morality. The Bordeaux judge, Pierre de L'Ancre, certainly assumed a missionary role in executing 80 witches in Pays de Labourd between 1609 and 1614. Yet across the border in Spanish Navarre the Inquisition had found no sign of witchcraft.

Significantly, it was precisely in countries where the Inquisition investigated most cases – in Italy, Portugal, Spain and the Spanish Netherlands (after 1568) – that a stay on convictions is most apparent. The Spanish Inquisition tried more than 3,500 people for magic and witchcraft between 1580 and 1650, but fewer than 1 per cent were put to death. Similarly, though nearly half of the 558 cases brought before the Roman Inquisition between 1595 and 1610 concerned witchcraft, very few resulted in death. Years of experience had taught inquisitors to be wary of false accusations; moreover, the Inquisition placed little faith in torture and required tangible proof from at least two witnesses before it convicted. In Castile, for example, few deaths occurred after 1526 when inquisitors were ordered to be more circumspect. In 1532 all sentences had to be submitted to the Inquisition for confirmation; six years later, inquisitors were warned by the Suprema not to believe everything in the *Malleus Maleficarum*. In fact, the Inquisition was more interested in discovering the motives of alleged witches than in handing out harsh sentences or reacting to popular demand. Thus, the Spanish inquisitor Alonso de Salazar pronounced after investigating 1,802 alleged cases in Navarre in 1612 that he had not found any evidence 'to infer that a single act of witchcraft has really occurred' but that 'three-quarters and more have accused themselves and their accomplices falsely'. He was convinced that 'there were neither witches nor bewitched until they were talked and written about' and proceeded to dismiss all 289 cases brought before him in Vizcaya in 1616. In contrast, the civil courts remained powerful in Catalonia, where 300 witches were burned between 1616 and 1619, and in Aragon, at least until the 1620s, when local persecutions declined in the face of the Inquisition's restraining influence.

3 A third important legal change occurred in 1468 when the Papacy ruled that witchcraft was a *crimen exceptum*. This opened the way for the suspension of normal legal procedures and the official use of torture. Though confession was required to convict in cases of diabolism (dealing with the Devil), not one in a million according to Jean Bodin would have done so without the methods of torture such as pulleys, screws, pincers and the rack. With the implementation of *tormentum insomniae*, thousands who were not witches confessed. As Johannes Junius of Bamberg explained to his daughter in 1628: 'For whoever comes into the witch prison must become a witch or be tortured until he invents something out of his head and – God pity him – bethinks of something.' The use of torture on a woman of 70 at Ellwangen in Germany led to her naming several accomplices who, in turn, under torture named others, resulting in 260 victims in 1611–12. More deaths followed over the next six years until the alleged coven was finally broken. Significantly, countries that did not use torture (England, for example), or applied it sparingly (Denmark, Sweden and Norway), had a low number of executions.

4 Many trials were conducted by local and regional courts and resulted in a larger number of convictions. This was particularly true in Germany where each of the states had its own courts and applied its own brand of justice. Though some adhered to the *Carolina* of 1532 – Charles V's revised criminal code – many did not. As a result, strict rules governing the use of torture were often relaxed or ignored altogether.

KEY TERMS:

Crimen exceptum

A *crimen exceptum* was an exceptional crime which fell outside the usual civil law conventions. Different methods of torture were approved: the *strappado* was a pulley that lifted the victim by his arms, which were tied behind his back, with weights attached to his feet.

Tormentum insomniae
This method of torture was forced sleeplessness, the most feared of all punishments.

Judges, for example, should first have established that a crime had been committed before permitting torture to be used, and then they should have ensured that it was applied once only on a prisoner. In practice, formal procedures were often ignored by local and provincial judges, which facilitated witch-hunts throughout the Empire. In the Rhineland, for instance, princes, abbots and bishops exercised judicial autonomy and in the 1620s were able to transform a communal hatred of witches into legalised murder. 'The behaviour and motivation of the ruling élite is crucial in explaining the new fashion for witch-hunting', suggests Richard Bonney. There does appear to be a correlation between the response of local authorities to rumours and accusations and the prevailing judicial system as to whether a witch-hunt was initiated or ended.

5 Popular culture

Where there were demands for action out of personal, confessional or political reasons, and a collaboration existed between people, pastors and magistrates, witch-hunts began, trials followed and panic set in. At Burg in Saxony in 1617, for example, the town council was forced to investigate six prominent women named by Maria Guldenpfennig, who had earlier been found guilty and burned as a witch. Some locals, believing Maria was innocent, accused the six women as 'whores of the Devil', and so initiated a personal and political feud between the accusers and relatives of the accused, some of whom were town councillors. The council ultimately succumbed to popular threats and burned two women and arrested four more, in spite of their innocence.

Why did intelligent and level-headed judges find defendants guilty of crimes which they had not committed? Their conduct cannot be explained simply in terms of responding to political orders from above or social pressure from below. Historians acknowledge the importance of anthropology in throwing light on this issue. Witchcraft was a sociological phenomenon, and the key to understanding it lies in the mentality of sixteenth-century rural communities. White and black magic were central elements of medieval culture accepted by everyone. White magic was practised by 'cunning' people and witches. It entailed harmless pursuits such as curing illnesses, protecting cattle against infection, and making love potions. Black magic, in contrast, was evil invoked to harm others, ruin crops and cause distress.

In the course of the fifteenth century, intellectuals developed a theory which led the Papacy to pronounce that witchcraft was an aspect of devil-worship. That witches could fly, dematerialise and, by the glance of their 'evil-eye', cause death and misery may seem contrary to reason, but in a culture which accepted the Aristotelian cosmology, it was reasonable to believe in demonology.

The publication of *Malleus Maleficarum* two years after the Papacy officially acknowledged the existence of witches, universalised their characteristics, explained how to identify them and how to proceed with their arrest, interrogation and trial. This book provided unwarranted confirmation and proved extraordinarily popular. By 1520 it had been reprinted 14 times (though not between 1521 and 1576) and had run to over 30 editions by the late seventeenth century. Popes, kings, philosophers, judges, churchmen and scientists alike believed in it. Jean Bodin, Europe's finest philosopher, identified in his *Demonomania of Sorcerers* (1580) 15 crimes specific to witches; James I and Emperor Rudolf II believed in witchcraft, and both Kepler and Descartes wrote in support. In Italy one of the most influential works was the *Compendium Maleficarum* written by a Milanese friar, Francesco Maria Guazzo. He drew upon earlier publications in German, French and Italian, and complemented his guide to witchcraft with a series of illustrations of witches liaising with the Devil.

Through the dissemination of pamphlets, listening to sermons and hearing evidence read out at executions, most people believed witches not only existed but consorted with the Devil and had to be hunted down. In Italy, for example, the Friuli Inquisition had regarded the *benandanti* (witch-beaters) as an agrarian cult throughout the Middle Ages. Each quarter day the *benandanti* defended their children and harvests by waging 'night battles' with the 'witches of the Devil', but from 1580 and throughout the seventeenth century they were convinced they were witches and were persecuted as such. In contrast, only a minority condemned the persecution of witchcraft, most notably the Italian philosopher Girolamo Cardano (in 1550), the German Lutheran Johann Weyer (1563), the English Anglican Reginald Scot (1584) and the German Jesuit Friedrich von Spee (1631). Understandably, in a climate of suspended disbelief, fear and credulity, these and other non-believers were voices in the wilderness.

Conclusion

Historians now recognise that the witch-hunts which plagued western Europe between 1580 and 1640 were multicausal. In the fifteenth century intellectuals had cross-fertilised white magic and black sorcery to produce an anti-Christian cult which was perceived by the Church and state as a threat to society. Thereafter, fear of and belief in supernatural forces grew by its own momentum, rising in periods of rapid social and economic change, of religious and political instability, and falling during times of domestic peace and communal stability. Specific witch-hunts only ended when a community believed that all witches had been identified, that innocent people were also being persecuted, and when magistrates refused to prosecute or courts of appeal overturned sentences. In general, witch-hunts ended when confessional and political conflicts receded, especially in frontier regions, when there were changes in judicial systems and governments asserted more control over local authorities, and when demonology was gradually banished from the world-view with the advent of natural science, Cartesianism and the Christianisation of the population. Progress would be slow and variable: the last recorded death of a witch in the United Provinces was in 1595, in Luxembourg 1630, in France 1745, in Germany 1775, in Switzerland 1782, and in Poland 1793 – which is further testimony to the enduring rural belief in witchcraft.

Tasks: analysis

1 Look at the list of factors above which historians have used to explain witch-hunting during the early modern period.
   a Put the factors in your own order of importance, giving your reasons.
   b Do you think this list helps you to explain the precise timing of the witch-hunts? Explain your answer.
   c These factors have been deliberately separated. Do you think that convincing explanations of the European witch-hunts need to stress how factors acted together, rather than separately? Explain your answer.

2 What can you work out from this chapter about the kinds of evidence historians rely on when they give reasons for the witch-hunts?

3 'A study of local rather than national history will provide us with a better understanding of the European witch-craze.' Do you agree?

Further reading

G. Scarre, *Witchcraft and Magic in 16th and 17th Century Europe* (Macmillan, 1987) – a very readable and stimulating introduction.

C. Ginzburg, *The Night Battles: Witchcraft and Agrarian Cults in the 16th and 17th Centuries* (Routledge Kegan Paul, 1983) – a lively introduction to this topic.

C. Larner, *Witchcraft and Religion in the Politics of Popular Belief* (Blackwell, 1984).

B. P. Levack, *The Witch-Hunt in Early Modern Europe* (Addison Wesley Longman, 1987) – provides a good survey of the main issues.

K. Thomas, *Religion and the Decline of Magic* (Weidenfeld and Nicolson, 1971, rep. 1978) – contains a mine of information and, although mainly drawn from English sources, it is indispensable for a study of European witchcraft.

H. R. Trevor-Roper, *The European Witch-Craze* (Pelican, 1969) – a little dated but still a powerful interpretation.

Index

Addison Wesley Longman Limited,
Edinburgh Gate, Harlow,
Essex CM20 2JE, England
and Associated Companies throughout the World

First published 1997
© Addison Wesley Longman Limited 1997

Set in 10/13 Meridien Roman
Produced by Longman Singapore Publishers (Pte) Limited
Printed in Singapore

ISBN 0 582 08403 2

Acknowledgements

We are grateful to the following for permission to reproduce photos and other copyright
material:

AKG London, pages 31, 241; Ancient Art & Architecture Collection, page 60; Bridgeman Art
Library, pages 30 & 90 (Galleria Degli Uffizi, Florence), 119 (Museo Del Castello, Sforzesco),
159 (Museo Lazaro Galdiano, Madrid), 162 (Royal Geographical Society, London), 223
(Varez-Fisa Collection); British Library, London, page 29; Photo Bulloz, pages 131 (Musee De
Chantilly), 134; by permission of the Syndics of Cambridge University Library, pages 143,
231 above, 266; E. T Archive, page 255; Mary Evans Picture Library, pages 68, 81, 120, 141,
149, 190; The Fotomas Index, page 142; Germanisches National Museum, page 252; Getty
Images, pages 44, 89 above, 231 below, 273.

We were unable to trace the copyright holders of the following and would be grateful of any
information that would enable us to do so, pages 21, 71, 80, 86, 89 below, 203, 300.

Cover photograph: Dome of Florence Cathedral, by Brunelleschi. Photo: Bridgeman Art
Library.
Series editors: Eric Evans and Christopher Culpin
Publisher: Joan Ward
Editor: Steve Attmore
Designer: Michael Harris
Picture researcher: Louise Edgeworth
Artwork: Tony Richardson

The Publisher's policy is to use paper manufactured from sustainable forests.